The Advent

To Everything-
There Is A Season

Mary A. Jansen

Published by
M.J. Press

Published in obedience to Habakkuk 2:2

Additional copies available. Use order form in the back of this book.

Published by M.J. Press
P.O. Box 187
Mountain, Wisconsin

First Edition
First Printing • 1000 • 1996

ISBN 1-57502-152-8

Front cover Illustration by M.J.

All Scripture references are from the
King James Version of the Bible.

Printed in the USA by

MORRIS PUBLISHING
3212 E. Hwy 30
Kearney, NE 68847
800-650-7888

INTRODUCTION

Along the banks of the Flint River lies the town of Roberts Junction, perhaps you've been there? I'm sure the place will seem familiar and the characters like old friends. Let me introduce you to a few...

SARAH DANIELS is twenty-five years old and the recent mother of a young son, Nicholas. We find her adjusting to the new role of mother and accepting the fact that others will be walking beside her husband where she used to stand.

BEN DANIELS age twenty-eight is a very stable Christian, wise, strong willed, confident. But is he? More than once we find him shaken by his feelings of inadequacy.

SUZANNA RHODES is the fourteen year old daughter of the local preacher. Her honesty about and to herself often place her in unpredictable circumstances.

RICHARD McALLISTER, also twenty-eight, is an old school chum of Ben's. He's been out of touch for ten years. Ten years in which some very disturbing things happen to him that leave him bound in guilt.

PATRICK RHODES, the seventeen year old brother of Suzanna, has assumed the role of her personal guardian.

JEFF JOHNSON seventeen, is struggling through the recent break-up of his parents marriage.

DENNIS LITTLE. In Dennis we find a young frustrated teenager taking the steps that lead to manhood; honesty, responsibility, and trust in God.

These are but a few of the people you'll meet at Roberts Junction. Doc Martin is there also, and Captain Omaha; the preacher Edward Rhodes, and Sarah's zany friend Chrys. You'll get just as frustrated with Brady Downing as Suzanna did, and laugh at the antics of Bob and Mike.

You'll meet family, friends, and yes, enemies, for this is not a story but more of a journal...three weeks in the lives of those that I hope you'll enjoy as much as I have.

CHAPTER 1

TO EVERYTHING THERE IS A SEASON

Tuesday, September 13, 1983

It was dry for September and around the farm there was evidence of the approaching harvest. Golden corners appeared on the broad green leaves; tinges of red, yellow and orange escaped and hid in the dark foliage of the Maple's branches.

The contrasting white of the freshly painted farm house gave it an air of country charm, nestled among the Maples and Pines with the bold red barn and stables in the distance. White fences lined the pasture where the browns, chestnuts, greys and buckskins grazed contentedly. All was at peace, a peace that was soon to be shattered.

There was a sound on the back porch just as Sarah was peeling potatoes for supper. It was followed by a bang on the door.

"Hey, are you home?" Came a call.

"Where else? My baby-sitter's been at school all day." Sarah laughed as Suzanna Rhodes hurried into the room.

"How's my little buddy today?" Suzanna asked.

"Precious..growing up a little too fast though, Mom can't seem to keep up."

"That's what you need me for, not everyone has a baby-sitter as responsible, cheerful, creative, intelligent and obedient as me!" Suzanna answered with a giggle as she took a seat at the table. Absently she grabbed a potato and began tossing it in the air. "Well Mom, what's for supper?"

"What's this Mom business?" Sarah asked putting the peeled potatoes into a kettle to boil.

"Well, I told you, that if I ever ran away from home, I'd come here. So, here I am."

"Yeah, sure. And tomorrow night your father will preach a sermon against harboring fugitives from the parsonage." Sarah laughed. "Well tell me, what happened?"

"I didn't do anything you wouldn't do." Suzanna said defensively.

Sarah grinned. "That is probably true, but just tell me what happened."

"That no good, useless Johnson said,..."

"Hold it." Sarah interrupted a little sternly. "Start over."

"MISTER Johnson started picking on me in class again today, and I sorta lost my cool."

"Really? What did he do?"

"It was terrible. There's this documentary on television tonight and he asked the class to watch what they could of it and write a report. Then he takes the huge book, it must have at least 600 pages in it, and hands it to me and says,.. in front of everyone... 'And for those who consider themselves too Holy to participate in the innocent practice of watching television you can read this book and have a report for me tomorrow.'" Suzanna leaned forward in her chair and exclaimed. "I almost died."

"You almost died" Sarah repeated "But what did you do?"

"I told him off."

"In front of the whole class?"

"No way! I haven't got the guts to do that!" Suzanna continued "I waited 'til after class, then I walked up to him, returned his book and said.. 'Thank you Mr. Johnson for teaching so faithfully about the American Government, the example you gave was excellent.. if you don't do things their way, you suffer."

"Well," Sarah began, "It's not as harsh as I expected, and it is true in some ways, How did he respond?"

"He didn't say anything, he just looked at me, and then I turned and walked to the door, but before I left I added. 'But the United States Government has one thing up on you, *Freedom of Religion.*"

"And now" Suzanna continued "He's probably called my father and I'll have to answer to him when I get home."

"Well you're actually worse off here. Ray, I mean, Mr. Johnson stops by almost every afternoon with his son Jeff. Jeff's horse Misty is about ready to foal, and they are really concerned about her."

"But," Suzanna pointed out "He doesn't come to the house, where I intend to stay." Just then a little whimper was heard coming from the direction of the nursery. Suzanna jumped up quickly. "Hey buddy, Aunti Suzie's here to save you from the diaper monster." She headed down the hall toward the stairs.

"I'll call your mother and tell her that you're here."

"Creep!" Suzanna called back.

The table was just being set when Suzanna returned from an errand to the barn.

"The boss says to put another plate on."

"Oh?" Sarah asked "Company?"

"Uh huh, Never seen the guy before though, he's really tall, pretty ugly too." Suzanna laughed "Especially next to Tom."

"Don't worry, Tom knows your crazy over him."

"Oh? Is it supposed to be a secret?"

Just then voices were heard as Ben Daniels and a tall man, wearing tattered jeans and an old army jacket entered the kitchen.

"Sarah" Ben introduced "This is my old buddy from school, Rich McAllister."

"Hi Rich, I pity anyone who had to put up with him back then."

Rich laughed "Remember he had a few of us loco's to put up with himself."

"Well Rich," Ben began "Let's have some chow, then I'll show you around the farm."

"Sounds fine to me." He agreed as they all gathered around the table.

Sarah enjoyed listening to the conversation that took place. Hearing about her husbands days of drinking and drugs, only proved more in her eyes the miracle working power of Jesus Christ. She hoped that Ben's friend would see the great change that had taken place in him and find deliverance for himself also. She glanced across the table at Suzanna. Suzanna who had never taken a drink in her life, who, since she was able to talk was taught the ways of the Lord,... well, Suzie was watching and listening intently as the men talked and laughed about their experiences. 'I'll have to ask her later what she things of this guy.' Sarah said to herself.

With Nick in capable hands Sarah was able to wander down to the arena, where Jeff Johnson and Tom VanDyke were riding two mares that Ben had recently purchased. Her friend Chrystal Shephard joined her there shortly after six.

"It's not often I see you empty handed." Chrys stated when she arrived.

"It's been awhile. Suzanna stopped after school, and I must admit it's a welcome break."

"Won't last long though, the boss'll see those idle hands and put you to work."

Sarah shrugged. Secretly she would enjoy working around the stable once again, she missed it.

"Speaking of the booger, here he comes now and he's got someone with him."

"That's Rich McAllister, he was in school with Ben."

"Poor Guy, and they still speak to each other?" Chrys said sarcastically.

"Apparently." Sarah watched as Ben approached the arena, he leaned against the fence for a moment and just watched. Rich looked slightly uncomfortable but his gaze also followed the horses.

"Hey Jeff!" Ben called "When did I hire you?"

"Hire me?" Jeff exclaimed "It took everything out of me to persuade Bill to let me ride. He only did because he knows that Misty is out of commission."

"You've got some pretty nice horses here boss." Tom commented as he rode past where they were standing.

"I hope so." Ben smiled "By the way Tom, I'd like you to meet your new boss. Richard McAllister."

"Hey! we've got enough bosses around here already, I know I'm the bottom guy on the totem pole you don't need to bring in anyone else to boss me around." Tom said as he rode up, He held out his hand to Rich. "Put 'em there boss." He laughed. Rich smiled as the two shook hands and Ben continued.

"I knew I'd be needin' more help this fall, Tom. You and Dennis are both back in school and Sarah is at the house with Nick, it seems that Rich came by right when I needed him. God sure had his hand in this.' He stated as he put his arm around his new employee. "Sarah, I've offered to put Rich up in the apartment over the garage, it's vacant and I'd like to have someone around the place." He smiled at Sarah before turning toward the barn with Rich. "Come on fella, I want you to meet Dennis, He'll be your number one man."

Ben Daniels was a dreamer, and it was because of that that he'd built up as nice of an establishment as he had in the six years he'd been at Horseman's Unlimited. Now at twenty-eight, his dreams were expanding, plans were in the making for a new stable and the purchase of a second stallion to join his Quarter Horse 'Cruisers Buck'.

Richard McAllister hadn't been part of the plan and although Sarah had nothing against Ben's friend she felt hurt that she hadn't been consulted before he made the decision to hire Rich. She left them at the barn finishing up a small tour of the facilities.

As Sarah was taking off her boots in the back hall she could hear sounds coming from the front room.

"Can you smile for Aunti Suzie? Huh can you? I know you can,.. there, that's it."

"Hi Suez" Sarah greeted as she entered the room. Suzanna was laying on the floor with Nick on the floor in front of her and they seemed to be having a blast.

"Hi little one, did you miss mommy?" She picked him up and cradled him in her arms. He looked up at her and began to gurgle. She smiled.

"Your momma loves you, she thinks the whole world of you,.. but too bad you had to born with my big nose."

"He's got his daddy's appetite." Suzie said. "I almost started calling him 'Draino'"

"He's got his manners too, ever hear anyone make so much noise drinking a bottle before?" Sarah laughed. The two sat awhile playing with the baby before Suzanna began.

"I must have scared Mr. Johnson off, he didn't stop by tonight. Did he?"

"No he had a meeting. Jeff came alone." Sarah informed her. "I don't think he's really concerned about what you've said, believe me, he's heard worse. And remember I talked to your parents and they don't seem upset. He never called them."

"I know, but I was so mad." Suzanna said. "At him, at myself, I just didn't want a hassle when I got home,. especially from Cindi."

"I understand, don't forget I've got a sister too and I know it's no picnic." Sarah agreed, then added. "Just guess who my husbands new helper is."

"It's Jeff isn't it" Suzanna asked. "I noticed his fathers truck is still here."

"No, but I'll give you a hint, he's tall, and he's ugly especially next to Tom."

"Richert Whatever" Suzanna laughed "How did he manage to get hired?"

"I'm not really sure, all I know is that Ben needed help and Rich showed up. Ben believes that God was supplying his need so he hired him."

"I wish I could get a job that easy."

"Come on, you're only fourteen." Sarah remarked. "Besides, I don't want to lose my best baby-sitter."

Sarah made a large batch of popcorn anticipating her husbands return and had just settled down to a game of cribbage with Suzanna when the phone rang.

"Howdi" Sarah answered "No Mr. Johnson she isn't..."

Suzanna made a nasty face.

"She must have left around 6:30,.. No I haven't any idea, .. I assumed your wife was home...I didn't see Jeff leave.. well they should be coming in any time now. Bye, see you tomorrow."

She shook her head as she sat back at the table. "You and your faces, people can read you like a book."

"So?" Suzanna challenged. "I've got nothing to hide,.. except maybe a few pimples."

"Just be thankful you have fewer pimples than I have grey hairs.

At nine o'clock Suzanna got up to turn in. "I'll check on Nick before I hit the sack. I just can't seem to get enough of that kid."

"Thanks Suzie, but I can do it, I'm going up to bed myself soon." Sarah watched intently, out the window, into the darkness toward the barns. Ben had not yet returned. She never noticed Suzanna leave the room. It was after nine-thirty when Sarah finally noticed four figures on horseback approach the barns and dismount under the dim light from the tackroom.

"That's strange," She thought, "Ben never rides on the trails at this time of night, and he definitely wouldn't approve of others riding this late either. Maybe something was wrong?" Hurriedly she slipped into her boots and sweater and headed down the path. Before she neared the stable a car pulled away. "Well, that looks like Denni's car, Ben's not going to be happy that he neglected his horse after such a late ride." As she rounded the corner of the arena she noticed the figures of her husband and another man. They were talking together as they unsaddled the horses.

"I'm sorry Ben for sticking my nose in this." The stranger was saying "But I overheard too much and was curious about what they were up to."

"Don't worry about it, I'm just sorry that you don't agree with the way I handled it."

"Well it was a pleasant ride anyway." Rich McAllister added as Sarah walked up. "Now I've had a tour of the place in daylight and at night."

"Nick in bed for the night?" Ben asked Sarah. "Oh no! don't tell me you left him alone in the house with that juvenile delinquent. Who knows, she may be putting strange idea's into his mind right now."

"They're both sound asleep. It wasn't them I was worried about. You never go riding this late at night. It's not normal for you to be out like this."

"Well Rich, no normal person would be doing what we just did. But then I never claimed to be normal and I don't think that you have either."

"On the contrary, I have. But only recently." Rich said quickly.

"Oh Sarah, after talking, Rich has agreed to return on Friday. I'm having Bill go up and see that everything is in order at the loft. Can we expect you for chow that evening?" Ben asked turning once again to his friend.

"Oh anytime." Rich laughed as he picked up two saddles and carried them into the dimly lit tack room. Ben followed with two more. As Sarah turned back toward the house Alfalfa a large Husky-Golden retriever mix came from the door of the barn and followed close at her heels.

"Well Alfie," She sighed. "It looks as though I've been left out of things again." They walked side by side to the house. Sarah let her hand drop to the top of the dogs head. Here was a friend from her past, a confidant. Yes, things were changing. Ben and Sarah had always done things hand in hand, sure they still did now, but it seemed like more people were joining him in the things that they once had shared and enjoyed so much, while she remained at home with Nick. True, she wanted to be a mother more than anything, and she did want to spend time with her son, but she also wanted the freedom to do the things that she enjoyed so much. "Must there be this conflict?" She wondered "Am I wrong to feel like this." What had happened to that perfect peace that God had given her. No, Alfie didn't have the answers,-Only God did.

The season of change had come to Sarah Daniels and she rose to meet it. On her knees she accepted the change,..not fully understanding all he had in store for her.

CHAPTER 2

A TIME TO EVERY PURPOSE

Wednesday, September 14, 1983

When the sun first shone through the Maples and Pines along the path to the Stable, Sarah was there, dressed in her ever present boots and a heavy cardigan sweater. Alfie wandered up from the stable to meet her.

"Hi fella" Sarah greeted. "You must be hard up for company if you want to be with me." The dog just sighed, and lay at her feet as she saddled Moses her bay Quarterhorse gelding. "I just don't understand the changes that are taking place. There are times when I wish things would return to the way there were." She mounted and headed toward the nearby woods and the golden fields of hay.

It was early and Bill had not yet let the horses out to pasture. The pasture was empty, the path was empty, the woods were empty. Sarah was alone; or so she thought. There was an unseen presence that remained with her. It never left her side, never failed to be on hand when ever she called. Like the faithful friend that ran along beside her, the Lord was there also, a friend who had travelled many weary miles at her side and would never leave nor forsake her.

The dew was still damp on the grass and the air was still crisp but, as Sarah rode she appreciated the beauty of the moment. The moment when all nature seems to waken to a new and wonderful day.

The birds were singing sweetly from the tops of the trees. "Oh to be like a bird." She thought "Free. Free to come and go as I please, to be able to soar above the tree tops with seemingly no trouble at all."

The fields were ripe, the men would begin harvest next week. The plants had grown so freely all summer. They stood straight and tall and golden in the morning sun. "I wonder why they grow so tall and straight" She questioned herself and almost immediately she gazed upward. 'The Sun' the plants grow toward the one that gives them life.' Tears came to her eyes as she thought of how she must also keep her eyes on the one who gives life.

The path ahead grew rockier as they neared the woods. Moses knew the place well, but still as he approached he was wary. He had stumbled here once before, he had once stood unsteady as he nicked the side of a large boulder. He had been here before and knew that if he was not alert he might stumble again. Sarah, knowing this allowed him to go a his own pace, for he alone could find the best route to the woods. Yet, as he walked Sarah's mind went back to the places she herself had gone that had caused her to stumble or slide, or maybe just to struggle a little. 'I sure need to be more alert and to keep my worries and cares from being in control of the peace within me.'

She stopped at the gate to the woods and dismounted. All around her the whole of creation was trying to tell her something. The birds, were given the power to fly above the house tops and trees, she had that power too. No, not the physical power of flight, but she had power from God above to rise above problems and situations at home, and from others. She had only to chose to use that power. The fields, if they chose not to strive after the sun who gave them life would cease to grow. Would she also cease to grow spiritually if she chose her own desires above that which God had chosen for her, and not only would she cease to grow but would she whither and die? and Moses, precious Moses, her friend who had carried her,.. carried her! Yes, God was there. He was there always to carry her along when she became too weak. Her eyes filled with tears, her knees were weak beneath her, as she knelt in the open field and poured out her heart to God.

Later that morning Sarah, with little Nick bundled up against the early September chill, made her way to the barn and stables.

"Want to go see Da da?" Sarah asked, bouncing Nick happily as Alphie jumped up and down and ran circles around her.

"Da da da da" Was all Nick could say.

The Daniels farm was quite large, with one barn mainly consisting of an indoor arena, along with a tackroom, office and lounge. Beyond were two other barns, both referred to as 'the stables'. The first contained horses that were owned by others who boarded there, and the second was occupied by Ben's horses, including 'Cruisers Buck' his pride and joy.

Ben was not in his office so Sarah walked across the open lot to the boarders stables hoping to find him. She glanced toward Misty's stall, but seeing no one headed down the next alley from which she could hear Bill Winters voice softly singing.

> Oh, Lord my God when I in awesome wonder
> consider all the works Thy hands have made
> I see the stars, I hear the rolling thunder
> all power throughout The universe displayed.

Bill looked up from where he was trimming the hoof of a Saddlebred, Sarah joined him.

"Oh, you are a blessed sight Missy. I'd just about forgotten the looks of you, but seeing your smiling face puts me at peace knowin' you're well."

"Oh, come off it Old timer." Sarah teased "I'll always pull through."

"Well I can tell you're havin' a rough time of it, and it is as I said, a relief seein' yer face."

"Am I that obvious?" Sarah questioned.

"Only to those who know yew as well as I" He answered with a twinkle in his eye "And knowin' yew reminds me that even though ye ain't no fighter, yew ain't a quitter neither."

Sarah smiled content again as she settled down on a bale of hay holding Nick in her lap.

"Well whipper snapper, seems to me that in a few months I could use some help from yew. All this bendin' over I's doin' 'll put me down one day, and it'd be no trouble a'tall for yew." Bill smiled then continued. "Ben tells me that he's got a new honcho comin' soon. I'll be goin' over to check on the place come quitin' time, but I spect there'll be a few critters livin' in there after all this time."

"Just give me the word when they're all gone and not a moment sooner. I'll be goin' tomorrow to clean a bit, and I'd rather be alone." Sarah laughed.

"Everything should be in order." Bill added "I'll get the juice to the place as soon as possible and if anything's shot, I'll either fix it or retire it and create somethin' new to do the same thin'."

Sarah smiled, she was well aware that the Old timer did know his stuff when it came to mechanical as well as general horse care. She always felt safe knowing he was around.

"Have you any word from the Doc or Johnson on Misty's condition. She should have that foal anytime now."

"No, no. Misty'll be around fer a few more weeks yet, but I've not heard from Johnson's a'tall, usually gone when Ray gets here, and then the missus, she never comes back this way."

Slowly Sarah nodded, and rose from the hay. "Well, I hope it doesn't take too long. It makes me nervous seeing a seventeen year old kid act like an expectant father." Bill chuckled. "Nick and I'll be heading out to find Ben, It was good chattin with you."

"Well Missy, he came by earlier to say he'd be a leavin' to do business. Haven't seen hide nor tail of him since, yew may be in luck though, it would be best to look."

"I'll do that." Sarah stated as she left the stable and walked into the chilly September breeze.

Ben pulled his car in front of the large two-story home on Broad street and was relieved to see the 'Clunker' parked in the drive. The home was kept up nice and the yard was well taken care of, a skateboard and a basket ball lay about the driveway but all else was neat as a pin. "Sister Rhodes will have the house neat as a pin too." He surmised.

"Brother Ben!" Elizabeth Rhodes exclaimed when she answered the door, "What a wonderful surprise. Ooops, You haven't come to complain about my daughter have you? I give you my word that she will not intrude on your homelife once more."

Ben held up his hands. "Hold it! We love having Suzanna around, I just stopped by to see if your husband was busy, I'd like to speak with him a minute."

"Of course Brother, he's in the study. Go right in." Ben thanked her and turned away. Later, seated beside his pastor in his small but comfortable study, with a full cup of coffee, he relaxed.

"Ben, I've never seen you so uptight, what's the trouble?"

"It's hard to explain, I don't fully know what is going on."

"Well, let me have it, maybe I can help."

"But this has nothing to do with you, or God, or even the church." Ben stated. "I guess what I really need is a friend to talk to."

"I'm here" His pastor interrupted.

"Well" Ben began, "I may as well let it out. First of all what do you think of Ginni Little's son Denni? Not from a pastors view point now, just as a person."

"I usually don't answer questions like that, mainly because everything I say is taken as the 'Pastors' view point as you called it. But you're his friend more than his employer, and if you've come to me I know you want the truth." He paused. "Dennis is a fine, courageous, intelligent,... boy"

"That was mild." Ben said.

"But that is just the beginning, first I did not say sensible. He tends to be very easily swayed but deep down he really wants to do what is right. Secondly, I said boy, though he's seventeen he is still very much a boy; he cannot handle responsibility as well as that other fellow you have working for you."

"But Dennis is the Christian." Ben said confused.

"Responsibility and accepting it come from maturity, not necessarily from God. Does that help you at all?"

"Far from it." Ben continued. "Do you feel that Dennis, deep down in his heart wanted to live for God?"

"Oh yes definitely." His pastor added "Overlooking his age and haphazard tendencies, his real love is for the things of God. Now it's my turn to start the questioning. Why are you asking me this? Has Dennis done something? or can't you tell me."

"Well, I intended on telling you." Ben started "Last night I was about to overtake him and a friend as they were riding in the woods. I'd say about 8:30. When I was summoned by someone who also seemed to be following them. Come to find out it was an old friend of mine. He'd been at the farm yesterday and overheard conversation concerning the delivery of cocaine on my property. Well to make the story short, the two of us followed the boys and sure enough another guy met them and made a delivery. Rich wanted me to stop them, but I talked him out of it. We did meet up with them, as they left the woods and I let Denn know that I disapproved of him riding that late at night. I never let on that I had witnessed the deal. The two of us escorted them back to the barn but I am not sure that this is the end." Ben settled back in his chair, having the burden lifted in a small way, just by sharing it. The Reverend Rhodes remained silent.

"Thank you for listening" Ben said after a few minutes. "I just need your prayers to sort this all out."

"No" His paster corrected him. "Dennis needs your prayers. Whatever he is getting involved in both you and I know is wrong. He needs your prayers. We must remember above all that there is a young boys soul at stake here. Just pray that God will show his love and forgiveness to Dennis before it's too late."

The service that night had been beautiful. Sarah again rekindled the thoughts that God had laid on her heart early that morning. "Look not where your feet are treading now but look beyond, at your goal, your victory, the glorious reunion with your father in heaven." Sarah wondered if

Pastor Rhodes realized how really close he came to speaking to her at that time.

"For he is here to comfort us and keep us from evil if we do not let our eyes stray from his face or our feet from walking in his truth."

The lesson tonight on 'He leadeth me in the path's of righteousness' was one of a series of lessons on the twenty-third psalm. Brother Rhodes continued.

"He will lead us, he must lead us. The path of righteousness cannot be found but by the righteous, only he is righteous. Only he can lead us, and we must be led. If we fail to completely place our life in his hands, he cannot lead us to the fullest, for our own desires would become a snare and hinder our walk. But, if we keep our eyes on him, our leader, he will carry us through."

The words echoed through Sarah's mind, she had heard them before. That morning, from the trees in the woods, the crops in the field, the whole of creation all seemed to be crying out the same message. She relaxed more, relieved of a little more of her burden as she glanced at her husband beside her on the pew. Yes, he looked more relaxed also, yet those lines of worry on his face seem to have remained, or had they always been there? He caught her glancing at him and smiled, yet the lines still remained, they framed his whole face and seemed to enhance his smile. Yes, his whole face seemed affected by that smile. She was indeed blessed, to be the mother of a fine healthy boy, but also to be a wife. She realized that the path she was on did not cause her to be alone, but the man beside her travelled one also, one he may not be too happy to accept at times. Maybe together hand in hand with hearts and minds and souls kindled with love they could make it. They both had the same ultimate goal. They had the same purpose.

CHAPTER 3

A TIME TO BE BORN

Thursday September 15, 1983

Sarah could hardly believe that the time had gone so quickly. Nick slept peacefully in his playpen sucking contentedly on a tiny pink thumb. Around her lay the work of the afternoon, needless to say, only half done.

"Well" She muttered to herself. "I'll never make it in this world as a maid."

It was another beautiful day. How she longed to go down to the stables and maybe take Moses around the arena a few times, even Nick enjoyed that, she could have gone down the lane toward the fields and back. This would have been a beautiful day for that,.. but why was she fussing? She had assured Ben that she could handle the cleaning and she would. She would force herself to. Thus she continued scrubbing the floor of the small apartment's kitchen, amazed at times at the change that a little soap and water could do. She was determined that by the time Richard McAllister returned with his belongings tomorrow, that the place would be spotless. "I'll probably offer to come in once a week and clean again, although I hate cleaning other peoples messes."

The windows were open wide to the September breezes which brought with them the sweet smell of hay and horses. As it blew over her she couldn't help but look up, through the kitchen window toward the barn and the fields beyond. It was a beautiful day all right, birds were singing in the nearby trees, and she knew that old Bill Winters was probably singing in the nearby barn as well. She also began to humm softly to herself.

'Well' she chided herself 'A minute ago I was ready to throw in the towel, now, I feel so at peace.' She scrubbed the countertop and sink and then made her way quickly to the bathroom. As she passed the playpen she glanced down at her sleeping child. There he was, that complete version of peace, yet, so dependent upon someone else for everything. She continued to gaze down at him and recalled the times she had felt the most peace were the times she had taken her whole self and placed it in God's hands, depending completely on him to supply her needs. 'I guess there is one essential ingredient to my peace' she thought 'I must depend on God, for he alone really knows our needs.'

The bathroom needed quite a bit of work but she worked diligently and as she was putting away the last of the cleaning supplies in a small cabinet by the door, a voice called up.

"Hey Sarah, aren't you through yet?"

"It's just like you." Sarah answered "To pop in just when I get through for the afternoon."

Suzanna Rhodes climbed the outside steps two at a time, but remained quiet when she noticed Sarah's finger to her lips and glanced toward the playpen.

"Oh," She whispered "Little bit is sleepin"

"Still, but he shouldn't be for long, I'll let him sleep. Let's go out on the landing." The two sat down on the top step of the stairway that led to the tiny loft apartment.

"Well, tell me. How did things turn out with Mr. Johnson."

"Oh, not too bad. He kinda ignored the situation, which isn't like him at all."

"Oh come on, he isn't that bad." Sarah could not help but feel that Suzanna had blown the situation out of proportion, after all she knew Ray.

"But Sarah, you don't know him! We don't get graded on how much we learn or our test grades. Our grade depends on things like class participation, behavior, attitude, and whatever else he could try to judge you on; not to mention how much you learn about the United States Government, which in my case is already -0-. I really haven't got a chance." Suzie answered.

"Sure you do, but leave it in God's hands. He can take care of it."

"Isn't that a cop-out? My father thinks so."

"Leaving things in God's hands is never a cop-out, in fact it's a commandment. I believe the scriptures says, 'cast all your cares upon him for he careth for you.'

"Sure, sure, 1Peter 5:7" Suzanna replied "But my father says that if we leave everything in God's hands nothing gets accomplished because God needs us to labor, not just to sit around and do nothing and expect him to do miracles."

"And your father is right. But this is a completely different case, unless you really feel as if you've been wrong and need to make things right." Sarah continued.

"But how would I do that?"

"Do what?"

"You know. Make things right. I don't think what I've done is enough to condemn me but I do feel I need to make things right."

"Apologize to Mr. Johnson."

"Apologize! to that ugly, useless, excuse for a teacher?" Suzanna exclaimed, then broke out laughing. "Just kidding, I think I've known for awhile what I need to do, for instance since about two seconds after I said what I did to him. But, I was kinda hopin' that you might come up with a better suggestion that would be easier to accept."

"I know it's hard but I'll repeat my familiar phrase,... TRUST GOD."

Sarah looked around the table at the people about her. To her left sat her husband, strong, handsome, she could add more to describe him. But as she watched him now she was aware of how much of his inner being was revealed in the things he did. His light wavy hair was windblown and tossed, the look of a man not over zealous with his outward appearance, yet he was clean and well shaven. His eyes always giving that little hint of a twinkle reflected the joy that was settled within, yet his gaze was straight and steady, solid determined as was his nature. His feet were planted firmly beneath the table as his steps both naturally and spiritually had always been, yet, his body was relaxed, content with his life, his home, his family. A wonderful man, Sarah thought, a pillar.

Beside him sitting across from Sarah sat a tall, dark, refined looking young teenager. His brown eyes were soft and tended to speak with kindness and gentleness, his voice was rough, but his words were cultured.

At his left sat Suzanna. Sarah smiled to herself. She could just imagine Suzanna's remarks to her friends about how she managed to sit next to Tom VanDyke. The son of wealthy Charles Bronson VanDyke, Tom was valedictorian of his class and an editor of the school paper. Right this moment Tom was sitting next to a punk preachers kid whose looks resembled more an oversized Teddy Bear. Suzanna Rhodes was short and plump, with merry eyes and a ready laugh, she had thick dark hair that normally was pulled into a pony tail while she was visiting around the farm. Her black eyes and olive complexion contributed to the numerous rumors about her escape from the reservation.

Suzie listened with half an ear to what Tom, (Her current flame) was saying as she carried on a separate conversation with a tiny fine featured, young lady with piercing blue eyes, and soft blond hair that was pulled into a knot at the back of her head. She had a timid smile, reserved actions, and an unlimited stack of manners and courtesy. Her name was Peggy Winters, and she sat next to her Grandfather, Bill. The old codger always clean and neat had the same piercing blue eyes as Peggy. They seemed to look through you with an unknown wisdom. His face, though aged and wrinkled, had a settled look from years of completely trusting God in all things. To his left and to Sarah's right, only hidden from view by Nicks high chair sat Chrystal Shephard. Chrystal was the proper name for her, Sarah thought for she is truly a Jewel. She was well kept and proper yet had such a giving attitude about her. She deeply cared about each little thing that concerned anyone she knew. Sarah looked at her clear complexion, the rosy cheeks and faultless hairstyle. Yes, Sarah thought, she is a jewel.

Little Nick was playing happily with a small set of plastic keys, so, Sarah continued her meal in silence. She still marvelled at the ways God had shown her his blessings in the last few days.

It was still early evening, the sun was barely beginning to set beyond the horizon. Suzanna, with Alfie close at her heels headed toward the stables. Ben had loaned her the use of Old Faithful Camalot, a beautiful but aged Palamino mare and she intended on taking advantage of the opportunity.

It truly was a beautiful evening, the sounds of the night were just beginning and above it all Suzanna could hear the sounds of the farm still alive with excitement. The thud, thud, of horses hoofs in the arena, the occasional whinnies, the dull sound of conversation, car doors opening, phones ringing, the motor on the pop machine, all of them added to the wonderful sounds that enhanced her being. But the one that Suzanna picked out most was of course the most familiar, the steady, though often out of tune whistling, of Bill Winters.

She rounded the corner of the barn deep in thought and inadvertently disrupted a meeting beside Mr. Johnson's truck. Dennis Little, Jeff Johnson, and Brady Downing were grouped about the front hood when Suzanna turned the corner and walked right into Brady.

"Oh!" Suzanna said startled "Excuse me, I'm sorry, I'm terribly sorry."

"Oh, anytime." Brady said with a laugh. "I don't mind at all."

"It's about time you came down to earth Rhodes." Jeff remarked.

"I guess I did let my mind get away from me." She added as she hurried past them toward the Daniels family stable.

"This is just great." Brady scoffed after she had gone.

"What's that?" Denni wondered.

"Don't be a fool, she heard every word we were saying."

Jeff Johnson looked after Suzanna's retreating form with concern. "You sure?" He asked.

"You saw the look on her face didn't you, she's a narc if I ever seen one. Isn't she some preachers kid or something?" Brady asked, he and Jeff looked at Denni who was busy regarding the designs his boots were making in the sand.

"She is isn't she?" Jeff asked Den pointedly.

"Yeah" He mumbled.

"Oh just great, and it's too late to change my plans." Brady complained.

Jeff looked concerned. "What are we going to do?"

Brady thought a moment, finally a smile spread across his face.

"Just leave it to me. I can handle her." His grin let them know that he had everything under control.

Suzanna had just reached Cam's stall and was leaning against the gate talking soothingly to her when she felt rather than heard someone come up alongside her.

Startled she turned once again to look into the cold blue eyes of Brady Downing.

He came and stood beside her looking in at the large mare.

"Going riding?" He asked.

"Uh huh, Cam here and I are old friends, we're gonna spend some time together." Suzanna managed to smile but was uneasy.

"Alone?" Brady asked, and when he saw Suzanna's bewildered look, he grinned. "Do you mind if I join you?"

"Why ah,..no, not at all." Suzanna stammered, still uneasy. "Your welcome to come along if you don't mind my backwoods riding style."

"How's that?" He asked.

"Oh, I just hang on for dear life and hope I don't fall." She laughed.

"Now that's got to be an exaggeration."

"Well, I have been known to stretch the truth at times.." Suzanna admitted. "But only in fun."

"I'm sure." Brady laughed. "Den, is letting me take Prints out, I'll meet you outside the tack room." He turned, and began walking away, but before he got far he added. "I'm looking forward to it."

Suzanna, having an over curious nature anyway, wondered at the sudden interest, especially from someone such as Brady whom she barely knew. But, she could only continue on. She led Cam to the hitching post outside the stable door, then went for a saddle and bridle. She was surprised to see Prints already saddled and Brady nowhere around. She soon gathered her tack, and headed back toward Camalot. She was just leaving the tack room when two strong arms reached out and enfolded hers.

"Here let me take that for you." It was Brady.

"Thanks" Suzanna smiled as she allowed him to take the load. He watched closely as she saddled the mare, then turned toward her.

"Need a leg up?"

"I can manage." She answered.

"Just trying." Brady grinned, his eyes twinkling.

Suzanna had never been one at a loss for words, but now as she mounted Cam and turned to meet Brady on Prints she seemed to be at a dead end. What do you say to someone you barely know? She glanced over at Brady, yes, he had those cold blue eyes that seemed to shut everyone out, but otherwise he had the looks of the athlete that he was. Tall, strong, and yes, quite handsome. She decided to make the best of it and just be herself.

"What are you grinning at?" He laughed "Do I look that funny? I sure feel it."

"Just pretend the reins are a football, then you'd feel more relaxed holding them."

"And about your backwoods riding. I haven't seen you hang on yet. Talk about exaggeration."

"Only in fun, only in fun." Suzanna laughed. Maybe things wouldn't be too bad. "Have you ridden a lot?"

"Does it look like it?" He asked, but added "No, no. Den got me up here once before. That was it. I rode once or twice around the building and I was ready to surrender."

"Why's that?" She wondered.

"I like to have control of things, and when I get up here I guess I feel as though I lose that."

"Oh, but you don't! Think of the control you have, to be able to persuade the horse to go where you want. Now that's control." She continued. "I feel I have more control being here, than anywhere else. I can go places that I wouldn't even think of going alone, I can go for hours and never tire, but it's not really the control I enjoy the best, it's just the oneness of a horse and rider. I feel part of the horse many times when I ride."

"Well, I've been referred to as part of a horse at times too." Brady said with a laugh, when he found that she didn't share in his laughter he continued. "You know it's really neat."

"What is?" She asked.

"Watching you ride." And when Suzanna blushed he added. "Well I have to learn from someone."

"Just watch it, I might pull something on you." She ribbed.

"Like what?" He wondered. Before the words were out of his mouth, Suzanna gave Cam a swift kick and rode off at a fast gallop. Brady being caught off guard was not able to keep Prints from following close behind so he rode "Backwoods Style", meaning he hung on and hoped he wouldn't fall. At the end of the stretch of path that bordered the corn field Suzanna pulled up. Soon Brady joined her.

"Well" Hc said catching his breath. "I learned the backwoods method and a lot more. Next time, I'm bringing a pillow."

Sarah quickly dodged into the stable door out of the breeze. It smelled of the sweet hay that was being distributed among the horses. She made a face at Tom as she passed the stall that he was working in, on her way to see Morning Mist's (Misty's) new filly Lady Falene.

Ray Johnson, Jeff and Bill were still gathered around Bills work area amid halters, blankets, shoes, and other paraphernalia, discussing the filly's future. Sarah could tell that Bill was on his way out, having stayed much later than planned to be with the mare.

"Well Missy, You's getting out a lot these days. Come to see de little filly that ain't supposed to be here for a few weeks?"

"Don't worry, I've heard you make false predictions before and would never consider you as a prophet."

"No Isaiah am I, but them hosses has young un's when they's good'n ready."

"So do people" added Dr. George Martin as he approached from the stalls where his horses were kept. "She's a mighty pretty picture isn't she?"

Sarah walked over to the large box stall, Misty was up and so was a tiny sorrel colored bundle of legs, or at least almost up. Nick had been close to horses all five months of his life but this was indeed the funniest looking one he had ever seen. As soon as his eyes focused on it his hand were reaching in that direction, wanting to grab.

"Don't worry little guy, You'll have one of these for your own someday." Sarah told him.

"Probably sooner than most do." Jeff commented. "It'll make his daddy's day to see this little one astride one of these fine creatures."

"So true." Sarah agreed. "It's probably one of the biggest events that daddy's looking forward to. Me I think on a small scale. When he was first born I couldn't wait for that first smile, then his first giggle, now I can't wait until he starts putting words together. Each are little milestones for us."

"And I bet, in crossing all the little milestones, it's been usually just between you and Nick" Ray Johnson spoke.

Sarah thought a moment, surprised. "Why,..yes, but how did you know?"

"I'm a father, remember. All fathers go through the time when Mom and baby share these little treasured moments, while we're off at work. It is a privilege that you have, to be a mother." He let his words stop at that but Sarah knew then how very true they were. The birth of a young filly had reminded her that life was always on the verge of a new beginning.

CHAPTER 4

A TIME TO DIE

Friday September 16, 1983

'Charlie's Cafe' was a small joint at the corner of Cedar and Spring streets in down town Roberts Junction. It was, of course, a hole in the wall where all manner of characters patronized, but it was clean and neat and Charlie was an excellent cook. Ben had never been a prominent man in town, had never wanted to be, but in this spot he seemed familiar with most that came and went and they all seemed to have good to say about him.

Rich enjoyed the friendship of his new employer. He was returning to town after ten years and had not been sure how his former neighbors and classmates would receive him. Most of the people he met on the street were strangers, but each time he glimpsed a familiar face, memories of that person from ten years or so before would be brought to mind.

As the two enjoyed their meal along with each others company, their talk wandered from discussions of the farm, former classmates, changes in town, til it finally rested on the strange occurrence of Tuesday night.

"Well did you get rid of the Dennis fella?" Rich asked "Your only askin' for trouble if you keep him on."

"No Rich, I disagree. He is a good young man, capable and hardworking." Ben began

"But is he trustworthy?" Rich asked "Ben don't be stupid! He's using his familiarity with your property and the access that his job gives him to be a party to illegal transactions. Ben, what makes you think that you can trust him not to pull something on you?"

"Rich, I've known Dennis since he was eight years old. I'd give him the shirt off my back if he needed it."

"He just might steal it first." Rich interrupted. "Those who become involved in any form of illegal practice lose all sight of what's right and wrong."

"Your talking as if you've encountered this type of person before." Ben mentioned.

"Yes, but not completely of my own choosing..." Rich let the statement drop at that, so Ben continued.

"Rich believe me, Dennis is different. He's been kind of an outcast and loner all his life. Right now Jeff and this other fellow, whom I know nothing about, are paying him a lot of attention. In other words it appears he's doing this to maintain their friendship."

"But Ben he *is* doing it, and he's doing it of his own free will. He's allowing them to use his job, while you allow them to use your property."

"I'm sorry you feel that way Rich, Dennis is too fine a fellow and friend for me to get too excited about this. He's a kid, a seventeen year old punk kid, and I myself and you know it, may have been caught up in the same under similar circumstances."

"Then Ben, if you insist on keeping him on, confront him with it. Because if you don't it may become too hard for me not to. As of right now I'm going to be watching him like a hawk, for I'd hate to see you get taken."

"If you do speak to him Rich," Ben began "Which I prefer you didn't, please keep in mind all I said. He's a kid, don't treat him like a man, and please don't expect him to behave as one."

The two men closed their conversation and began gathering their things. It was barely 7:30 and the town was beginning to bustle. As they moved toward the door, a tall young man, clean shaven, neat, yet modestly dressed entered the cafe with a load of books under his arm. He hailed Ben sincerely and noticing Rich nodded his head in gretting.

"Hey Brother, I didn't realize you were with someone. I just poked my head in to say Hi!" The young man stated. "Haven't much time for more that that, school starts soon."

"It's good to see ya, you've never met Rich, but he'll be around the farm when your out."

"Oh!" The young man exclaimed. "So this is the infamous Richard McAllister. My sister filled me in on all the so called jolly times both you and Ben shared 'way back in the dark ages.' He extended his hand "Hi, I'm Patrick Rhodes, older brother and part time guardian of that kid sister of mine Suzanna. Whom you undoubtedly remember as in inquisitive loud mouthed bratt."

"Not quite loud mouthed, open mouthed maybe, and amazed." Rich started. "But I am pleased to meet any friend of Bens."

"Pat's forgetting that 'loud mouthed bratt' turns into 'quiet young lady' whenever Tom VanDyke is around." Ben added with a snicker, that vanished quickly as he glanced across the street at a young couple on their way to school. The girl was obviously Suzanna.

"Well guardian, you'd better get to work, you've been sloffing off." Ben nodded in their direction.

"And that" Rich pointed out "Is not Tom VanDyke." The two men watched as Pat waved and followed after the pair, grinning. After he had gotten beyond hearing distance Ben slowly added.

"That friend of Denni's that I said I knew nothing about?" Rich nodded for him to continue. "Well, I just learned something about him, and I'm not sure I like what I've learned."

If Ben had been startled at what he had seen from the doorway of Charlie's Cafe, how much more startled was Suzanna barely five minutes before, when upon turning the corner of Broad street onto Spring, she had come face to face once again with Brady Downing.

"You may have gotten yourself out of a ride into town from the farm last night, but you can't stop me from sharing the sidewalk with you, especially seeing that we're headed in the same direction."

Suzanna smiled but looked soberly at him "But Brady, you live nowhere near here, we may be headed in the same direction but, it sure seems as if you went out of your way to do so."

"And I'll be doing it again if you don't mind."

"But I do mind." Suzanna said once again looking at him. "Brady, listen to me. If you want a friend, you've got one. But you've got plenty more too, and a number who'd be willing to accompany you to school if you can't seem to find the place yourself." She grinned trying to cover her straightforwardness with humor, but not succeeding in the least.

"So now I'm doomed to be deprived of a few enjoyable minutes in your company this morning?"

"Well, join me then if you've got it in your head to do so." Suzanna added for she did enjoy his company. "But let me warn you, I'm not alone."

Brady looked at her quizzically, bewildered at her last statement, but said nothing.

Suzanna had spent a sleepless night. She had enjoyed the ride last evening more than she had enjoyed anything for a long time. 'I could kid myself' she thought 'and believe that we could build a friendship even a close one but I won't. I know any friendship at all will be completely destroyed unless I let Brady know from the beginning that nothing will ever go beyond just being friends. Unless,.. but, I won't even consider that, boy would he think it a joke if I even mentioned it.' Determined once again to be that straight forward no nonsense loudmouth that she was, she knew that if he still appeared interested in her she would have to let him know. 'A friendship is better than nothing.' She had concluded.

After a while Brady began "By the way? What is this friendship deal, I've got plenty of friends."

"You can have one more if you want it." Suzanna answered.

"We'll see" Then after a pause he continued "You'll let me walk you to class though?"

"Fine with me," Suzie laughed "I usually walk to class with friends."

"Lets leave them out this time." He added quickly "By the way, when do I get my next riding lesson? I've got the hang on and hope I don't fall part down. What's next?"

"Lesson number two." Suzanna remarked. "Never go any faster, or slower than the horse."

"Oh boy, I don't know if I'm ready for that." He answered recalling the agony of the ride last night. "I can only imagine what this will be like.

"Be thankful that I can tell you instead of having to learn it by experience."

"I have a feeling that if this goes any farther, I'll be experiencing plenty." Just at this moment a horn honked beside them and Brady turned to wave and holler a few words to a friend who was driving by. Noticing this, Suzanna turned around to face her brother, whom she knew was following and just shrugged her shoulders. She wanted Pat to know that she was in as much doubt about this young man as she knew he himself must be.

"Let's see," Brady began as they entered the school "Classes start in ten minutes. What do you have first hour?"

"English with Mrs. Grant. But I was hoping to stop across the hall at the Social Studies Office first. I guess it'll wait."

"It won't have to if we hurry, come on." Before Suzanna knew it, he had taken her by the arm and headed up the main flight of stairs. They hurried and got to the office in plenty of time.

"Thanks Brady" Suzanna said "Wish me luck, I'm not sure what's going to happen when I get in here." She nodded toward the door to the office.

"Trouble?" Brady asked "You?"

"Yea, me." She grinned "I'm human see?" And she pinched herself.

"Oh, I'm sorry, I guess I never considered you being in any form of a scrape, in fact on the way here I began to think that you didn't want anything to do with me, and that was why you were so cold about only being friends."

"Silly," Suzanna smiled "But I meant every word I said. That you will find is my chief problem. I mean what I say and I say what I mean." She nodded her head as she entered the office.

The receptionist Mrs. Roman was an older woman, slightly over fifty. She was heavy set with graying hair made into tight curls all around her head. She wore small wire glasses that slid down to the end of her nose as she worked. She would have to replace them every time she glanced up.

"Yes, May I help you?" She asked.

"Yes, Ma'am, I'm Suzanna Rhodes, and I'm wondering if Mr. Johnson is around. I had wanted to see him before he went to his classes today." Suzanna answered politely.

"Oh, I'm sorry miss. He hasn't come in yet this morning, but if I give him your name, I'm sure he'll get a hold of you."

"Oh, there's no need," Suzie put in "I've got him for class third period, I had just hoped to see him before then." Suzanna thanked the lady and hurried away quickly. She wasn't sure of the time but knew she should be getting to class.

As she entered the hall she glanced quickly at the groups of young people heading for their classes. Then turning to her left she noticed Mr. Johnson coming toward her.

"Good Morning Suzanna" He said sternly "I've just had a talk with Mrs. Grant. She won't be expecting you in class right away and I want to see you in my office. Go on in. I'll be with you soon." and he was through the door, past Mrs. Roman and out of sight before Suzanna could respond.

Mr. Johnson shared an office with two other teachers. It contained a desk, four straight backed wooden chairs, a large table piled a foot high with various newspapers and pamphlets and shelves and shelves of books, some still in mint shape but others in need of great repair from their hours and hours of use. Suzanna took a seat in one of the chairs and waited nervously.

It seemed an eternity that Suzanna sat and waited, she tried to put together a speech that would kind of make her look a little better, but nothing would work, she had been wrong. She must pay the price,.. whatever that would be.

Footsteps sounded in the hall outside and the door opened. Mr. Johnson entered, quickly tossed a pile of mail on the desk, collapsed into the chair and leaned back. Suzie looked at his face, it seemed as if she had never seen him before. His graying hair that had always been combed to perfection was tossed wildly, only a faint hint of a part remained. His face seemed to have a gray ashen look, and his eyes,.. as Suzanna looked at his eyes she saw, not the solid steady gaze that had been there before, but eyes that wouldn't look at her. Weary, tired, bloodshot eyes. He sighed and ran his hands through his hair. Resting his elbow on the desk he supported his head with his hands and just sat there awhile. Suzie wondered vaguely if he had fallen asleep when he pushed back from the desk, opened the top drawer and brought out a stack of papers.

"Mr. Johnson" Suzanna began "I had stopped by to apologize for my outburst the other day, I was wrong in losing my temper and for saying the things that I said."

Mr. Johnson looked up for the first time since entering the room. "But that is how you felt isn't it?"

Suzanna thought awhile. "No Mr. Johnson, it isn't really. I didn't feel you were forcing anything on me that I shouldn't have been able to accept. But I felt humiliated, I felt like you were singling me out and something in me had to fight back."

"Do you still feel I was singling you out?" He asked.

"Yes, I know it must be hard having one person in class that seems to always have to do things different than the rest, but you had no business singling me out and ridiculing me that way."

"You don't expect to get ridiculed?"

"Yes I do, but not from you, or any of my other teachers."

"Maybe you better start expecting it, in a few short years, you'll be walking out the doors of this school for good. No one will have consideration for your differences then."

"I guess not... I should probably expect to be singled out constantly. I guess I have no business getting upset with the way you handled it. If you want I'll begin reading that book tonight."

"That won't be necessary." He smiled for the first time. "I have the papers from the classes that I had asked to fulfill the assignment. I've chosen a few of the better ones, I'm going to ask you to read them. You can make a report on their views of the issue, it should be an interesting project."

Suzanna took the papers he offered and placed them inside her folder. "Thank you Mr. Johnson. I hope that in the future I won't become a problem to you again." She glanced up at him and he was smiling at her.

"Suzanna you have been far from a problem. I'm just glad that you have accepted the fact that your differences can become an inconvenience to those of us who don't understand them."

Suzanna got up to leave but before she did Mr. Johnson stopped her. "Suzanna" He started "I'm going to meddle a minute if you'll allow me. Your parents and I may not have the same ideas and goals about your immediate future, but I'm hoping that it doesn't include that young fellow I saw you with both last night and again this morning...Brady Downing."

Suzanna was standing now, shocked at what Mr. Johnson had to say, but knowing deep down how right he was. She left the office toward class, her heart lighter because of the apology she had made, yet at the back of her mind was the strange change of appearance in Mr. Johnson, and the last statement he had made.

The hallways of Kennedy High School can become pretty chaotic between classes. But each morning after first period three young boys meet without fail beside their lockers on the east wing. The first, a shy timid young man, small of build yet strong of character is none other than Dennis Little. The second, a tall lanky lad, with sandy hair and dark brown eyes rimmed with glasses, his name is Jeff Johnson. The third blue eyed young man of course was Brady Downing.

"Ready for the game tonight?" Brady asked Jeff.

"Yeah, sure" Jeff shrugged.

"What in the world is up with you, you look as though you lost your best friend."

"In a way I did,.. but then not really" Jeff's answer sounded confused.

"Well, I'm excited. We're gonna slaughter 'em. The comets haven't a chance against the Patriots. No Way! remember the game last year with them? Talk about Tender Feet."

"That's right." Dennis said "I heard the way they played was a joke.

"They aren't any better this year." Brady commented. "It'll be a cinch."

"What's up after the game?" Jeff asked "I want to know what I'll be missing."

"Missing? You mean, I'll be on my own? Dennis sure isn't the partying type, in fact I'm lucky he even associates with me at all." He wrapped his arm around Dennis' shoulder and pointed at Jeff "Now you are gonna weasel out too? Well go ahead, I'll party alone."

"Hey man," Jeff added. "I don't mean anything by it. I just feel it's best if I head right home with Pa. It's got nothing to do with you."

"Sure, sure, Dennis is probably wearing off on you. But it won't happen to me."

"But" Jeff added jabbing him with his elbow. "You're the one that seems to be associating with those so call 'Holy Rollers' more and more."

"Hey what does that mean?" Brady was surprised. "I'm just teasing Dennis, he can take it."

"I'm referring to your new sweatheart." Jeff chided. "Suzanna."

"Hold it guy, you know I've got things all under control. It's part of my plan." Brady stopped "Besides in her very own words, we can only be friends so cool it."

"It won't take you long to change that." Jeff laughed.

"Oh, don't underestimate Suzanna" Dennis put in seriously "if she said friend, that's all she'll be. You can try Brady, but you won't get far, and you may even lose that friend."

"All I need to do is keep her yap shut until after tonight." he said pointedly "Than I don't care if we're arch enemies."

Denni shook his head.

"Don't think I can handle it huh?" Brady asked.

Denni shrugged. "Just kinda shocked that you'd even try."

"Well I can't afford a slip up now, there's too much at stake. Well, it's getting late.. I'll see ya." Brady smiled as he headed down the hall toward his class.

"What a joke" Jeff laughed.

"What is?" Denni wondered.

"Brady and Suzanna together." The two just smiled at each other. "But, He'll try." Jeff continued.

"But Jeff," Dennis said "So will Suzanna" They both laughed.

Dennis turned to Jeff seriously "Hey guy, What's up. Something's bothering you."

"Den, I can't tell you." Jeff started. "But you've claimed that God answers prayer. Den.. I haven't any answers for anything, not one. Everything it seems is being pulled out from under me. Could you pray for me."

"Jeff. I've been praying for you. Now it's your turn. My prayers won't answer your questions, and my prayers won't put anything solid under your feet. You say it seems like everything has been pulled out from under you. Jeff I'm trying to base what I do and live directly on the word of God. It has stood for centuries. Nothing can take it away, nothing can pull it out from under me. You can have the same Jeff, if you just pray and ask God.

Suzanna was glad fourth period was over. The morning had seemed so confusing to her. First of all there was the strange encounter with Brady on the way to school, then the meeting with Mr. Johnson, and what he had to say. Then third period Mr. Johnson had sent in a substitute teacher. "He must be sick, he looked terrible." Suzanna reasoned aloud.

She hurried toward the Home Economics class rooms where her and Peggy usually met before going down to lunch. She was just turning the corner when she felt a hand on her arm.

"Hey where ya headed?" Was the question.

"I'm meeting Peggy." Suzanna answered coldly as Brady stepped beside her. They continued down the hall.

"Is she expecting you?" Brady asked.

"Oh, yes. We always eat vittles together."

"Vittles huh"

"That's what Gramps calls 'em and what's good enough for him is good enough for us too."

"Peggy's the quiet one, that doesn't say much but thinks a whole lot right?" Brady asked.

"I guess you could say that." Suzie laughed. "She really is a honey down inside." The two were now approaching Peggy as she was gathering her lunch and a note-book from her locker. She turned and saw the two of them, recognizing Brady she blushed slightly but smiled.

"Peg, have you met Brady Downing? I've been trying to shake him all day, but it hasn't worked."

"Hi" Peggy answered.

"Hi Peggy" Brady replied then turned his attention back to Suzanna, "Hey, I'd like to walk you home from school tonight O.K.?"

"She might let you but I won't" A deep voice sounded behind Brady. Startled he turned and was met face to face with Pat Rhodes' gentle smile.

"No offence fella, but I'm gonna steal this young lady after school to see her home safely."

"Pat, come on." Suzanna complained.

"No, Suez, I'm serious, I need you. I'll explain it later. Meet me at the south entrance at 3:00 O.K?"

"I suppose." She answered.

"I've gotta rush, I'll see ya then." Pat ended.

"Hold it!" Brady demanded as Pat turned away "What's going on here?"

"I often wonder that myself" Pat laughed as he disappeared into the crowd.

"Hey" Brady said "who is that guy? is he the reason you've been trying to get rid of me all day? If he comes between us, I'll take care of him." Brady jokingly held up his fists.

"Brady,.." Suzanna insisted. "there is nobody, not you, not him, no one. I'll be repeating that as long as you continue to feel differently."

"And I will continue trying to get you to change your mind." Brady said with a grin "Although I've been informed that that is impossible."

"Oh, oh," Suzanna said looking at Peggy. "Someones been talking about me."

"Just some small talk with Denni and Johnson, Denni seems to think you're pretty sure of this friend business,.. and Jeffer, he's kinda on my side."

"Spare me the details please." Suzanna laughed.

"Sure, but if you've got plans with your friends right now, I'll go look up a few of mine." He also headed down the hall.

"Suzie?" Peg asked after quite a silence. "What's going on?'

"I will rephrase my brothers answer." Suzanna quoted. "I often wonder that myself." Then breaking into a laugh she added. "Imagine, thinking that Pat and I were interested in each other."

"He really had no idea that Pat was your brother, just wait until you tell him."

"Who's gonna tell him?" Suzanna remarked.

"Suzanna Rhodes you wouldn't"

"Just wait and see" Suzanna said "and by the way, that deal that Johnson's trying to push, well he has no idea what he's doing. Brady thinks that in my be-coming more than a friend to him, he'll be winning. But I know, that if I can introduce him to my dearest friend and see him open his heart and soul to God, We'll all be winners."

"Suzanna, I've never heard you talk like that. I hate to say this but you sound like,.. me"

"Well, who do you think has been my example all these years?" Suzanna smiled back "Pray for that fella Peg. If anyone can pray a hole in heaven it's you. And maybe with me helpin'..Praise God! I can't begin to imagine what God will do."

Pat Rhodes was on a mission that sent him home during his short lunch period to borrow the family 'clunker', when Dennis Little hailed him before he ever left the school building he welcomed the younger boys company.

"So, your getting the car huh?"

"Yeah, Do you remember Michelle Morrison?" Pat asked rather timidly.

"Well, yeah, I think so. She dated Joe Jamison, they came to church awhile before Joe left for the service."

"Mmm Hmm" Pat nodded. "Well, it's her last day of classes, I offered to help cart some of her books and stuff home after school."

"Her last day?" Denni looked confused.

"I guess you haven't seen Michelle lately." Pat guessed.

"You know I don't pay a whole lot of attention to girls." Denni reminded.

Pat nodded rather hesitantly. "Michelle's baby is due in a few weeks."

"Her Baby?" Denni gasped. "And Joe's?"

Pat nodded.

"Wow." Was Denni's only comment. "I guess I'm pretty out of things."

"She kinda keeps to herself, and being a senior you wouldn't have any classes with her anyway."

"Your driving her home?" Denni asked.

"Yeah,.. with Suzanna, to please Pa of course." He grinned.

"That aught to keep you both in line." Denni grinned.

"Both?.. Has my kid sister been having problems staying in line?" Pat asked.

"Not yet, but that buddy of mine, Brady Downing, is gonna do his best to Monopolize her interest. He's a very persuasive guy. She's gonna need to be quite strong to stay on top of things. Some of us aren't that strong."

"You've always appeared to stay on top." Pat added.

"Appearances can be very deceiving." Dennis continued "It looks as though this one fella," Points to himself. "Has bitten off too much of the world, and when it began choking him he tried to spit it back out only to find that damage was already done."

"We all make mistakes, Den" Pat put in "don't be down on yourself, God knows what's in your heart."

"Yes, and he sees the sin and the filth as well as the good intentions. No Pat, I'm a sinner, one of the lowest. I don't know if I can ever except forgiveness. But at the same time I still can't refrain from sharing God with the very ones who have witnessed my sin. Pat! I'm a hypocrite. I can't help it. I love the Lord, he's all I'll ever need, but I still get dragged in continually with what my friends are doing. I've justified it in the past, because I thought I could win them to God by being just like them. But Pat, I can't continue. I've got to make a choice. Actually I've made the choice, years ago. My friends need to be told that I've been wrong, but,.. I haven't got the guts to do it." Dennis rattled on. "I was supposed to meet them at noon today but I couldn't bring myself to do it. I know that the next time I see them I'll have to make some sort of confession, or apology or offer some explanation and I really wish to avoid that."

"Dennis, I'll be praying for you. Meet them today after school, point out where you were wrong, explain that you've repented and God will forgive you, ask them for forgiveness also. Denni you may lose some friends, they may have liked the compromising Denni better. But, I'll be praying."

"Thanks Pat." Den said "I know you will."

Later after a short trip to the Rhodes house and a reminder from Pastor Rhodes to drive safely, Pat and Denni returned to school for their afternoon classes. They were just entering a parking stall in front of the south entrance of school when Denni noticed Jeff pulling in a little farther from them. Brady was in the seat beside him.

"I'll get going on that explanation right now, instead of waiting until after school. Thanks Pat." He opened the car door and was gone in a flash.

"Hey guys!" Dennis called as he hurried to the car.

"Well if it isn't our missing link. Where have you been." Jeff asked smiling.

"I took a walk with someone."

"Yeah, sure." Brady laughed.

"You guys got a few minutes? I want to talk to you about something."

"Oh oh," Brady began. "I think I feel some preaching coming on."

"Brady hear me out this time." Denni begged "It's really important to me that you hear this."

"O.K. Shoot." Brady answered as he joined Jeff on the front hood of the Johnson truck.

"I don't want to preach to you but I do want to tell you what has been happening to me. When school started this year and Jeff and I became partners in Chemistry and then the three of us in English together, I thought that it was great. That I had some friends that I could keep for a long time."

"O.K. Den, what did we do?" Brady wondered.

"Hear me out Brady, You haven't done anything. I have. I began to do things to keep your friendship, things that I knew were wrong. Guys I was wrong to have anything to do with your deliveries, or to be with you while you drank or used drugs, or shoplifted. I know I never got involved but I was wrong, just being there was being involved enough. I justified myself in my mind guys, but I was no innocent bystander. I know what is going on, I can no longer have part of it and still live for God. I've asked him to forgive me, I know he will, although I don't see how he can. I'd like you to forgive me also. I want you to know, I've changed my life. You may not want to remain my friends, but I really think you are both neat guys, I'd like to continue our friendships. But guys, I love Jesus, I've given him my heart. There are things you will just have to count me out of."

"Count yourself out right now." Jeff the more passive of the two declared. Both Brady and Dennis were surprised at the anger in his voice.

"Don't be so hard on him Jeffer." Brady started, but Jeff went on.

"I'm sick and tired of people claimin' to be Christians, and living hypocritical lives. We talked before Chemistry today, remember Den. I was wrong to think your prayers or your God could do a thing when the very skunk that is causing my whole life to crumble is claiming the same power and the same God."

"Come on Jeff, Settle down." Brady asked again.

"No I won't settle down. I've been settled down long enough. My family is suffering because of 'so called' Christianity, and 'so called' Christian beliefs."

"Jeffer, what are you talking about? Have you gone off your rocker?"

"No, Brady" Jeff said settling down. "That church has, everyone of them. If they think that they can claim to be above sin and living holy, and having Jesus in their lives while they live just as sinful as the rest of us, if not more.." Jeff had changed abruptly from an angry temper to almost a weak voice full of emotion. "Denni, you love the bible and claim it is the source of your strength, at the same time it was through a bible study that my mother met the fella she's having an affair with, real Christian behavior if you ask me." Jeff scoffed. "We thought nothing of it when Ma first started going to these 'bible studies' at the Daniels, we trusted them, they were 'good Christian's' so we thought. Now our whole life is falling apart and I can't help think that Ben Daniels is behind it somehow." Jeff was really shook up and by this time both Denni and cold hearted Brady were pretty emotional. Jeff buried his head in his hands and just sobbed.

"Jeff, I don't know what to say." Dennis stated. "I had no idea what you were going through. True I think the world of both Sarah and Ben Daniels, but surely they can't be at fault."

"Don't take it out on Denni, Jeff. He's always been straightforward and honest with us. This situation may have ruined your family don't let it ruin a good friendship too."

"Jeff" Denni tried again "My father left us a little over a year ago. My whole life fell apart because of it. But Jeff, I had something solid under my feet to hold me up, God's word. I had friends that lifted me up in prayer daily. Ben Daniels being one of them. What you've said is heart-breaking, but I'm sure if you talked to Sarah Daniels she'd be as heart broken as you are."

"Oh Denni, I'm just sick and tired of this whole thing. I'd be a fool to say I didn't love my mother, but what has happened has been very hard on all of us, especially my Dad."

"Let's keep our heads about this thing." Brady started. "Class starts in five minutes and the three of us need to be there, and in good form so straighten up."

"I'm not going" Jeff stated. "I don't think that I could handle seeing anyone else today. I'm going to find my Dad. Maybe if I talked to him we could both figure something out."

"Fine. See you at the game tonight." Brady called as Jeff climbed back into his truck.

"I'll be prayin' Jeff" Dennis added "You can't stop me."

And in the parking lot of J.F.K. high school the spirits of two young boys had died. Dennis' with the realization of how far his life had drifted from what God intended it to be had died to the flesh when he openly confessed his sin to his classmates' and Jeff, star athlete, tough guy, and even keeled, had died to the flesh while relating the incidences that were happening in his life. The scripture mentions where Paul says he 'died daily', we can just be thankful that for Jeff and Denni we know that there is life after death.

CHAPTER 5

A TIME TO PLANT

Friday September 16, 1983

Judy Johnson, wanting to refrain from an embarrassing confrontation with her husband, did not go directly home that morning after working the night shift at the Good Samaritan Hospital. Instead she headed toward the nearby town of Lincoln where she had breakfast with a gentleman that for now remains anonymous.

Returning home much later than expected she entered her living room at 10:00 and found her husband waiting. That he had been drinking was obvious for he was really a sight. The incidents involved around his recent condition had deteriorated his outlook drastically, in reality he had just ceased to care. Judy's heart went out to him, for part of her truly loved him. He didn't acknowledge her entrance but knowing that the time had come to speak the truth she walked over and took the chair that had sat beside his for years. She put her hand on that seemingly feeble weak one that rested absently on the arm of his chair.

"Ray darling, let me explain." She started.

"I've been waiting" He stated.

"Ray, I didn't want it to come to this."

"Yes, I know, You never planned for the children and I to find out." He interrupted sarcastically.

"Oh, Ray, That's not it. I didn't want to see you in this condition. Hurt, broken. Ray, I should have come to you long ago. I should have told you long ago,.."

"Your things are packed." He stated bluntly.

"So you are going to send me off then?" She asked.

"Isn't that what you want?"

"Ray, I love you, I love the children, I don't really want to leave."

"What!" Ray was furious "You make a laughing stock out of me and my children, go running around with another man and you have the audacity to come in here and tell me that you love me. Judy, love doesn't work that way. Love binds families together, it doesn't tear them apart. It's obvious to us all that something is going on, the kids may still accept you, but I can't. I can't live with it. I love you so very much. You always knew that. Don't make me live in a dream world thinking that you love me in return. If you can't love me and only me and be happy, please go."

"Ray I do love you, believe me. I won't lie to you and say I hadn't been unfaithful. But Ray, that doesn't mean I love you any less than I ever did."

"Don't you feel anything toward him?"

"Oh Ray, he's a wonderful man, understanding, courteous, the kindest man I've ever met. Ray he's done so much for me, I love you, your a wonderful man, and father. But Ray, so much more was missing in our relationship, I've found what was missing."

"So your not going to stop seeing him?"

She sighed "I've tried to stop, many times."

"How long has this been going on?"

"About eight months." Then seeing the shocked look on Ray's face added. "We kept it secret as long as we could, I just wish I'd come to you sooner."

"Will you be wanting a divorce?"

"Ray! I don't even want to leave!"

"Jenny packed your things. She is really shook, we all decided it was best."

"So you've gone to discussing this with the kids'

"Judy, you wouldn't. You told us nothing at all."

"I'll put my things in the car and I'll be back for more." Judy replied stubbornly. "There are a lot of things here that are special to me."

"To bad the people aren't." Ray began "I'm warning you, you're free to go. You're free to live you're fulfilled life. But that life does not include my children. I will fight you tooth and nail on that point if I have to. They are my children and nothing you do can keep me from being their father.

"Your forgetting, I'm the one that gave birth to them and raised them."

"And deserted them. No Judy, I won't listen. You've chosen your lot, take it. Have your fulfilled life, we'll try our hardest to have ours, without you."

Suzanna was only half concentrating on the textbook before her. Her mind was a million miles away, totally consumed with hopping from one idea to that next, yet never resting on her accounting assignment.

"Psst" Suzie heard amid her wandering "Suzanna" Suzanna turned quickly. Miranda Helms the girl sitting across the aisle from her was attempting to get her attention.

"How did you do it?" Mandy asked.

"Oh, I'm sorry" Suzanna apologized. "I wasn't thinking about accounting."

"Neither am I, I just wanted to know how you did it."

"Did what?"

"Get Brady Downing interested in you. I think he is s-o neat." Mandy rolled her eyes. "I'd do anything just so he'd talk to me."

"You would?" Suzanna asked surprised. "I hope I haven't done anything." She said sincerely.

"Oh come on, he's been following you around like a lost puppy all day, you must have charmed him somehow."

"I'm afraid not." Suzanna laughed. "You know me better than that, I'm just me. I don't try to charm or come on to anyone. Hope I never do."

"So do I, the rest of us would really be in danger if you did."

"What?" Suzanna was shocked.

"It was a compliment, silly, not an insult. You've got such a natural honest way of doing things that makes most everyone like you. I can't imagine what it'd be like if you felt you needed to start flirting."

"There indeed is no threat that I will start either. But still I wasn't aware that people thought that of me."

"No you wouldn't. That's the unselfish part of you." Mandy smiled. "I know I'm not one of your close friends, but I enjoy being around you and so do the rest of the gang."

"They do?"

"Yeah, hey, I've got an idea. Bonnie, Dana and I are meeting at my house before the game tonight. Why don't you come too?"

"Oh, I'm sorry Mandy, I've got plans tonight. Besides you know I don't attend those types of functions."

"Well, I tried, but I'm sure Brady will be disappointed that you don't come to see him play."

"I don't think he expects me." Suzanna laughed. "We're just friends."

"Yeah, yeah," Mandy smiled. "I sure wish that I had a few friends like that."

The conversation baffled Suzanna. Mandy Helms had barely spoken to her all year, yet, she considered herself Suzanna's friend. She was also pretty shocked at the compliment Mandy paid her. Was she really that likeable? She'd always been able to make friends but to have people like her personality made her proud of that determination to be herself. Maybe if she did try harder, .. but no. She'd be herself,.. nothing more.

Once again the halls of Kennedy High were total chaos between classes. Suzanna dodged quickly into the hall that led toward her locker.

"I'll spend study period in the library." She thought. "I've got to read these papers Mr. Johnson gave me."

Peggy greeted her with a smile as she reached their locker.

"I've got the best news." She exclaimed.

"Shoot." Suzanna said, "I need some exciting news."

"Angie Arnolds, my Physics partner is coming to Youth Service tonight."

"Really, That's great!" Suzanna smiled. "I hope our skit goes well."

"It will if you can remember to say your lines without giggling."

"And if we can keep Luke from over-acting." The two girls smiled a little recalling Suzanna's younger brothers attempts at theatrics. "Mr. Johnson was quite fair with me this morning." Suzanna changed the subject.

"Oh, really? He accepted your apology, I'm glad." Peg said sincerely.

"Yes, he did, and we had a really neat talk. I still have a paper to write, but it's not as drastic of an assignment as before."

"That's good, he is a good teacher." Peggy added "as good as any teacher can be." She made a silly face.

"And you're the one who likes school." Suzanna accused.

"Correction. I like learning, I tolerate school." Peggy laughed.

"Well I'm on my way to the library, to get started on this paper. I'll walk with you to class." Suzanna said as the two closed their locker and headed down the hall. They hadn't gone far when they noticed Brady Downing heading their way.

"Oh oh" Peggy said in mock despair "Should I hide you?"

"Don't bother, I can't win him to God if I avoid him." Suzanna pointed out.

"Just be prepared." Peggy reminded.

"Good afternoon Ladies." Brady stated as he approached.

"Hi" they both answered.

"I thought we got rid of you before." Suzanna added.

"It'll take more than that to get rid of me." Brady laughed "By the way, where are we going."

"We?" Suzanna asked rolling her eyes. "The last I recall, I was walking Peggy to phy-ed class, you can come also, of course, if your taking aerobics."

"That's got to be a lot safer than taking riding lessons from you." Brady remarked. The three walked in silence until they reached the girls locker room.

"Bye Suzanna, I won't see you 'til tonight. Gramps and I are picking Angie up on our way in." Peggy stated. "Bye Brady."

"I'll remember to say a prayer." Suzanna added as Peggy entered the locker room.

Once alone with Suzanna, Brady began.

"Sounds as if you've made plans for tonight."

"It's just a goofy little skit. But we've had a blast with it. My name will be 'Blanch Perfectio' and needless to say, I'm the preachers kid."

"I'm not surprised." He smiled. "But then nothing you do would surprise me."

"Now I don't know about that, I tend to amaze people at times with my warped ideas."

"I was hoping I'd see you some time tonight, at the game maybe."

"I thought you knew better." Suzanna stated.

"Huh?" Brady was confused.

"I'm sorry" Suzanna laughed. "But with all the discussing your friends have done I assumed that Denni had informed you that I wouldn't be there."

"I don't recall it ever coming up." Brady stated. "But now, where are you headed?"

"I've got some studying to do and thought I'd stop at the library."

"It's Friday, couldn't you finish it over the weekend and come with me now, for a coke at the canteen?" Brady asked.

"I guess it could wait." Suzanna answered reluctantly.

"Thanks." Brady smiled. "I was hoping you would."

Sitting at a table in the schools snack shop with Brady Downing was the last place in the world Suzanna expected to be, or should be, yet not necessarily wanting to be overly rude and secretly enjoying his companionship and complements, she had agreed. They found a table after getting their cokes.

"I see 'ol Johnson's out today." Brady said "You'll have to wait for a meeting with him. Maybe Monday."

"Oh, I saw him early this morning." Suzanna informed him "He came in right after you left. I had a nifty apology to make, and now I've an ever niftier assignment to makeup." She smiled patting her folder.

"He came in today?" Brady asked. "I'm surprised. But he's home now probably. Jeff's gone too. He couldn't hack being in school any longer today."

"Really? Why is that?" Suzanna asked puzzled.

"That's right, you wouldn't know. But I guess good Ol Johnson's wife's been having an affair with some guy."

"What!" Suzanna's mouth dropped open in surprise. "Mrs. Johnson, That's terrible... Oh the poor man, and Jeff, Oh Brady, Jeff must really be shook up. I don't know him very well but I know that something like this is hard on everyone."

"Yeah, he's kinda beside himself." Brady admitted.

"Was Denni able to talk to him?" She wondered

"Yeah, Denni talked." Brady answered. "That kinda fed the flames a little. I've never seen Jeffer so mad. Told Denni that he didn't want to be his friend and all that. I was pretty embarrassed about the whole thing."

"Why would he lash out at Denni?" Suzanna wanted to know. "Denni went through the same thing a year ago."

"They may have similar cases but frankly I think there's a lot of people around that are pretty blind to reality. Denni gave us a cute speech about wanting to live for Jesus, which kinda started the whole mess."

"But what would that have to do with Mrs. Johnson?"

"Well it seems that she met the fellow she's involved with at a bible study,.. he must be a Christian."

"Lot's of people say they're Christians."

"Do you mean you don't think this man is a Christian." Brady wanted to know.

"Brady, I may be weird, but I have very firm beliefs. The only Christians in the bible were called Christians from others because of the way they lived. Christian, means Christ-Like, if people live for Christ they become more like him, then folks can really call them Christians. No Brady. If he's having an affair with a married woman, I would not call him a Christian. That is in no way Christ-Like."

"Does your church teach this?" Brady wondered.

"Our church teaches the bible. It's in the bible that adultery is sin."

"But what if I told you that this was a bible study from your church? Would you believe me?"

"Brady, What are you driving at? Do you mean to say that Mrs. Johnson is having an affair with a member of my fathers congregation?" When he didn't answer, she continued. "I hope they've got evidence."

"I guess they have." He shrugged.

"Your gonna tell me who it is now and quit this guessing game aren't you?"

"Who the guy is?" Brady asked. "Somebody named Daniels from what Jeffer said."

"Daniels!" Suzanna gasped.

Brady nodded.

Brady had been hoping to get a reaction out of Suzie, but what happened next surprised him and a few others that sat near them who witnessed it. Suzanna's face got deathly pale, she closed her eyes for a brief second then grabbing her books she fled from the room, her chair falling to the floor beside her.

Brady had no choice but to follow Suzanna as she fled the room. Luckily for him she had stopped nearby and just gazed out a window. She was standing so still he was almost afraid to approach her.

"It's okay Brady." She surprised him by responding. "I'm okay now. I just hope you realize I don't normally react this way."

"I guess I wasn't being wise myself." Brady admitted. "I did kind of keep you guessing; I didn't expect that reaction."

"Brady don't ever play games with me." Suzanna stated seriously "I detest them."

"Won't happen again." He agreed then smiled. "It seems we've both made foolish mistakes."

Suzanna nodded then turned to face him. "Brady, I need to know something. Was all you told me back there the truth or was it part of your game?"

"Suzanna believe me, I repeated things exactly how I heard them from Jeff."

"It's that bad huh." Suzanna asked.

"I guess there's no doubt."

"I didn't want to hear that, I think the world of Sarah, you must know that, and I guess my heart is broken because of her, and oh,.. poor Nick, my buddy." Again tears came to Suzanna's eyes. She turned her back on Brady embarrassed by the show of emotion. She was crushed inside, Ben and Sarah seemed so happy. Little Nick had his whole life ahead of him with a father that was a first class,.. she couldn't think of anything to describe the hatred she was beginning to feel toward Ben Daniels. Never in her life had anything affected her like this. She quietly sobbed uncontrollably, so shook by the whole incident and so furious at Ben, that she didn't object when she felt Brady's strong arms around her shoulders. He leaned his head close to hers and whispered.

"Don't let it get to you, they'll pull through somehow."

"Buy why Sarah? Why must she suffer?"

"Who knows?" Brady shrugged.

"I guess I just need to get a hold of myself and face facts."

"Is there anything I can do to help?" Brady asked.

"First of all, you get your arms off me. I shouldn't have allowed it in the first place." She answered giving him her usual grin.

"Well, I enjoyed it while it lasted. "He quipped back. "But, with my hands free I can easily take these now." He reached for her books.

Suzanna was still quiet when she met her brother after school, silently she climbed into the backseat of the Rhodes old beater, only slightly aware of the conversation going on between her brother and Michelle.

"I'm glad you waited." Pat told Michelle.

"Thanks for the lift, I guess I'm too proud sometimes to admit I need help."

"No problem at all, Have you made arrangements with your teachers about your classes."

"Yes, I'll be studying at home, and hopefully be able to pick my classes up again when I return after Thanksgiving." Michelle stated. "The teachers, most of them anyway, were really good at making allowances for me. I know I shouldn't expect it."

"I'm glad." Pat smiled "things will be easier now for you without school pressures."

"Oh, it's not too bad. I just get so weary." Michelle stated honestly.

"I'll tell you what I'll do. I'll stop over one night each week and keep you up to date on what we're learning in Physics."

"Oh, Pat. Thanks for offering, but I'll be Okay. This is my decision and I'd rather go it alone."

"But your not alone, you know that."

"Now your gonna say, the Lord is with me and he loves me, he loves Joe too and he loves the baby."

"Yes, he does, and he cares." Pat added.

"Pat, if Jesus cares, why is this happening? I would have followed Joe anywhere you know that. Why did it hapen this way? Why must I go it alone? Why must this child remain fatherless?"

"Michelle, don't get bitter toward God. He's given us all a will and a choice to make. Joe made his choice, you yours."

"I often wonder if I've made the right one. I listened to your advice when I was at my weakest point and sometimes I regret that decision I made."

"But you made the decision and it's up to you now to make the baby's life happy, and you can't do that being bitter toward Joe, or the baby or God."

"You'll make a good preacher someday, you know that." Michelle laughed.

"I'll forgive you for that remark," Pat stated seriously "But don't give up on God Michelle. Remember he cares about each and every one of us and about that little one not yet with us."

They were pulling into Michelle's driveway when she turned to both Pat and Suzanna.

"I want to thank you both, for the lift naturally, and emotionally. Pat, I'll try to remember your words. It's a little late to start feeling sorry for myself."

"But you can't do it alone, many have tried." He stated earnestly.

"We'll see." She said as she got out of the car. Pat watched until she was safely inside before he backed from the driveway and headed home.

"Your gonna have to watch yourself now." Suzanna threatened "I don't intend on forgetting that remark Michelle made about you being a preacher."

"Thanks a lot Kid." Pat answered."So, what was keeping you so quiet."

"I was busy." She answered "My parents taught me to be quiet and sit still and listen during the preaching."

"You never seemed to listen to my preaching before." He reminded her.

"I guess once in awhile a person needs to quit thinking and just listen a little bit."

"Do you want to talk about it?" Pat asked pointedly. It was a game between the two of them, they always seemed to know when the other was in need of a friend.

"Not really, You'll hear sooner or later, and I can't bear to put it in words."

"I'm sorry to hear that." Pat said "It's never good to keep things to ourselves long."

"I think you and I are the only ones around here that feel that way." She added. "When my heart gets full and ready to spill over I'll come to you."

"By the way" Pat wondered "Who's your new friend?"

"Some creep" Suzanna stopped herself. "No I shouldn't say that, he's fun to be around, polite, nice looking, popular, but,.."

"But what,..?"

"I wouldn't trust him an inch" She stated simply.

"Then don't" was all her brother said.

Suzanna barged into her fathers office the moment she got home from school.

"Where does one go around here to find the truth?" She asked.

"Try right here." Her father stated, lifting his well worn bible up and holding it out to her.

"Does it say anything in there about Bible Study?" She asked.

"Study to shew thyself approved unto God, a workman needeth not be ashamed rightly dividing the word of truth."

"Yeah, right Timothy isn't it." At her fathers nod she continued. "Did Timothy go to a bible study at the Daniels farm?"

"No, but I know several who have." He stated simply.

"Did they all find lovers while they were there?" She questioned further.

Her father looked confused, "Run that by me again." He asked.

"Did they all find lovers there?" She repeated.

"I hope not, your mother went to several of those meetings." He attempted lightheartedly.

"Did you go?" Suzanna asked.

"It was a woman's bible study, I thought I'd stay out of it. Sarah usually kept me up to date on the response though."

"It was a women's bible study? Didn't Ben go?"

"Not that I know of. He's a very busy man Suzanna."

"So I heard." Suzanna scoffed.

"Young lady, what are you trying to get at? It's not like you to interrogated me this way."

Suzanna crossed the room and dropped into a chair, shoving her hands into the pockets of her skirt.

"I guess Jeff Johnson's mother went to a few of those bible lessons."

Her father was thoughtful for a few minutes. "Johnso-n,...yes, Judy Johnson."

"That's where she met the fella she's having an affair with."

"Suzanna how many times have I warned you about believing gossip." He corrected her. "This was a women's bible study, one even the Pastor of the church didn't attend because he was a male."

"But Jeff said."

"Jeff could be wrong."

"He even told a friend of his that the man was Ben Daniels." Suzanna insisted. "Couldn't Ben have possibly been at a few of the Bible studies."

"Of course, it's even probably that he was, it is his home you know." Her father spoke slowly "But Ben Daniels is not having an affair with Judy Johnson."

"Tell his son that." Suzanna stated.

"I will... if I have to." Edward Rhodes regarded Suzanna for a moment. "Ben Daniels is a fine man Suzanna, one without any intention of...." Edward shook his head.

"But it could have happened."

"Yes it could, and I could have shot the mayor and robbed the Washington State Bank. Forget it Suzanna, you need more than accusations to get me to doubt Ben Daniels. And you need to learn to take the words spoken against the brethren as folly if they are not backed by fact."

It was just becoming twilight when Jeff Johnson approached his home. He had wandered all afternoon, not going anywhere particular but just wandering. He looked at his home. HOUSE he should call it, just an empty building, full of happy but misunderstood memories. He lowered himself onto the back steps and gazed at the yard.

Memories flooded his mind, his mother hanging up clothes while he and Jenny ran laps around the clothes line poles, his mother pushing him on a swing, teaching him how to go higher. The swing set was gone now, but the memory was there. He recalled the games of croquette, the old pup tent that his mother had helped him set up, the pigeons they had kept, his first patch of pumpkins that they had tended together. More recent were the times spent this past summer cooking on the gas grill and playing games of domino's and cribbage. And the farm. How could he ever bear to go out there knowing that, that was where it all started, or rather ended.

"I was worried son," Said a voice behind him.

"I'm sorry Dad. I should have called."

"I understand, really I do." His father said honestly as he sat beside him. "Things will never be the same, you know that."

"Yeah," Jeff nodded. "Is Mom gone?"

"Uh huh, she left late this morning."

"How is Jenny?" Jeff asked.

"Pretty deflated, she hasn't said much, and barely ate a bite, are you hungry?"

"No Dad, I couldn't eat."

"I'll let you go today but remember life must go on." His father said, "And you both need to eat decent."

The two sat in silence for awhile. The stars were beginning to appear, and the crickets had begun their evening serenade.

"Dad?" Jeff wondered. "I just don't understand. I don't know who to trust anymore. I love mom and I thought she loved me."

"She does son."

"But why this then? And Daniels, I've always thought a lot of Ben."

"He hasn't done anything Jeff." His father answered.

"I find that hard to believe." Jeff scoffed.

"Your mother would have found someone with out spending time at the Daniels'.

"Is that what Mom says?"

"That's what I know to be true Jeff. Your mother is a very unhappy person. This relationship has changed that."

"She wasn't happy with,... us."

"She wasn't happy with *Me*." Ray said pointedly.

"And you believe that, with all the lies she's given us lately."

"I find it hard to believe any of this, Jeff, lets just say I'm accepting it. I told the fella so myself."

"You talked to him?" Jeff was surprised. "What did you say? Hey I don't even know who he is."

"All I said to him was that he made a good choice, but a very unwise one in my opinion."

"Oh Pa, be serious."

"I'm very serious. He can have her if he wants her. I'm not that forgiving of a person."

"Does he want her?"

"Huh?" Ray laughed. "I really don't know. I've only met him a few times."

"That's right, you know who he is. Aren't you gonna tell me?" Jeff asked.

"Oh I'm sorry son, Sure,...His name is Steve Williams."

"The Cop?" Jeff asked suddenly.

"I don't know if he's a cop." Ray answered. "He's the fella that owns Special Export."

"Yeah, he's the cop. You'd think a guy in his position would be straighter than that."

"It's only a job son." Ray added.

"But it should be illegal. Dad." Jeff said angrily.

"They're both adults son, and both should know what they are doing."

"Wait until I see that guy." Jeff said angrily.

"Don't do anything stupid. I've already made many unwise decisions and had to suffer."

Jeff thought awhile, and then quickly got to his feet. "Oh no! I've got to find Denni"

"Whatever for?" His father wondered.

"I let steam off at him today and I owe him an apology."

"It can wait." His father stated.

"Maybe, but I can't take any chances. I'll be home soon." Jeff started away.

"Where to?" His father asked.

"Church" Jeff replied. "Where else?"

Jeff pulled the truck to the curb before the small church on Willow street. A welcoming glow was coming from the lighted building, but Jeff didn't see it. The songs of praise were drifting on the air but he was deaf to them. He had but one goal, one aim, to see Denni. To apologize.

He entered the small building quietly. "I hope I can find him and lure him out of here so we can talk." Jeff thought, he approached the doors leading to the sanctuary. He couldn't miss the singing now. The jubilant voices of those few young people filled the air.

Love lifted me
Love lifted me
When nothing else could help
Love lifted me

Jeff entered the sanctuary and quickly glanced about. "That's funny" He thought, I don't see Denni anywhere." He glanced around once more before his eyes rested on the young person that was leading the group in song. Dennis Little.

"Well look at that" Jeff thought. "He's here, I just don't think It'll be that easy getting him away."

Jeff entered a pew toward the rear of the church to wait.

Dennis himself, was quite surprised to see Jeff enter. 'What now. Oh no! Ben's supposed to speak next, and after Jeff's accusations this afternoon I hope he's not here to create a scene." It became harder for Denni to lead in the singing and he stammered constantly while asking for testimonies. "Lord," He prayed silently 'Whatever happens tonight, have your will.' He was relieved when it came time to ask Ben to speak.

Denni descended the platform and was about to join the boys in the front pew when Jeff motioned to him.

Dennis quickly walked to the back and entered the pew where Jeff sat. Jeff looked nervously at him.

"Hey, can we get out of here? I want to talk." Jeff asked.

"Is it important?" Dennis wondered. "Ben will be done in a few minutes and I really want to hear what he has to say."

"Come on." Jeff urged. "I don't like it in here."

"You can wait outside if you want" Dennis stated, he knew that his decision this afternoon to put God first would include hearing his word, even a small five minute talk at Youth Service.

"Aww. I'll stay" Jeff whispered "What have I gotten myself into now." He thought. He began looking at the things around him. A few banners hung between the tall windows that extended to the high beamed ceilings. The first was red with gold lettering, and it read...

HEAR O ISRAEL
THE LORD, OUR GOD
IS ONE LORD

The one opposite was also red, with a family silhouetted along the bottom in black, the letters in white read,...

CHOOSE YE THIS DAY
WHOM YE WILL SERVE
AS FOR ME AND MY HOUSE
WE WILL SERVE THE LORD.

Jeff thought they looked kind of bold, not very appealing. 'I enjoyed looking at the ornate stained glass windows and statues at St. Bernards when Ma made me go' He thought. There he was thinking of her again. Maybe if he listened to what Mr. Daniels was saying he could get thoughts of her out of his mind and rid himself of some of the pain he felt.

The service closed with prayer and Jeff and Denni quietly left the building.

"It was a surprise to see you Jeff" Denni said honestly. "I hope I didn't offend you today, if I did, I'm sorry."

Jeff was silent a minute. This wasn't going as he had planned at all. He's the one that should be sorry, not Denni. "I came to explain to you that I was wrong to blow up like I did this afternoon. I was being a fool to blame my personal problems on you or your church."

"It's okay Jeff." Dennis began "You may not believe this, but I know how you feel."

"Yea, I guess you do."

"But Jeff," Denni continued. "Your life doesn't have to fall apart. Jesus still loves you and every time it looks like the world's gone black it seems he shines a light to get you back on the path."

"That's good for you Den. But not me. You may believe and live how you want, I don't think it makes a difference. Ma went to church every Sunday, she forced us to go with her, and Denni, look at her today."

"But Jeff don't you see?" Denni said. "Jesus is God, he loves you. Going to church doesn't make you a Christian, anymore than going into a barn makes you a cow."

Jeff laughed but added. "I get the point, but Ma prayed the rosary too, she took communion, she never ate meat on Fridays during lent and all that other stuff. I don't understand."

Denni didn't know how to respond but added. "Jeff, it's more than that. Jesus is my friend, not only that, I've got his Spirit within me. When I pray I'm not praying to someone far away and remote, I'm talking to a friend just like I'm talking to you. But that friend is the all powerful, all knowing God."

"I don't understand at all." Jeff repeated bewildered "Religion seems to me to be a sham just to get peoples money, and a platform to pump people full of opinion and self righteousness."

"I'm sorry you feel that way." Denni said. "But I'm also afraid you might be right."

"See!!"

"Sure, you've been talking about religion. Your mother's religion. But I've been talking about a real God. A relationship, I guess that ceases to be religion but becomes more a way of life."

"Your crazy Den, you know that?" Jeff smiled.

"Sure do." He answered.

Tom VanDyke was just replacing the last of the grooming supplies that evening when Rich returned from the stables.

"Everything in order?" Rich asked.

"Yea, looks that way." Tom responded.

"You heading out now?" Rich wondered.

"Yea, I'm just gonna leave a note here for Ben, I noticed a horse favoring a leg out on the trail tonight."

"Think it's serious?"

"Not if we've found it soon enough." Tom answered as he wrote on a small sheet of paper. "I'll just leave this here where Ben will see it." Tom added as he placed the note on Ben's desk.

"You really enjoy working with the horses here don't you?" Rich questioned.

"To the utter disappointment of my father,.. yeah." Tom admitted. "I'm supposedly going through a phase and will grow out of it."

"Ben didn't" Rich added laughing.

"And I hope I don't." Tom continued. "My father would have liked me to go into business with him. But I was never interested. It really broke his heart at first. But there is one consolation."

"What's that?" Rich wondered.

"I've three younger brothers." Answered Tom with a laugh. Rich joined him.

"I didn't come looking for a job when I stopped by Tuesday, all I needed was a place to board my horse, but I think I'll enjoy it." Rich said confidently.

"Ben is a fair person to work for." Tom returned. "He'll treat you the same as he treats Old Bill whose been here all his life."

"Yeah, Ben's always been like that." Rich recalled.

"That's right, you're an old friend of his."

"We were buddies in High school." Rich stated. "Did a lot of hunting and fishing together. We'd go up camping with our friends, and while they spent the majority of their time going from bar to bar, Ben and I did the hunting and fishing." Rich chuckled to himself. "Don't get me wrong, neither of us was without our trusty bottle or pipe."

Tom smiled encouragingly and Rich continued. "After High School, We kind of parted, I went off to college, I guess Ben continued working with horses."

"You went to college?" Tom stated.

"Yeah, I studied conservation and forestry. I got my degree back in '78. I landed a job right a way with a logging company out of Colorado scouting for them."

"Hey that sounds interesting." Tom commented sincerely "you travelled a lot?"

"Oh Yeah, I really enjoyed the work." Rich added then changing the subject asked. "Are you planning to go on to school?"

"Yup, there's a college up north with a real good program, I'll be majoring in Veterinary Medicine, and Minoring in Horse Science."

"A Veterinarian huh?"

"I've wanted to be one all my life."

"You'd think your father would be pleased." Rich added.

"Oh, I think he will be, he's just disappointed that I'm not walking in his steps. He had a lot of plans for me in the back of his mind, none of which I'm willing to fill."

The two moved quietly out into the moonlight. After walking in silence for awhile, Rich broke the stillness.

"Busy day tomorrow. Take it easy."

"You too." Tom answered as they parted. Tom toward his car and Rich along the path through the trees to the small garage apartment.

Jeff reluctantly agreed to join the young people after service for Pizza at Charlies. He wasn't surprised that after having a talk with Denni he no longer felt uneasy in the presence of the others, and besides he'd had nothing to eat since breakfast. Charlie out did himself and produced pizza's even the kids agreed could not be matched and all enjoyed the fellowship of one another. It was as they were leaving that Suzanna cornered her brother with a suggestion.

"Hey, Pat" She called "I'm gonna walk Angie home with Peg, tell Pa I'll be a bit late."

"We could cram you all into the jalopy." He answered.

"No Thanks, it's not far. And they are much better company."

"Ya, Ya" Luke lipped off as he headed toward the curb. "Better company for us,.. without you."

The girls walked slowly together along the darkened streets.

"I love fall." Suzanna said enthusiastically. "I love the crisp air and the smell, the sound of leaves, like this,.." She laughed as she jumped off the sidewalk and began trampling some of the leaves that had fallen in the park.

"Hey how'd you get rid of Brady today?" Peggy asked her as she rejoined them on the sidewalk."

"I guess I didn't"

"What do you mean?"

"I mean, I never made it to the library, we went for a coke instead."

"Oh really?" Angie spoke up "With Brady Downing? He seems so nice."

"I don't know" Suzanna answered "He seems nice but there's something about him I don't understand."

"What's that?" Angie wanted to know.

"Well, he could have almost any girl in the whole school if he wanted, why would he pester a bozo like me; who couldn't care less if you kick a football or throw it through a hoop; and wouldn't go to his parties? Actually when it comes right down to it, I'll not be dating him at all. If he ever does get around to asking that is."

"Oh, your dating someone else?" Angie wondered.

"Me?" Suzanna laughed "Are you kidding? I'll probably live to be an old maid with the prospects I've had."

"Brady Downing isn't a prospect?" Angie sounded confused.

"It's out of the question, first of all there is the 'Edward Rhodes' Rules on dating." Suzanna imitated her fathers voice. "There will be no dates until your sixteen and then it will be in a group setting."

"And then?" Angie wondered.

"It's still out of the question."

"Maybe someday." Peggy said with a knowing look at Suzanna.

"I doubt even then." Suzie answered. "I think I'm doomed."

"You?" Angie said shocked "If your doomed where does that put me?"

"I bet you'll have lots of dates." Suzanna assured her.

"I don't think so." Angie said. "I'd even be scared to death to say yes if I was asked."

"Well, maybe the two of us will be spinsters together." Suzanna added. "We'll send all the guys Peggy's way."

"No thanks." She responded.

"Are you dating someone special?" Angie asked a second time.

"I've had a few dates with guys but nothing serious,.. yet." She smiled.

"Really, Who did you date?" Angie wondered with girlish interest.

"Oh, a few guys from church, Matt Rankin, a fella named Scott Morris from Lincoln."

"Yeah, My sister Cindi is dating his brother Bob. They're going to that concert at his church tomorrow night. Did you hear about it?" Suzanna asked Peggy.

"Yeah, I did. I heard they were really good." Peggy answered rather reluctantly.

"Will you get to go?" Suzanna asked innocently.

"Uh, huh"

"Really? Is Gramps taking you?"

"No,..not really." Peggy answered.

"Okay" Suzanna said as she stopped abruptly "Who is he? Speak up."

Angie was listening with interest also. Peggy looked down at her feet. She would rather this idiotic questioning were over. She'd hate for Pat's own sister to raz him on her account. She looked straight at Suzanna.

"It's Pat."

"What!" Suzanna said shocked. "My straight-laced, fuddy duddy, do good and everything your told brother, has asked you for a date?"

"It's not that bad!" Peggy tried to apologize.

"No It's great!" Suzanna said sincerely "Maybe you can put a little more life into his decrepit bones."

"I think Pat is really nice." Angie said aside to Peggy.

"Well, at least he comes from a good family." Suzanna lipped off again. "Some of them anyway."

The Rhodes home was still quite lit when Suzanna returned from her walk. Both Cindi and Luke had gone to bed, but her mother had retired to her sewing machine, her father to his study, and Pat to the couch in the family room. Suzanna walked into the room and picked up the book she'd been reading the night before. Before she had it open however, her brother had put his aside.

"Well Angie seemed to enjoy youth services tonight." Pat stated matter-of-factly.

"You sure seem to be getting interested in my friends." Suzanna remarked with a smile. "Especially the cute ones."

"I'm only human" He retorted with a grin. "But I'm serious, Angie seems like a nice girl. I knew her older brother slightly, he was okay."

"She's got an older brother?" Suzanna asked.

"Hords of them. Jim's the youngest and Angie is the only girl. There must be six maybe seven other brothers I'm not sure."

"Whew, and I can barely stand the two I've got." She remarked. "I don't know much about Angie at all. In fact, I've heard her say more tonight than I have all the other times I've talked to her combined."

"She does seem quiet." Pat added "Her brother was kind of reserved too. He went on to Medical school if I recall. He spent a lot of time with Joe Jamison."

"Has anyone heard from Joe at all?" Suzanna asked.

"Not any of the guys at school, but I guess he keeps in touch with his parents okay."

"Michelle hasn't heard a thing huh."

"No" Pat continued. "Joe was really a swell guy, I can't imagine him taking off like he did. I never did understand it. He never said a word to me when he left and we had become so close."

"It's a shame that Michelle quit coming to church when he left. She's gonna really need the Lord after the baby is born."

"She needs him just as much now." Pat began. "We talked quite a bit when Joe first left, and she felt at the time that God had failed her."

"Really? What happened?"

"I guess after she first repented and began seeking the Holy Ghost her and Joe were so happy together. Then she realized that she was pregnant and didn't know how Joe would react. So she prayed. When she prayed she told God that she would live for him all her life if Joe would marry her and they could have the baby and be a family. When she told Joe, and he took off like he did, I guess it proved to her that there wasn't a God. Or if there was a God, that he didn't love her."

"Oh, that's so sad. If only she wasn't so closed to the word of God now."

"Well, after that your older brother stuck his nose into the situation. Michelle was so shook and as of yet no one but Joe and Myself knew of her condition."

"She didn't even tell her parents?" Suzanna asked.

"No one. Well anyway while her and I were talking after Joe left and I was trying to encourage her not to give up on Jesus, she mentioned her plans to have an abortion."

"No!" Suzanna was shocked. "I never would have thought she'd feel that way."

"She was pretty desperate, and confused. Well, we had a talk. I don't recall exactly what I said, but I got through and she decided against the abortion. A few weeks later she came to me and explained that if she couldn't have Joe, she wanted the next best thing, his baby. She had also considered adoption, but in the end chose to keep the baby herself."

"She still loves Joe then?"

"More than ever, It seems."

The two sat in silence awhile. Finally Suzanna spoke.

"Pat,.. All guys aren't jerks like Joe are they?"

"So Joe's a jerk, huh" Pat smiled, when Suzanna shrugged he continued. "Is that what this Brady fella is?"

"Beats me." Suzanna shrugged again. "I barely know him. I literally ran into him last night at the farm and I haven't been able to shake him since."

"Do you want me to scare him away?" Pat said with a smile.

"I don't think so." Suzanna responded. "I can handle it. Peggy and I are claiming him for the Lord. Now that would require nothing short of a miracle."

"He didn't take to kindly to me I noticed." Pat put in.

"That's because he thought you were my boyfriend. But I'll let Peggy have you."

"Come off it." Pat stated "don't start giving her a hard time because of me."

"Oh I didn't, in fact I told her that I thought she'd do you some good. You've been getting a little bit to serious lately. Peggy can be a blast if she lets herself. But if Cindi's there that might put a damper on it."

"Don't worry, Cindi's hopes are set for Bobby Morris, we won't even know she's there."

"That would be impossible for me." Suzanna stated.

"Are things that bad?"

"Not really, but I just feel so intimidated by her all the time. I really love her. We've been through a lot together, but if I don't get ahold of myself I find she gets me fighting mad. Pat, you know her, she is not that pure and Holy that she's above the rest of us. Yet it seems like she's looking down on me sometimes."

"Have you talked to her about it?"

"Yeah, I told her how I felt and she said I was imagining it and that I'd understand her more when I *matured* a little." Suzanna responded emphasizing the word matured.

"Did you pray about it?" Pat asked.

"It seems silly to pray,.. Oh Lord, please help my sisters rotten attitude." Suzanna laughed.

"How about praying,.. Lord give me the patience with my sister and the measure of love I need to show her?"

"Oh, so I am the immature one. Thanks a lot." Suzanna said reproachfully.

"Looks like you might need a little patience with your older brother too." Pat stated. "any changes in the situation are gonna have to start somewhere, and it might as well be in your heart. That might be what it takes to cure her stinking attitude."

"Ah ha,.. so you agree, it does stink!"

"Like a landfill." Pat laughed.

It was nearing midnight when Brady Downing returned to the deserted ball field. It had been a great game, and the party that followed was fun too. His movements were not as swift or accurate after the amount of alcohol he had consumed, but still, his night was only beginning.

Brady waited impatiently near the entrance to the park.

"Aww, come on guys." He spoke into the darkness "Don't stand me up tonight."

It was after perhaps five minutes, that the car he was waiting for pulled slowly through the entrance. Brady ran over to it as the driver rolled his window down.

"Hey, what took you guys?" Brady asked.

"We were busy man. What of it?" The driver of the car stated.

"I don't get my thrills out of standing around in deserted places at midnight." Brady muttered.

"Well, we got the thrills here." The driver stated as he handed a small envelope to Brady.

"Hey thanks guys. I'll enjoy it." He said sincerely as he shoved the envelope quickly into the pocket of his letter jacket.

"Where do I find you next Friday?" Brady asked.

"I like watching the fisherman at the dock in Liberty Park." Was the answer "10:30".

"Got it. You'll bring the usual?" Brady asked.

"Yep, sure thing." The driver answered.

"Hey Grub" Interrupted the fellow in the passenger seat. "Let's split, someone's comin'" The driver quickly put the car in gear and headed toward the street. It took Brady a minute to realize what was happening, by then he glanced up and saw a car approaching from the other direction. This time there was no mistaking the car, or it's occupants. Brady was off in a flash behind the bleachers. The car came to a halt behind him and all too soon he heard heavy footsteps pursuing him.

He was running scared. He knew he could outrun the guy, but what if he didn't. 'I gotta ditch this stuff." He thought. He knew the fella was gaining on him and realized that the amount of alcohol he had used that night was having an affect on him. As he turned to head toward the nearby woods he pulled the envelope from his pocket and was about to toss it where he'd be sure to find it when a hand reached out and grabbed his arm.

"Not so quick fella." A voice said. The envelope fell to the ground.

"Mailing letters this late at night?" Asked the man as he gained a firmer hold on Brady leaving the envelope where it lay.

"Get your filthy hands off me." Brady screamed "I haven't done anything."

"Don't talk so soon." The voice interrupted. "I've got a few formalities to take care of first."

"Hey Coop." He hollered toward the direction they had come "Hustle along with the cuffs will ya."

"Comin' Steve." Coop answered.

"Now fella" The man named Steve began. "you're under arrest. You need to know that anything you say and do can be used against you." Coop came with the cuffs and bound Brady's hands behind him.

"Hey! You can't do this!" Brady said again. "I haven't done anything."

"Well it looks like you dropped something." Steve Williams remarked as he gingerly picked up the envelope.

"You've gotta be kidding me." Brady answered "I've never seen that envelope before, it was just laying there."

"Come on Cooper. Let's get him down to the station. Cap'l want to meet this guy."

Thus another day ends in Roberts Junction, a day in which a seed of the word of God is planted in the lives of both Jeff Johnson and Angie Arnolds,. could a seed also have fallen into the hearts of Michelle Morrison, or even perhaps Brady Downing? Only time will show us what manner of seed it is.

CHAPTER 6

A TIME TO PLUCK UP

Saturday, September 17, 1983

Suzanna woke suddenly Saturday morning. Something hard was hitting her on the face.

"Get up slothful," Cindi Rhodes demanded as she once again aimed her pillow at her sister. "It's 9:00 and we've got cleaning to do."

"Why do you think I'm still in bed, if that's all I've got to look forward to." Suzanna rolled over and pulled the covers over her head.

"And I dear sister" Put in Cindi, "Am going to see that you get up and do your share, even if I have to get a bucket of cold water to drown you with."

"Oh, all right." Suzie moaned. "I'm coming."

Ten minutes later she entered the kitchen. Cindi was busy scraping dishes to be washed.

"Where is everyone?" Suzanna wondered.

"Pa and Luke went out to the Daniels." Cindi began "Ma's at a Ladies meeting at church, and Pat's playing Tennis with Matt Rankin. Now I don't have all day to be domestic let's get this over with."

"Can't I have breakfast first?" Suzanna asked.

"By the time you get going it'll be time for lunch."

"Well okay, where do we start?"

"I've already started dishes here, I'll finish up the kitchen. You can start stripping beds and getting the laundry going. Your lucky it's a nice day and the sheets can go on the line."

"Oh, I'm so thrilled." Suzanna said sarcastically as she left the kitchen.

One day a week, Suzanna thought dejectedly, that I get to sleep and this happens. Can't anyone just let me be?

Just once? Quickly she stripped the beds and sorted the Laundry. After getting the first load started she headed back upstairs to make the beds.

"I'm coming thru" She called to her sister as she entered the kitchen where Cindi was scrubbing the floor. "At least Luke's not in the way today."

"Thank Pa for that." Cindi sighed.

After Suzanna had changed the bedding, vacuumed the stairway and upstairs hall and cleaned the bathrooms she began to think. 'That useless Cindi. She hasn't don't half what I've done today, it's not fair that I have to sit back and let her make a slave out of me. I don't have to put up with this." She fumed as she stomped furiously outside making sure to slam the screen door. The sheets had already dried on the line so she began yanking them off and carelessly shoving them into the basket. "It's just no fair!" She thought again. As she grumbled inwardly she began to recall the conversation she'd had with her brother the night before, and his words.

"Any changes in the situation are gonna have to start somewhere and it might as well be in your heart." He'd said.

"Oh Lord," She prayed silently "Give me the patience with Cindi that I need. Lord, teach me to prefer my sister above myself, and to love her unconditionally." After a few more words of prayer, Suzanna went about her work much more peaceful than before.

"Well brother" She said aloud "Michelle was right. You will make a pretty good preacher some day."

She returned to the kitchen where Cindi was just taking a cake out of the oven.

"Oh that looks good! and it smells even better." Suzanna commented good naturedly.

"It's a recipe one of the girls at work gave me. I've been just aching to use it."

"Is it lunch time yet?" Suzanna asked.

"You can make yourself a sandwich but *please* don't make a mess. No one is expected home 'til two or so."

Suzanna opened the refridge and began digging around to see what she could find.

"Oh, there's some ham left." She stated. "Would you like me to make you a sandwich too?"

"Sure, that would be nice." Cindi answered then added, "I'll get us some milk."

After a quick prayer they began their meal.

"Are you looking forward to the concert tonight?" Suzanna wondered.

Cindi shrugged. "I don't know, I've been to so many like it, they're all about the same."

"At least you'll be with Bob."

"Yeah,.. *and* my brother." Cindi said flatly. "Why I've got to have my little brother tagging along all the time I don't know."

"Be thankful you're going at all." Suzie said "I don't think I'll ever get the chance."

"Oh some nice boy will come along." Cindi stated.

Suzanna tried to ignore Cindi's use of the word boy. "But Peggy dates all the time and here I sit."

"In my opinion the only decent fella Peggy ever dated is the brother of the one I'll be with tonight." Cindi commented "And to have Pat drag her along with us is disgusting."

"What do you mean?"

"Why she's just a kid." Cindi responded. "A friend of yours, Pat should date girls that are older and would appreciate him more."

"Your older and you don't appreciate him much."

"Oh skip it." Cindi stated. "But, your time will come, Suez believe me." Cindi smiled across the table at her, as Suzanna uneasily continued her meal.

The Rhodes old dilapidated jalopy approached the impressive Stables of 'Horseman's Unlimited'.

"Ya gonna come with me to see the horses, Pa?" Luke asked sitting on the edge of his seat.

"Maybe for a minute. Brother Daniels is expecting me."

"Brother Bill won't be here will he?" Luke asked.

"No but I'll arrange for Dennis to take you out with a group of riders."

"Really Pa? Really?" Luke asked excitedly.

"Really," His father smiled "But you'll have to promise me you'll listen and obey what he says."

"I will Pa, I will" Luke assured him.

Brother Rhodes had barely stopped the car when the passenger door flew open and Luke was rushing excitedly toward the stables.

"Come on Pa! hurry." He called as he entered the first barn in search of Misty.

By the time his father found him he was already admiring the tiny sorrel filly. Father and son stood awhile together.

"Isn't she gorgeous Pa?" Luke asked.

"I have to be honest don't I son." His father began. "And you are absolutely right, she is gorgeous."

"Thank you." Said a voice behind them. Startled Brother Rhodes turned quickly to the new comer.

"I'm sorry if we're in you way." He began. "We were just admiring the filly."

"Oh, I count that as a compliment." Ray responded, then held out his hand. "I'm Ray Johnson, and you're Edward Rhodes."

"Have we met?" The minister asked bewildered.

"Not officially, but I've had your older children in classes of mine." Ray responded then grinned at Luke. "I'll probably have another one before too long."

"Yes, this is my youngest Luke. He's the one with the fascination for horses."

"Very good fascination if I do say so myself." Ray nodded. "Jenny, my youngest is around here somewhere, her horse Poncho is pastured outside. This is my son's horse Misty."

"And that's Faleen." Luke put in. "Old Bill told me."

"That it is young man." Ray confirmed then was startled by the sight of his daughter coming toward them.

"Daddy!" She called as she approached. "She's here!" Tears were streaming down her cheeks, her face was a mask of confusion.

"Who's here sweetheart?" Ray asked as he gathered her into his arms.

"Mmmomm" Jenny walied. "With some Mmman."

"It's okay dear. Don't let it bother you. We've talked about it and you knew that you would see her sometimes."

"But I didn't think it would be so soon. I really didn't" Jenny wailed again.

Br. Rhodes and Luke slowly walked toward the entrance of the stables not wanting to attract attention to themselves. They were just nearing the door when Judy appeared.

"Good Morning Ray" She said, then turning to Jenny "Jen, sweetheart come here. Momma wants to talk."

Jenny sniffed a few times then went to her mother. "Okay," She whimpered, Luke and his father quickly left the building.

Luke hurriedly approached Tom. The money his father had given him clutched in his fist.

"Hi!" He said as Tom was saddling a small palamino.

"Hi" Tom answered. "Can I help you?"

"Yeah, I've got money to go out with Denni's next group."

"Oh, sure, I'll be right with you." Tom finished tightening the cinch then turned to Luke. "It's a great day for riding," He commented as Luke handed him his money. "Thanks, Have you ridden before?"

"Not enough." Luke smiled "I've ridden Ben's old horse Camalot in the arena a few times. I've gone on the trails twice."

"Well I'm glad I saddled this one in time then." Tom answered patting the palamino's neck. "This is Yankee. Denni will be back in about five minutes, you can wait over there if you want." Tom said motioning toward a picnic area.

"Do you mind if I stay here and watch you?"

"Oh no, go right ahead." Tom answered.

Luke climbed to the top of the fence to watch Tom. He took in every detail and acting as if he'd never get another chance to watch again. Tom felt himself being watched.

"So, what's your name?" He asked.

"Luke"

"My names Tom."

"Yeah I know." Luke answered frankly.

"Am I that popular?" Tom teased.

"My sister's mentioned your name before. And I know Denni. And your not Denni, so you have to be you."

"And who might your sister be?" Tom asked.

"Her name is Suzie, she's Nick's baby-sitter."

"Oh," Tom acknowledged. "you're Suzanna Rhodes' brother, which accounts for the fact that you've ridden Cam. Your parents are close friends of Sarah and Ben aren't they?"

"Uh huh, My Pa's talking with Ben right now." Luke explained.

"Hey, look yonder." Tom pointed "Here comes Denni my man now."

Luke shifted his gaze to the group of horses slowly returning from the fields.

"Well if it isn't Theodore Bartimaus Jones!" Denni laughed as he rode up, calling Luke by the name of the character he'd portrayed the night before.

"Hey, I thought you said your name was Luke and that you were Suzie Rhodes' brother?" Tom asked immediately confused.

"I am." Luke answered.

"I was just teasin' kid." Denni told Luke as he dismounted and prepared to help others that might need assistance.

"Guess what Denni!" Luke called and continued before waiting for a response.

"I'm going out with your next group."

"Hey, you'll enjoy that." Denni said truthfully.

"I get to ride Yankee. He's just my size." Luke added.

Denni stretched his legs and walked about a bit after the group he'd brought in had dispersed.

"I've got a fresh group of horses for you." Tom stated. "We'll give these a break. Still, you'll have to take three that you just brought in, Your next group is quite large." Denni glanced over toward the picnic area.

"Hey, I know most of those guys from school."

"So do I, Luke here looks like the youngest you'll have."

"I'll keep an eye on you kid." Denni smiled.

"I can handle it okay." Luke stated in return.

"Well, lets get you mounted then." Denni walked over to Yankee and took a few minutes to show Luke how to mount, then to guide the horse, left and right.

Ben and Edward Rhodes approached right when Luke was mounting Yankee.

"You look mighty small up there." His father commented. "Take it easy, I'll be here when you get back." Then turning to Dennis asked. "What time will you return?"

"Oh, about an hour and a half." He said. "12:30 there about."

"Well, take it easy," He repeated as the group of horses left the stable yard.

At the end of the lane that led from the stables Denni stopped the group. He had kept Luke directly behind him to see that he was handling the horse properly. Now he turned and faced the group.

"Hi" He began. "I know most of you know who I am but for those that don't my name is Denni and I'm your trail guide here. We want your time here to be enjoyable so if you have any questions or comments or problems I'll try to help." He paused a little.

"Horseman's Unlimited has been established so that anyone no matter what age or ability can have the opportunity to ride. Today is your opportunity. It may be your last time on a horse, but, it may also be the beginning of years of enjoyable riding. Now I know Tom saw to it that everyone signed a form. I hope you all read it."

There was a chorus of affirmative answers.

"Okay, I believe you." Denni laughed, then addressing one of the riders he continued.

"Pete, I know you've ridden here a lot, you know the trails fairly well. Why don't you take the lead today and go at your own pace."

"Thanks Denni, that would be swell."

The group of riders continued again, Luke kept back toward the end of the line and Denni moved back and forth, commenting on things and making suggestions. He had just explained to a young fella who was riding for the first time what the purpose of the saddle horn was, and how it was used.

"But," He added smiling. "It does come in handy the first few times you ride." Just then another rider motioned him over.

"You're a friend of Brady Downing aren't you?" The boy asked. Denni recognized him as Jim Townes a Senior and another member of the schools football team.

"Yeah, We've got a few classes together and such." Denni answered.

"Have you heard from him today?" Jim asked.

"No, I usually leave quite early for work in the morning." He explained.

"Well rumor has it that he was busted last night and they've got him in the can."

"You're kidding?" Denni was shocked. "What did they get him on?"

"I'm not sure, I didn't hear much." Jim continued.

"Hey," Called the girl riding behind Jim. "Are you talking about that Downing kid?"

"Yeah," Denni answered. "Did you hear anything?"

"Uh huh, they've got him for possession of cocaine. But, he's fabricated some story and won't crack."

"How did it happen?" Denni wondered.

"Well I figure someone must have tipped the cops off 'cause they got him right after he received the stuff, and how else could they have known where to find him?"

"So they got the dealers too?" Jim asked.

"No, that's another thing funny about it. The others got away in a car, the cops didn't even pursue them."

"That's not strange." Jim put in. "All they'd need on the other guy is his license number. But they may have had no idea who Brady was."

"But he's a nobody, just a user. It's the big guys they want. I think he was set up."

"Maybe they hoped that if they got him behind bars he'd talk." Jim suggested. "Who knows what he may have told them. Hey,.. you're pretty quiet Denni."

"I may be quiet" Denni responded. "But my mind is working overtime."

The phone interrupted Suzanna right when she was getting to the best part of her novel.

"I'll get it, it's probably for me." She heard Cindi call from upstairs. She was just returning to the story when again Cindi called.

"Suez it's for you."

Suzanna jumped from the couch and ran to the phone.

"Hi" She answered.

"Howdi" Suzanna knew the caller immediately for there was none she knew but Sarah Daniels who answered the phone with 'Howdi'.

"Sarah, Hi." Suzanna returned.

"I hate to trouble you Suzie" Sarah began "But, Ben wants to drive south this evening to look at some horses. I'd like to go along. Do you think you could come out and watch Nick?"

"Oh, sure." Suzanna answered. "I'd love to. What time?"

"Ben'll stop by for you around five if that's okay."

"Just fine."

"We may be kind of late. Ben suggested that if you'd like you could spend the night here we'll bring you to church with us in the morning."

"That sounds great, but I'll have to ask Ma."

"Your father was here before and he already Okayed it so we'll plan on it."

"Sure" Suzanna answered. "I'll see you then."

"You too, bye."

Suzanna hung up the phone and was just returning to her book when Cindi walked in.

"Sarah need a sitter?"

"Yeah," Suzanna responded opening her book as the phone rang a second time.

"I've got it." Cindi called as she picked up the receiver. "Hello?... Suzie?... Well ahh... Sure. Just a moment." She covered the mouthpiece with her hand and mouthed the words. "It's a boy." to Suzie.

Suzie looked bewildered as she took the receiver. "Hello, this is Suzie."

"Hi, Suzie. This is Jeff Johnson."

"Jeff, Hi" She answered with a smile, but frowned when she saw Cindi wink from across the room.

"It's about Brady." Jeff began. "The Cops got him last night he's in jail."

"In jail!" Suzanna asked. Cindi sat forward in her chair to catch Suzanna's side of the conversation.

"Yeah. I can't really explain. But, he assured me that they had nothing on him and that he'd be back out on the streets again today."

"Oh" Suzanna remarked.

"Suzie" Jeff continued soberly "If I hadn't gone to that silly meeting at your church last night, I'd have been with him. I just wanted you to know that."

"Thanks Jeff. I appreciate your calling." Suzanna said as she hung up the phone a second time that afternoon.

"Well?" Cindi asked.

"Well what?" Suzanna wanted to know.

"I gather that was Jeff Johnson on the phone. I also understand he's in jail, but what did he do and why did he call you?"

Suzanna laughed. "Oh Cindi, you are so far from the truth." But refused to say more.

"Hey Denni!" Jim called as they were approaching the stable after their ride.

"Yeah, Jim what is it?" Denni asked.

"You really have the life you know that?"

"What do you mean?"

"Landing a job where all you have to do is ride around on a horse all day."

"Try staying in the saddle for eight hours on a Saturday in July once." Denni suggested.

"It's still better then most jobs."

"Like shoveling out horses stalls."

"You do that too huh."

"And putting in my share when they harvest the hay and grain."

"What else?"

"Oh I clean saddles and bridles, mend fences, fork hay, get bit, kicked, stepped on,..."

Jim laughed.

"I can see you've never had a horse step on your foot." Denni remarked, then added. "I even wash windows, mow lawn, take out trash, sweep, scrub, paint and,.. I love every minute of it.."

Jim laughed "I'm sorry I mentioned it."

"No don't be. Most people never see what has to be done to keep a place like this going. I wouldn't take Ben's job for a million bucks."

"Oh, so your not gonna keep working here?"

"I will until I graduate but after school, I don't know."

"Hey man, I graduate in spring and I'm still undecided. It's pretty scary when you think about it."

They had just returned to the stable and Denni quickly dismounted and assisted some of the others who were less familiar with riding. Luke ran off quickly to find his Dad, but Jim hung around a bit to talk to Denni.

"Hey, what do you think will happen to Brady?" Jim asked as they leaned over the fence to watch the horses that were corralled there. Denni just shrugged.

"I hope he gets off the hook. The team needs him. I know some kids who've been sent to reform schools for less." Still Denni didn't respond. "Don't you hope they give him a break?" Jim asked again.

"Not really." Denni replied rather reluctantly.

"Hey! You're supposed to be his friend." Jim was startled at Denni's frank answer.

"Jim, it's because I'm his friend that I want to see him get help."

"You've got to be kidding!" Jim responded. "How will it help, the team especially, if they stick him in some reform school with a bunch of degenerates?"

"Hold it Jim, I never said I wanted him to go to a reform school, I just said I hope they don't give him a break. I don't know what they'll do. But I do know this. Brady was caught doing something he knew was wrong. Why should he get a break and not the next guy? Why should he be favored and not the next guy? No I don't want to see anything bad happen to him, but Jim I didn't like seeing him use Cocaine either."

"Aww come on. Lots of guys use the stuff. It's not like all those wild stories adults tell you to scare you away from the stuff. They're a bunch of hogwash, nobody believes them."

"Jim your wrong. I've seen kids lives ruined by the stuff. It's dangerous and I told Brady I thought so, right now I don't want to see him get put away, I just want to see him get help."

"Oh come off it." Jim stated "Your no better than him."

"You're right I'm not." Denni interrupted. "I'd be in his same shoes if I hadn't had help when I needed it. And no one could help me until I wanted help. You're wrong Jim I know I'm no better, I only know that there is a better way."

A patrolman led Brady into the room. Though it was large it was sparsely furnished, having a table with a few chairs, another side table containing a coffee pot, cream, sugar, and a few styrofoam cups. Over in a corner was what appeared to be video equipment.

"So this is the interrogation room." Brady commented to the officer.

"This is where Captain Omaha will be meeting with you."

"Omaha?" Brady asked "He's not from Nebraska is he?" Brady's laughter filled the room. The Patrolman didn't join in but motioned for Brady to be seated then took his place beside the door.

"Your not very sociable." Brady pointed out. "This whole thing will be cleared up as soon as I talk to the Captain so don't treat me like I'm a criminal yet."

"Just doin' my job." The patrolman responded as the door opened and three men walked in.

The first two were vaguely familiar. The third was a large muscular man. Although he wore a uniform it was more his looks that commanded authority. His hair was cropped short, his eyes small and piercing.

"Boy," Brady thought. "He's got to be the ugliest guy I've ever seen."

The man took the chair opposite Brady, Steve Williams, sat on his right with Mike Cooper to his left.

"It'll be a minute before my man get's here and we can start." Omaha began, then turning to Cooper. "Mike bring us some coffee."

"Sure Cap'n"

"So this is Brady Downing." He spoke, "I'm Captain Omaha Jordon. You've agreed to make a statement, and that is what we're here for. Have you spoken with council?"

"Yes sir."

"May I ask who will be representing you?" Omaha continued "and are you expecting him here when you make your statement."

"Yes," Brady began boldly. "My father, Bronson James Downing III of Downing, Hampshire and Willmington, will represent me. And no, he is not expected. He is in Chicago, I spoke to him and related my story. Needless to say, he blew his stack." Brady added with a laugh.

Brady thought he saw the corners of Omaha's mouth turn upward into a smile which was quickly erased.

"I'm not sure I'm familiar with your father." Omaha spoke.

"I'm not sure I am either." Brady smiled again "He practices in Chicago. I live in town with my Mother and Stepfather."

"Yes, I see" Omaha interrupted looking at the paper before him. "Marion and Fred Robbins, over on TrapLine road."

Just then the door opened and a secretary walked in followed by another officer.

"Ah ha," Omaha stated "We can begin, the Machine's set up properly today I hope." He stated with a slight trace of a smile.

"Yes Captain" The patrolman answered.

"Let's begin. Brady you notice that my secretary is prepared to record all you say, and the video machine will also be recording. Now once again I want you to remember this is an authorized statement and anything you say can be used in a court of law."

"Yes sir"

"Okay then, Tell us your story. I may be interrupting you with questions none of which you are required to answer."

"Well" Brady began "There isn't much to tell. I played at Legion field last night and after returning home realized that I had misplaced my keys. I felt I knew where they were so, being in training, also without the keys to our car, I jogged down to the ballpark to find them. I knew where I had probably lost them for I had tossed my jacket aside before the game. I had just entered the park when this car full of weirdo's pulled in. I mean, they were weird. They asked directions to 'Monty's bar' over on main street. After I gave the directions they took off. Pretty fast too. I again continued jogging toward where I thought my keys would be but before I got there, that cop, right there had stopped me." Brady pointed straight at Williams.

"Go on." Omaha stated.

"Well that's it. The creeps handcuffed me and shoved me in the back of their squad car. They brought me here."

"So then," Omaha began "You have never seen this before." He held up the envelope which Brady had dropped the night before.

"Oh sure, I've seen that." Brady stopped "The first time I ever saw that envelope, that cop right there had it." Again he pointed at Steve.

"Now what do you suppose was in this envelope?" Omaha asked.

"Come on now." Brady replied exasperated. "Be real will ya, You know very well that I know what's in there. At least three dozen people have told me, that it contained one gram of cocaine but I don't know that for sure, you see I never laid eyes on that envelope, and I never opened it. Why don't you ask the dude who planted the thing and for some reason is trying to get me to take a rap for something I didn't do."

"And who would that be?" Omaha asked.

"I've told you twice already. The only person I ever saw in possession of that envelope, cocaine or no cocaine was that cop right there." Brady pointed at Steve a third time. "Why he's playing this Charade, or whether your part of it I don't know, but I'll tell you one thing. There is a fellow down in Chicago right now who is ready to burn some things around here, and theres a few people, Mr. Williams." He looked steadily at Steve. "Who are on the top of his list."

Omaha cleared his throat. "Are you implying young man that you believe yourself to be the victim of a fabricated story set up by this Police Force?"

"If not by the police force, by at least one of it's patrolmen. And make sure you get that statement in your notes too."

Omaha looked steadily at Brady "It's no use kid." He stated "It won't work."

Brady smiled confidently back at him.

Back in his cell Brady was deep in thought.

'Things worked too clean last night for my comfort. It doesn't make sense that they'd leave Grub and Moonshine get away if they knew we'd just made a deal. But they had to know, why else would they follow me.'

'Wait a minute.' Brady thought 'Maybe Grub set me up, yeah, that's gotta be it. When I get my chance I'm gonna let this fist of mine make a permanent indentation on that fella's nose.'

Brady lay back on his cot pondering the events of last night. 'It doesn't make sense, Grub is a bigwig, I'm just a nobody. Why give him a break to nab someone like me?"

He shifted uneasily on his cot. He had to sort this out. 'Maybe they don't have enough on him and hoped I'd talk. That's gotta be it. Then someone must have tipped them off on the deal. The only ones beside Grub and Moonshine that knew of it were Jeff and Denni. I recall telling them Thursday night when I stopped at the farm.' Brady sat up suddenly.

'The same Thursday night that Rhodes made her appearance.' Brady's mind recalled. 'Right beside Johnson's truck where she barreled into us,.. So' He pondered, 'My attentions the past few days haven't proven very effective.'

"Am I ever a fool" He breathed "It's got to be her. I knew it all along. I thought I could handle her. Boy was I wrong. I should have called the whole deal off."

Rage boiled within Brady. He was furious. It was beyond doubt according to him that, that crazy, snott of a preachers kid, had blown the whistle. "I'll get her" He said revengefully "She'll pay." He chuckled to himself as he began to make plans "You just wait, Suzanna Rhodes, You just wait."

The papers were still scattered on his desk when Ben Daniels entered his office that day. He sat down and immediately began searching through the correspondence. Quickly he glanced over the letter he had received form Reynolds Marksman.

Reynolds Marksman
Rt. 13 Pounding Hooves Ln.
Duncan, Wisconsin,

Dear Ben,

Upon receiving your letter concerning the procurement of the yearling colt of 'Miraco DeMarks' I've chosen to respond thus.

If you are interested you are welcome to join us at our establishment at your convenience. There are several other parties that have expressed an interest so it would be wise on your part to act quickly. I am looking forward to seeing you again.

Your Friend and Colleague,
Reynolds Marksman

Smiling to himself he put the letter aside, then turning to his file cabinet began searching for the records of a few of his best mares. He had just pulled a few files when there was a knock on the door.

"Hey, it's open" Ben answered. Denni quietly entered. "Den, what can I do for you?"

"I just wanted to stop in before I headed home." Dennis began.

"It's been busy today."

"Yes sir" Denni agreed but still stalled.

"Is something up?" Ben asked after a pause.

"I guess I've got quite an apology to make." Denni admitted.

"Oh?"

"Yes, I don't know where to begin, but a lot has happened that I feel you should be aware of." Ben sat forward in his chair realizing how really hard it was for Denni to talk, yet, wanting to grasp every word.

Denni began to relate his association with Jeff and Brady to his employer. Of the times he was included with them yet felt justified because he never partook of their sins.

"I've really deceived myself." Denni continued. "It's gonna be twice as hard now to show the power of God after I had allowed myself to get entangled in their ways." Denni stated humbly.

"That's right." Ben began "But the Lord is with you and he will give you the power. You need to be thankful that it never went farther than it did."

"I'm hoping that it still doesn't" Denni said then continued. "One of the big reasons I came to talk to you is because my buddy, Brady Downing was arrested last night. I guess they caught him with cocaine. I wasn't surprised because I knew about the deal. But I began to realize what I had actually done, and then recalled the times Jeff and I would receive deliveries for Brady. We'd take the horses Ben, and go to that wayside south of here where someone would meet us. Ben to think that I put you in that position makes me sick. To think that transactions that you detest were going on right under your nose, and me being a part of the,.. and after all you've done for me."

"Hold it Den" Ben began "You don't owe me anything. Right now I'm just thankful that you have seen your wrong and have sought peace with God." He paused. "Now I'll be honest with you. I knew about your deal Tuesday night.

Rich and I had followed you, we came upon you later and cautioned you about riding at night."

"Yes I remember." Denni began. "But why didn't you do something then? Turn me in, Fire me, something?"

"I did do something." Ben interrupted. "I prayed for you."

Denni smiled. "Thanks Ben, you don't know how much I appreciate what you've done."

"Den, I can do nothing but what Jesus allows me to do. I'm only a man and an insufficient one at that. But Den, by the Power of God, we can walk everyday Victorious. Prayer works; and it'll work on your friend Brady just like I kinda feel it's working on your friend Jeff."

"Jeff's pretty confused." Denni added, then reluctantly told Ben of the conversations concerning Ben himself.

Ben just sat in thought, so Denni continued. "I better head home, I'm going to Lincoln tonight with some friends."

"Hey, have a nice time." Ben said as they both rose. Then instead of Ben's typical firm handshake he moved forward and embraced Denni with a hearty hug. "I love you Denni," He began, "and I want to see you grow and mature in God. Someday there's gonna be a Pillar where Denni Little used to stand."

Denni quickly left the office, a few unshed tears filling his eyes.

It was past seven P.M. when Tom VanDyke rode toward the barns with the last group of riders for the evening. Rich was already waiting to help him unsaddle the horses and prepare them for the night. The two worked side by side.

"Did you have a nice visit with 'Cowboy Bob'?" Rich wondered.

"Who?" Tom asked.

"That handsome fella with the Ten Gallon hat and Cowboy boots."

"Ya'all caint mean that dude." Tom answered imitating the man's phoney accent.

"Wa of curs I me'an theat dude." Both began laughing as Tom recalled the incident.

"You would have enjoyed it." Tom began "I took the group into the woods and it wasn't but a minute and a branch had swiped that hat plumb off the fella's head," Tom laughed. "He hollered so loud I thought someone had died but by the time he convinced me to retrieve it, it had the authentic marks of a true cowboy hat...Hoof prints." The two laughed again.

"Well" Tom continued. "It's really been a long day, I'm beat."

"Me too." Rich agreed "Ya hungry? I thought maybe you'd like to come up and burn a pizza with me after we lock this place."

"Now that sounds like something I could handle." Tom answered "Thanks."

The last door was secured and the last Bridle put back on it's rack when Rich headed back over the path through the woods to the Garage.

"I'll race you!" Tom had laughed as he headed toward his car.

"You haven't got a chance." Rich had added.

As Rich got near the house he could hear Suzanna singing happily to baby Nick.

Nick was a child that was being nurtured in the love of God and in the praise of his people, Suzanna Rhodes being one of them.

At barely five months old he responded enthusiastically with smiles and coos and often with clapping to all the songs both his mother and baby-sitter sang. He enjoyed hearing voices and often fell asleep peacefully at night as his mother read the scriptures aloud to him.

Tonight Suzanna had been singing with him as she gave him a bath in his small plastic tub.

What can wash away my sin?
nothing but the blood of Jesus
What can make me whole again?
nothing but the blood of Jesus

Gently she lifted the small child and carefully dressed him in a clean sleeper. After laying him in the crib she quickly emptied the tub and discarded his soiled clothing to the hamper. When she returned he was nearly asleep his tiny thumb securely placed in his small pink mouth. Quietly she left the room.

With Nick asleep Suzanna moved to the kitchen table where she had placed her folder when arriving.

"Now for that blasted assignment for Johnson." She thought.

Below at the stables not all was still. A silent figure dressed in dark clothes was sneaking quietly toward the building that housed the arena and office. With no trouble at all the door was open and the figure inside.

Suzanna's page of notes had grown quite full as she read the essays that had been given her. She was reading the third paper and had just come across a point that the previous two hadn't covered, when the phone rang. She quickly set her pen down and left to answer it.

"Hello!" She responded, then after a silent pause, "Hello?" Reluctantly Suzanna replaced the phone and returned to the table. She had just reached for her pen when the phone rang a second time. "Maybe it's someone looking for Ben, and after hearing my voice thought they had the wrong number." Suzanna thought as she reached for the phone.

"Hello, Daniels residence. This is Suzie." She answered then waited briefly. "Hello, this is the Daniels residence." Shaking her head Suzanna once again returned the phone.

The phone rang a third time just as she was locating the item she had planned to add to her notes.

"Hello this is the Ben Daniels home, Suzie speaking." This time a frown formed on her face for on the previous calls she had heard just silence. But now she was hearing a distinct sound, muffled, but she still heard it,.. laughter.

"I'm not going to spend all night walking back and forth to this phone." She thought to herself as she hung it up the third time. She remained standing by the phone. Sure enough after a few minutes it rang again. "I know," Suzanna thought "I'll answer like Sarah."

"Howdi!" She said as she picked up the receiver. Her face froze, for as clear as a bell on the other end of the line she heard laughter. Loud, clear, and haunting. "Is this a joke?" She asked, then thought a moment. "Luke? Is this you?" She heard no response so quickly hung up the receiver. Then after lifting it back up she set it aside.

"I'm here to baby-sit, not answer the phone." She thought. "I'll hang it up in a few minutes when whoever it is quits playing games."

Reluctantly she returned to her assignment.

A dark figure emerged from within the office of the stables. Quietly creeping into the tackroom, his dim flashlight scanning the rows of saddles and bridles. Finally resting on what he was looking for, a complicated set up for the electrical source that included the whole of Ben's property. First making sure that the lock to Ben's office did not look tampered with, he secured it. Then upon returning to the stacks of saddles, opened the box, He reached to the very top,... the main breaker switch.

Suzanna was just finishing up the last essay when the power went out.

"What now?" She wondered as she began to make her way from the table to the shelf in the pantry where she knew Sarah kept a flashlight and a few candles.

Less than thirty yards away in an upstairs apartment Rich and Tom had been enjoying a Pizza and a few of Rich's tapes when the breaker had been pulled.

"The power must be out." Tom commented.

"Great deduction, Watson." Rich laughed from somewhere in the darkened room.

"Do you think you've overloaded the circuit?"

"Shouldn't have, nothings running that's using extra power."

"Maybe you can't use the stereo, stove and electric lights all at the same time?" Tom laughed.

"It's possible that a breaker has gone out, but I seriously doubt it." Rich smiled as he moved clumsily from the table to look outside. "Impossible, everything's dark, the house too. And the light's down at the stables. Boy is it black out there." He repeated. "There must be an outage in the area, maybe a lines down. I hope it's not long 'til they get the juice going again."

Tom walked over to join him. "It's strange." Tom began, "How totally dark it is. I really take those yard lights at the stables for granted. I've never seen the place so dark."

"Maybe I should phone the power company?"

"Ben's probably called them by now, maybe you should ring him?"

"I doubt if Ben's even returned home." Rich began, then said startled. "Oh, I'd better call! Ben and Sarah went away this evening, Suzie Rhodes is baby-sitting Nick." He reached for his phone then after finding it in the dark he continued. "Ever try dialing a phone in the dark, I'd better get a flashlight."

"Oh I can get it." Tom offered. "Just tell me where."

"And how young man, will you find it if you can't see where I'm telling you it is?" Rich laughed as he handed Tom the phone and went to get the flashlight.

He returned quickly, then dialed Ben's number.

"Now that's strange, the line's busy."

"Maybe she's calling the power company? or her Parents?" Tom suggested.

"Could be. I'll call again in a few minutes meanwhile lets get some candles lit."

Slowly and expertly the doors to the arena were closed and a dark figure hurried toward the path that led to the Daniel's home. Still keeping as quiet as possible the silent shadow crept slowly through the trees toward the back of the property. The intruder looked searchingly through the various windows of the home until he found one where he could see the small glimmer of light from a candle.

Again Rich tried Ben's number. When he found it still busy he decided to walk over to check on Suzanna, Tom joined him.

"I'm sure she's Okay," Rich began, "But I'd hate to see her alone in the dark with the baby."

"Don't worry about Suzie. "Tom put in, as the two reached for their jackets "She can take care of herself."

"Hey, I forgot about this." Rich said as he passed the table and noticed the half finished pizza. "Might as well have a snack on the way over." He picked up a large piece.

"Don't mind if I do." Tom said as he also chose a piece.

Suzanna had taken the flashlight and a candle and wanting to be near the baby had brought them into the nursery. She placed the candle on the dresser and sat back on Sarah's antique rocker. She was puzzled. First those strange phone calls, now the power outage. She felt on edge, really nervous. She rocked quietly and began to pray and talk to God. "Oh Lord," She began. "Give me the peace I need and the assurance to know that you're with me. Calm my spirit father, and grant me your perfect peace that I may rest in your presence." She rocked quietly for a while. Thinking back she began to recall a few things that had happened to her recently. She had just recalled the trip home from school and her talk with Pat about Michelle Morrison when she was startled by a sound.

"What was that?" She wondered anxiously as she sat up in the chair. She was positive she had heard something. There it was again, there was something outside the window. Sure enough, she heard it a third time.

Something was hitting the window from outside. Cautiously she approached, ashamed of her fears. She glanced out. There was nothing there, nothing at all. No lose shutters, no branches blowing nearby, nothing. She stepped back, sure enough, something struck the glass. But what was it? The darkness prevented her from seeing anything, the moon though bright, still did not allow her to see clear enough.

Suzanna felt her way to the dresser and retrieved the flashlight. She shone it out the window but it did no good, she saw nothing. "I can see better without it." She thought. She was holding the flashlight toward the window and saw it's shadow. An old pine cone hit the window and fell slowly to the ground below. "Oh Suzanna, You ignoramus." She said out loud. "Those pine cones are falling from the tree outside the window there is nothing to be afraid of. The wind must just blow them enough so that they hit the house before they fall to the ground." Just at that moment another one hit the window. Suzanna was startled, they definitely were NOT falling from the tree, for pine cones did not fall up against the law of gravity. Right at that moment she heard muffled thudding coming from down stairs. Completely beside herself and regardless of the baby who slept peacefully in the crib beside her,.. she screamed in fright.

Rich and Tom had just reached the front door, not before Rich had kicked the leg of a porch chair and almost sent it sprawling, when they heard Suzanna scream.

"She must have heard you and thought you were some Wild Critter." Tom suggested to Rich as he knocked on the door.

"Maybe she's right." He whispered. "She must be upstairs." He paused then quietly turned the door knob and opened the door.

"Suzie?" He called inside, "It's Rich McAllister, Tom is with me, we came to see how things are."

He paused to listen for a response; faintly he heard it.

"Come on in." Suzanna called from the nursery where she was now holding a wide awake Nick. "You sure know how to scare a person half to death."

"Come on Tom." Rich said as he entered, but was surprised to find that Tom was gone.

Suzie was coming down the stairs holding Nick in one hand, shining the flashlight in front of her.

"I'm sorry to have alarmed you like I did." Rich said.

"Don't apologize," Suzanna insisted. "I was being really paranoid."

"I tried to phone a few times before coming but you must have been using the phone."

"No." Suzanna began "I haven't used,.. Oh I took the phone off the hook right before the power went out."

"Oh?"

"Yeah, some yoyo was calling every few minutes and laughing over the phone." She paused, "It was probably my brother Luke. Wait'll I see the twerp."

"Phones in the kitchen right?" Rich asked, and when Suzie nodded "I'll go hang it up and call the power company to see what they're doing about this."

"Thanks" Suzie said as she sat on the couch with Nick still in her arms.

Tom had been standing on the porch looking out toward the stables as Rich had entered the house. He was surprised to see a small light moving through the woods toward the stables.

"What in the world is that?" He wondered, "It looks like a flashlight." He vaguely heard Suzanna's response from inside as he quietly left the porch to follow the dim light.

Sure enough Tom could tell by the way the light moved that it was a flashlight and someone was carrying it. But who? It wasn't Suzie and everyone else was gone for the day. Because Tom was familiar with the area he quickly and quietly gained on the intruder. He was a few yards behind him when he called.

"Who are you? Stop."

They were just nearing the arena and when Tom spoke he could see the fella was startled enough to jump almost out of his shoes. His resonse though, was to take off running; with Tom in pursuit. Past the stables, and parking lot and toward the road. Tom quickly overtook the fella and after wrestling with him awhile he managed to pin him down and get the flashlight from him. He shined the beam down on the now fighting captive.

"Sorry to have cause a halt to your departure so suddenly Old boy."

"Let me up VanDyke, will ya."

"What was the running for?" Tom asked as he let Brady up from the ground. "All you had to do was say who you were, You didn't have to take off like a scared rabbit."

"Get off my case will ya." Brady said as he brushed off his clothes.

"Do me a favor," Tom requested as he handed Brady back his flashlight. "Next time you and your sweetheart want to spend time together don't go sneakin' around here."

"Lay off VanDyke," Brady repeated as he walked toward the road where he had parked his car. Then after going a few paces turned and called back.

"Hold it VanDyke, what were you doing hanging around this time of night?"

"Eating Pizza." Tom laughed as he returned toward the path through the trees.

Tom contemplated the situation. He had always held a certain dislike for Brady Downing, although the two tolerated each other well enough. "It surprises me." Tom thought "That Suzie would have him out here while she's babysitting. Maybe she's not as straight as I always thought her to be." He frowned, "But Ben's straight. He'd be pretty upset about it, it's probably best if I not mention anything at all."

Rich had just finished starting a fire in the Daniels fireplace when Tom joined them.

"I've got news." Rich began "While you were gone I called the power company, and no lines are reported out. None of the others along this area are having trouble it must be a breaker somewhere."

"It would have to be the main one then." Tom put in. "Because nothings got power down at the stables. I'll go check the main switch." Tom turned to go.

Rich was aching to join Tom but after hearing about Suzie's evening, decided to stay put, at least until the power was on.

"It should only be a few minutes now." Rich commented. "If that's the trouble." Suzie remained uncharacteristically silent. Rich was puzzled Suzie was always so happy and bubbly, it seems at times you almost had to gag her to get a word in. True he'd barely met her, but still he could tell something was on her mind. Maybe it had to do with Tom. Hadn't her brother Pat mentioned something of her infatuation with Tom. Well Rich liked both young people and decided, that must be the problem.

"Rich" Suzanna interrupted his thoughts. "When I was upstairs with Nick, right before you got here. I could have sworn someone was throwing pinecones at the nursery window. I can't imagine why, except just to scare me, that's what made me so paranoid."

"Should I go out and see if anyone besides us is around?" Rich offered.

"No." Suzanna began "They'd be gone by now I suppose anyway. It's not that important."

"I'll check in the morning, and see what I find." Rich offered again. He noticed Suzanna still seemed quite upset. They talked a few more minutes before the power was restored.

'The Remnant' turned out to be a great group. They had no intention of going professional with their work they stated, but, wanted to use their talents to glorify God. Their spokesman explained their Love for the old paths their fathers had walked and the need to preserve them. In so doing they played the older hymns avoiding the contemporary music that the majority of their peers enjoyed.

"I really enjoyed that." Peggy said to Pat as they left the church. "But then those songs are extra special, my being Whistlers Grand-daughter and all."

Pat laughed "Even my straight-laced father would have approved." The two walked in silence for awhile.

"You're worried about Cindi aren't you?" Peggy asked.

"Huh?" Pat looked at her wondering if she could read minds.

"I noticed she was missing. But they'll be at Perkin's. They did say that they would meet us there."

"Yeah, I suppose," Pat said "But, I wish I wouldn't have to act as her baby-sitter all the time."

"Then don't" Peggy put in. "She's nineteen years old, and has a will of her own There is nothing you or your father can do about it."

"I know, and I want to just forget about it. But, Pa thinks the sun rises and sets on her. He kind of wants me to protect her."

"Protect her from what?"

"From being human I guess." Pat laughed.

"Quit fretting, nobody can stop that."

They had reached the car and were about to enter when Denni and Becky Franklin came running up, laughing. Becky was a tall, slim, red haired, athlete of a girl, who quickly left Denni behind her.

"Sorry to keep you waiting Pat, but I had to talk to a few of those guys. They really did a great job." Denni apologized as he caught his breath.

"Denni plays a trumpet." Becky put in. "I don't know how he's kept it a secret so long."

"That's right, I remember those hideous band lessons at school years ago."

"Well I played for a few years, but, I quit when I came to God three years ago. I didn't feel right playing the school's idea of music."

"Hey, you'll have to get it out again." Pat told him. "I've got lot's of music you could borrow. If you can use piano music."

"I hope it's survived the accumulation of three years of dust from the back of my closet." Denni started. "Besides I could never play like those guys tonight."

"Nobody expects you to." Pat began "Just take it out and if you feel comfortable with it maybe you and I could work on a few songs together. Maybe there's others who can play too."

"Don't the Rankin's play instruments?" Becky asked.

"They sure do." Peggy answered. "But I'm not sure which ones."

"I'm sure Mike can come up with something to play too." Pat grinned. "You'd never believe what that fella's got up his sleeve. I think he's determined never to grow up." Pat laughed then went on. "He's got one of those things, I'm not sure what you'd call it. A 'Hum Strum' or a 'Stompffiddle'. I think."

"Is that the pole with the baseball at the bottom and the noise makers and bells and stuff?" Becky asked interested.

"That's it." Pat went on. "He's played it for me a few times, can't get a whole lot of music from it but it sure is an attention getter."

Peggy was laughing. "Sister Chrys is always telling us that nonsense is normal. Just think of what that wide range of talent will bring us. I might even attempt to learn to play something quick so I don't get left out."

"Not me." Answered Becky "I want you guys to play good! You'll do better without my untalented efforts."

Pat was releived to find Bob Morris' car parked outside the restaurant. Peggy smiled at him and gave him an 'I told you so' look, He grinned back. They were barely parked when Cindi and Bob approached.

"I'm glad to see you made it." Pat said looking directly at his sister. She smiled broadly back at him.

"Ah Ha! Some one did miss us, Bob." Cindi stated "But then Pat never misses much."

"I hope we didn't worry you." Bob began but Pat interrupted.

"Whether I was worried or not isn't the point. Your both old enough to spend a few hours together without a kid brother around."

"Thanks Pat." Cindi said. "I knew you'd understand.

The group entered the establishment. As they were being seated Becky whispered to Cindi.

"You missed a great time."

"No Becky, I didn't miss anything." Cindi answered sincerely.

The food was excellent, and as they were preparing to leave Bob turned to Pat.

"I'll be driving Cindi home tonight Pat." He stated.

"If you prefer too, that's fine." Pat began "But you don't really have to bother."

"No, I want to." Then turning to Cindi he asked. "Do you think your father will be up?"

"There's usually one or the other pretending not to be when ever we get home." She answered and Pat laughed. Cindi glanced at Bob and when he nodded she went on, looking steadily at her brother. "We've got something to talk to Pa about, but it seems I can't keep quiet until then."

Becky looked up quickly, excitement in her eyes. "Congratulations." She laughed.

"You would be the first to guess." Cindi smiled back.

"Guess what?" Denni asked bewildered.

"Bob and I plan to get married." Cindi stated.

Pat was pretty taken back by the announcement, but as he contemplated it, he became quite pleased, and a smile spread across his face. He held out his hand to Bob who was beside him, yet instead of shaking hands the two embraced. He then licked his finger and making an imaginary tally in the air exclaimed.

"One down, One to go." Then turning back to Bob. "I just hope you know what your getting into."

"Your loss is my gain." Bob answered sincerely.

Sure enough, there was a light on in the Rhodes home when Bob pulled his car to a stop before it. The two quickly approached and after entering went quietly to the door of the Reverend Edward Rhodes study. After a pause, Bob knocked boldly.

"Come on in." A voice was heard.

"You wait out here, I want to see him alone." Bob whispered to Cindi before he entered the room. The study was extremely orderly, shelves of books lined the walls, along with numerous file cabinets. The desk at which he sat was clean of all clutter but the papers stacked neatly before him, and a bible laying open beside them. Edward Rhodes was a middle aged man, barely graying at the temples. He was a kind man, considerate of all, forgiving. He was strong in what he believed, yet humble in living it. He adored truth of all kinds, and honesty was his trademark.

Still he was not perfect. In one area of his life he still struggled. In one aspect he still at times became blind. That one element in his life involved his family. He loved his family and thanked God daily for his children, but yet somewhere down through the years he had never learned to turn them over to their Creator. He still longed to protect them and would risk all to prevent anything from happening to them. Cindi being his special pet. He had hopes and dreams for her life as most fathers do. He had thought often of the day she'd marry, of the fine Christian husband and provider, who would see to all her needs. He even glimpsed in his feeble mind, grandchildren climbing on his knee and reaching into his pockets for the pennies he would save for them. Bob Morris didn't fit into the picture. He quietly entered the room and stood before Brother Rhodes.

"Good evening sir." He began.

"Bob, Hi, Take a seat." Edward began, "You've brought my daughter home I see, did you have a nice time."

"Yes sir, we did." Bob answered honestly.

"I've heard nothing but praise for that group of young people, you don't find many like them. Were they good?"

"I'm not sure sir," Bob began, "I heard very little. You see Cindi and I were so busy talking outside that we never bothered to go in." He smiled sheepishly. Brother Rhodes was kind of shocked at this announcement, but continued.

"You must have been having a pretty important conversation."

"Yes sir, we were." Bob began. "Sir, Cindi and I have been seeing each other steady for six months, and both of us feel strongly toward one another." He paused, then after a minute came right to the point. "We love each other sir, and plan to be married." Again Brother Rhodes was quite taken by the statement, but after a minute he replied.

"Just like that, You like each other and are gonna get married."

"No sir," Bob interrupted "We love each other. I think so much of Cindi sir, I'd like to spend the rest of my life with her."

"There's more to it than that Robert." He answered. Bob cringed at the formal use of his name. "To decide you want to spend the rest of your life with my daughter is not enough."

"But I love her sir." He answered.

"Love won't put a roof over your head, dear boy." Her father answered.

"Sir, I've got a job, and although I admit it's not the best, I enjoy it and I'm sure we'll manage." Bob continued. "the important thing is that we're together."

"Young man, you have a run of the mill job pumping gas and tinkering around smashed up cars at a filling station miles from nowhere. There is no way that you can keep up a home, and a family on the little you make." He paused. "Listen to me. You've had this job less than two months, the one before it didn't pan out, and before that it was the same. Face it, you are not marrying material. You have no business even considering it until you can hold a steady job and provide for your family."

Bob looked crushed, as brother Rhodes continued.

"Bob, I've got nothing against you. You're a fine young man. A fine Christian. You are a fine worker, I know someday you will find steady work and be able to provide. But, Cindi is my daughter, As a father I don't want to see her struggle if this job doesn't last long either. I'd like to see her happy, living a good life, well provided for. Bob you can't offer that. Maybe in a few years, but not now." Bob sat uneasily after the man had finished talking. Then he spoke reluctantly.

"We've discussed it sir, our decision's made. I'm just sorry you don't feel the way we do."

"So you'll go ahead regardless of what I have to say?" Brother Rhodes asked.

"Yes, sir, we will" Bob began "I'm sorry you feel the way you do but sir I owe it to Cindi and to God to try my hardest at whatever I find to do. I enjoy my job sir. You may not feel it's secure but sir, there are few things that are secure. First is the love that your daughter and I have for one another. Second is the love that God has for us. He promises in his word to provide, the strength, comfort, and peace we need. I'm sorry, Brother Rhodes but I feel with a love for one another and a sincere love for God, nothing could destroy our happiness together.

Brother Rhodes sat solemnly behind his desk, slowly the dreams he'd harbored began to crumble. Gone was the beautiful home, and clothing. Gone was the table always laden with the best food, and a new car in the garage. Yet still he saw his daughter and in his minds eye, she hadn't changed. The same happiness he'd wanted for her was found in far less than he felt she deserved. Or was it less?

He looked across his desk at the young man who had just come to him desiring to marry his daughter. Bob had his head down, as he studied his hands. Hardworking hands they were, doing what they enjoyed. Brother Rhodes' heart softened toward young Bob.

"You realize" He began with fatherly pride. "Of all the girls around you've chosen one of the best. I'm very partial to her. Be good to her Bob." There were tears in the mans eyes.

"Yes sir, I will" Bob agreed quietly.

Thus we find at the end of another day, those in Roberts Junction looking closely at their lives and facing change. Young Denni Little made the first step toward change when he plucked the seed of sin from his life during his talk with Ben Daniels, likewise, Edward Rhodes relinquished the harbored dreams for his daughter when he faced the honest sincere plea of Bob Morris. You see change doesn't always involve new beginnings, and new happenings, sometimes one must look at themselves and realize that some things must go.

CHAPTER 7

A TIME TO KILL

Sunday, September 18, 1983

It was already quite late when Suzanna came down for breakfast. Ben was busy frying pancakes and Sarah was trying to feed cereal to a very obstinate baby.

"Well, Good Morning." Ben said enthusiastically. "It's about time you were stirring, I thought for a minute I'd have to use persuasion to rouse you."

"I'm not awake yet." She mumbled.

"Nick either." Sarah added. "Being up that little while last night must have really put him off his schedule."

"At least he's got a schedule." Suzanna complained. "The only schedules I ever have to follow are those that others enforce on me."

"Hot Cakes and fresh Maple Syrup! come and get 'em." Ben announced, as he set a heaping plate of pancakes on the table. "There's plenty more where that came from." He added as he returned to the skillet.

After a short prayer the two, Sarah and Suzanna, began filling their plates.

"Ah ha!" Ben declared. "Rich is in for a treat this morning. He's coming this way. It's been years since he's had my hotcakes."

"Good then I won't have to warn him." Sarah answered as they heard footsteps on the porch.

"Come right in fella!" Ben called. "I'm making my famous Flatcakes as you always called them."

"I thought I smelled a peculiar odor." Rich answered as he entered the kitchen. He took a handful of pine cones and held them out to Suzanna. She glanced at them and nodded.

"It's not your imagination, that isn't even a pine tree outside that window. Things don't add up."

"Whatever are you referring to?" Sarah asked bewildered. The Daniels upon returning soon after the power was restored had been made aware of the outage, but, neither Suzanna nor Rich had mentioned anything about either the phone calls, or the noises at the window. Rich related what he knew.

"You mean you think someone had deliberately done all that?" Sarah asked, "But why? Why would someone do that?"

Rich didn't answer. He was confused also.

"I'll have to get myself a few Pitt Bull's to guard this place." Ben added only half seriously.

Sarah felt uneasy. Something could have happened to Nick while she was gone. She didn't blame Suzanna the same could easily have happened with both Ben and Sarah home. Soberly she looked at Ben.

"You were joking about the Pitt Bulls, but maybe that's the answer." Sarah began. "Not Pitt Bulls, but another kind of dog. One that would bark if we had people come on the place at night. I'm afraid old Alfie isn't much of a watch dog."

"Sure he is." Ben smiled. "If he see's someone on the place he just sits there and,... watches them."

Everyone laughed.

"Well," Ben continued. "I'll have to do something, especially after taking the plunge that I did last night."

"Oh really?" Rich asked.

"Yup, I bought that colt I told you about. I worked out quite a bargain, had to sacrifice two of my best mares in the deal and I still had to fork over a mint.

"But from what you told me, that fella will be worth it with that bloodline."

"That's what I'm hoping." Ben stated. "Old Cruiser is gonna have to learn to share the spotlight."

"Ben's having the builder come this week, to make plans for the private stable." Put in Sarah.

"So soon?" Rich asked.

"I've thought about it." Ben began "and I won't really be gaining anything in waiting. So I figure I'll get it started as soon as possible."

"You sure know what you want."

"That's right." Ben said "I know what I want and I'm gonna do my best to get it."

Ben Daniels had the extreme privilege of being the Youth Teacher, for the Sunday School department. He enjoyed working with the kids and challenging them to seek in the word of God for their answers. Most of the class was there before Ben arrived.

"Hey, Did you hear the news?" Becky asked her friends.

"What news?" Connie Little asked.

"Cindi's getting married." Becky placed a special emphasis on the word married.

"Really?" The girls echoed.

"She was engaged just last night. She's getting married to Bob Morris."

"The Pastors son, from Lincoln?" Debbie Davis asked, Becky nodded.

"Oh, he's a hunk." Jeanni Van De Lou said as she rolled her eyes.

"When's the wedding?" Connie wanted to know.

"I don't know," Becky answered "But I just love weddings, don't you?" All the girls agreed. A few of the boys had been listening also.

"I heard that Bob Morris was in a terrible accident." Matt Rankin said loud enough for all the hear. "He survived all right, except for one thing. His head, hasn't been the same since. Keeps getting these strange idea's..."

"Such as?" His brother Mark asked with false curiosity.

"Oh, marriage and stuff." Matt answered.

"Nah." Mark said with mock astonishment.

"Hold it Bozo's" Debbie Davis interrupted. "How come anytime a couple decide to get married you all act like it's taboo or something?"

"Hey" Matt responded "There's a fella's whole life at stake here. It's serious. Why would a fine, good looking guy like Bob, decide to throw his whole life away for a girl. It doesn't make sense."

"It's called *LOVE*" Becky stated. "and one day each of you will be smitten with the same disease."

"Hopefully it won't affect any of us." Connie Little said with a laugh.

"Don't worry." Matt responded "I think you're all safe."

There was general laughter in the room when Ben entered, Suzanna was right behind him.

"Morning troops." He said as he made his way to the front table.

"Good Morning Brother Daniels" A few replied. There was still a few minutes before class began so a few of the girls cornered Suzanna.

"I heard the news, isn't it exciting." Connie Little began.

"You must be thrilled." Debbie Davis added. "Do you get to be in the wedding?"

"What Wedding?" Suzanna asked bewildered.

"Why your sisters, who else's?" Jeanni laughed.

"Cindi? She's not getting married." Suzanna informed them.

"She sure is." Becky responded, when eyes turned toward her. "She told me last night, or I should say, I guessed it."

Suzanna looked toward Peggy who had remained out of the conversation.

"That's right," Peggy affirmed. "She got engaged to Bob Morris last night."

"Really?" Suzanna asked shocked. "It's no joke?"

"Nope." Peggy answered.

"Bob, huh."

"Yup, Bob."

"As if I don't have enough problems with the brothers I have." She quipped toward Pat who sat quietly in a corner. "Now I'll have In-Law's to contend with." The girls laughed and returned to their seats, as Ben began class with prayer.

Early Sunday morning two young men left their car parked near the entrance to Liberty Park and, Bouncing a basket ball between them, jogged toward the courts.

"You haven't told me yet about Friday." Jeff began.

"Nothin' much to tell." Brady started.

"Yeah, sure." Jeff laughed. "You get stopped by the cops and they take you to jail, and you say there's nothin' much to tell."

"Cool it Jeffer," Brady stated. "I got into the whole mess from talking too much. I'm just lucky my talking also got me back out."

"Hey," Jeff seemed offended "Since when did you quit trusting me? We're in this together. It was just coincidence that I wasn't along with you Friday."

"Yeah, I know." Brady began, "But I do know who narked on me, and I'll see it doesn't happen again."

"You mean someone did blow the whistle?" Jeff stated surprised. "Who was it?"

"That crazy female I've been trying to keep quiet the last few days."

"Who?" Jeff asked confused.

"Blabber mouth Rhodes." Brady stated.

"Suzie?" Jeff interrupted.

"Yes, one and the same."

"You told HER about Fridays deal?"

"No meathead, You and I were talking about it Thursday when she came eavesdropping. Why do you think I've been paying so much attention to her. I wanted to keep her trap shut." He paused. "I guess I didn't succeed."

"You mean you're not really interested in her?"

"Are you kidding? What have we got in common? The whole idea of us together is a joke."

"She won't fall for it Brady." Jeff said seriously.

"I can see that already, the little Nark."

The two reached the court and began to shoot a few baskets.

"You really think it's Suzie huh." Jeff asked.

"It's gotta be. But it won't happen again." Brady began. "And I'll see that she pays for the damage she's already done."

"You're not gonna hurt her or anything?" Jeff asked uneasily.

"Are you kidding?" Brady began, "I'm not quite that dumb, but I can make life miserable for her."

"Like how?" Jeff wanted to know.

"Well I began last night." Brady stated. Then he related to Jeff the various innocent pranks he had played the night before. "The funny thing about it is that Tom VanDyke caught me leavin'. He thought I was a prowler so he tackled me. When he found out who I was, he thought Suzie and I had been fooling around and I was sneaking off before I got caught." Brady laughed. Jeff joined him although he didn't like the idea of Suzanna Rhodes being the subject of Brady's escapades.

"*He* tackled *You*?" Jeff put in. "We should recruit him for the team. You're not that easy to tackle."

"He played a few years ago. But he quit. I guess he didn't feel it to be as important as that job of his."

"He practically lives out there." Jeff commented. "By the way, do you have any jobs that look promising?"

"Not anything better'n what I've got. I'll probably stick to stacking shelves and bagging groceries three nights a week for the rest of my life."

"But it's something. My mother had arranged a job for me at the hospital, but I told her no."

"Really, why not?"

"I guess I want to make my way without others help... especially hers."

"You sound pretty upset about that split fella." Brady began, "It's not the end of the world, life goes on. Look at my parents. They've been separated for twelve years. I've got a Step-Father, Step-Mother, Step-Brothers, Step-Sisters, Half-Brothers, Half-Sisters, not to mention umpteen Step-cousin's that I've never seen." Brady laughed but Jeff remained quiet.

"It was just such a shock." Jeff finally said.

"Especially with that Daniels fella involved?" Brady asked.

"Ben Daniels isn't involved." Jeff informed him. "It's some guy by the name of Steve Williams."

"Who?" Brady stopped in his tracks. "Did you say Steve Williams?"

"Sure," Jeff answered "Do you know him?"

"Know him? He's the cop that tracked me down Friday night."

"That's right, he is a cop." Jeff stated.

Brady laughed. "I guess I'll get even with him for you then." Brady began. "I convinced my Pop that I was innocent and that Williams planted the cocaine on me. He bought it hook, line and sinker. And knowing my father, and his reputation, Your mother's sweetheart will be taking the rap."

"Really?" Jeff asked, secretly excited at the prospect.

"Sure, Pop's dug out bugs in all kinds of places. He's almost notorious for cleaning up crooked operations."

"But Brady, Your forgetting that this isn't a crooked operation, but a fabricated story."

"Now Jeff, you and I and Steve Williams are the only ones who know that for sure. And no one has proof contrary."

"I just hope your father can swing it." Jeff said sincerely. "You'd be taking the rap if Steve doesn't."

"And may the best man win, I always say." Brady declared, as he tossed the ball toward the hoop. "Bravo" He stated as he made a difficult basket.

Richard McAllister had just plugged in the coffee, when there was a knock at the door of his apartment. He hurried to answer it.

"Mom, Dad! It's good to see you." He exclaimed, giving his mother a hug.

"So this is the apartment you told us about." His father said as he looked about the place. "Kinda small isn't it?"

"I think it's quaint." His mother responded.

"I'm glad you came, would you like some coffee?"

"Yes, I'd like that." His mother answered.

"Ya got anything stronger than coffee, son?" His father asked.

"George! You promised." Riches mother exclaimed.

"It's okay mom." Rich laughed. "No Dad, coffee's the strongest you'll find here."

"What's the matter son, can't handle anything stronger?"

"You might say, I don't want anything stronger than coffee handling me."

"Dear, you promised before we came that you wouldn't talk about it." Rich's mother said to her husband.

"It's really okay mom, I can take it."

"We got a phone call the other day," His father began. "They're looking for you,... again."

"Really?" Rich was surprised. "I was planning to call them tomorrow and give my change of address, and information on my employment. I guess they missed me sooner though."

"You behaving yourself?" His father asked.

"Dear! You already covered that." Rich's mother exclaimed.

"If you mean, have I been drinking? The answer is no."

"What about the other stuff?"

"I'm still off it Dad, I'm gonna stay off." Rich responded.

"That's good to hear." His father replied, then continued. "Did you talk to this friend of yours about it?"

"If you mean does Ben know. I'm not sure. I didn't say anything, the time just never seemed right, but I did lèave reports with him when I started work Friday, whether he read them or not,..I don't really know."

"But you didn't talk to him?"

"No Dad, I didn't" Rich admitted. "Now enough of the questions, lets go outside, I'll show you around a little."

"Oh son, I'd really like that." His mother answered.

The three descended the stairway and followed the path to the stables. On the way Rich related about the power outage last night, refraining of course from any reference to Suzanna's phone calls and the disturbance at the window.

"Ben made a good decision then, in having you stay right on the farm." Rich's mother stated.

"We both like it. I needed a place, he had one and needed someone else here. It's working out okay."

"You could always have come home, son, your room is still there."

"Mom,.. I'm twenty-eight years old, I'm not going to go running back home like some teen-ager or something."

"I was only suggesting." His mother apologized.

"Does Ben have a family?" George McAllister asked changing the subject.

"Yeah, a wife and young son, Nicholas. He's only a few months old."

"Ben always seemed like a fine boy." Rich's mother added. "Did I know his wife?"

"No I don't think so. She was a few years younger than us. I knew a few of her brothers and sisters vaguely, but even I had never met her."

"What was her name?" His mother asked.

"Sarah James. Her sister Kelly was in our graduation class, and her brother John was a year or two older than I."

"Oh Look, here's your horse." Mrs. McAllister exclaimed as they stopped outside 'Spirit's' stall.

"I still can't see, why you're so interested in horses, son." His father stated.

"I'm not that interested, I enjoy them, true, but I'd really like to return to doing the kind of work I had been. Maybe not scouting, but something in the line of forestry."

"You want to go climb trees again." His father said sarcastically.

Rich remained quiet. It was beginning to seem almost impossible to please his father. Although his mother tried hard to cover it up, Rich knew he was not in his fathers favor, probably would never be. His father considered him a weakling, without any stamina. Something inside Rich hurt desperately. He wanted to try hard to restore peoples trust in him, but, it seemed his fathers trust was not repairable.

Most of Brother Rhodes congregation had dispersed and gone on home. Only old Bill and his grand-daughter remained at the church. The girls had arranged for Suzanna to spend the afternoon with the Winters.

Brother Rhodes and Bill stood at the entrance to the church watching their families make their way the their cars.

The old timer turned to his Pastor. "Yer eldest young 'un looks a mite happier this mornin'"

"I only wish I was a pleased." The preacher remarked.

"Tell ya what, I'll swap ya." The old man stated.

"Huh?" Brother Rhodes asked confused.

"I'll be prayin' fer yew and that daughter of yern, and ye be a prayin' fer me and that meetin' at the home today."

A smile broke out on the man's face as he looked at the old man.

"I'll make a swap like that any day." He answered.

Quietly Suzanna shared with Peggy the incidents of the night before.

"You really think someone was trying to scare you?" She asked.

"I don't know what they were trying to do. If they were trying to scare me, they sure succeeded. But then again, they may not have known that Ben was out of town and it may have been aimed at him."

"I'd hate to think someone would deliberately want to scare people."

"I almost went through the ceiling when Rich knocked on the door."

"I haven't met Rich yet." Peggy began, "But Gramps says that he seems to be a good worker and knows his stuff."

"You have no idea how relieved I was to see him when I did." Suzanna began "Tom was with him."

"Oh, oh." Peggy said with a grin.

"Don't start that. Like always he completely ignored me." Suzanna remarked, and when Peggy grinned back, she continued. "I bet you weren't being ignored last night though."

"No Ma'am I wasn't" Peggy laughed. "I was with too fine of a gentleman for that. But Becky and Den didn't seem to have any trouble getting along either."

"Becky went too?" Suzanna asked. "With Denni?"

"Sure, I thought you knew."

"No," Suzanna paused. "I didn't" Suzanna was pretty discouraged, it seemed like all her friends were enjoying themselves, and she felt so,... left out. On one side there were girls admiring her and the attention she was receiving from the notorious Brady Downing, and on the other hand she knew that was not what she wanted. She sighed loudly.

"What's so serious?" Peggy asked.

"Just thinking." Suzanna began. "For as long as I can remember I've been complaining about my brothers; and right at this moment I wouldn't mind if there were a few more Patrick Rhodes' in this world. But, only in different families." Peggy joined in Suzanna's general laughter.

The Gold Abode was a large sprawling building on the shores of the Flint river, that flowed through town. Each Sunday afternoon Bill Winters went to hold a small Bible Study and worship service for the elderly that lived there.

Both, Peggy and Suzanna accompanied him that Sunday. They planned to help lead a few songs of praise and worship. Suzanna played the piano quite well. Although not as talented as her older brother, she was able to support the faltering voices by playing the few simpler tunes. Peggy's voice led the chorus' easily, mixing a bit of youthful excitement that some of the group hadn't seen in years.

The message Bill delivered in his teaching had the same simplicity and was presented with a humble spirit of Love and deep concern. Many that now lived here had been dear friends of his for years. He'd worked side by side with them. Their children had grown up together, yet, every week he brought to them truths they had never heard, and a revelation of who God was, that they had never dreamed.

By Bill's patient continuation, many had secretly been led to a closer walk with him. Although none publicly professed the change. Each week they returned and each week they were more receptive to the word of God.

Before they left, Bill sought out each one and gave each a special word of support or maybe just a firm handclasp. The girls also felt a strong need to help these people and chatted freely with them. They left much later than they had anticipated.

"Well young'un's" Bill began as he started his car. "I always feel a bit blessed to meet with these people."

"Grandpa, it's so sad." Peggy started. "Those people have nothing left to live for. Even if they come to know the Lord, their lives are already over. Some of them can't even leave their beds. Some no longer even talk or think coherently anymore."

"But Missy it's not this world and this life we're awaitin' on. It's the one hereafter. The one up yonder we'll be spendin' with our Lord. That's all that's on a lot of their minds. They're all through livin' here, they're just bidin' their time."

"I want to spend eternity in heaven." Peggy stated. "But I sure want to enjoy a little of life down here too."

"They've done a lot in their lives most don't regret it."

"But going through day after day, year after year, without the peace of having the Holy Ghost within you?"

Old Bill smiled broadly at his grand-daughter. "You know Missy, I's mighty glad to see that decision firm in your mind. Don't ever lose it. It'll take you far. Maybe not with man, but with the one who counts."

"I plan on it Gramps."

Suzanna remained silent, deep in thought. Not only about the elderly, but of young people too whom she knew to be lost; Brady, Michelle, Jeff, Angie, Tom, ... even Rich McAllister. 'How can I, as useless as I am be an example to them when I haven't made a firm decision myself?'

The noon meal was later on Sunday, and the McAllisters had already gone. Sarah invited Rich to join her and Ben. He readily accepted the invitation.

"Tomorrow, evening." Rich stated. "I'll be the cook, you're invited to my place or should I say,... your place?"

"It's yours as long as you want it." Ben answered. "But as for your cooking,.. I'm not quite sure."

"Now I have never seen you turn down a meal of fish, so don't start now." Rich laughed. "You don't do much fishing anymore do you?"

"I fish a bit in winter, summers are always so busy. I take off 'up North' a week or so early in May. But usually I don't have the time."

"He's so out of practice that he stops off at the local grocers and gets fish sticks out of the freezer." Sarah made a face.

"Your slipping." Her husband responded. "You just stated an all out lie and your conscience never bothered you one iota."

"That's what I have you for." Sarah continued "But let me bring something,.. desert maybe. My apples are ripe and there is nothing better than fresh Apple Pie."

"You're on." Rich smiled.

The three entered the kitchen and Sarah began serving the meal. It was a simple meal and afterward the two men wandered out to the back porch to relax. Sarah took Nick upstairs for a well earned nap, she also went to her room for a rest.

"Your parents enjoy their visit this morning?" Ben asked.

"I doubt it." Rich began "My father kind of enjoys making life uncomfortable for people."

"I've met people who do that." Ben recalled. After a short while Rich picked up the conversation.

"Did you take a look at the papers I left with you Friday?"

"No need. I already know as much as I need to about you."

"Are you sure?" Rich prodded.

Ben thought about the question. "I can't imagine what you had to inform me of that would change your job standing here. I trust you Rich, what I need is someone I can trust."

"Ben, You have absolutely no business trusting me."

"Why not?"

"If you had read the papers I left with you, you wouldn't have to ask that question."

"Well I'm asking anyway."

Rich remained silent for a while looking down at his hands as they lay in his lap.

"Ben, I know how much you love your wife and son. They are your whole life. I can tell that. How would you feel if they were suddenly taken from you?"

"I've never thought about it." Ben began "I'd be heart broken,.. that's for sure. Lonesome too. I really don't know."

"What if someone was at fault. How would you feel toward that person?"

Ben thought awhile. "Probably angry at first. I'd want to go beat somebody up. But I know that's not the answer."

"But what is the answer?" Rich asked.

"I'd pray for the person of course, I'd have to do a lot of praying for myself first. Then I'd pray for that person that God would open his heart to receive his love and his spirit. You see Rich, my wife's life has already been sacrificed. She's made a decision to live for God. If she goes I know I'll see her again. I feel the same about Nick, although he's made no decision he is too young to comprehend, and my wife and I make those decisions for him."

"But how could prayer help the other person? The one who caused the death of your wife and son?"

"Rich there is hope in the Lord for everyone. It doesn't matter who. He is no respecter of persons. That person can be saved and receive the promise of eternal life just as my wife has."

"I wish I could believe that" Rich said impatiently. "But I can't. Now I'll tell you what I had to include on the papers I left with you. No, I'll tell you more." Rich decided then began quietly.

"When I got out of college I had that job out of Colorado. I loved it, wouldn't trade it for nothing. But, there were other things I wouldn't trade either. One of them was alcohol, the other was drugs. That was my life, one big high, day in, day out. I was having the time of my life." Rich became quiet, a stifled sob escaped him before he continued. "One afternoon, I stopped at one of my favorite places after work. Must have been three years now. Well anyway, I did the usual number, same amount of alcohol, same amount of drugs. I can't recall taking more or less than normal." He paused again covering his face with his hand. "I never saw her Ben." He sobbed. "I was so wiped out I never saw her." Rich began crying. Ben put his arm around him. In a minute he had stopped.

"I'm sorry Ben, I usually am able to control myself better than this. But I've tried to put the whole thing out of my mind. I hit her car, head on. She didn't have a chance. Her two kids were with her, a little girl of two and a boy about Nick's age." Rich paused again.

"If you don't want to talk about it, I understand." Ben spoke at last.

"No Ben, you don't. I have to talk about it. I've been trying to get a grasp on it for three years. I spent the next two years behind bars. I got counseled for Alcoholism, drug abuse, Depression, aggression, anything they could think of. They stuck me through every program they had, to try to keep me straight, but by then they needn't have bothered. I had already decided never to touch another drop of alcohol, or take any more drugs. But Ben, I decided too late. Three lives were lost. I was at fault." Rich sobbed inwardly again. "After I got out last July, I had to see them. I had to see the graves. I knew it was too late, but there was some reason I had to go. It was one of the hardest things I've ever done in my life."

Rich quit talking and once again buried his face in his hand. Ben had kept his arm around him and said.

"Rich there is hope, Jesus loves you, he alone understands if no one else does. He forgives when no one else can. Rich, I don't feel any differently about you. You've made your mistakes but you've also accepted the fact that they were wrong."

"No Ben I can't believe that, I caused the death of three innocent people, nothing you or anyone else says can make me believe that God loves me." Rich was almost whispering, but his voice gained strength. "God does not love, Richard McAllister."

Chrystal Shephard and her brother Mike sat quietly together that afternoon. Chrys was working on a piece of needlework, while Mike caught up on the local news in the paper.

"I heard news today that won't be in the paper." Chrys smiled.

"Oh?" Mike said absently.

"Yeah, Sis Rhodes mentioned to me this morning that her daughters engaged."

"Cindi? Really" Mike asked, putting his paper aside. "Bob Morris?"

"Yes, I don't know him to well." Chrys began.

"I do." Mike interrupted.

"What's he like?" She asked.

"Like 80% of all other twenty one year old fella's."

"Well what does that mean?"

"Nothing." Mike added absently.

Chrys looked at her brother. He seemed to have returned to his paper. She had to draw him out, they both needed to talk.

"Mike." She began. "It's none of my business,.."

"I know." He interrupted again and returned to his paper.

"Mike" She stated sternly. "Will you put that paper down for one minute and carry on a decent conversation?"

"With *you*?" He asked teasingly as he laid the paper aside. "What's on your mind?"

Chrys paused before answering.

"You Mike. I'm worried about you. You're a nice guy, except maybe once in a while to me. You're good looking, intelligent, you've got an excellent job, lot's of friends,.."

"So what's up?" He interrupted again.

"I'm curious." Chrys continued. "You never seem interested in dating anyone."

"So?" Mike asked.

"I was wondering why."

"Do you really want to know?"

"If you'll be serious."

"I'm quite serious." He began "I just haven't met anyone I'm really interested in."

"How do you know Mike?" She asked again. "You never spend time with any."

"Sure I have." Mike continued. "I just haven't dated them.

"Why not?"

"There's no purpose in it." Mike answered honestly.

"Sure there is. That's how you learn about one another, being together."

"I've learned a lot about the girls I know and I never dated a one of them."

"Come on Mike, be real."

"No. You be real." Mike returned. "I'm only twenty-one years old, and you've got me written off as a confirmed bachelor, or a weirdo. Well if you'd really like to know I'm neither. I'm just as human as the next guy. I don't intend on spending the rest of my life alone, just give me time. When the right one comes along, You'll be the first to know."

Chrys sighed and went back to her needlework. "You know," She hesitated. "I'd always harbored secret hopes that you would be the one interested in Cindi."

"What!" Mike was astonished.

"What's wrong with the idea." Chrys wondered. "You would have been good to her."

"And she would have destroyed me," Mike laughed "Chrys do me a favor, and leave my so called love live alone,...-please."

"Alright,.. alright." She relented.

"Besides," He grinned. "Who are you to talk."

Mother and daughter sat together in the sunlight that shone through the windows of the Rhodes kitchen. Luke had gone off to the park, while both Pat and his father had chosen to spend the afternoon studying.

"Oh Honey, I am so happy for you." Elizabeth Rhodes began.

"Mom I never guessed that I would feel like this." Cindi stated. "I'm so excited, life seems so perfect. You know mom, I want to have the perfect wedding."

"Oh?" Her mother asked.

"Yup. Don't you think a spring wedding would be lovely? I could have it outside with hordes of flowers. I want everyone to have a part in it. Just think, I could have six maybe eight attendants. I'll wear white of course, and I'll have Bob get a white tux,.." Cindi rattled on.

"Have you and Bob talked about this?" Her mother asked.

"Yes, and no." Cindi admitted. "He told me the wedding was up to me. I could do what I wanted. Hey, I've got an idea! I'll have the remnant come and play after the meal."

"I thought you didn't like the Remnant?" Her mother asked.

"Oh mom. You know what I meant when I said I didn't like them. But they'd be great for a wedding."

"Dear, don't you think it's a bit early to be making plans, maybe the two of you should talk more?"

"Oh, we will mom, we will." Cindi stated, then went into thought again, after a minute or so, she exclaimed. "I've got it! I was a bit worried about what to do about a preacher. But I think I worked it out."

"Oh?" Her mother asked.

"Uh huh, I'm gonna want Dad to give me away of course, so then he couldn't meet us at the alter.. That would be Brother Morris, he could say the vows with us and then when it comes time for us to receive the blessing,.. they could both pray. I want Daddy to say part of my wedding but I wanted him to give me away too..." Cindi rattled on.

Elizabeth Rhodes looked at her eldest daughter. The Apple of her husbands eye. She was very much like her father, she had the dark complexion of her mother and her mothers tiny mouth, and dimples, but there the resemblance stopped. The eyes that now looked back at her were the same vivid blue as her husbands, they were large and clear. Her hair was fine, smooth, and golden, highlighted with lighter shades. Elizabeth realized how truly beautiful her daughter was.

"We'll miss you dear." She interrupted her daughters rattlings.

"Oh Mom, I'll miss this place so much. But I won't be far. And I'll visit all the time."

"It won't be the same." Elizabeth stated. "You won't be ours anymore, we'll have to share you."

"But just think, the Morris' will have to share Bob also." The two smiled at one another.

"Let me tell you a story." Sis Rhodes requested. "I've never told you this before, I guess I was waiting for a special time."

Cindi nodded as her mother continued.

"It was twenty-five years ago. I was nineteen, the same age as you. I was dating a great guy. He was handsome, kind, thoughtful, and when he asked me to marry him, I thought I was on cloud nine. But you know the way I am. I never was much for words, and I kept putting off my decision. I hadn't accepted his proposal yet, when some friends of ours went with us to that Tent Revival I've told you about so often."

"The one where you repented, and got the Holy Ghost?"

"Uh huh, Well we went, and I've told you how that night went. How confused I had been and suddenly God took that confusion and cleansed me."

"You got the Holy Ghost that night."

"Yes I did. But you know, the boy I was dating didn't. When we left that night I was so happy and never noticed how quiet he was. I couldn't wait to gct back, so I asked if we could go the next night. He said 'Go ahead.' so I did. I went every night during the rest of that revival. Each night I asked him if he'd join us and it was always 'Go ahead without me.' Finally the last Sunday of the revival, we were having the Baptismal Service, there were twelve of us baptized. My boyfriend wouldn't come. I begged and I pleaded but he always said,.. "Go ahead without me." That was when I woke up to the fact that when my old flesh died, that relationship died too. Cindi I never realized how much I loved him 'til I lost him. I cried for days, it hurt so bad. I decided that I'd pray him saved. That if I prayed hard enough and long enough. If I fasted enough, that God would hear me, and God can do anything can't he?"

Cindi nodded reluctantly as her mother went on.

"For two years I prayed for him. He no longer would talk to me. I rarely saw him. But I kept praying. I loved him and felt that I could never love anyone else. I tried to ignore the other girls he dated, although some of them were close friends of mine. I quite praying for him though, after those two years."

"Why Mom?" Cindi asked.

"Because he married someone else honey."

"Oh Mom, I'm sorry!"

"You'd better not be sorry!" Elizabeth exclaimed. "I only thought I knew what love was. I was crushed again, but I had to face reality. For those past two years while I was praying for my lost love, there were those who knew it and prayed for me. They knew how young I was in the Lord and how I needed to learn to trust him."

"Uh huh." Cindi nodded for her to continue.

"Finally I became aware of the wonderful family I had in the Lord. Our young people had become so important to me. They were my strength, my comfort, especially one young fellow."

"Dad?"

"Yes dear, your father."

"How did you first get together."

"It was him dear. I was so crushed and blinded about my first love that there was no room for anyone else in my heart. Not for a long time. But your father was there. It seemed wherever our group would go he'd arrange somehow to be near me. I never was the wiser. I just accepted him, He was the youth leader at the time. I never dreamed that God had someone else for me. Someone of his choosing, not my own."

"It was about a year after the wedding that we went as a group canoeing, and who do you suppose arranged to be my partner?"

"He was the Youth Leader, but he sure didn't act like it that day. He was an instigator of an all out war with the canoes. We all tried to flip the next boat over, I guess the last canoe standing would be the winner. Well it looked like it would be between us and another couple. The other canoes were already overturned and the young people in an all out rampage after the ones who had caused it."

"We were getting into swifter water though, it was about two feet deep, finally your father, determined to overturn the other canoe stood up and stepped onto the side of theirs to overturn it, and sure enough, he did. But he overturned himself also which left me in the one remaining canoe alone and with only a paddle, which I didn't keep too long."

"What happened?" Cindi asked.

"Well, I hit a rapids that we hadn't anticipated and away I went going wherever the current took me, which in the end included over. When that canoe capsized I was swept down river with the current and I realized that I'd be okay if I just let myself go, so I did. When the current slowed down I was able to pull myself to shore and I waited there. I couldn't see any of the gang but I knew they'd be coming. They wouldn't just leave me."

"But only one came." She smiled at her daughter. "He gave everyone orders to stay put and your father came for me." Elizabeth laughed. "He was hollering my name and looking left and right down the river and he never saw me. I don't know why I didn't answer, I might have been too weary or I might have still been upset about the whole thing." She laughed again. "He must have thought I'd drowned because when he reached the river about twenty feet from me I called out 'Hey Mister! got room in that thing for one more!' He looked like he was seeing an angel. I'd never seen a fellow look so relieved to see something in my entire life."

"After he'd pulled the canoe up on shore, he let me know how he felt. He loved me then Cindi, like he loves me now, but Cindi, I didn't love him. My love grew. The love I have for your father now surpasses any I'd ever felt for another but I didn't feel that way immediately. Love is something that is built, and if it's built on the right foundation, a solid one, a foundation of truth and honesty it'll last a life time." Elizabeth finished and looked at her daughter.

"Now you run on over to the park and get Luke, it's about time for me to start supper."

Young Luke had gone to Liberty Park quite early that afternoon. He'd carried with him his rod and reel and tackle box, hoping to catch a few perch from the Flint river that flowed through the park. He recognized Jeff and grinned at him as he passed the basketball courts and headed toward the peer.

A few others were fishing also, and the afternoon passed quickly. He'd landed only two nice perch but had enjoyed himself on the smaller ones that insisted on pestering his lure.

Jeff and Brady had played the majority of the afternoon and were heading toward the car Cindi Rhodes entered the Park.

"Hey Jeffer." Brady began as he saw her. "Who's that beauty? Do you know?"

Jeff looked up and smiled. "Sure do." He stated.

"Well?"

"Well what?"

"Who is she you meatball?"

Jeff pondered a bit before answering "Her name is Cindi, she's a bit older than you so behave."

"Hah, that never stopped me before and you know it." Brady laughed.

Jeff refrained from commenting.

"Do you know her well enough to talk to her?"

"It's whether or not she'll talk to me that's the questioning."

"Stuck up huh."

"I don't know if that's it, she's just older than us."

"Well try, Okay." Brady whispered as Cindi approached.

"Cindi, Hi" Jeff called.

Cindi Rhodes glanced over and seeing the two smiled.

"Jeff" She acknowledged "Hi, isn't it a beautiful day."

"It'll probably be one of our last." Jeff commented.

"You're right, it did get quite chilly last night. Oh, by the way, congratulations. All I've been hearing today from my brother is Faleene this and Faleene that."

"Oh, has he seen her?" Jeff asked interested.

"He spent yesterday morning out at Ben's pestering Denni." Cindi laughed. "My mother sent me where to fetch him, he must be down at the peer. It was nice seeing you." Cindi started to leave but stopped when she saw Brady watching her. "I'm sorry." She began "I don't believe I've met you."

"Name's Brady." He smiled. "And your Cindi I gather."

"Yes. It's nice meeting you." She turned again. "Oh, by the way Jeff, rumor has it that Denni is preparing to resurrect his trumpet. Do you think you can handle it?"

"With the forewarning you just gave me perhaps." Jeff laughed as they parted. The boys walked in silence until reaching the Johnson's truck.

"Now that girl was beautiful." Brady stated. "I'm gonna make it a point to see more of her."

"Not at all like her sister is she?" Jeff asked smiling.

"Sister? There's another one?" Brady asked looking around.

"Uh huh, a year or two behind us in school." Jeff stated still grinning.

"Oh? What's her name?" Brady asked interested.

"Suzanna Rhodes." Jeff smiled again.

"What?" Brady sounded shocked.

"Like I said, she's not at all like her sister."

"You can say that again." Brady said deep in thought, as he opened the passenger side of the truck and entered.

"You know." Brady continued. "I just might find reasons to see more of this Cindi and at the same time get that loudmouthed sister to clam up."

"You never learn do you?"

The small congregation that gathered for the evening worship service had great cause for rejoicing. After a heart moving song service, Br. Rhodes delivered an anointed message entitled, "It's never to late." Although he was a minister that frowned upon begging people into repentance, he laid the scriptures at their feet and opened the alters to all that wished to pray.

Having delivered what was on his heart he felt weak and empty. Turning from the pulpit he also knelt and cried out to God for the congregation.

No there was no wild rush to the alters, not even a steady flow. Yet silently, very silently, people slipped from their pew and made their way to the front. First a young tow headed boy of twelve came forward, and looking through blue eyes washed with tears he made his way to the alter. In a minute he felt a hand on his shoulder and knew that his older brother had joined in the prayers for his soul.

Also coming forward was a newcomer. A young girl left her seat beside Peggy Winters and also made her way forward. Peggy accompanied her and the two knelt at an old fashioned alter as another soul made her way to God.

Old Bill left the pew after them, not for their sake or for his own, but to make his way to an elderly gentleman in a wheelchair who's heart was ready to turn to his saviour.

Suzanna Rhodes was left alone in the pew she had shared with the Winters and Angie, which was probably best for her heart also was feeling the steady tug toward repentance. Not bothering to go forward she turned and knelt at her seat, while the Lord looked down upon her and cleansed her, refilling her once again with a measure of his spirit.

Yes the church had great cause to rejoice, three souls had found a place of repentance and a fourth had found a place of restoration. Great miracles were wrought that night in the hearts of those few who's lives would no longer be the same.

For young Luke Rhodes, Angie Arnolds and Simon North, life now held something more, and for Suzanna Rhodes it again held something she had once neglected and lost.

Late Sunday evening Suzanna sat at her desk putting together the last pieces to the paper she was writing for Mr. Johnson.

"Aren't you coming to bed, yet?" Cindi asked.

"It'll be just a few minutes." Suzanna replied. "Then I'll turn the light out."

"What is that your working on anyway?"

"Oh, not much, a paper for Mr. Johnson's class. I'm already behind on it, so I want it for tomorrow."

"He's really a bear of a teacher isn't he?" Cindi continued. "He was so particular about stupid dates and names, I'm surprised I passed at all."

"This is for his 'United States Government' course." Suzanna continued. "I guess I don't mind the work because it's interesting. In fact I thought I'd hate this particular assignment but I guess I surprised even myself."

She continued to write for a minute or so, then put her papers together in her folder.

"There I'm through now, I'll flip the light off so you can get your beauty sleep. Not that you need it." Suzanna answered as she flipped off the light.

"What did you say?"

Suzanna shrugged. "Just that I'll turn off the light now."

"No, I mean about the beauty rest." Cindi stated.

"Oh nothing." Suzanna answered.

"No, you said something." Cindi insisted. "Did you say I didn't need a beauty rest?"

"Sure."

"You said that!"

"Sure and I meant it, I don't say things that I don't mean."

"You mean you think I'm pretty." Cindi asked astonished.

"Cynthia Marie Rhodes." Suzanna began, "For all of my fourteen and one half years I've been the other daughter, or the homely sister, or the simple one. Now you have the nerve to ask me if I think you're pretty, when I've heard it from everyone else all my life."

"But you've never said it." Cindi said severely.

"Okay, I agree, you're extremely pretty, but please don't be quite as honest with me, I'd rather not know my downfalls."

"You don't need to be pretty." Cindi sighed.

"Why is that?"

"Because everyone likes you. You're fun to be around. I'm a dud."

"What!" Suzanna was shocked.

"You heard what I said. I mean it, you'll have lots of friends because you're friendly, I've got friends because I'm pretty."

"I may have friends." Suzanna began, "But you've got Bob. I'll probably never have that."

"Oh don't get so worked up about not dating. You'll do fine. Didn't Jeff Johnson call yesterday?"

"Not because he's interested in me." Suzie stated.

"Your not fooling me sis." Cindi continued. "He's a very nice looking boy, and on the football team. I bet he's pretty popular with the girls too."

"I wouldn't know." Suzanna mumbled.

"Oh, you're jealous already, and you want me to believe he's not interested. Well if he's not interested in you, why'd he call huh?"

"It's none of your business." Suzanna stated firmly.

"He's not in jail, that much I know." Cindi began. "I met him and a friend of his at the park today. Hey, now that guy, Jeff's friend, he's another good looking boy, maybe you've met him? His name is Brady, do you know him?"

"Yup I know him." Suzanna paused. "They must have let him out."

"Out? Out of where?" Cindi asked.

"Out of jail, Bozo." Suzanna answered irritated.

"That nice looking young fella was in jail? You've got to be kidding."

"No it's you that's got to be kidding. You've been encouraging me to become interested in Jeff Johnson, someone you know is not a Christian. What's gotten into you?"

"All I said was he was nice looking and was probably popular."

"Well, I agree on both counts. But he's a lot more too, and I'm not interested in either him or in Brady Downing."

"Downing, huh, is that the kids name?" Cindi asked then after a pause. "Suzie, why would Jeff Johnson call you to say that Brady Downing was in jail?"

"You promise you won't tell?" Suzanna asked. "I don't want him to know I said anything."

"Sure, I promise."

"Well, he said that he would have been with Brady when Brady was arrested if he hadn't come to our youth service. He wanted me to know that."

"Suez, that's great! God could be leading him, and keeping him at the same time." Cindi stated excitedly, "Maybe you two will get together after all." She hinted.

"Don't count on it." Suzanna responded, "I'm not interested."

The two lay in silence for a little while, before Suzanna continued.

"By the way, congratulations."

"Oh, Suzie thanks!" Cindi said sincerely. "It's still hard to believe it's true."

"Well it appears I was the last to know." Suzie responded.

"Well, you know the mouth that Becky has." Cindi stated. "But at least what she says is true."

"What was it like?" Suzanna asked. "What did he say."

Cindi laughed to herself before continuing.

"Well I said most of it."

"You did?"

"Uh huh, he was so embarrassed. So I just told him how I felt about him, and he said he felt the same about me."

"Now that doesn't sound romantic at all." Suzanna said disappointed.

"That's because your not in love with him. I am!" Cindi laughed. "I'm gonna want you in the wedding you know."

"Really?" Suzanna asked.

"I want you to be my Maid of Honor. Will you?"

"Of course, if that's what you want."

"I'm planning on having Sis. Chrys, Becky, and Peggy as attendants as well as Bob's sisters Mary, and Martha."

"Six!"

"Sure, why not. I want a huge wedding, I only get one you know."

"I hope Bob picks someone decent for a best man." Suzanna mused. "I'd hate to have to be paired with a scuzz-ball."

"Bob doesn't know any Scuzz-Ball's Suzie." Cindi rebuked.

"Oh excuse me." Suzanna said in mock apology. Both girls began giggling, then Cindi continued.

"I'll try to arrange it though that Pat does not get paired with Peggy."

"You don't like him dating her do you?"

"She's just a kid."

"She's sixteen."

"Barely,.. she's a kid."

"He'll only be turning eighteen next month."

"But he's mature."

"So is she."

"Then why is she a friend of yours?" Cindi said.

"She's very particular about choosing her friends." Suzanna shot back.

The conversation would have gone further if the phone hadn't rung just then.

"Pa asleep?" Suzanna asked.

"Long time ago." Cindi responded.

"I might as well get it then." Suzanna said as she slipped out from under the covers and headed toward the hallway, where there was a phone outside her parents room. She picked up the receiver just as her father appeared in the door.

"Hello" She answered.

"Yes, uh, this is Michelle Morrison, I ah,.. ah,.."

"This is Suzanna." She answered quickly then added. "Are you okay?"

"I will be soon, I just need to know that you and Pat will say a prayer for me. The baby isn't due for three more weeks but I guess it's decided to come now."

"Oh!" Suzanna said "I'll tell Pat and we'll be praying for you." Then she paused. "Do you need anything?"

"Just your prayers Suzie, please."

"Sure, but feel free to give us a call anytime."

"I have right now, haven't I?"

"I guess so, but you take care of yourself - good bye." Suzanna slowly hung up the receiver, then looked up at where her father was watching her.

"That was Michelle Morrison," Suzanna began, and when her father nodded. "She's going into the hospital and wanted Pat and I to pray for her."

"Come on then." Her father said as he placed his arm around her and the two headed toward Pat's room.

And on an evening when a new life was making it's appearance, four others had sought to push aside once and for all the works of the flesh that burdened them. Killing the roots of fear, bitterness, and sin that had snared their souls Luke Rhodes, Angie Arnolds, and Simon North also stepped aside for a new life to make it's self known within them.

Each day more and more changes were taking place, but then life is full of changes.

CHAPTER 8

A TIME TO HEAL

Monday, September 19th, 1983

Suzanna knocked on her brother's door early Monday morning.

"Come in." Pat called.

"Hi!" She greeted as she slowly opened the door.

"What's on your mind kid?" Pat asked.

"Have you prayed yet this morning?" Suzanna questioned.

"Why,.. ah.. no I haven't." Pat admitted as he picked up his textbooks from the desk and put them together.

"Well," Suzanna began reluctantly, "We had such a wonderful time praying late last night after Michelle called, I thought maybe we could make more of an effort to pray together, before school."

Pat stopped, and turned from where he was making his bed.

"What happened to you?" He teased. Suzanna just smiled back.

"I'm serious."

"I can see that, and it is a good idea." He admitted then motioned her to join hands with him.

The two knelt in prayer together besides Pat's half-made bed, on a rug littered with dirty socks and empty pop cans. God met them there, two hearts bound together before their God. As they prayed a small figure entered the room and a tiny hand joined theirs in prayer. In unity the three brought before God the praise of their hearts.

Pat nudged Suzanna and nodded toward Luke, his face was shining, and tears of joy were falling down his cheeks. On an impulse Pat embraced him.

"Thank you Jesus." Suzanna sighed.

"Amen to that." Said a voice from the door.

"Oh Pa!" Suzanna laughed. "You're late for the prayer meeting."

"I can see that," Brother Rhodes smiled, "But I don't mind at all. Welcome to the family son." He said to Luke. "There may have been rejoicing in heaven last night, but, there's rejoicing at the Rhodes home this morning."

Luke just beamed, and Pat playfully socked him on the shoulder.

"Let's get breakfast, I'm starved."

"It's waiting." Their father smiled as the four of them left the room and made their way to the kitchen.

Elizabeth Rhodes was frying eggs at the stove, and Cindi sat at the table drinking a cup of coffee with the morning paper before her. The boys found places at the table as their father walked to the window. He stood looking out while Suzanna seeing a stack of toast beside the toaster began to butter them.

"I'll take care of these ma." She offered, picking up the butter knife.

"Thanks sweetie." Her mother answered. She filled the boys plates with eggs, and bacon and then turned back to the stove.

"It's gonna be a nice day." Edward remarked. "I've got time to rake those leaves this morning."

"Oh Pa." Pat began, "Hambones been digging again. When I fed her last night I noticed it."

"Has she gone through yet?"

"No I just saw that the floor was all scratched in one corner and the wood was beginning to splinter."

"The fool was probably trying to bury a bone." Cindi stated.

"I'll take her for a run today." Their father replied.

"Pa, can I go too?" Luke asked.

"I don't see why not." His father answered, "Hurry home from school and we'll go right before supper."

"Okay, I'll be here." Luke said excited.

"Oh, by the way Mom" Suzanna began, "I won't be coming right home after school."

"Oh?"

"I thought I'd stop at the Samaratin and see Michelle."

"Don't bother her dear if she's too weak." Her mother advised.

"I won't, I promise." Suzie answered.

"Michelle had her baby?" Cindi questioned. "So soon, I thought she had plenty of time."

"She thought she did too." Suzanna answered.

"She may not have had it yet." Their mother stated.

"But ma she called last night surely it will be here by now." Suzanna stated.

Elizabeth Rhodes just smiled, "Dear, I was in the hospital fifteen hours before you were born. And it was almost twice as long for your brother." She tossled Lukes hair.

"No wonder you didn't have anymore." Cindi stated.

"I'll ask at the desk before I go up." Suzanna assured her mother.

"That'll be best." Her mother returned.

"You'll let her know that she should call if she needs anything." Pat reminded.

"Sure," Suzie said as she pushed away from the table. "I'm in a hurry, I'll see you all tonight."

"Good-bye dear." Elizabeth called.

"Bye Ma, bye Pa!" She called as she grabbed her books and lunch from the hall table and headed out the door.

She had agreed to meet Angie Arnolds at the corner this morning, before heading to school. She was thrilled when she saw her. Suzie could already see the remarkable change that had taken place the night before.

"I feel so great this morning." Angie began as Suzanna approached.

"I'm glad. You know, my brothers and I had a regular prayer meeting this morning."

"Really?" Angie said with envy. "Help me pray for my family. They need to know the Lord too."

Just then Suzanna noticed Brady Downing walking toward her. Angie noticed too.

"Do you see who's coming?" Angie asked.

"I'm trying not to." Suzie stated.

"You really don't like him do you?" Angie asked.

"I don't know." Suzanna said honestly "I wish I knew what he was up too."

Brady smiled as he approached.

"Ah ha!" He began "You've brought a chaperon." He winked at Angie. "But seeing that there's two of you that makes me out-numbered so I guess I have to behave."

Both girls remained quiet. Then Brady continued. "But I'll take these." He said as he reached for Suzanna's books. "And that other nice fella that's coming up right behind you can take hers." Brady stated.

Both Girls turned quickly. Pat was right behind them.

"Good idea, Downing." Pat said as he reached for Angie's books. Embarrassed she allowed him to take them.

"Oh so you've got one up on me." Brady said looking directly at Pat. "You seem to know who I am."

"You seem to be pretty notorious." Pat smiled. "My names Pat, and I am not dating Suzie." Angie giggled uncontrollably "But then you aren't either."

Pat motioned Angie to go ahead and the two proceeded on their way to school. Angie looked back nervously at Suzanna, but she just shrugged.

"There that's two down." Brady said smiling at her.

"I guess so." She answered.

"Still friends?" He asked. Suzanna shrugged again as they continued toward school. "Okay what did I do?"

"Oh nothing." Suzanna began, "and everything." She sounded confused.

"Can't friends talk?"

"I guess so, but." Suzanna decided to be honest. "I think it would be best if you just leave me alone."

"But I don't want to leave you alone." Brady began "I want to spend as much time with you as I can." He smiled at her.

"It's hard for me to believe that." Suzanna stated.

"Don't try to believe it. Just accept it." He smiled and continued. "Now you didn't answer my question. What did I do?"

Suzanna didn't answer, she knew Brady had just spent time in jail, for what she had no idea. She knew he wasn't a Christian and also that for some reason she just couldn't trust him completely.

Angie and Pat were already quite a bit ahead of them. Brady continued. "You like that fella up there huh?"

"Oh yes." Suzanna laughed.

"Well, what's so funny?" Brady asked.

"I'm sorry." Suzanna giggled. "That fella, is one of my favorite people." Brady looked at her funny before she continued. "And he's right, we aren't dating. He's my brother." Suzanna laughed again. After a minute Brady laughed also.

"You sure kept that a secret."

"You never asked." She returned.

"Any other family member that I haven't met." He asked slyly.

"Just a kid brother, Luke. He's twelve."

"No sisters?" Brady asked confused.

Suzanna looked right at him. "Just the one you met yesterday?"

"I met your sister?" Brady pretended surprise.

"Well, she mentioned that she talked to Johnson yesterday, and that he was with somebody named Brady."

"Oh," Brady acknowledged. "You mean, whats-er-name."

"Cindi"

"Yeah, I had no idea she was your sister." He lied.

Suzanna continued walking.

"Your not at all alike." Brady stated.

"Uh huh," Suzanna began. "I know,.. I'm ugly."

Brady stopped in his tracks and when Suzanna turned his clear blue eyes looked deep into hers.

"I don't think so." He stated with a smile.

"You probably need glasses." Suzanna said looking down. But Brady wouldn't listen.

"Look at me." He said, and when she did he smiled. She smiled back. "There, that's what I like to see. And I'm gonna to my best to see it as often as I can."

Brady made a complete nuisance of himself all day. It began as Suzanna was leaving her English class after first period. Peggy met her at their usual spot and they began walking together.

"What's up?" Peggy wondered.

"What do you mean?" Suzanna asked.

"Angie was pretty shook up when I saw her this morning."

"Oh? She seemed fine to me."

"She came pretty unglued when I saw her. She thought I'd be upset with her for what happened."

"Really?,... What happened?"

"Pat walked to school with her and carried her books."

"Why would that upset her."

"She thought I'd be jealous."

"Really, why?"

Peggy shook her head at Suzanna. "You really don't see do you?"

"See what?" Suzanna was bewildered.

"Think will you, we talk Friday night and I tell her that Pat is taking me to the concert on Saturday. Monday comes around and,.."

"Brady con's him into walking her to school" Suzanna finished.

"She thought I'd be furious! It was hard to convince her otherwise."

"You know, sometimes that Brady causes more trouble than he's worth."

"But he's worth something." Said a voice behind them.

"Hi Brady" Suzanna said sarcastically without turning around.

"You don't seem to excited to see me."

"I'm not." She answered.

"Well get used to it. I told you I want to see as much of you as I can."

"Even if I object?"

"Even if you object." He smiled as they continued down the hall. Suzanna glanced at Peggy and rolled her eyes upward. Peggy shrugged. They hadn't gone far when one of Brady's friends joined them.

"Hey Downing, How'd it go?"

"Can't talk now." Brady said impatiently.

"Aw come on. What'd the pigs do to ya?"

"Not much." Brady answered.

"Aw come on Brade. What's the rap?"

"I'm out man, isn't that enough?"

"They don't just let people out when they're found with cocaine fella." The other responded.

"I didn't have the stuff." Brady responded.

"Yeah, sure, and I'm George Washington."

"Lay off it. It was a set-up, I'm out now. Some dude will have to pay. It ain't me."

"What do you mean?"

"I mean the cop that stopped me fabricated the whole story and planted the stuff."

"Oh, is that what you told the cops?" The other acknowledged with a laugh.

"That's what happened." Brady replied.

"And I know you better than that." The other said chuckling as he went on his way.

Brady walked in silence for a minute.

"I'm sorry you had to hear that."

"I knew you'd been in jail Brady." Suzanna stated honestly.

"I thought you would." Brady said firmly. "But I was clean I had nothing except what that crummy cop planted."

Suzanna said nothing. Brady continued. "Is that why you've been acting so formal today. You of all people, it surprises me, I thought you'd show a little compassion. I get carried off to jail, accused, abused, for no reason and you're gonna snub me for it?" He paused. Then he stated firmly. "I knew it. You're just like the rest. Preach love and being like Jesus and bla, bla, bla.. well I know better now. You're a hypocrite just like the rest, wait 'til a guys down, then kick him in the face."

His false accusations hit home. Suzanna felt it. She didn't want to be labeled a hypocrite, she believed she was a Christian. Wouldn't Christ accept Brady? Brady had played his game well, Suzanna looked at him.

"Hey, I'm sorry." She began. "I really shouldn't have let that affect the way I act. I'm wrong."

Brady once again caught her glance with his and smiled his enchanted smile. "Does that mean we're still friends?" He asked.

"Yes it does." Suzanna answered sincerely.

Brady left them at their typing class, they entered the room just as the bell rang. Peggy was quiet 'til they had taken their seats then she whispered.

"Do you think he's telling the truth?"

"It doesn't matter Peggy. How would Jesus treat him?"

"But your not Jesus. Your Suzie Rhodes."

"But I'm supposed to be like him. Right."

"Your supposed to be like him, not be him." She whispered. "Let Jesus accept him. You watch it. I don't want you hurt."

"If I don't accept him who will.? and if I don't show God's love, who will? I'll be careful."

"You'd better." Peggy stated.

Brady was waiting outside the typing lab when class dismissed. Suzanna smiled when she saw him, and waved to Peggy as they parted.

They talked very little as they continued toward her class. Brady was quite popular and greeted many he knew, Suzanna was deep in thought.

"Hey Denni" Brady called as they met up with Denni and Becky Franklin. Becky noticed Suzanna and looked surprised. Suzanna smiled.

"Hi!" Becky called then whispered "Are you dating?"

Suzanna laughed then whispered back. "No soul winning." They both laughed together.

"Denni dusted his trumpet off. He's gonna try playing again." Becky began.

"Hey that's neat." Suzanna said sincerely. "You're gonna resurrect it huh."

"Yeah, but I'll be playing different music."

"I'm glad." Suzanna stated honestly.

"I know it was a tough decision, packing it away."

"Mark plays a sax, and Matt a trombone." Denni began "We're getting together Wednesday before service. Pat, and Mike are gonna meet too."

"It sounds interesting." Suzanna put in. Brady took her arm and steered her forward.

"We've got to be getting along" He called. "Tell Jeffer I said hi will ya."

"Oh sure!" Denni stated as he and Becky began talking again.

Suzanna was hurt. Why? She didn't understand, she liked Becky Franklin a lot, but for some reason seeing her and Denni together bothered her. Yet here she was with one of the best looking athletes in the school.

Suzanna had dreamed for years about boyfriends, dating and what it would be like. Still, here she was accompanied by one of the most popular boys and she wasn't happy. She knew why not. Her whole heart ached. She wanted a fine Christian boyfriend who was courteous and fun not a handsome athlete who'd spent time in jail and showered her with flattering words. The ball was in her court. She could tell Brady how she felt but she also knew that there would be no one to take his place. No one seemed interested in her, except of course Brady and she wondered why.

She was pretty down by the time they arrived at Johnson's class room.

"I'll be here after class." Brady stated. His clear blue eyes looking steadily into her face. "I hope Johnson's in a better frame of mind today."

"Oh, I'll do fine." Suzanna said as she turned toward the class but Brady caught her arm.

"I'll be here, remember that." He repeated as he gazed at her.

"Uh,.. Uh,..Sure." Suzanna mumbled as she pulled herself away and entered class.

Suzanna quickly took her seat and glanced at her papers before handing them into Mr. Johnson. All was in order so she felt she'd give them to him before class began. Quietly she left her seat and made her way to the front desk.

"What can I do for you today?" Mr. Johnson said as Suzanna approached him.

"I came to return these to you." She handed him the papers he'd given her Friday. "And also to give you this." She offered him her essay.

"What's this?" He asked blankly then recalled "Oh yes, yes, Thank you Suzanna."

Suzanna smiled and returned to her desk. Something about Mr. Johnson bothered Suzanna. He seemed different somehow. She couldn't put her finger on it, and tried to put it out of her mind.

Throughout the class period Mr. Johnson's attitude bothered Suzanna. He had always been so alert, so sharp. Today he seemed so absent minded, and rambled on and on about things of no importance. 'The poor man' she thought as she recalled the circumstances of his wife's leaving. 'He must really be having a rough time.'

After class Suzanna was not surprised to find Brady waiting.

"Well, how was Johnson."

"O.K. I guess." She answered still concerned.

"He should be pretty sauced by now." Brady stated.

"Sauced?" Suzanna asked.

"Yeah, Jeff said he hasn't put the bottle down for very long since Friday."

"He's drinking?" Suzanna asked. "In school?"

"He must be, I guess he'd stashed some somewhere." Brady answered. "Jeff is pretty concerned. I told him he was making a mountain out of a mole hill. He's acting as though it's the end of the world. These things happen all the time."

"But not to Jeff." Suzanna answered seriously.

"I guess not." Brady said. "By the way will you be letting me take you to Charlies' for lunch today."

"Oh Brady" Suzanna sighed. "I'd rather not."

"Then I was right. I'm not good enough for you." Brady accused.

"It's not that, it just wouldn't work. Beside I've brought a lunch with me and already plan on spending my time with my friends."

"Aren't I a friend." Brady asked.

"Sure, you can join us if you want."

"We'll see!" Brady commented to himself. "Who else are you meeting."

"My friend Peggy, and Becky Franklin, and the girl you forced my brother to walk to school with Angie."

"Hey, is Franklin the one I saw with Denni this morning."

"Yea" Suzanna answered.

"The old son of a gun." Brady laughed. "That's the first girl I've seen Denni even look at more than once. Well let me see. Seeing that I'll be dining with your friends you shouldn't mind a few of my buddies joining us would you?"

"I suppose not." Suzanna answered wearily.

"Good, I'll see you then." He announced as he left her at the door of her next class.

Suzanna couldn't concentrate. Her mind kept wandering from Brady's being in jail to Mr. Johnson's drinking, to being anxious over what would happen during lunch. She'd been a fool to let things get this far out of hand. But if she refused he'd claim she wasn't a Christian. What, Suzanna wondered would be the best reaction? Do what she felt a Christian should do or do what she wanted? If she were really a Christian she'd accept him, but wasn't she a Christian and wasn't her initial response to him that she should put on her brakes and stop the relationship now? Frustrated, she buried her face in her hands.

True to his promise Brady and company met the girls for lunch. Suzanna had just met Peggy and Angie when they approached.

"Good Morning, Ladies." Brady grinned gallantly. "May we join you for lunch?"

The three looked at one another as Becky walked up.

"Hi!" She smiled "What's this?"

"The back woods welcoming committee." Suzanna said under her breath. She looked up just in time to see both Denni and Jeff chuckle.

"Well Ladies, we best be off." Brady answered taking Suzanna's arm. Denni nodded at Becky, and Jeff at Angie. The fourth fella of Brady's clan, Jim Townes joined Peggy. The girls were quite bewildered, yet they reluctantly followed.

"We're taking you to 'Charlies'. That is if you don't mind."

"I mind." Suzanna said.

"Uh, uh, uh," Brady reprimanded.

"I don't mind." Becky said smiling at Denni.

"Then let's be off. Suzie and I will ride with you Jim, we'll meet the others there."

Suzanna and Peggy were ushered toward Jim's car. In spite of the circumstances both girls were impressed with Jim's car. He helped Peggy into the front seat while Brady and Suzanna got in back. The minute they were inside Jim lit up. Sweet smelling smoke filled the whole car. Brady followed suit. Both girls were relieved they were sitting by open windows.

Brady nudged Suzanna and offered the joint to her. Hastily she shook her head and turned away. Brady smiled to himself. Things were working out fine so far. Sure she was a stubborn old bear, but he felt he could handle her.

In the second car, Jeff turned to Angie.

"Sorry to inconvenience you like this." He began. "But Brady was pretty determined to spend lunch with Rhodes, and he usually get's his way." Angie didn't reply but smiled shyly.

"I'd like to know how he got the two of you to play his game." Becky asked.

"His suggestion seemed okay to me." Denni grinned at her.

"But what about Suzie?" Becky wanted to know.

"She can take care of herself." Denni said. "I've seen it."

"But does she like Brady? Does she want to have him manipulate her like this?"

Jeff and Denni both looked at each other and shrugged.

"No she doesn't" Angie said from the front seat.

"What do you mean?" Jeff asked her.

"She told me that she doesn't want to be with Brady."

"She told you that?" Jeff asked.

"Sure, she told Peggy and I that Friday night."

"It's only lunch!" Jeff exclaimed.

"It's more than that to her." Angie responded. "But I don't completely understand why."

"I'm ashamed to admit, that I do." Denni answered again. Becky also nodded.

"Well" Jeff shrugged. "We might as well make the best of it." The others looked at one another uneasily.

The group found a large table at Charlies and seated themselves.

"What'll it be" Brady asked Suzanna, who just shrugged.

"Hey the pizza in this joint is excellent," Jeff stated.

"You bet." Denni agreed.

"Sounds okay to me." Brady said. "What about you." He asked Suzanna she just nodded.

Things were getting way out of hand and Suzanna knew it. It was beyond her control, far beyond it. Becky seemed to be doing okay, but Peggy was quite muddled and Angie was as white as a sheet. Charlie came and took their order.

"You like Pizza so much you come back for more?" He smiled.

"I bet you didn't expect to see us so soon." Jeff smiled.

"No, but den nothing you young'un's do surprises me." He laughed.

Brady looked at Jeff after Charlie had gone.

"Hey, Jeffer you sound as though you come here a lot."

"No. I was here last Friday night for the first time." He added.

"I almost didn't get him to go then." Denni added.

"I'm glad you did." Suzanna added smiling at Jeff, and recalling their phone conversation Saturday.

"Hold it!" Brady stated firmly "Am I to understand that the three of you were here together Friday." He looked accusingly at Suzanna.

"I come here all the time." She stated.

"That's not what I asked." He interrupted, then switched his gaze to Jeff. "Okay Jeffer what's up?"

"Nothing that I know of. I just wanted to talk to Denni Friday night and after I found him we came here for Pizza."

Brady glared at Denni. "Just the three of you huh. It makes a cute alibi doesn't it." Brady's mind was busy seeing both Denni and Suzanna and his best buddy Jeff all turning narc. His blood began to boil. Jeff sensed it. Jim did also.

"There was more than the three of us Brady." Jeff smiled reassuringly.

"I was here too." Becky put in. "So was Angie and Peggy."

"And my two brothers, and My sister." Suzanna counted on her fingers.

"And the Rankin brothers, and Ben Daniels." Peggy continued.

"My sister Connie and her two friends." Denni added.

"Chrys Shephard and her brother Mike." Jeff continued. "Is that all?"

"Give or take a few." Suzanna answered.

"What was it, a party?" Brady asked.

"It was the Youth Group from our Church." Suzanna stated.

"What!" Brady said startled then looked at Jim. "Did you hear that Townes? Johnson went to church Friday night instead of playing at the game. That's gotta be a first." Brady laughed. Jim joined him, Jeff surprisingly laughed too.

"I told you Brady, I had to talk to Denni. Where else would I find him?" Jeff laughed. The tension at the table was eased suddenly when Brady realized that the three had not been plotting against him.

Charlie joined them with the pizza. Conversation around the table didn't lag. Brady, Jeff and Jim talked mainly about Football, while the girls discussed different things among themselves. Denni listened attentively to the boys and put in a few words now and then.

Suzanna's mind had strayed back to her problems with Brady. As she pondered how to deal with him she saw a familiar face enter 'Charlies'. Rich McAllister entered and took a seat at the counter. Suddenly she wanted desperately to get rid of Brady and hoped for an ally in Rich. She motioned to Peggy, the two left the table and headed toward the Ladies room. As they passed Rich Suzanna stopped as if looking in her purse.

"Rich" She whispered quietly. He looked up at her, but before he could acknowledge her she went on. "See that fella at the table I'm with. He's been after me all day. I can't get rid of him what do I do?"

Rich glanced at Brady who was still engrossed in conversation and didn't notice. "Don't worry." He began "I'll think of something."

The two girls quickly went their way to the restroom, once inside Peggy asked.

"Suzanna Rhodes! Who is that man you just talked to, and what is going on?"

"Peggy Winters" Suzanna imitated."That man is Richard McAllister, and I have absolutely no idea what's going on."

"Then what are we doing here. And with them! Me! with Jim Townes of all people."

"What can we do. How much of a Christian would I be if I told them to get lost?"

"A very wise one, I'd say." Peggy stated determinedly. "Poor Angie. You know how deathly afraid she is of people. At least Jeff Johnson's a little more civil then what we've got."

"Becky seems to enjoy it."

"But what about Denni. You'd think we could trust him not to pull this kind of stuff on us."

"I don't know Peggy. All I know is I've got us into this mess. We might as well make the best of it."

"Yeah sure. It's not gonna be that simple for me." Peggy answered. "It'll be a long time before I'll forget this. And how do we know we'll even get back to school today. I've heard a lot of things about Jim Townes and I don't doubt a one of them."

Suzanna stopped suddenly and covered her face. "Oh no!" She sobbed. "I never even thought of that. Have I ever been dumb."

"Do you realize that Brady just spent time in jail! For what we can only guess, yet you're encouraging him by not telling him to get lost."

"But what about his soul Peggy?"

"He's not concerned about his soul, he's only interested in getting something from you. We're both treading on pretty shaky ground girl."

"And it's my fault." Suzanna sobbed again.

It was then that the door of the Ladies room opened and 'Charlies' wife entered.

"There you are." She smiled at Suzanna.

"The man at the counter said you dropped this." She stated handing a folded piece of paper toward Suzanna.

"Important, no?" She asked.

"Yes" Suzanna remarked. "Very important. Thank you."

After the woman had left the two girls huddled over the note as Suzanna opened it.

Will stall boys when you leave 'Charlies'
The rest is up to you.
good luck,..

Rich

"Well, it's our chance." Suzanna stated.

"See that this doesn't happen again will ya."

"I'll try." Suzanna said soberly.

The two returned to the table. Rich was just leaving the building and nodded at them as he went out the door.

"Hey, was that Rich?" Denni asked as Suzanna sat down.

"Uh huh," She answered.

"I wished I'd seen him sooner, I would have said hi."

"I did" Suzanna commented as they finished their meal.

Soon the group was preparing to leave. The boys were paying the check and the girls had a chance to talk.

"Get ready to leave quietly" Suzanna said. "A friend is gonna stall the boys and were gonna disappear, get it."

"Sure." They chorused.

"Let's act natural about it though and not draw any attention to ourselves."

"Do you think they'll try to stop us." Angie asked.

"Maybe but stay cool."

"Denni'll do his part." Becky stated.

"I find that extremely hard to believe." Suzanna said bitterly.

"He had no idea what Brady was up to."

"Jeff either." Angie added.

"Sure that's what they say." Suzanna remarked. "I just wish this whole thing was over."

Moments later the young people left 'Charlies' and headed toward their cars. They had walked only a few yards when Rich hailed them from under the hood of his truck.

"Hey Denni," He called. "It must be my lucky day. Can you guys give me a hand?"

"What's the trouble Mr.?" Jim asked approaching Rich.

"That's what I'd like to know." Rich laughed. "I know next to nothing about cars. I've seen Denni fight with that old tractor yesterday, maybe he can help here."

"Well if he can't I'm sure I can." Jim stated as he looked under the hood of the car, Brady joined him as Jeff and Denni looked on.

The girls had taken their cue and had quickly and quietly made their way down the street.

Brady and Jeff sat at their table at the back of the class room. Denni was busy finishing up some lab work so Brady took the opportunity to talk.

"I'm meeting the Grub again tonight."

"Oh yeah" Jeff answered. "Where'll you be."

"That woods worked out great last week."

"No way I'm not risking that again."

"I don't expect you too. The horses worked out fine last time but today I'll just be waiting with my car. We'll be careful. You want to come?"

"Hey man, I'd like to but I haven't been with Misty since Thursday, I planned on spending some time at the farm tonight."

"No problem. I can bring you there after we get the load."

"What about Jen, I promised I'd take her. Pa's been kinda useless lately." Jeff continued. "I wish I'd known but I don't want to let her down, not now."

"Sure." Brady answered. "Maybe, I'll take a trip by there before I head back to town."

"Dennis is working tonight. He'll be around." Jeff added.

"You really went to church Friday?" Brady asked changing the subject.

Jeff laughed. "Yeah, I almost walked out too after I realized Denni wasn't going to leave with me. But there was only a few minutes left so I stayed."

"Did they converted you?" Brady laughed.

"They tried." Jeff answered with a grin. "They seem to be such fine people. It's a shame that they're such fanatics about everything."

"Are they?" Brady asked. "I've got a repellent mind it rejects all useless garbage, such as Religion and Chemistry." He stated holding up his Chem note book.

"Man are they ever. Denni doesn't say much, But I've heard and I'm amazed that anyone would willingly choose to live that way."

Suzanna left school that afternoon with Becky Franklin who baby-sat after school a few blocks beyond the Good Samaratin Hospital.

"How was your afternoon?" Becky asked.

"Okay." Suzanna answered.

"You didn't have any escort between classes huh."

"I kinda dodged him a few times."

"Why do you think he's pestering you?" Becky asked.

Suzanna just shrugged.

"He is nice looking." Becky began "He can be really nice and fun to be around too." She continued. "He's one of the most popular kids in school."

"But,.." Suzanna put in.

"Yeah, but,.." Becky smiled. "I guess it's out of the question then."

"You sound disappointed." Suzanna stated.

"Aren't you?" Becky asked.

"Not at all" Suzanna stated "I just wish I could get him to realize that I'm not interested in him."

"Did you tell him?"

"That's the first thing I did. But I also left it wide open when I said we could be friends."

"I think he's interested in more than just a friendship." Becky observed.

"I know, but how do I get rid of him. If I just tell him to get lost that I want nothing to do with him I'm not being very Christian am I?"

"I guess not." Becky pondered. "Maybe you can report him?"

"He hasn't done anything!" Suzanna stated then laughed. "I can just hear myself saying 'I'd like to file a complaint against Brady Downing.' 'Yes Ma'ma what is the nature of your complaint' 'He's been walking me to school, carrying my books and he took me to Charlies Cafe for lunch' 'And your complaining ma'am?'" Both Becky and Suzanna burst out laughing.

"Does Pat know?" Becky asked after a while.

"Yeah, but I told him I could handle it."

"You could tell him what's up."

"I guess I could but I hate to get him involved."

"You aren't planning on telling your parents are you?" Becky asked.

Suzanna looked shocked. "Are you kidding, I can just see my Dad fly off the handle if he even knew I was in a car with Brady."

"You don't have to tell him everything." Becky stated. "Just ask how to get rid of a guy who likes to follow you around."

"I don't know. I really don't. Peggy and I were claiming him for the Lord. I want to do what's right. I guess there's only one solution."

"What's that?"

"Pray." Suzanna answered.

The Good Samaratin Hospital was a large Modern building also built along the Flint River in Roberts Junction. It served a vast area, which was sparsely populated, therefore Suzanna was not surprised to find Michelle alone in her room.

She quietly knocked on the partly open door.

"Michelle" She asked. "Can I come in?"

"Suzie!" Michelle exclaimed "You'd better come in, if you don't I'll never forgive you."

Suzanna entered the room and took a seat beside Michelle's bed.

"Did you see her?" Michelle asked.

"Yes I did." Suzanna answered "Just a peek as I went by."

"Isn't she the most beautiful thing you've ever seen?" Michelle began. "Suzanna I never dreamed it would be like this, she's gorgeous, so tiny, so perfect."

"You look great." Suzanna commented.

"I feel great! Oh Suzie,.." Michelle added. "Thank Pat for me will you. He'll understand."

"I will" Suzanna began. "He told me to say Hi."

"He would" Michelle stated. "He's been a good friend. I named the baby Joanna Michelle Jamison, I doubt if it will please Mrs. Jamison, but when they asked me what the name would be I knew it would have to be her fathers name. She's all I have now."

"No she's not Michelle." Suzanna began. "You've got friends like Pat and Myself and there's a God in heaven that cares too."

"But none of you can be Joanna's father." Michelle stated simply. "It will be just the two of us."

There was a slight knock at the door and a woman entered. Her face was completely hidden by a huge bunch of roses. She set them on the table, and smiled at Michelle.

"Congratulations. Mom." Chrystal Shephard laughed.

"What's this?" Michelle asked.

"This is from the Youth Group." Chrys smiled. "I'm acting as flower girl today. There are three roses from each of the young people. A red one for you, a white one for little Joanna is it?" Michelle nodded. "And a third pink one for the union between Mother and Daughter." Chrys paused. "We love you Michelle.."

Michelle was quiet for a while, tears began to form in her eyes. "Thank you." She stated. "You'll never know how much this means to me. I was so excited about my new life, about my daughter, and now it looks as though I'll have special friends to share it with too." She dabbed at her eyes with corner of her sheet.

"There's another too Michelle, a friend that sticketh closer than a brother." Chrys began.

And amid the clean smell of Antiseptic and powder, in a brightly lit hospital room, the heart of a lonely rejected, seventeen year old girl began to hope. With the first act of hope a healing began.

CHAPTER 9

A TIME TO BREAK DOWN

Monday, September 19th, 1983

Luke ran quickly into the house, the screen door crashed behind him.

"Young man how many times...?" Elizabeth Rhodes began.

"Aww Mom. Not now. Where's Pa, he said he'd wait." Luke interrupted.

"Your father was called away, he will be home soon, now you go back and shut that door properly. Do you hear?"

"Yes Ma'am" He responded as he turned back to the door.

"I've made some molasses cookies, would you like some?" His mother asked when he returned to the kitchen.

"Do you have to ask?" He grinned. "Of course I'd like some." He reached for a cookie, as his mother poured him a glass of milk.

"Tell me," His mother began. "How was school."

"The same." He answered quickly. "Unbearable." Then he laughed. "Sonny Abrams put an alarm clock in Mr. Monrovies desk today when he was out of the room."

"Oh?" His mother asked smiling.

"It went off right during the Civil war. You should have seen Mr. Monrovie jump. I thought he'd never come down."

"It wasn't quite that high now was it?" His mother admonished.

"No, but I'd like to think it was." Luke smiled. "Sonny had to stay in during recess, but he insisted he didn't do it, that it was his brother, so Mr. Monrovie made Junior stay too."

"Junior is Sonny's brother?" Mrs. Rhodes asked confused.

"Sure, they're twins." Luke stated matter-of-factly. "Christopher John, that's sonny, and Jonathan Chris; That's Junior."

"I see" His mother sighed. "I guess I'm lucky I had my children one at a time."

"Just think ma," Luke responded "You could have been blessed with two of me."

"That's exactly what I was thinking. I repeat, I'm lucky." She smiled as she mussed his already unruly hair. "Are you ready to go? I think I hear your father drive in."

"I'm off." Luke called as he jumped from his chair. He almost collided with his father as he left the kitchen.

"Slow down son." His father stated. "I haven't forgotten, and No I won't leave without you. Why don't you get Ham ready. I'll be right out."

"Sure Pa!" Luke responded as he headed out back.

His parents watched as he left the house.

"If everyone had that energy and enthusiasm, Life would be a lot less complicated." His father commented.

"You might even have gotten those leaves raked today."

"Today's not over yet, I'll be back shortly. I'm just gonna run over to the woods by Ben's place. I might even be able to con my energetic son into using a rake also."

"Good luck, energy like that is extremely hard to tap." Sister Rhodes stated.

"Hey I appreciate the ride." Suzanna stated as her and Chrys left the hospital.

"Sarah mentioned that you'd offered the take Cam out as often as you can. It'll be nothing to swing by there and while I'm seeing Sarah you can get some riding in."

"I need it." Suzanna responded. "Ma let me know, when I called that supper'd be a little late anyway. Pa's off with the dogs."

"Dog's?" Chrys asked.

"Yeah, Hambone and Luke." Suzanna laughed and Chrystal smiled. They rode in silence awhile before Chris asked.

"How's the new convert today?"

"Ang? Oh, she seems fine, considering."

"Considering?" Chrys asked "Considering what?"

"Considering the fact that she's a friend of mine."

"Now what does that mean?"

"Oh I just got her into a few peculiar situations, and you know how shy she is.

"With you, I can imagine just about anything."

"I doubt if you'll imagine this." Suzanna said seriously.

"Try me." Chrystal suggested.

"Well, I hate to admit this." Suzanna began. "But there's this guy at school, and he's got a problem."

"Most of them do." Chrys stated matter-of-factly.

"This one likes to kind of manipulate things."

"That's the worst kind." Chrys agreed.

"Well he likes to be with me." Suzanna shrugged "So he tries to get rid of all my friends."

"No!" Chrys seemed shocked.

"It's not that bad." Suzanna began. "He's being good about it, but he's still doing it. Take this morning for instance. Angie and I were walking to school together, and because he wants to walk with me he cons a complete stranger into walking with Angie. Just to get rid of her."

"And you let him?" Chrys asked.

"What do you want me to do? Say get out of my life scumface!"

"You could have tried something."

"That wasn't too bad. It kind of backfired. The stranger was only a stranger to him, not us."

"Who was it?"

"Pat." Suzanna answered. "Brady wanted to get rid of Pat too because he thought Pat was my boyfriend."

"No." Chrys was laughing.

"I set him straight though."

"I'm sure you did." Chrystal stated.

"Later he decides that he wants to take me to 'Charlies' for lunch."

"Uh huh" Chrys nodded.

"Well, I was planning on having lunch with my friends, so doesn't that meatball come with dates for everyone of my friends, and poor Angie ends up at 'Charlies Cafe' with Jeff Johnson."

"Jeff seems nice."

"But Chrys, that's not it." Suzanna insisted. "Brady manipulated the whole thing. I stated out right away that we didn't want to go with him."

"And he used brute force to get you there?" Chrystal asked.

"Well,.. ah, not really. We kinda went along with the whole thing."

"Why?"

"Oh Chrys you don't understand. I can't just snub the guy. That wouldn't be Christian." Suzanna sobbed.

"You like him don't you?" Chrys asked pointedly.

Suzanna sniffed a few times then answered. "I did at first. But now that I see him manipulate people I like him less and less. And Chrys I have no business liking him at all."

"Why not?"

Suzanna sobbed again. "Can you imagine my fathers reaction - his innocent daughter spending time with a *heathen*! Spare the thought will ya."

"Suzie, you are only 14. You are not getting married to this guy, you are not even as of right now dating this guy, why can't the two of you just be friends if you like each other?"

"He claims he has plenty of friends." Suzanna answered. "For some reason he's singled me out, and I can't allow it."

The two rode in silence for a while. Then Suzanna continued.

"Here I am, one of the best looking, star athletes in school is singling me out and it seems like all the guys I could go out with, want nothing to do with me." Suzanna stated. "It doesn't seem fair, I'll be fifteen in two weeks and all my friends will be dating and there I'll be alone,..and I can't even blame it on my father's old fashioned rules either."

"If I recall correctly most of your friends are older than you."

"Sure, so what?"

"Peggy and Becky are both sixteen aren't they?"

"You mean I've got another whole year of this mess??" Suzanna asked surprised.

"You think it'll be over then? That dear, is when the trouble starts. Life is seldom fair." Chrys stated. "It was different for me when I was in high school."

"It was?"

"Sure, I wasn't living for God. I was living for Chrystal. I had dates all the time. I had a blast. Life was on continual party for me. But my best friend was the one who didn't date. It's funny though, she didn't care, not one iota. We did things together all the time, and often we'd go in a group. There were all kinds of guys around but she never dated."

"She must have really been ugly." Suzanna remarked. "Or had a personality problem."

"Oh no, she wasn't ugly at all." Chrys stated. "She thought she was. Maybe that is why she never got upset about dating. She was fun to be with too, but kind of quiet."

"You mean she's gone thru all these years and never dated once?"

"Hold it, I never said that!" Chrystal remarked then laughed. "Maybe she hasn't. You see I don't know if her and her husband actually dated like you and I would consider dating."

"She's married!" Suzanna exclaimed "How did that happen?"

"I guess it was my fault." Chrystal said. "If I tell you, do you promise not to repeat this?"

"I'll try."

"You'd better do better than that young lady." Chrystal laughed as she began her story. "Well, I met your mother about that time, and she invited me to church. I was eighteen a Senior in High School, my friend was too. We were both rowdy, her probably more than myself. Well anyway I began attending your Dad's church."

"I thought you always went to church there."

"You were only seven then, you wouldn't remember. Anyway, there was a fella in the church then, that I really liked. One of the finest people I'd ever met, so after I'd gone to church awhile I thought it would be neat if I could get him to ask me out."

"Oh, oh," Suzanna laughed.

"Oh! oh! is right. I did whatever I could to impress him. It didn't work, he was too busy with the church to notice. So I decided it was a lost cause and just began living for God. I still am." Chrys smiled.

"What about your friend."

"Oh, her, she was in trouble with the law. Nothing too serious, but she was pretty shook up. I invited her to church, and I have never seen anyone hit the alter as fast as she did. It was great."

"She got saved?" Suzanna was surprised.

"Of course." Chrystal stated. "She was baptized two nights later. Three years after that she was married to the guy I had tried so hard to impress."

"Your kidding?" Suzanna asked.

"No I'm not and the two of them are the dearest friends I could ever ask for. We even joke about my 'Former Infatuation' as we refer to it."

Suzanna was quiet for awhile, then looked at Chrystal. "Sarah and Ben Daniels?"

"That's them."

Along Twilight Road about halfway between Homestead lane and the Highway that runs between Roberts Junction and Lincoln, there is a small turnaround in a wooded area, bordering the back property line of Ben Daniels. The owner of the woods is insignificant but many are the picnics folks have enjoyed under the shade of it's trees. Many are the times the paths were used as bridle trails, deer roamed there as did an abundance of smaller game, squirrel, chipmunk, and rabbit. One of the tallest oaks held the nest of a hawk, and the fields nearby held plenty of brush for pheasant, partridge and quail.

On this particular afternoon it held more.

"Hey Pa!" Luke shouted. "There's 'ol longears!" The rabbit headed right toward them, Hambone right behind.

"You're in luck." Edward Rhodes said addressing the rabbit. "This is just a practice run, but I'll be watching for you next time." He laughed as the rabbit ducked quickly into it's hole, leaving Hambone slightly bewildered, but not enough to keep him from running off in another direction on a different scent. Brother Rhodes sat down to rest on an old fallen tree trunk, his son settled down beside him. They sat in silence a few minutes as Hambone made his way back and forth through the woods stirring up all sorts of trouble.

"Boy it feels good to get out in the fresh air doesn't it?"

"It smells a bit like that farm we passed on our way here." Luke responded with a smile.

"That's country, son. I miss it plenty." His father answered.

"Surely there's nothing keeping us from living in the country now." Luke said hopefully. "You could have a woods to hunt in and,.."

"You could have a pasture for your horse." His father returned smiling a little at the thought. "No son, I need to be in town. I'm needed there, I miss the country but I can't run from what I feel God wants me to do."

"I guess so." Luke answered forlornly.

"Son, when I first had children. "His father began. "I wanted them to have every opportunity I had, and more. I wanted them to enjoy hunting, fishing, farming. But I wanted to give them the opportunity to do things I never did. Things they themselves longed to do."

"Like Pat with his building?"

"Yes," His father laughed. "I couldn't even build a decent rabbit trap 'til he showed me himself. He was eight at the time. But yes, like that, and also music, I've tried not to push but encourage you to learn music. Suzanna and Pat seem to enjoy it, but Cindi,.. well give her a recipe and she'll make a top notch meal, where the same recipe will be only hard balls of charcoal if Suzanna attempted it." Luke laughed as his father continued. "And you've seen some of the gorgeous things your sister has sewn,.. that girl is almost capable of making something out of nothing,.. I guess she will make a good wife." He finished lamely.

"Didn't you think so Dad?" Luke asked surprised.

"Oh don't mind my words son, It's just hard to see her go."

"I hope you feel the same when I leave." Luke smiled.

Brother Rhodes slapped his son firmly on the back as they got up from the log.

"I was thinking son." Brother Rhodes began. "Of working out some arrangement with Ben to give you more opportunities to ride."

"Oh really Pa, would you." Luke said excited. "Suzies been riding Cam a lot, and she doesn't like horses near as much as I do." Luke insisted.

"I'll have to talk with Ben soon, it wouldn't be your own horse. I just can't swing that, but if you really show your responsible we'll see what we can do in a year or so."

"Really Dad, really" Luke exclaimed.

"I said, we'll see." His father emphasized with a smile. "There is nothing I'd like better than to see you have your own horse, but if it doesn't work out there's nothing we can do. Understand?"

"Sure Pa," Luke answered, secretly harboring forbidden hope.

The two were just nearing their car when a second car pulled into the turnaround. Brady Downing knew he was running a risk when he pulled in behind the Rhodes car, but, he knew also that Grub was not a dude to trifle with and that if you'd planned to meet him you'd better be there. Reluctantly Brady stopped the car, determined not to look suspicious he opened the door and stepped out.

"Good afternoon!" He greeted pleasantly as Edward Rhodes walked up, Hambone at his heals.

"It is good isn't it." The preacher responded with a smile.

"Someone looks like he enjoyed himself." Brady continued, nodding at the dog.

"Not near as much as I did." Brother Rhodes admitted. "I don't take time enough to enjoy life. Time goes to fast."

The two talked a little longer as Luke put Hambone in the car. Brady walked a few yards down the path as they drove away, before returning to his car.

Sure enough no sooner had the Rhodes car disappeared from sight when Grub pulled up beside Brady.

"Hey man, thanks." Brady said as he accepted the packet and handed Grub some cash.

"Be a little more careful with this stuff will ya." Grub responded.

"You bet." Brady agreed. "But I've found out who tipped the cops off and it won't happen again."

"Better not." Grub answered as he started his engine. "Enjoy yourself Downing." He called as he drove off.

Brady took the packet and went quickly to his car. He slid the cocaine into the glove compartment then turned the ignition, the engine came to life only to be snuffed out.

"What in the,.." Brady began as he tried the engine a second time.

Nothing.

"Oh you idiot!" Brady said to himself as he looked down at the empty gas gage. "How could I be so dumb." He hollered as he got out of the car.

There he was stuck out on some country road, miles from nowhere with an eight of a gram of cocaine on him, and not a cent to his name. Frustrated he gave his car a sturdy kick before he glanced forlornly down the road where both cars had recently gone.

The road to town was about a mile in the distance, then it was a good five more along that highway to Roberts Junction. He was about to start walking in that direction when he recalled that Jeff had told him he'd be at the farm all evening.

"Hey" Brady smiled to himself. "Daniels' farm is just on the other side of the woods, I'll cut through there then wait for Jeffer he's bound to give me a lift into town."

As Brady made his way out of the other side of the woods he could see the outbuildings of Ben Daniel's farm about three quarters of a mile in the distance, it was still long walk but there were bridle paths to follow and it was nothing compared to the walk into town. He was about to step onto the trail when he noticed a lone rider approach on a Palamino mare.

"Ah ha." Brady smiled to himself. "I'm really gonna enjoy this." Once again making sure his contraband was secure in the breast pocket of his jacket he stepped out onto the trail as Suzanna Rhodes approached on Camalot.

Suzanna was greatly enjoying the quietness of the late afternoon in the woods. She'd finally began to relax after her hectic day, when a figure emerged from the trees directly in her path.

"Ah" Brady said gallantly. "My knight in shining armor upon a trusty steed."

"Brady?.." Suzanna gasped.

"That's me." He smiled. "And you're just in time."

"In time?" She questioned.

"Yep, it isn't every day you get called upon a mission of mercy." He laughed. "Let me explain, I was on my way out here and my tank went dry. I know it's my fault." He held up his hands defensively. "But I thought I'd step through the weeds here and corner Jeffer to give me a lift into town."

"Oh" Was all Suzanna could say.

"So, how about a lift to the farm." He nodded toward Camalot.

"Oh, ah sure. I guess so." Suzanna stammered. She slipped her foot out of the left stirrup so Brady could get a boost.

"Thanks much." He grinned as he climbed up behind her. She encouraged Camalot to continue, as Brady went on. "You know I couldn't believe I did what I did. I always keep that tank full. I'll be more careful from now on believe me."

"I hope so." Suzanna said soberly. Once again she felt uncomfortable in Brady's presence. 'I'm really being stupid.' She thought. 'He only needed a ride and I happened along, there's nothing more there.' But still his arms around her waist bothered her, his body so close to hers made her uneasy.

"Your being quiet." Brady said interrupting her thoughts.

"Uh huh." She nodded. "Nothing to say."

"No impromptu riding lesson huh?" Brady questioned. "What's lesson two again?... Don't get the cart before the horse?"

Suzanna laughed in spite of the situation. "Close enough but I'll save that lesson for,.."

"Another time huh?" Brady finished. "Do you realize that is the first positive statement I've ever gotten from you! Every time we talk." Brady continued. "You make it sound like we're saying good-bye forever, but it's not that way is it?"

"Could be." Suzanna said sober once more.

"You know I don't know what to make of you at all." Brady responded exaggerated.

"Then don't make anything at all." Suzanna quipped back.

"That's harder to do than you think." He responded. "How can I ignore the fact that I'm at present astride a golden steed with my arms around a beautiful girl?" He tightened his hold on her waist and leaned forward to whisper in her ear. "I'm kind of pleased myself."

"I'm not." Suzanna responded. "By the way, did you bring your pillow? Because if I'm gonna have to tolerate this trip I'm gonna make it as short as possible."

"Don't try anything funny." Brady said half in alarm, for he still felt uneasy around horses.

"I'm not the one who's been pulling shady things all day." Suzanna reminded him as she kicked Camalot into a fast gallop.

Suzanna led Camalot swiftly over the trails toward the farm, Brady holding firmly behind her. They were just reaching the lane leading to the stables when she stopped abruptly. Brady, startled, lost his balance and slid off, almost taking Suzanna with him.

"Lesson number two,.." She laughed down at him. "Never go any faster or slower than the horse." Brady lay in the discarded stubble of a hay field, dirt and grass covered his jeans and he held his head as he looked up at her.

"Nothing like first hand experience huh?"

Suzanna laughed, Brady joined in, neither of them noticed a rider approach. Suzanna helped Brady remount and when she turned Camalot back toward the Stable, she met Tom.

"Enjoying your ride?" Tom questioned sarcastically for he had seen most of what had transpired.

"Just taking lessons." Brady answered.

"You've got a lot to learn Downing." Was Tom's reply.

The Rhodes family bowed before their meal while Br. Rhodes said the blessing. Young Luke at his fathers side shifted anxiously in his seat. Pat sat beside Luke, stealing glances toward his sister across the table. Suzanna sat on the opposite side of her mother, she was quiet and subdued tonight not at all like the Suzanna that normally turned the place upside down with her vibrance. Cindi sat beside Suzanna next to her father, she looked tired after a long day at work, yet she was encouraged by the fact that soon she'd be on her way to Lincoln once again to see Bob. With the prayer over, Elizabeth served the meal.

"How did Michelle feel when you saw her?" Pat asked anxiously of Suzanna.

"She looked great. Is that baby ever a doll. Her name is JoAnna, after Joe of course. You should have seen her face when she got the roses from the young people."

"I'm glad to hear she's fine." He paused. "Do you think it would be proper for me to see her?" He asked his mother.

"I really don't see why not." Her mother paused. "She'll probably have plenty of visitors."

"I think, I'll stop over tonight. There's a new job starting this week and I don't know how much time I'll have later."

"What's the new job?" His father asked. "Ben's meeting with Girard isn't he?"

"Yup, and that's the job. I'm excited about it. Having a hand in building at Ben's is gonna have extra purpose because he's such a good friend."

"What is Ben up to now?" Cindi asked bewildered. "He's not building a new home is he?"

"No sweetheart." Her father responded. "Ben's investing in some prize stock and is building a new facility for them."

"A barn?" Cindi asked then looked at her brother. "Your excited about building a barn?"

"It'll be more than a barn, sis." Pat answered. "In fact it's quite fancy. It'll look like the old fashioned Carriage Houses."

"To each his own." Cindi responded.

"Mike will be stopping by for me after school tomorrow, Ma." Pat continued. "He'll be able to fill me in on the job then."

"Just don't neglect your school work, son." His mother smiled. "By the way how was school today?" She asked turning to Suzanna.

"Okay I guess." Suzanna answered feebly. "I gave Johnson that report I told you about."

"I'm glad." Her mother seemed pleased. "Did you meet Angie this morning? She seems like such a nice girl."

"You might say I met her." Suzanna smiled, then grinned across the table at her brother. Pat knew better than to mention Brady's behavior in front of his parents especially at the table so he just smiled.

"She seems to be doing fine but she is concerned about her family." Pat answered. "She asked us to pray for her parents, she really wants them to accept the experience she's had. Her brothers too."

Cindi looked sternly at her brother, then added. "Patrick, I think you've been spending entirely too much time with your little sister's friends."

"Cindi that was uncalled for." Her mother rebuked.

"But mom, it's sickening. Every time Suzanna brings home a new friend he falls all over them."

"That's not true!" Suzanna defended. "He probably wouldn't have even spoke to Ang today if it didn't just work out that they were together and besides there is nothing wrong with my friends."

"But they are so immature. Don't you think so Dad?" Cindi asked.

"No comment." Brother Rhodes said with a smile.

"Well, *I* think it's sickening." Suzanna said severely. "First you pick Pat apart for dating Peggy, then you pick him apart for talking to Angie, and in my opinion he's twice the guy Bob is."

"Leave Bob out of this."

"Gladly." Suzanna retorted.

"Now when you two are done fighting over me can we get back to our meal." Pat asked. "I never realized so many people cared about me and my almost nonexistent 'Love' life. The next time I talk to any one of the opposite sex, I will first seek your approval. He nodded at Cindi.

"This family is nuts." Cindi remarked. "all of you."

"No." Luke laughed as he pointed his finger at his oldest sister. "I think maybe just one of us."

Suzanna lay forlornly across her bed, her accounting book lay open before her, but her mind far from the subject. Cindi's clothes were strewn over the room where she had hurriedly flung them as she rushed to get ready for the evening. Suzanna was startled by a light rap on the door.

"C'min" She called.

The door opened and Pat stuck his head in.

"Miss Perfect gone?" He asked.

"Finally." Suzanna sighed, as she sat up on the bed. Pat entered the room and after throwing Cindi's jacket off the rocker sat down. Suzanna noticed that he had dressed carefully and must have spent extra time on his hair.

"Where are you off to?" She asked.

"The hospital, remember." Pat answered.

"Oh" Suzanna responded. "But you're here. What's up?"

"You know what's up."

"I try to ignore it."

"Tell me about this Downing character."

"There's not much to tell. I don't know that much about him."

"He seems to know a lot about you."

"He knows almost nothing about me." Suzanna insisted. "Or he'd leave me alone."

"Which it appears he doesn't want to do." Pat continued. "Did you enjoy the pizza?"

"How did you hear about that?" Suzanna asked.

"I've got connections. Actually I talked with Denni. He's pretty upset."

"I should hope so,.. the skunk!"

"Dennis is not a skunk, sis."

"But he sat back and let Brady manipulate him."

"So did a certain young girl that I know." Pat said simply. "Denni like I said is pretty upset. I guess Becky set him straight on how you felt. Up until then he thought you liked Brady. He had no idea. Jeff either."

"But they're all in it together Pat, don't be fooled."

"I'm not. Brady is doing this of his own accord. Don't snub the others for it."

"But what do I do about him?"

"We'll think of something. But in the meanwhile try prayer."

Contrary to what Elizabeth Rhodes had thought Michelle was alone in her room when Pat arrived.

Quietly he entered. Michelle lay facing the window, a discarded novel lay on the bed beside her. Pat cleared his throat.

"Oh Pat!" Michelle spoke. "You startled me."

"I didn't mean to."

"Oh I know that. Tell me,.. have you seen Joanna?"

"No I haven't, but tell me about her."

"Do you really want to hear?"

"Why of course." Pat said honestly.

"Well to begin with her name is Joanna Michelle Jamison." Michelle paused to see Pat's reaction, then continued. "She weighs 8 lb's, 2 oz, she is 19 inches long," Michelle paused again, shakily. "and everytime I look at her I think of Joe." Tears well up in her eyes.

"I'm sorry." Pat began.

"Oh no Pat! Don't be. Joanna is all I have. She's beautiful. I already feel a special bond with her, but Pat she wouldn't be here today if it wasn't for you."

"Not me Michelle, The Lord."

"Whoever." Michelle said quickly. "Why I ever let you talk me into keeping her I never figured out, but Pat this is the best thing that has ever happened to me."

"I'm so glad to hear you say that."

"Your sister was here. And Chrys, she brought the roses."

Pat glanced up at the humungous vase of roses. The pink, the red, the white, all blending together. They were the only flowers in the room and immediately he felt bad that he hadn't thought to bring something on his own."

"How are you feeling?" He asked.

"Real good, they've got me pretty doped up though. I've already taken a few walks up the hall to see Joanna while she slept." She sat up and slipped her feet into the slippers beside her bed. "Let's take a walk down their now I personally want you to see her."

"Sure," Pat helped her to her feet and then held the door for her.

"I can't believe how really great I feel." Michelle continued. "My mother was with me last night, she's so shot, she spent the whole day in bed." She laughed. "She told me I was in such good spirits because all I had to do was lay their the Doctor did everything else."

"Who'd you have?"

"Martin. I was worried at first for he was out of town all weekend but they finally reached him at about 10:00. I'm so glad. Even though I've never seen Dr. Peters as a patient, I couldn't possibly have argued about him treating me."

The two had reached the nursery window and were looking in on the tiny babe as she slept.

"She's so small!" Pat commented as he watched the little child.

"She won't stay tiny long, they tell me." Michelle began. "They grow pretty fast."

"She's too small yet to see really who she'll favor."

"Oh,.. I hope she looks like Joe, he is far the better looking of the two of us."

"That dear girl, is a matter of opinion." Pat stated. "If you recall, Joe is built like the quarterback he was, I'd hate to see a girl like that." He laughed. Michelle joined in the laughter.

"You know exactly what I meant." She laughed.

"You're right I do, but I also disagree."

They talked a bit more, then turned back towards the room. They were passing the elevator whan an older man stepped out. He seemed embarrassed to see them.

"Michelle." he said as he held out his hands to her. She took them both, as she stepped toward him.

"I'm sorry." The man began. "That you had to be alone."

"I'm used to it." She said flatly.

"Can I see her?"

"Sure, she's right down here in the nursery." She took the mans arm and led him back down the hall. He gazed at the baby silently for awhile.

"You had to do it didn't you?" He stated. Then when Michelle looked confused he added. "Her name."

"I hope you don't mind." Michelle began to stammer. "I felt she needed to have her fathers name. Joe is the father, nothing can change that."

"I believe you." He admitted, "But, well, Eileen is a different story. She won't be pleased."

"I didn't do it to please her." Michelle stated testily.

"Of course not." He assured her, then after a pause he spoke as he took an envelope from his jacket. "This is for the two of you, I'd like to do what I can to help, although it's not much."

"That's not necessary, you know that." Michelle responded as little Joanna began to squirm and cry in her crib. "look, she's awake. Let's go back to the room. The nurse will bring her in, and You'll be able to hold her."

"Maybe just this once." He spoke quietly as they turned toward her room to wait.

Pat had slipped back to the room when Michelle had led Mr. Jamison to the nursery. He was seated on a chair near the window when they returned.

"Patrick, I didn't mean to ignore you back there, it is good to see you again." Mr. Jamison began.

"It's good to see you also sir." Pat answered as he stood to shake the man's hand.

"Here comes the nurse now." Michelle stated, "Here put this on." She handed a sanitary gown to Joe's father. Pat helped him into it. The nurse entered the room and handed Joanna to Michelle.

"Oh," She stated. "You have visitors, well they can stay for five minutes. Then we'll let mom and baby alone." She turned quickly and left the room.

Michelle brought the baby to where Mr. Jamison now sat on the foot of the bed.

"Joanna." Michelle said talking to the little one. "There is someone special I want you to meet. Joanna Michelle Jamison, this fine man is your Grandpa." She carefully placed the baby in the man's arms.

"Thank you." He said amid tears.

It was a few minutes before six when Brady entered the breakroom. He quickly punched in, then hurried to the store room. He eyed the skids of cases that needed to be shelved with frustration.

"There's no way I'll get done with this mess by ten." He mumbled to himself as he began to load cases of cans onto a nearby dolley.

It was a long job, although not requiring a whole lot of brains or ingenuity. By 7:30 Brady was wishing he'd never seen a Campbells Soup label. He had just opened a new case and was beginning to place the cans securely on the shelf, when he glanced up.

Coming toward him, up the aisle was Brother Rhodes, his son Luke, and Suzanna. Brady cleared his throat. When Suzanna looked his way he smiled.

"Brady?" She asked.

"Yup, that's me." He smiled. "and this must be your father?" He asked nodding at Brother Rhodes.

"Yes I am." Edward smiled broadly "Did you enjoy your walk this afternoon?"

"Oh yes certainly." Brady lied. "But it looked like it would be much longer than planned."

"Oh?" Brother Rhodes asked.

"Yeah, the tank was empty on my step-fathers car. I was quite stranded."

"Oh, You don't say."

"I made it to Daniels' farm though, and my buddy Jeff, gave me a lift into town. In fact I barely made it to work on time."

"I'm glad to know you got help." Rhodes continued. "That's quite a walk back to town. Well we won't keep you from your work any longer, take care of yourself Young man, and don't go to far from home without a full gas tank."

He moved up the aisle with Luke after him. Suzanna stayed behind pretending to examine the labels on a few cans.

"Thanks Brady." She said quietly.

"Whatever for?" He asked.

"For not mentioning that I gave you that ride. He wouldn't have been too happy."

"I think he's Okay, he would have wanted you to help someone who was stranded, you know 'The Good Samaratin' and all that stuff."

"Well thanks anyway." She repeated as she turned to leave.

"Sure, by the way, I'll see you in the morning. And decide where you want to go for lunch."

"How about the school Cafeteria?" She answered absently.

"It's a date" He stated.

"No,.. It's not!" Suzanna was flustered. Then when he began to chuckle she continued. "I never know what to expect from you."

"Expect the best." He grinned.

"Yeah, sure." Suzanna said sarcastically as she went on down the aisle to where her father and Luke were picking out groceries.

Suzanna slammed the trunk after loading the last bag of groceries, then climbed into the front seat beside her father.

Brother Rhodes cleared his throat a little as he started the car.

"Ah." He began hesitantly. "That fella back there, seemed like a nice chap. Do you know him well?"

"He's a friend of Denni's." Suzanna answered immediately hoping to stop any further questions.

"That doesn't tell me a whole lot." Her father smiled at her.

"His name is Brady Downing, he's a junior, he plays football, has his license,.."

"And he was busted last Friday night when they caught him with cocaine." Luke interrupted.

Suzanna was shocked at Lukes words. "Where did you hear that?" She hissed.

"They were talking about it Saturday when I was out at the farm. Denni and some other guys from your school."

"Do you know anything else?" Suzanna asked.

"I guess he made up some story and they let him out."

"How come you didn't say anything to me you dirt ball." She reprimanded.

"I didn't even know that you knew he existed." Luke defended himself.

"And what may I ask." Brother Rhodes began, "Makes my youngest daughter so interested in Denni's friends all of a sudden?"

Suzanna felt her face grow hot from embarrassment.

"As long as you didn't hear what we said." Suzanna whispered to herself.

A frown appeared on her fathers face. "I've always hoped that my children would never say or do anything that they'd be too embarrassed to tell your mother or myself."

"Oh Pa, I'm sorry. I didn't mean it that way at all."

"I should certainly hope not. And I hope my youngest son learns to keep tales that he knows no facts about from being repeated."

"Yes sir." Luke said quietly.

"We'll talk about this Brady fella another time. Maybe when you're ready to tell me."

"That might be never." Suzanna responded.

It was after ten that night, when Cindi returned from her evening with Bob. After saying Goodnight to her mother she quietly entered the room she shared with Suzanna.

The room was completely dark, and Cindi began preparing for bed without switching on the light.

"If you throw your jacket on the rocker like you always do, you'll hit me right in the face." Suzanna said quietly aware that Cindi didn't know she was there.

"Oh!" Cindi said startled "Your not in bed?"

"Just thinking." Suzanna responded. "Go ahead, get some sleep don't let me bother you."

Cindi finished dressing and climbed into bed. She lay there a while before she spoke. "Are you upset with the way I criticized your friends today?"

"Not much. I've learned to expect it from you. But I wish you'd lay off Pat."

"I guess so, he takes it too well, but when anyone attacks you! It's fun to see the fur fly."

"Yea I know I've got quite an impulsive temper. "She answered, then continued. "Maybe you can help me."

"Oh?" Cindi asked "Algebra? Accounting?"

"No, no," Suzanna paused. "Boys."

"Boy's,..you? That's a joke."

"I wish it was." Suzanna commented.

"What's the trouble?" Cindi asked.

"Well" She began reluctantly "There's a kid at school who likes me and I can't seem to dissuade him."

"Do you like him?" She asked.

"Well,.." Suzanna was puzzled. "I don't know."

"I bet he does."

"What do you mean?"

"I just mean that there are some things that guys know. And they can tell if a girl likes them. No matter how hard we try to convince them otherwise, they can tell."

"So what do I do?"

"Why do anything? That is if you like him?"

"But Cindi, He's not a Christian?"

"So what?"

"What about all the scirptures that talk about believers and unbelievers and such."

"What about them, that's marriage. You're only talking about some kid going looney over you, he'll grow out of it."

"Man, I sure hope so." Suzanna put in.

"Just don't tell dad."

"I think he already knows." She responded.

"Oh,oh,"

"Oh,oh, is right. He told me I could come and talk to him about it when I'm ready. But he's waiting."

"How did this slip out? To Dad I mean." Cindi asked and Suzanna relate as much of the conversation in the car as she could.

"You mean that good looking guy that was with Jeff Sunday likes YOU?" Cindi asked.

"I guess so."

"And you want to get rid of HIM?" What is wrong with you? I bet all the girls would fight for his attention. And is it true about the cocaine?"

"I don't know. I don't really doubt it. Partly because of Jeff's call Saturday. He seemed pretty sure and they're best friends."

"Stay clear of the stuff yourself will ya." Cindi stated.

"Of course." Suzanna responded firmly. She turned down the corners of her bed and climbed in.

"Oh,..Sue?"

"Yeah, what is it?"

"Enjoy yourself will ya. You're only gonna be a teenager once."

Slowly in the midst of daily life and the struggle thereof the facade of the ideal and perfect Christian that Suzanna had formed began to crumble and break giving way to the hand of God to form in her mind the true image of his child. But what would this image include,..and would Brady Downing be a part of it?

CHAPTER 10

A TIME TO BUILD UP

Tuesday, September 20, 1983

Ben entered the stables where his private horses were and quickly walked to the end stall. Leaning against the gate he looked silently at 'Cruisers Gal'. Tom had ridden her last evening and then Bill had spent extra time on her. Now here she stood, all ready to be loaded onto the trailer that would take her to the farm of Reynolds Marksman.

Reynolds Marksman indeed owned the finest farm of it's kind in the area, he was a man in his mid-fifties and had been working on his line of horses for years. Ben had a secret longing to have a set up much the same and had made quite a start in the few years he'd been at it.

Actually at twenty-eight, Ben had become quite noted in the area as one who both knew and loved his work, and one who also strove for perfection. Opening the door he quickly entered the stall, taking the halter in his left hand he gently stroked the fine features that had become the Daniels' trademark. Cruisers Children. The rich brown coat with it's darker markings, the telltake dorsel stripe, the strong legs made for both speed and power, the arch of the neck, the ears so alert.

"Your Cruisers Gal alright." Ben commented, the awesome fact of what he had done in the way of business sobered him. The realization that if his venture with Marksman's tiny colt should fail, Ben would be facing severe financial difficulty was a chance he chose, a risk, to see that dream become,.. a reality.

In the next stall stood Wonder, a green broke filly who also had been part of the deal. Rich would be taking the two of them south this morning, and returning with the colt.

Ben had placed clean straw and fresh water in the trailer before he hitched it to his truck and drove it around toward the stables. Both his truck and trailer were quite impressive. They were a deep midnight blue with light blue racing stripes, and white letters outlined with light blue. His personal logo which appeared on all his correspondence and also on the sign at the entrance to his place was on both the drivers door of the truck and also on the back doors of the trailer.

'Horseman's Unlimited' was a pretty impressive name for a place as young as his. Barely eight years in existence Horseman's Unlimited was known throughout the state as a fine establishment for any who desired an experience with horses.

Rich approached him as he climbed out of the cab of his truck.

"Hey fella." Ben laughed. "How's our breakfast coming?"

"We're waitin' on you." Rich answered as the two headed toward the Garage "Bill's been chompin' at the bit since he got here."

"Sorry to keep you waitin' I wasn't watchin' the time." Ben apologized.

"Hey, no problem. I got through a bit earlier than I'd planned."

Five minutes later the three sat around a breakfast table laden with food. Fried eggs bacon, toast, and hashbrowns.

"Great meal Rich" Ben commented, through a mouth full of potatoes.

"Well if you like to eat good food you have three choices, either learn to cook yourself, or spend your substance in restaurants."

"What's the third one?" Ben wondered.

Rich eyed him. "That's the one you chose,.." When his friend gave him a questioning look Rich replied. "Get married."

Ben and Bill both grinned. They had both married, and knew what he was talking about.

"Well young man, I sure does like eatin' but my cookin' leads a lot to be desired." Old Bill commented. "I jist started, eatin' good vittles agin. My Peggy's gonna be the cook her grandmammy was."

"Now the Mrs. she was a cook, she was. Went through the depression she did, and never lacked. Always had the best laid table, never none of this store bought stuff either. Everything from her own kitchen. Peggy, now she's got the cookin' down, she just needs to master the bakin' and the cannin' and stuff."

"You've got a first rate young lady there Bill you know that." Ben commented.

"Yes, I have, yes indeed I have." The old man stated with a satisfied smile on his face.

Rich began clearing the table and placing dishes in the sink.

Ben pushed back his chair and rose. "Hey guys, if we're planning to send these horse out we better get goin'."

An hour later Ben Daniels stood at the door of the stable and watched as his truck hauling it's midnight blue trailer carrying 'Cruisers Gal' and 'Wonder' two of Ben's best mares turn onto the road, leaving 'Horseman's Unlimited' behind.

"Hate to see 'em go don't ye." The old timers voice interrupted his thoughts.

"MmmHmm." Ben mumbled. Then shrugged. "But that's business."

"Yeah,.." The old timer turned toward the alley, and the two empty stalls. "I best get to work. I'll be makin' a place for that new critter in the same stall you just had Gal in last night. Will that be fine."

"Absolutely, He should be getting here about 1:30 - 2:00 perhaps, so stick around this afternoon, I want you to inspect him right away."

"The critter got hiself a name doesn't he?"

Ben nodded looking soberly around at the red buildings, green pastures, and white fences that made up his lively hood. "His name is 'The Mark of Fortune'."

It was midmorning when Steve Williams' Jeep pulled up in front of the stables. Ben was in the outdoor arena training a yearling on a longeline, he waved in greeting and continued his work. Steve headed toward the field where 'Special Export' was pastured, but Judy walked purposely toward where Ben was working. He continued with his work although he was a little uneasy."

"Don't you ever get dizzy doing that?" Judy asked.

"Sure." Ben responded. "I just try not to do it very long at one time."

"Is that one of 'Cruisers' foals?"

"Uh, huh. in fact this is from one of the two mares I just shipped out this morning. This is Surprise, She's Cruiser's Gal's filly. Should be getting a saddle on her in spring."

"Do you think Jeff will have a hard time with little Faleene? I mean most foals are born in spring, is there any problem with those born in fall?" She asked.

"Shouldn't be. I've never encountered any yet. I'm sure if he keeps his eye on her she'll do fine. Have him let me know if she seems to have problems."

"Oh I'm sure he'll be after you constantly asking questions, he's as bad as a new father."

"I'm glad of it. Not many teenagers are interested in horses. He's really lucky he had the opportunity to work with his own so young."

"I guess so." She answered. Then after a pause she continued. "You know, I'm really ashamed about the fact that people have misunderstood my relationship with Steve and have some how figured you into it."

"That wasn't your fault." Ben stated "Tongues will wag no matter what the true facts are."

"Oh but it was my fault. If I'd been honest with my family months ago none of this would have happened. I just wish Ray wouldn't have gotten so riled up."

"Well, he does love you,.. and it's hard to lose something you love."

Judy looked down at her feet. She wanted to tell him that she was loosing something too, that she loved Ray, and the kids... but no one believed that anymore. Finally she spoke.

"Thanks for being fair to Steve and myself through this whole thing."

"I try to keep out of the affairs of other people." Ben said honestly. "I admit it does get hard sometimes but I try."

"Well, thanks, we both appreciate it." She continued, as Steve walked up to join them. He put his arm around her shoulder and smiled at her.

"Well did you ask him yet?" He asked, Judy shook her head.

"Ask me what?" Ben questioned.

"It seems we have a problem." Steve smiled. "There's two of us, and the last time I looked, I only owned one horse."

"We thought maybe you could show us a few of your sale horses." Judy continued. "Something nice and gentle."

"Of course." Ben began. "Do you have anything in mind?"

"Well, I have been showing Special export and Judy would like to join me so we'd like one that has good linage. A Quarter horse, unless you suggest something that would work better with her. A five or six year old would be best."

"I like Cruiser's foals." Judy admitted.

Ben nodded as he led Surprise back to her stall. They discussed various horses Ben had in his stables.

Old Bill led a four year old gelding into the arena. He walked her back and forth in front of the group at the fence.

"This fella is 'Flasher'." Ben began, "Cruiser's Morning Flasher to be exact. Morning his mother is a mare I obtained from a fella down south. She's not quite as stocky as most quarter horses and this fella's not either, he doesn't have as nice of a gait as the others but he's gentle as a lamb. Extremely well trained."

"You trained him yourself, I suppose." Steve asked.

"Oh, no, Not this one. He's been here since birth but he was one of my wife's projects. I'm kinda partial to the trainer you see." Ben smiled.

"He looks calm enough." Judy commented.

"Would you like Bill to saddle him up for you?" Ben asked.

"I'm still trying to decide between him and that Buckskin mare."

"I'll tell you what. I'll have Bill saddle both of them. Both Flasher, and Charade, the two of you can take them out and then decide. Charade isn't Cruiser's but she's got an excellent bloodline. She'll have a much smoother ride."

"Which do you suggest." Steve asked.

"I'll answer that after you've ridden the two of them." Ben answered. "They're both excellent show stock." He turned to Bill. "Saddle him up and Charade also, they'll be taking them both out."

"Sure boss." Bill answered as he led Flasher to the hitching rail at the side of the arena. Steve and Ben were busy discussing the horses when two men joined them.

"Oh Frank." Ben exclaimed. "It's good to see you."

"Hi Ben," Frank Girard began. "Looks as though the weather will be holding out for you."

"Oh I'm praying it does." Ben added then smiled at the second man, Mike Shephard.

"You've already met Mike I've heard." Girard continued.

"Yes, we've been friends for a number of years." Ben added. "Good friends."

"Well lets get to work." Girard declared.

"I've got all the plans and figures in my office." Ben spoke as they headed in that direction, turning back he called to Steve. "Bill will be ready for you in a minute. If I'm not through when you return Bill will take the horses, I hope to get back to you soon."

"No hurry." Steve smiled.

Francis Girard was a short balding man, with large muscles and a strong will. He had an uncanny sense in building that few had. Ben had contacted him for that very reason. He had been pleased that both Mike and Pat Rhodes would have the opportunity to work on his project, it became more personal to him.

Girard walked with Ben to the sight while Mike went back to the truck for surveying equipment. He studied the plans intently before giving Mike further instructions. Girard got right to business after studying the plans a second time and making a few notes then left Mike to survey the area and stake out the outline for the foundation. Ben assisted him and the job was finished in record time.

"Thanks for the help, it wasn't necessary."

"I know Mike, but I guess I just couldn't keep my hands out of it."

"Just watch it around Girard. He's an excellent builder, but his personality and manners could use a little help."

"You seem to get along fine."

"Oh! I've learned early in life to stay clear when storms start comin'." Mike commented. "Actually I take the, hear no evil, see no evil, speak no evil, attitude. It works but I sure don't plan on doing it for the rest of my life."

"I should hope not." Ben laughed.

"I'll be heading to Lincoln, right now. I've got a load of supplies to get. I'll be back around one or so, to deliver them. Then after I unload I've got a stack of forms at the shop that have to come out. I'll have a crew with me. It shouldn't take us long to set the forms for the foundation we'll pour it tomorrow.

"So soon?" Ben was surprised.

"Sure, it'll need to sit a day or so. Let's see that'll be Friday. I'll tell you what, we'll start on the actual frame work Monday. Should have the thing completed by next Friday at the latest. What do you say?"

Ben shook his head as if to clear it. "I don't know what to say? I hadn't expected you to get after it so fast."

"Well, if I pushed to start it Friday it would sit over the week end, I personally prefer to get after a job and finish it in consecutive days. The inside would be rough of course but you wanted it that way I gather."

"Yes I did. We'll work that part out ourselves. I'm really pleased it is working out so well." Ben smiled, excitement in his voice.

"Well, I've gotta run, I'll be by later."

"Take care, Michael." Ben called as Mike headed back to his truck.

Rich had plenty of time to think as he drove to Marksmans stables. Ben had been so good to him, it had only been a week since they had rediscovered their friendship and already Rich owed him so much. Rich thought about the past few days and how he had enjoyed the work. Ben knew what he wanted from his employees and expected them to perform it. Rich admired that. He enjoyed the work, the people, the setting. No one seemed in a rush for anything, no one seemed to wonder about his past life. It was a relief.

The past years had made quite an impression on Rich. That one careless mistake would be with him always, it was something that he just couldn't forget. Not once since that time three years ago had he gotten behind the wheel of a vehicle and not remembered that day, those faces. Not once since that day had he been able to look at a woman with two young children and not be reminded of the lives that were lost. It was such a waste. Why hadn't the careless one been wasted and the innocent set free.

Those questions seldom left him. True they didn't drive him to depression, or cause him to consider acts of irrationality or suicide, he was to level-headed for that, now. It was as if the questions kept him alert, kept him striving, kept him aware enough to keep himself from his previous ways.

It was 10:30 when he approached Marksmans' stables. He was awed by the meticulous quality of the buildings and property. 'Talk about a post card to send home to Mama.' He smiled to himself.

Reynolds Marksman was on hand to see the mares the instant one of his grooms had backed them from the trailer.

"Nice, nice,..." Was all he said as he nodded his head. His son also was on hand. He was a tall young man in his early twenties, lean and agile with just a trace of a beard beneath a lopsided grin and soft brown eyes.

"Hi ya." He said.

"Hi, I'm Rich McAllister" He held out his hand.

"Joel." The lad said as they shook. "It looks like the Old man's pleased." He commented.

Rich smiled and returned to the cab of the truck for the files on the two horses.

Later, over a cup of coffee in the elder man's office, Rich related a few remarks and comments from Ben.

"Let the young fella know that I'm well pleased, very well pleased. I'll do business with him anytime." Marksman responded as he lifted a manilla envelope from his desk that contained information on the Marksman colt.

"Everything he needs to know is right here." Reynolds tapped the folder. "Have him give me a call if he has any questions."

"Yes sir. I'm sure he will."

"I'm having my men load him now. Do you mind if we go on out so I can have a last look at him?"

"Not at all, in fact Ben spent most of his morning mooning over those two mares before he sent them out."

"When you put your whole life into something, it's not easy to say good-bye."

A kettle of chicken dumpling soup was being heated on the back of the stove when Ben entered the kitchen slightly before twelve.

"We're in here." Came a voice from the laundry room. Indeed they were too. Sarah was busy tossing white T shirts and socks into the wash machine, Nick sat in a laundry basket surrounded by clean bath towels.

"Hey sport." Ben said as he picked his son up. "Don't you know this is women's work?"

"Da da." Nick answered as he grabbed a handful of his fathers hair.

"Yikes kid, you've got some grip." Ben teased as he disengaged Nicks tiny fist from his head.

"How was your meeting with Girard?"

"Better than I expected." Ben began "He's a businessman believe me. They're not wasting any time though. Mike said they'll be done a week from Friday."

"So soon? That's great!" Sarah said as she closed the wash machine "Lunch is ready. I'll make us a few sandwiches too."

"Looked good when I walked through, smelled even better." Ben responded as they entered the kitchen. He set Nick in the high chair then went to wash his hands. "You know, I delayed widening that lane for a few years."

"Oh?" Sarah responded. "Will you be able to get the trailer back there?"

"No problem." Ben began, "The cost right now would've been the problem."

"Then I'm glad you decided the way you did." She answered as she set sandwiches on the table, she returned to the stove and began ladling soup into bowls. "What time do you expect Rich to return."

"Not til after one. I plan on giving that critter extra attention."

"I should hope so." She smiled. At this time young Nick took his bottle and threw it, hitting his father squarely on the head.

"Ouch, I think I need to give this critter extra attention." He commented as he tossled his sons hair.

The countryside around the Marksman stables was tranquil and calm, gently rolling hills pastured lazy cows that rested in the shade of broad Oak trees that grew along the fence lines.

The fields mostly tilled under, were patterned like a quilt across the countryside. Some corn fields were left just stubble. Other fields of hay were ready for the last harvest before the frost. The road Rich drove wound in and out of tiny villages, that consisted of a store building with a gas pump, two bars and possibly a church.

He had just passed the town of Wheaton when he noticed a farmer before him on a tractor. He was pulling a full load of hay slowly along the side of the Highway. Rich smiled to himself as he drew nearer, the load rocked from side to side as it was brought along the rough side of the road. Rich slowed up. He was in a no passing zone and although the farmer allowed him plenty of room he still chose to remain behind.

Rich could not see beyond an approaching curve in the highway, but knew that on the next stretch he'd have his chance to pass the tractor. He relaxed and glanced in his rear view mirror. Coming up behind him was a newer model sports car. The driver was obviously in a hurry for he gained on Rich quite rapidly. As it pulled up behind him without another moments hesitation the driver pulled into the oncoming lane and prepared to pass. Rich moved over nearer the side of the road as the small car sped quickly past him. Rich wasn't sure what happened next. He recalled seeing a movement, and light reflected off a second car as it sped around the corner less than fifty yards ahead. He gasped, quickly breaking he attempted to ease the truck and trailer off the Highway, but things happened too fast. The impact of the collision that was inevitable forced the small sports car against the load of hay which toppled. Rich's reflexes although swift were not quick enough to avoid impact with the wagon. Both he and the farmer had been going quite slow by the time of the catastrophe so not much damage was done to either vehicle, but the sports car was smashed beyond recognition.

'Wow' Rich remarked half dazed, then recalling the responsibility he had, jumped from the truck to check the trailer where the colt, shaken yet uninjured was kept.

The farmer was climbing from his tractor at the same instant Rich jumped from the cab.

"You got something in that trailer?" The farmer asked.

"Well, ah yeah." Rich responded bewildered.

"Well get it out! Then give me a hand. Nothing burns faster than hay. We'll have a regular inferno here in minutes.

"But what about,.." Rich began then noticing the remains of the driver of the sports car he turned quickly to the back of his trailer as the farmer headed toward the second vehicle.

Rich took only a minute to lead the shaken colt a few hundred yards down the road and tie him to a fence post. Upon hurrying back he heard the faint siren of approaching police. Help was on the way. Although to late for one.

Ben was once again working in the arena with one of his yearlings when Sarah found him.

"There's a call for you." She said, "In the office. I answered it as I was walking by."

"Who is it."

"I didn't ask but he sounded pretty important. Nick is with Bill right now, I can take over for you."

"Thanks" He said, then after taking a minute to explain what he was doing with the filly, he hurried to his office and the phone.

"Hello, Ben Daniels speaking, may I help you?"

"Mr. Daniels, this is Deputy Bundy from the Woodland County Sheriffs department. I've been asked to notify you about a delay in receiving your colt."

"A delay?" Ben asked. "Where's Rich?"

"There's been an accident."

"An accident? Is he okay?"

"The horse is fine sir." The voice reassured him.

"Not the horse, Deputy, Rich McAllister, the fellow that was driving the truck."

"Oh, he's fine. He's being delayed for questioning. He explained that you were expecting him and asked me to call."

"That's a relief; where is he?"

"Just a few miles north of Wheaton on highway 76."

"What shape is my truck in? Can it be driven?"

"Definitely, it's got a small dent in the front hood but no serious problems. Mr. McAllister is making an informal statement, a witness but he will be along shortly."

"Thanks Deputy" Ben sighed as he hung up the phone. He quickly left his office.

"Bill" He called "Take that bugger from Sarah, we'll be gone for an hour or so."

"Sure boss, You needn't wake the little tike though he's a sleepin' on the hay in the corner of my shop."

"You don't mind him here?"

"Not at all, gives me someone to talk at, sides the horses."

"Thanks I appreciate it."

Ben quickly joined Sarah and asked her to accompany him and in minutes they were in their car heading toward Wheaton on highway 76.

"I should have asked you to drive." Ben said to his wife as they sped along the Highway. "My mind is not at all on what I'm doing."

"Well pull off the road, I can take it from here."

"No, no, that would take to long. I need to see Rich."

"Didn't the man from the Sheriffs department say he was Okay?"

"Yes, but that doesn't mean much. I need to see him."

"Why?"

"I guess I'm curious. I feel rotten thinking like this. Almost as though I'm letting God down, but Sarah, this is not the first accident Rich has been in."

"Oh? But I've been in an accident once too. How does that matter?"

"The other accident was his fault and three people perished because of it."

Sarah was quiet, though slowly she let out her breath. "Poor Rich, Can you imagine living with that guilt?"

"Poor Rich! What about the father and husband of that woman and her children?"

"Ben!" Sarah exclaimed.

"I'm sorry hon. Like I said I feel like I'm letting God down. When Rich told me of his accident I thought nothing of it. But now that this has happened, I'm getting all kinds of crazy notions." Ben began, "Like,.. maybe he stopped in one of those small towns for a drink or maybe he got careless and began taking risks. And what about the colt, I can imagine what it looks like if it's still alive that is."

"Settle down, Ben. Worrying and tossing this back and forth in your mind will get you nowhere." Sarah began "You trusted Rich, you had no idea this would happen. Now lets just trust the Lord to work this all out."

"I guess so." Ben began "But you know, Rich seemed like such a sober minded fellow. I'd been hoping I could trust him responsibly."

"Don't start thinking like he's already been tried and found guilty. Let's leave the situation in God's hands, and pray that above all he would restore your peace."

Ben looked upset at her words, then after nodding slowly began "Your right dear, lets say a word of prayer right here and now. And I'll harbor a glimmer of hope that I'm wrong about Rich."

It was mid afternoon when Ben and Sarah came upon the scene of the accident. The small sportscar had been totally crushed and there had been no hope at all for the driver. The other car fared much better although totalled it's occupants remained alive, a middle aged couple, they were injured and being treated now at the nearest hospital. Rich was just preparing to continue on his journey home when Ben pulled up.

Ben got slowly out of the car. His eyes took in the scene, the smashed glass; the blood; the twisted chunks of metal that had once been someone's car. 'Oh Lord,' he said under his breath. He walked slowly over to where Rich stood holding the halter rope of the young colt. Slowly he walked around the animal, and looked him over. "Everything seems fine." He murmured.

"Ben," Rich began "You don't know how sorry I am this had to happen. It all happened so quickly, so swiftly,.."

Ben remained silent for a while. It was an eerie silence. Finally he spoke.

"How did it happen?"

Rich proceeded to relate the incidences and was pleased, yet at the same time disturbed to see the anxious look on Bens face relax.

"And how are you?" Ben asked.

"Oh, I'm pretty chipper, bruised up a bit but nothing more."

"I'm glad to hear that." Ben smiled for the first time that afternoon. "Let's hook this bugger up so we can get something solid under his feet."

The two worked side by side, in silence. The colt was quickly loaded and Rich prepared to enter the cab. Ben stopped him.

"Hold it." Ben said as he came closer. "I happen to be a man of few words but right now I owe you an apology."

"You doubted me then?" Rich had been suspicious.

"It had crossed my mind. Plenty had. But I'm wrong Rich. I'm sorry I misjudged you."

"Ben I really don't blame you but think about what it must be like for me. That one incident will cause plenty to mistrust me and with cause."

"I'm sorry Rich, but I believe the story you gave me. I just hope I can keep my imagination from running wild again."

They shook hands firmly, and Ben returned to the car where Sarah was waiting.

Mike Shephard and a small crew, which included Pat Rhodes were unloading the truck when Ben and Sarah returned to the farm, with Rich right behind them.

Sarah quickly found Nick and hurried to the kitchen to prepare for supper. Bill joined the men as they unloaded the horse from the trailer and led him to the arena.

"Wheewwee." Bill whistled. "That's some critter boss. I hope he has a whole passel of young 'uns."

"Me too." Ben laughed. "There's an awful lot at stake with that fella."

"Marksman almost hated to see him go." Rich commented. "But those two mares helped to persuade him."

"He's spent a lot of time and money developing this line of horses and he's pretty particular as to how they're treated."

"I can believe that." Rich continued. "I have never seen a set up quite like his before. Everything was in top notch condition and he had the finest equipment around."

"It's been in the family for close to a century." Ben remarked. "His father is still kickin' but not much. From what I've heard it was his grandpa that settled the place in the late eighteen hundreds."

"His son seems to be a friendly fella, although he does lack his fathers wisdom."

"Don't let Joel fool ya. He may appear to be a scatterbrain, but he's still a Marksman, that place will be his someday so he'd be a fool not to take it seriously."

"Is he the only son?" Rich wondered.

"No, there's a second son, a few years younger. Off at college now. His daughter must be seventeen, or around there. Can't quite recall."

"That there Julie is a fire cracker if ye ask me." Bill put in, "She's got more monkey business up her sleeve than a truckload of orphan boys, that young 'un. The stories I heard would make your hair stand on end."

"Come on now." Ben teased. "When did you start believing the stories you hear?"

"When they come from my Peggy, I believe 'em." Bill said defensively. "She prednear had to hogtie Julie to keep her in her bunk during 4H camp a few years back."

"Then I'm glad I didn't have the chance to meet her." Rich laughed. "I've had my share of feisty teenagers for a while."

"Oh? Why's that?" Ben asked curiously.

Rich chuckled and related the experience he'd had at Charlies the afternoon before, and about Suzanna's earnest plea for help.

"It looks like Pat's been slippin again." Ben laughed. Pat and Mike approached and the comment was made intentionally for him to hear.

"And why is that?" Pat asked pointedly, smiling.

"Are you not the self appointed guardian to one Suzanna Rhodes?" Ben asked professionally. "And did you not unwisely let her venture on her own with strange men of unknown character. Only to be rescued by one knight in blue jeans and flannel?" He nodded at Rich.

"Oh that!" Pat laughed. "My personal detective filled me in on all the details. Plus more, so don't worry."

Ben and Rich both grinned as they joined Mike at the trailer.

"Fine horse," Mike said as he looked at the colt.

"That Michael, is my newest investment." Ben began "Straight from Reynoldds Marksman's Stables,.. this is 'The Mark of Fortune."

"Mighty long handle for a little tike." Bill laughed.

"He'll grow." Ben commented.

And should we see into the future we would find that it is not only Colts and young babies that grow, we find in the midst of building up his herd the faith and trust Ben Daniels has in his friend and employee Rich McAllister begins building a confidence within the man that no program or prison term could. Such is life, when change often comes when least expected.

CHAPTER 11

A TIME TO WEEP

After the last bell had rung for the day Jeff headed toward the Social Studies Department to meet his father. He wasn't anticipating the meeting much for his father's drinking had been getting steadily worse. His father was changing drastically right before his eyes. In the last few days he'd gone from a care-free, happy, clear minded father- to an irrational, loud, yet, slow minded, Jelly Head. Jeff was shocked at the change and he knew that Jenny was even more baffled for as far as Jeff knew, Jen was unaware of their father's drinking.

Jeff entered the department office and heard loud voices coming from within. He found himself a chair and waited.

"Settle down Ray." Said a steady voice.

"SETTLE DOWN?" Jeff heard his father scream. "YOU QUESTION MY BEHAVIOR, AND THEN WANT ME TO SETTLE DOWN?"

"These were only things that concerned me."

"CONCERNED YOU! MY LIFE IS NO CONCERN OF YOURS."

"It is when it affects your performance as a teacher."

"WHAT! WHAT ARE YOU SAYING?"

"I'm only saying that I've beeen noticing the fact that you've been drinking. I understand. But, it's getting to the point where it's affecting your behavior."

"YOU'RE A LIAR."

"And you are screaming. Ray, you've never so much as raised your voice around here before. Now all of a sudden things change. We can't allow that."

"YOUR AFTER ME FOR RAISING MY VOICE?"

"No Ray, That's not it."

"THEN JUST WHAT IS IT?"

"That's just one of the things. The biggest thing is the students can tell what's going on. It's not a good example."

"YOU NEVER CARED ABOUT EXAMPLES BEFORE."

"But this is different Ray. We just want to help. We want you to know we're behind you but we want you to know also that drinking isn't the way out."

"YOU DRINK!"

"Yes, I do. But we're talking about you Ray. You've been teaching here for twenty years and you've worked hard to gain the respect of your students. We don't want you to lose that respect."

"WHO CARES!"

"You do, Ray, and we do. You're one of the best teachers this school has ever had. Don't let this one little thing ruin what you've got here. Put the bottle down. Get a hold of yourself. Life will go on, but Ray when things go wrong,.. don't go with them."

"THANKS." Ray said sarcastically. "FRIENDS."

Jeff looked up when the door opened. Two other teachers, Marv Jordon and Phil Walters left the room. Mr. Walters walked over to Jeff.

"Things will work out." He said as he laid his hand on Jeff's shoulder. "Take care of your father will you."

Jeff was glad that they left quickly, for neither of them saw the tears that had formed in his eyes.

Suzanna had just left Angie at the corner and was heading toward home when she heard footsteps behind her. Brady soon joined her.

"I must admit you've been in a better frame of mind today." Brady smiled.

"Only because you've been less of a pest." Suzanna said honestly, as Brady took her books from her.

"I realized I was fighting a losing battle." He lied. "So is it possible to go on from here,.. just friends?"

"Really Brady? Are you serious?"

"Sure am."

"Thanks, I'd like that." She answered honestly. The two continued in silence as they neared the Rhodes home.

"Is your father home?" Brady asked.

"I doubt it. There's a meeting or something."

"Do you mind if I stay?"

"Oh no, not at all, in fact Luke would probably like it."

"He's your kid brother right?"

"Yup, see, he's already got his basketball out."

"Hey, I think I can handle that." Brady answered as the two joined Luke in the driveway. Brady caught the ball and threw a difficult shot successfully, while Luke watched wide-eyed.

"How did you do that?" He asked.

"Watch, I'll show you." Brady began.

"I'll fix us a snack." Suzanna suggested.

"Great!" Brady answered as she turned toward the house.

"She never offers to make me snack." Luke whispered when she was gone.

"Don't worry kid, someone will in a few years." Brady said with a lopsided grin as he tossled Lukes hair.

Five minutes later the three sat around the table in Rhodes kitchen with generous slices of Pound cake in front of them. Elizabeth Rhodes was chopping carrots for the stew she planned for supper.

"This tastes great, Mrs. Rhodes." Brady announced politely.

"Thank you Brady, help yourself to another if you'd like."

"I think I will." He began. "You know" He turned to Luke "You're gonna be quite good on the court if you keep after it."

"You think so?"

"Sure do, I can tell. All you need is someone to coach you a little more."

"Really?"

"Uh huh, I'll give you all the pointers I can, but I'm much better in football than basketball."

"You play football?"

"Uh huh, in fact I had practice right after school tonight, that's why I had to run to catch up with your sister."

"And you work too? Boy your busy."

"I only work two nights a week." Brady began, "I worked steady during the summer when people were on vacations."

"My brother Pat is working tonight, He works for Girard. He's a builder."

"Oh? Hey, that must be fun."

As the two continued talking Suzanna got up and cleared the table. She brought the dishes to the sink where her mother was working.

"Need any help?" She asked.

"No, no, you entertain your company."

"He's just a friend ma, and he seems to be doing fine." Elizabeth looked at the two at the table.

"You're right dear he is." Then she continued. "You can peel these potatoes if you like. I'm gonna make a cheese cake to replace the pound cake we would have had for dessert." She winked at Suzanna and they both laughed.

"Mom!" Luke called from the table. "Can I do my homework after dinner, please. Brady's gonna show me some shots, if it's okay."

"Go ahead son, but no complaining later when it's time to hit the books."

"Thanks Ma."

The two left the house.

Everything at the farm had returned to normal, or as much as could be expected. Mike Shephard and his crew were busy setting the forms for the foundation of the stable. Bill, no longer a baby-sitter was back in his shop preparing shoes for an old aged gelding. Both Tom and Denni were aloft, forking hay down to the horses. Rich, with a very sober attitude, was preparing a stall next to Special Export for Steve and Judy were in Ben's office at the moment closing up on the purchase of 'Flasher'. Peggy had joined her grandpa and was perched on a few bails of hay at his side, playing with three small kittens.

In the arena, Doc and Sylviah Martin were exercising their Saddlebred's and Jenny Johnson had just finished Saddling her small quarter horse. Jeff had haltered Misty and was leading the mare while the tiny filly Faleen followed close behind.

Ray Johnson had retired to a bench by the arena where he watched his children in noticeable silence.

Ben's office door opened, and Steve emerged with Judi right behind. Seeing the riders she walked over to the fence a moment.

"Son," She called to Jeff. "That little one is not gonna let you out of her sight."

"I see that." Jeff replied awkwardly, for he'd seen little of his mother lately. "I don't want to go fast though, I'd hate to see her take an unnecessary tumble."

"Mom, are you going riding?" Jenny asked.

"No dear, I've been riding all afternoon, but I did do something you'd be interested in."

"What's that?" Jenny asked. Jeff listened also.

"See that fine looking bay Quarterhorse that Rich is leading this way?"

"Uh huh." Jenny answered.

"That's 'Flasher' I just finished signing his papers."

"He's ours?" Jenny exclaimed. "I mean,..yours?" She corrected.

"Our's is right dear. We'll plan a day soon to go riding, just you and I." She answered. Jenny beamed.

"Could have done that years ago." Ray commented sarcastically.

"Oh Ray, don't start now, please."

"You're the one that started it. I can't forget that."

"Can't we stop the hard feelings right now Ray, and go on."

"That's easy for you to say Jud, your not the one who's been hurt." Ray remarked. Steve joined them then and Ray continued. "And you! Aren't you the lucky one. Just keep on your toes Mister or she'll pull the same on you that she did on me."

"I'm not worried." Steve smiled.

"Oh no, Not You!" Ray said obnoxiously.

"Don't start anything Ray, please." Judy begged.

"What's the matter, afraid I'll get a good shot at the fella and damage that pretty face of his?" Ray said standing and moving toward Steve, Jeff moved from the arena and was beside him in a minute.

"Dad,.." He began.

"Don't stop me son," Ray insisted. Steve stood his ground as Ray drew near.

"Ray," Judy interrupted again. "Don't do anything that you'll be sorry for."

"Sorry for! Your the one who should be sorry, and I'll have you know any man would do the same as I!" at this point he violently and blindly realed forward with his fists, striking home, but not the party he was after for when he recovered from his fury, before him lay his son. Jeff was bleeding from both his mouth and nose from the blows he had sustained. At the sight of him Ray's heart broke. He rushed to the boys side and helped him to sit."

"Jeff,... son. Why? Why? Why?" He cried confused.

"Dad I'm sorry." Jeff mumbled. "I had to. Too many people have been hurt to let another suffer. I'm suffering already so I don't mind, and Pa I understand and I forgive you. Steve might not." Doc Martin came to the lads side just as his father broke down in uncontrollable sobs.

"There, just as good as new." Doc Martin stated as he finished cleansing the cut on Jeffs face.

"Thanks Doc." Jeff said, then laid back for his head still ached.

After the fight Doc Martin and Steve had helped Jeff to the house while Ben had a stiff talk with Ray. Now Ray stood sheepishly in a corner, ashamed of the damage he'd done to his son, yet still uncertain of his feelings toward Steve.

"Leave the lights low for awhile and let him rest." Doc spoke again. "It'll be best just to leave him. He'll be up again in no time." And so saying he ushered both Ray and Sarah Daniels from the room, the others had gone long before. Jenny was in the kitchen with Nick, she looked up anxiously when her father entered.

"He's fine." was all Ray said as he walked quickly through the room and out the door.

Jenny looked up at Sarah, tears were forming in her eyes.

"Mom want's me to go with her." Jenny stated as Sarah gave her a tender hug. "She said it wouldn't be safe with Dad." Jenny broke into hideous sobs.

"It'll be okay Jen." Sarah whispered gently.

"No, no it won't. First Mom leaves, and now Dad starts acting like this. What if he hit me Sarah, what would I do?"

"He didn't mean to hit Jeff, dear." Sarah said soothingly.

"But he would have hit Mr. Williams if Jeff hadn't stopped him."

"I know."

"Mom's waiting for me outside. I think I'll go. Will you tell Jeff?"

"Yes, Jen I will." Sarah agreed then continued. "Remember if you need anything or if you just need a friend. Give me a call,.. okay? Promise?"

"Uh huh." Jenny nodded as she wiped her last few tears and hurried out the door.

Sarah went quietly about her work. Little Nick played happily on the floor with a few wooden spoons and a bowl, while Sarah finished preparing. She was just putting a loaf of French Bread in the oven when she heard a stifled sob coming from the next room. Hurrying in she found Jeff sitting up on the couch, his face covered with his hands. She was about to comfort him when she noticed something else. Slowly she left the room, unseen. Knowing that she could give no more comfort then the author of the book that laid open beside him on the couch.

Edward Rhodes was indeed surprised upon returning home to find his son and Brady Downing shooting baskets in the driveway. Suzanna was sitting on the front stoop a textbook in her hand. After tooting the horn he was able to pass the boys and enter the garage. The boys continued their game and Rhodes walked over and took a seat beside his daughter.

"What's this?" He asked.

"Punctuation and capitalization." She answered never looking up from her book.

"That's not exactly what I meant." He stated.

"I know." She smiled. "But don't I bring friends home with me all the time?"

"Too often I must agree." He returned smiling. "Let's have a talk, before today is over,.. okay?"

"Sure Pa." Suzanna mumbled and tried to return to her punctuation and capitalization. Brady soon joined her.

"The kid went in to see his Dad." Brady began then looking at Suzanna's book he groaned. "Egads I remember that class."

"I wonder if it's worth studying?" Suzanna said mildly frustrated.

"Definitely, you wouldn't want to take it a second year would you?"

"Spare the thought please." She closed the book and set it beside her.

"Do you have plans tonight?"

"Just homework, and a stack of it too. I've got a test in accounting tomorrow."

"No church, or youth meeting, or trip to 'Charlies' or anything like that?"

"Nope, just homework."

"Me too, Physic's test, and first period at that. I'll never have a chance in the morning to even glance at the book."

"Same with this." She lifted her text book. "Mrs. Grant will probably have tons of exercises for us to do in the morning."

"Tell you what, Seeing that we're both gonna spend the evening studying, why don't we spend it together?" Brady began, Suzanna started to protest but he continued. "I know we're studying for different classes, but it'll be fun. Mom wouldn't mind having us around at all. Why don't you ask yours?"

Suzanna looked uncertainly at her feet. "Brady I'm sorry, but I can't. It just wouldn't look right to my parents and they'd say no." She shrugged. "And I guess I wouldn't feel to comfortable with it either."

"What's the problem?" Brady asked bewildered. "Go ahead and ask, I'll stop by and pick you up at 6:30. You can be home by 9:00,..go ask." He urged again.

"Not without an adult around Brady."

"You've got to be kidding." He laughed, then after seeing the serious look on her face he continued. "Ma and Fred will both be there. I'll even have Mom pick you up if that's what it'll take." He pleaded.

"Okay, I'll ask." Suzanna said reluctantly. "Wait here."

She entered the house and gave a sigh of relief when she noticed that her fathers office door was shut. Her mother was alone in the kitchen.

She could almost hear the conversation now. "Young Lady, you are not to be spending time alone, even studying with anyone who is not a Christian." She shrugged. It wouldn't matter to her father if Brady's mother was there, it was the principle of the thing - especially if he found that they didn't even have corresponding classes to study for.

"Mom?" She almost whispered.

"Yes dear?" Her mother asked looking up from her work.

"I'm wondering,.. Brady wanted someone to study with him tonight, and asked if it would be okay if He stopped by for me at 6:30?"

Liz looked concerned. "He asked for your help?" She questioned.

"He said his mother wouldn't mind." Suzanna avoided the question.

"I suppose you could ask your father."

"I already know what he'll say mom." Suzanna said soberly.

"I suppose you do." Her mother laughed easily.

"It's not funny mom. It's kind of a touchy situation."

"Is it?" Her mother interrupted.

Suzanna nodded. "What will he think if I'm not allowed to go? I can't lie and say I have plans, how would it sound if I told him that my father didn't trust us together - that doesn't sound very Christian."

"I guess I can see your point. Leave his home number with me, and I'll talk to your father."

"Thanks mom." Suzanna said with a smile. "His mom will be by to pick me up at 6:30 and I'll be back by 9:00."

"I'm sure you will dear."

She left the kitchen and hurried to the front stoop where she had left Brady to wait.

"It's fine with Ma." Suzanna began.

"Great!" Brady added obviously pleased. "I'll be by later. Now I'd better be getting along, I'll see you then."

Brady was smiling to himself and for obvious reasons. The girl who yesterday was doing everything she could to shun him was now playing right into his hands. He was satisfied, he'd spent all day yesterday getting her to realize that he liked her, now he placed himself as just a friend and she began responding. He laughed. This was going to be easier than he thought. "I'll teach her a lesson she won't ever forget."

Sarah had the meal on the table in plenty of time in spite of the disturbances during the afternoon. Jeff had gone home, sore but in fair spirits. Sarah had guests for dinner that evening and they had arrived and were seated.

"I forgot to mention Sarah." Ben began "I sold that gelding you trained a few years back."

"Which one was that?"

"Flasher, and you'll be surprised to know who bought it,... Judy Johnson."

"Oh, that's great! Then Flasher will stay here. I always hate to see my horses go."

"Maybe it would be better to see Flasher go." Rich commented. "And Special Export too."

"No Rich, Judy and Steve haven't caused us any problem. Ray wouldn't have either if he'd stay off the bottle."

"Mr. Johnson's been drinking?" Peggy asked alarmed for she admired the man.

"Johnson's are going through a lot right now and he just chose the wrong way to handle his problems." Ben informed her.

"I'll say." Rich commented.

"But can't you do something?" Peggy asked again. "tell him he's wrong? tell him about Jesus?"

"We've tried Peg, but when a man drinks he tends to get very irrational, it alters the way he thinks." Sarah spoke.

"But the Lord can deliver him from all that." Peggy said sincerely.

"Only if he surrenders to God and he's not in the frame of mind to do that." Ben commented. "Maybe if he were sober he'd be easier to talk to."

"He used to be sober all the time." Dennis commented dryly. "Maybe if I hadn't been such a wishy washy Christian both him and Jeff would have heard the truth long ago and believed it. It would have saved them all a lot of grief."

"Don't think that way." Dennis' mother commented. "God has a time for everything and although we can always be better Christians then we've been it's God alone that changes the heart nothing else. Nothing you or Ben do can save either Jeff or his father if they chose not to except Jesus on their own."

"...and." Sarah interrupted. "I don't think they've been rejecting the word as much as most of us think." She smiled to herself recalling the open bible she had glimpsed before Jeff this afternoon.

"But can't something more be done?" Peggy wondered. "Mr. Johnson has always seemed like such a good man."

"Tis only the Lord above that makes us good Honey." Her Grandfather commented. "What that feller had tried to be all his days is nothing for he trusted in hisself. Meybe that's what the feller needs to realize thet they's a greater one to lean on."

"I hate to think that anyone would have to go through that just to acknowledge God. But you could be right." Ben commented.

"There is something we can all do, though." Sarah mentioned as she glanced around the table at everyone. Ben,

Bill, Dennis, Rich, Mike and Chrys Shephard, Ginnie and Connie Little, and Peggy.

"I know what it is." Peggy answered solemnly. "Pray."

"Amen." Her grandfather responded.

Rich sat uncomfortable during the discussion at the table. He wasn't familiar with people who talked so openly and freely about God. God had always been more of an attitude, then anything real. He'd grown quite embarrassed by the comments that were made for many of them fit him also. 'People can not be good of themselves but only if they trust God.' He scoffed at the thought.

It was true though, that no one can make a decision for another to change. Rich knew that all to well for he had had to decide on his own many times. The conversation had made him uncomfortable, for he knew it was only a matter of time before he became their target and they would try to cram religion down his throat and begin their futile prayers for his lost soul.

He had wandered over to the stables and was leading 'Spirit' from her stall when Mike and Chrys approached.

"This is your horse, huh." Mike commented. "She's a beaut."

"I think so." Rich spoke honestly. "She was given to me by a good friend."

"Really?"

"An Indian fella I met, his family raises them. Has for years. Nez Perc Indians, decedents of the original Indians that developed the Appaloosa."

"Really?" Mike was impressed. "She must have a pretty good bloodline then."

"I don't think so, no one is concerned about that. I doubt if it's even recorded. Wynn's family just eliminate the horses from their stock that are inferior, in fact that's how I got her. She didn't have quite the markings and color that they desired. She's a bit larger than the regular Appaloosa too."

"You mean, they rejected her?"

"Uh huh, I'm lucky Wynn knew I was interested in one of their horses, when he found out she'd be sent out,.. he thought of me." Rich commented. "I was really impressed with the horses when I went there, they had old dilapidated farm buildings. Fences consisting of one row of electric wire, and a corral full of the most beautiful horses I'd ever seen. It was such a contrast to what I saw today at Marksman's. Sure he's got nice horses, not compared to these though, and his buildings and property are immaculate."

"Hey," Chrys interrupted. "I heard about your accident this afternoon. I hear you're lucky to be alive."

Rich was quiet awhile before he answered solemnly. "It wasn't the first time."

True to his word the Robbins' car pulled into the Rhodes driveway at half past six, it was Brady however who was behind the wheel, his mother was nowhere around.

"Well?" He began as Suzanna reluctantly joined him in the front seat. "What did your father say?"

"His exact words." Suzanna answered. "Were, ... study hard." She laughed.

"I'll see to that."

"I thought you hated Capitalization and Punctuation."

"Truer words were never spoken."

"Does your mother mind having me around?"

"Mom?" Brady asked. "Are you kidding? She's thrilled to death. I almost never bring FRIENDS home, she was probably afraid I didn't have any. You should have seen the look on her face when I told her you were the preachers daughter."

"Oh, Brady! You didn't!" She exclaimed.

"Sure, why not? You don't mind do you?"

"It's a little late to object now." She commented.

"Boy are you ever hard to please."

"Oh Brady, I'm sorry. It's just that all my life I've been 'Brother Rhodes daughter' or 'Cindi's sister'. It seems like no one seems interested in just Suzanna Rhodes the individual."

"I am." Brady answered quietly.

"That's what I was afraid of." Suzanna mumbled to herself.

"What's that?" He asked.

"Nothing important." Suzanna answered as she slumped down in the seat. 'How do I get myself in these messes.' She thought, 'All I want to do is enjoy life like Cindi said, why do emotions always have to get in the way and make things impossible?'

"Cheer up." Brady smiled. "I can't be that hard to get along with."

Suzanna smiled back as they turned onto the road leading to his home.

The houses were farther apart now, separated by clean white fences, or rows of hedges. They were set back from the road with long driveways and winding walkways that led over manicured lawns. Brady's home was at the far end of Trapline Road, built on a ravine, in a cluster of Oak and Evergreen trees overlooking the Flint River. It was a large home built of fieldstone, three large chimney's towered above the center of it, double doors graced the entrance, where small windows with etched glass designs welcomed any visitor.

"You live here?" Suzanna questioned.

"Unfortunately." Brady answered. "It can really be a pain."

"It can?" Suzanna was flabbergasted.

"Uh-huh"

Suzanna was confused, she couldn't understand why anyone would be unhappy living in such splendor as this.

"Come on in." He said as they left the car in the garage and headed toward the back door.

Just as Suzanna had been impressed with the outside of the home she equally admired the inside. It was tastefully decorated and although it was quite elaborately done it had a comfortable quality about it.

Brady led Suzanna through to the kitchen.

"Brady is that you?" His mother called from the next room.

"Yup." He called back. "We'll be in, in a minute." Then turning to Suzanna he suggested. "Let's grab a soda quick."

After the two had grabbed cans of soda from the well laden fridge and found tall frosted glasses, Brady led the way to the family room.

Marion Robbins was a young woman of thirty-five. She was slight of build with gorgeous blue eyes and full blond hair that hung below her shoulders. A young boy of about five was sitting beside her and a baby was in her lap as she held a picture book. Two young girls were watching television with their father in another part of the room.

"Hi dears." Marion Robbins began. "I see you've found the soda." She smiled at Suzanna. "It's nice to meet you Suzanna."

"It's good to meet you too, Mrs. Robbin's."

"Oh, call me Marion please, everybody does."

"Um, yeah, sure,..Marion." Suzanna said flustered.

"I'll introduce you to the rug-rats." Brady stated. "That little fella, the baby, that's Forrest; next to him is Sherwood; the girls are Courtney and Whitney; and that's Fred." Everybody nodded in Suzanna's direction, and after exchanging a few more words, Suzanna and Brady left.

"I usually study upstairs." Brady commented as he led Suzanna through a large formal dining room and into a magnificent entry. There was an open stairway that led to a large landing. Bookcases lined the walls of the landing and one corner contained comfortable chairs and a table. Hallways led to the bedrooms from two sides of the landing.

After the two were seated Suzanna ventured to speak.

"You know, I just realized after meeting your family, that I know so little about you. I noticed you never talk about them."

Brady just shrugged. "They're okay I guess. I can't complain, but the kids are Fred's kids, they're just there, a bunch of babies."

"They are young." Suzanna agreed. "Sherwood must be the oldest."

"Yup, he's five. Courtney is four. Whitney is two and Forrest will be a year old right before Christmas. You might say that Mom and Fred have been pretty busy."

"How long have they been married?"

"Seven years. I was ten when Ma got remarried. It was neat those first two years but, you see, .. I'm a lot like my father and although him and Ma aren't the kind to be bitter or angry at one another they still remember things and I think sometimes I remind Ma and Fred too much of my father."

"That's too bad." Suzanna stated.

"Not really," Brady grinned. "I think the world of my Dad. I miss him a lot."

Suzanna did study. She reviewed all the material, then Brady drilled her on it.

"I guess you do know more than just how to ride a horse." He quipped after she had successfully answered a few of his drill questions.

"And I guess you can do more than run back and forth across a field carrying a football with a group of boys trying to stop you."

"Thanks a lot." He said sarcastically.

"Your welcome." She smiled.

Brady was quiet a while and just watched Suzanna as she piled her books and paper together.

"I think it's contagious." He finally stated.

"No!" Suzanna said in alarm. "What is?"

"Your outlook, the honesty and sincerity you have. I really admire that,.. a lot." He reached across the table and put his hand on hers, Suzanna could tell he was troubled about something.

"You know," He began. "I've said things tonight, that I've never even considered telling anyone else. It's as though your honesty with me has allowed me to trust you with my feelings... Thanks."

"Um,... ah." Suzanna began to stammer. "I'm a friend Brady. And you've got my word, I'll be there if you need a friend... and you can trust me."

"I want to,.. you know that."

"Then do."

The uneasiness left his face and he relaxed. His smile returned.

"It's getting late and I'm getting rigamortis from sitting so long. It's beautiful out tonight, why don't I walk you home instead of taking the car?"

"I don't mind." Suzanna said. They stood and Brady reached for her books.

"Allow me." He smiled.

It was later when Chrystal and Mike said their good byes and left the farm.

It was a beautiful fall evening. The air was crisp and the sky was clear as the car headed swiftly down the highway toward Roberts Junction.

"Do you mind if I take a detour before going home?"

"It depends on where to." Mike answered.

"I just want to stop at the shop a minute. I've got an appointment to keep early tomorrow and thought I'd go to it before opening the shop. I need to grab my portfolio."

"Sure." Mike answered. "You know, I really like that friend of Bens, don't you?"

"He's friendly enough."

"Is that all?"

"What do you want me to say?"

"I thought maybe you'd have noticed a few other things. Like his interest in horses, and outdoors, his knowledge of Indian History, he is rather jolly to be around."

"So?" She asked giving him a sidelong glance.

"So. I just thought you'd notice a little more about him."

"Oh,..He's ugly." Chrys answered.

"Ma ma mia!" Mike cried throwing up his hands in despair. "When are you going to begin to take a serious interest in men sis?"

"Maybe when you take a serious interest in girls." She laughed.

Trapline Road was on the opposite side of town from the Rhodes home. The distance was only a little over a mile through the streets of town. Brady and Suzanna walked slowly along, gazing up at the stars,.. stomping playfully through fallen leaves,.. taking crunchy bites from apples picked from a neighborhood tree.

"I really enjoyed tonight." Brady began.

"Me too." Suzanna paused.

"You did?" Brady wondered "I'm glad, I had begun to think that you weren't too keen on being in my presence."

Suzanna paused before she answered. "I guess I wanted myself to believe that, til I realized that I was the only one being fooled."

Brady stopped, he took her hand in his. His clear blue eyes seemed to shine in the semidarkness. "You really mean it?" He asked.

"Uh huh." Suzanna was pleased at the touch of his hand in hers. The uneasiness she'd felt around him this past week began to fade. She enjoyed being with him and felt relieved in the fact that she'd let him know her thoughts.

They continued on in silence, just enjoying the walk, at least Suzanna was. They had reached town and the streets were more crowded now, she began to feel awkward.

"Let's take the backway." Brady answered as if reading her thoughts. They turned down the alley behind Charlie's Cafe'.

Tall shop buildings on either side of the alley kept it quite dark. A few of the back entrances were still lit and a few of the owners cars were parked outside. The two had not gone far when Suzanna heard a noise behind her. Turning quickly she saw four large teenagers, clad in dark jackets with stocking caps pulled down over their faces following them. She gasped.

"Brady." She whispered. But he didn't respond. His hand just held hers more firmly in his. It was then she noticed four more similarly clad fellows standing before them. "Brady who are they?"

"Don't know." He whispered. Both groups began approaching.

"What do we do?" Suzanna asked shakily.

"How should I know?"

One of the four before them stepped forward.

"Well if it isn't a couple of love birds." He feered "Or should I say jailbirds, huh Downing?"

"What do you want?" Brady asked.

"What? Did I say I wanted something?"

"If you don't want something let us pass."

"Afraid I can't do that."

"Why not?"

"First of all." He said walking over to Brady and looking at him through his ski mask. "You are far to big of a wise guy, and you,.." He moved over to stand before Suzanna, "Are far to cute."

"Brady." Suzanna whispered. "Do something."

"It's a little late for that sweetheart." The masked boy responded as two of his friends subdued Brady who naturally was fighting like a wild cat. "Your friend is kind of incapacitated." The boy laughed wickedly.

Suzanna prepared to run, but as she turned strong arms grabbed her also.

"You won't be leaving quite yet, sweetheart." He said as two of his other cohorts held her.

"Leave her alone creep!" Brady hollered.

"Shut that wise guy up will ya." One of the thugs wrapped his arm around Brady's neck choking out his words while the second held him and a third stood by with a knife. "Take him away guys, me and the sweetheart want to be alone."

Suzanna had never been so terrified in her life. The other boy had a knife, she knew this fella did too. She also knew that there was nothing physically she could do to defeat him and the others that still held her.

"Dear God!" If you're there, help me." She silently prayed.

"Now, lets get down to business, sweetheart." He moved closer to her.

"Leave me alone... please." She stammered.

"Oh, I'll leave you alone. After I have my fun." He laughed again. "Gag her will ya." He nodded to his friends. In a matter of seconds a rough cloth was secured tightly in her mouth.

Terrified Suzanna stiffened. She had heard enough in her short life to expect the worse. As she fought for freedom the two that held her dragged her to a darkened entry.

"Now sweetheart, I'm not gonna hurt you. I like you." He laughed again. He came toward her and began to tear at her clothing. His hands were everywhere, rough and clumsy, his breath wreaked of alcohol as he breathed heavily in her face. Suddenly one of the others yelled.

"Let's split! car's coming."

And the car did come, quickly too. It scattered the remainder of the little group and left Suzanna slumped unconscious in a heap on the gravel.

Chrys pulled into the alley and saw figures in the doorway to the back of her shop.

"What's going on?" She asked Mike. "Are they breaking in?"

"I don't know, but step on it, We'll try to catch them."

But when she sped up and the fella's fled she could tell by the figure that lay slumped on the ground that something else was a foot.

"Oh Jesus." She screamed covering her face. "Is she dead?"

There was no answer, for before the car had come to a complete stop Mike was out of it and kneeling beside the young girl.

Unaware of who she was he lifted her gently off the ground and hollered to Chrys.

"Quick, open the shop. She's gonna need help!"

In the light of the shop's work room Mike was startled when he recognized who it was he still held in his arms. Chrys was in shock herself and just stood there.

"Call the police." Mike began. He carried Suzanna over to a couch in the corner and placed her on it. Running to the bathroom he grabbed a soft rag and ran cold water on it. He was bathing Suzanna's face when Chrys returned. "Have you got a blanket of some kind around?" He asked.

In response Chrys left the room. He could hear her rummaging in the shop.

"Lord Jesus" He whispered in prayer "Only you know what has transpired tonight, only you can heal. Oh father touch this body, restore it oh Lord, but more so father, restore this mind that it be not tormented, heal it completely. I pray."

Suzanna gained consciousness slowly. Someone was stroking her face, gently with a soft cloth, someone was speaking to her softly in soothing words.

"It'll be okay. The Lord is here Suzanna, nobody will hurt you anymore." She vaguely wondered if she had gone home and it was the voice of the Lord. But this voice was familiar. Slowly she opened her eyes.

"M,..Mike?" She whispered. "W,.. what?"

"Shh" Mike answered quietly "Don't try to talk, Chrys called Doc. Martin, he'll be here soon. You just rest." Mike's heart went out to the poor girl who silently closed her eyes although her body wrenched with the sobbs that poured forth involuntarily.

"Why?" He whispered. "Why?"

Not far from Chry's shop, in an old beat up van a group of teen age boys gathered. Both the bottle and the pipe had been passed among them.

"You guys were great!" Brady said. "It couldn't have worked out better if it had been real!"

"To bad the car had to come when it did. I could easily have finished the job."

"I'm sure you would have enjoyed it." Brady continued. "Me, I plan on getting it the right way... willingly."

"Yeah, sure Downing. I think you're dreaming."

"No I'm not the dreamer." Brady continued. "She is. But I can be a likable old cus can't I."

"Perfect ladies man... a liar and a hypocrite."

"Can I help it if that's what they respond to?"

"What happens now?"

"First of all, I've got to get away from you guys and go back and look for sweetie pie." Brady laughed.

"She's in pretty good hands Downing. That Shephard fella took her into his sisters shop after we split."

"That's where I'm off to then."

"Good-luck dude."

"Thanks guys, Thanks a lot." Brady called as he opened the door of the van.

"Anytime, anytime at all." Was the response.

Brady had returned to the scene of the accident and found Doc Martin already there, although the police had not yet arrived. He looked quite bruised and beaten and claimed that the hoods had taken him down along the river, then let him go, to find his way back.

"I'll take a look at you too young man, just in case." Doc stated.

"No really Doc. I'm fine." Brady began. "I'm more concerned about Suzanna, you're sure she's okay."

"By the looks of her she faired better than you did yourself." The doctor commented. "She just gave us a scare when she passed out."

There was a knock at the back door, Chrys left to answer it, then returned with, Reverend Rhodes, his wife, and son Pat. Officer Williams followed them into the shop. Coop had remained outside where he was searching the alley.

Elizabeth ran to her daughter.

"Honey, are you okay?" She asked.

"Yeah mom. I'm fine, I guess I just passed out."

"How is she Doc." Her father asked.

"She's quite shook up, but there's almost no physical damage at all." Doc said honestly.

"Thank God." He breathed quietly.

"Is she up to answering questions."

"Shouldn't hurt any." The doctor responded to the officers inquiry.

"Can you tell us what happened?" Steve Williams asked her.

"We were just cutting through."

"We?" Steve asked. "You weren't alone?"

"No, Brady was with me." Suzanna pointed to the dishevelled dirty bruised boy that had retreated to a dark corner of the room.

"You were with Brady Downing? Whatever for? Oh don't answer that, it does explain a lot though." Steve said then added. "Who were the others Downing?"

"I have no idea." Brady said soberly. "They were wearing dark clothes and I couldn't see them well."

"That's hard to believe." Steve stated.

"Don't try to blame this on me too Mr. it won't work."

"He's right officer. Brady had nothing to do with it. In fact he's the one that they beat up. They knew who he was though." Suzanna interrupted. Brady grinned to himself to think that Suzanna would try to defend him.

"Why don't you tell us exactly what happened." Steve spoke once again to Suzanna. After she had related the incidents, she once again broke into sobs. Her mother held her. Her father paced angrily the length of the room. Pat sat with Mike Shephard quietly in another corner while Doc worked over a few of Brady's cuts and wounds.

"Can you tell me anything about the boys?" Steve asked when she was through.

"Nothing particular, they all seemed to be pretty big guys though."

"You're telling me." Brady answered. "At least the ones that tackled me were."

"What about you." Steve asked, can you tell us anything about them.

"I don't know their names if that's what you want."

"Anything that will help us locate them."

"Well, the one that held the knife,.. he was left handed at least that's the hand he held the knife in. One of the others, had an accent, a southern one. Y'all and stuff like that, he wore cowboy boots that must have been a size 19. Boy were they water ski's."

"Anything else."

"The third guy, he didn't say anything but he was shorter than the others, big and strong, but short. I'd say around 5'5" maybe."

"Thanks." Steve said when Brady was through. "We'll write this up, then I want both of you to stop by the station tomorrow and sign it. Okay?"

"Sure" they agreed.

"Now. The only ones who are aware of what happened are right here in this room. The only others are the culprits themselves, lets keep this hush and maybe the boys will say something to give themselves away."

"You mean you don't want us to tell anyone?" Brady asked.

"No one."

"I'd just like to find some other explanation for my mother that would hold water." He remarked sarcastically.

"I intend on speaking to your mother." Steve stated.

"You do?"

"Yes," He answered. "When I bring you home in a few minutes."

"Oh boy." Brady said as he sank back in his chair.

"We'll be quiet about it officer." Brother Rhodes stated.

"Same here." Mike put in.

The group dispersed quietly to their cars only Mike and Pat remained behind a minute.

That Downing's a skunk, you know that." Pat said. Mike nodded. "To bad he's got my family buffaloed." There was a pause.

"She's extremely lucky Pat." Mike stated finally "I just hope she can forget."

CHAPTER 12

A TIME TO LAUGH

Wednesday, September 21st, 1983

Pat awoke quite early the next morning. He hadn't slept well, he doubted if his parents and Suzanna had either.

Suzanna. Just the thought of her brought tears to his eyes. She was so young, so innocent. Why? Why? It was a miracle that Chrys and Mike had come when they did last night or something serious could have happened. It was serious enough as it was.

Pat reached for the bible he kept beside his bed. He held it a moment before opening it in search of a peace that could subdue him, for the day at least. He'd been reading for awhile when there was a hesitant knock at the door.

"C'min" Pat mumbled.

The door opened and Suzanna peeked in, she had showered and dressed and seemed ready again to tackle anything.

"Is it time for our daily prayer meeting?" She asked.

"Sure" Pat answered "But first,..how are you this morning?"

"I feel great!" Suzanna's face was beaming. "But you don't look to good."

"I'm having a hard time putting things together."

"Quit trying." Suzanna laughed. "I feel guilty being so happy about what happened to me last night but let me explain."

"Please do."

"Well, you know the way I am. I always say what I'm thinkin' and it gets me in trouble, and I'm always trying to take control of situations and it gets me in trouble. Well last night there was nothing I could do. My words fell on deaf ears and my actions didn't deter those muscle heads that held me. I had only one choice. Ta da! I realized that I could do nothing, I was powerless, but all my life I'd heard of the one that had all power. I placed my life in God's hands Pat. Physically, I did, as well as spiritually. There is no doubt in my mind that God intervened, no doubt at all. It just proves to me that if I truly trust him, he'll be there."

Pat was silent a moment before he spoke, "That's an excellent testimony."

"And I can't even tell anybody." Suzanna said exasperated, Pat laughed.

"Remember all the times in the bible when Jesus would heal someone and then tell them not to tell anyone?" Pat asked.

"I know how they feel!" Suzanna remarked.

Their time in prayer was a joyful one, for God was there.

Kennedy High School was in it's normal state of pandemonium when Pat entered close behind his sister and her friends. He had but one objective beyond his classes,.. to keep a protective eye on Suzanna. Brady and Angela were both at the corner when Pat and his sister arrived. Brady looked a fright for his friends had marred his appearance quite a bit, and he had taken it willingly. No reference was made to the previous night and conversation had lagged. Now as they entered the school Pat fell behind.

Jeff met Brady at his locker, they both stared at each other.

"What happened to you?" They both asked in unison, then burst into laughter.

"No comment." Brady answered.

"Same here." Jeff agreed.

Pat smiled to himself he'd heard of both accidents and felt he was in on a little secret. Comments flew back and forth concerning the pair yet neither would respond. Most who saw them concluded that they had a spat. Neither minded for they both knew differently and the two let popular opinion rest as it was,.. opinion.

After successfully seeing that Suzanna made it to class Pat hurried on to his own. His mind was in a muddle and he doubted if he'd function well in class but as always he'd do his best.

Pat got quickly to work, the class was involved in a complicated study and he was determined to grasp it. The fellow who sat beside him had more of a problem then he did, shifting in his seat almost constantly and failing to give even a faint response to the teachers inquiries.

"Wake up Jed." Pat laughed. "It's Wednesday."

"That won't help me none, I think I need a brain transplant."

"And I need a longer attention span." Pat whispered absently.

"No, just a shorter class period." Jed yawned as the two went back to their work.

When the dismissal bell rang after first period, Pat sprang up and hurried quickly to the door. He wanted to see that Suzanna got to her second class before he went to his.

"Hey, Rhodes, where are you off to in such a hurry?" Jed Bently called as he hurried toward him.

"Nowhere special...I just wanted to see someone."

"A girl,..huh?" Jed said knowingly as he nudged Pat.

"Sort of." Pat answered vaguely.

"What about the other one."

"Other what?"

"The other girl." Jed asked. "She was in class with us. Michelle? Yeah, Michelle."

"What about her?"

"How's she gonna take you meeting other girls behind her back?"

"You don't understand." Pat tried to explain.

"Sure I do, most of us guys would do the same."

"But Michelle is <u>not</u> my girlfriend." Pat insisted.

"No?"

"No. And the girl I want to see right now is my sister,.. Suzanna."

"Sorry Pat, I really am. A few guys had mentioned that you had a thing going with Michelle. I should have known better than to believe it."

"Hey, it's okay Jed, as long as you know where it stands. We're friends. The poor girl's alone and needs as many friends as she can get."

"When is the baby due?" Jed asked.

"She had it late Sunday night. A little girl."

"Oh." Jed answered slowly "But you're not dating her or anything like that?"

"No Jed I'm not."

"Why not?"

"Huh?"

"I asked why not? Why aren't you dating her. She seems like a nice girl and you two seem to get along real well,.. so."

"So,.. she just gave birth to Joe Jamison's baby if you recall." Pat said shocked at the idea.

"Well, where is he then?" Jed asked. Pat shrugged. "It seems to me" Jed continued. "That if anybody could date Michelle now it would be you. Face it Joey's been away since Graduation. I don't think he's planning on coming back."

"Wheew." Thought Pat as Jed left him and headed toward his class. "Imagine, thinking that there was something between Michelle and I." He smiled to himself.

To his great relief Suzanna was in one piece when he found her. She had already entered her classroom and waved as he peeked in. He smiled back then headed quickly to class. His locker was near his next classroom so he stopped quick to dispose of his last hours text books. When he opened his locker, a large envelope with his name on, fell to the floor.

"What's this?" He wondered. He glanced at it quickly, but because he was in a hurry left it in his locker. "Probably a note from Mark or some music from Denni." He thought.

Mr. Harper, Pat's second period teacher called him aside when he entered.

"I hear Michelle Morrison will be out of the hospital soon."

"Yes sir, in fact I plan on stopping by during my lunch period and getting her."

"Oh?" The teacher asked and gave Pat a strange look. "That's extremely kind of you."

Pat stood there awkwardly before Mr. Harper continued.

"Michelle was in one of my classes. I'd like to see her keep up her studies. Do you think perhaps you could bring her up to date on our progress so she won't have to repeat the class next semester."

"Yes sir, I'll try."

"Thanks Pat, I knew you would."

Pat walked absently to his desk. Mr. Harper had given them problems to work on in class. Pat enjoyed it, he liked figuring puzzles, especially if he knew that somewhere there was a correct answer. Obviously the pair who sat behind him didn't share his desire.

"Did you get a load of Old Man Johnson today?"

"Is he tipped again?"

"Tipped isn't the word. He ain't been straight all week. Can barely stand on his feet the old coot."

"Is he still teaching his classes?"

"Sure, I think they're afraid to send him home. I guess he's been making a few scenes lately."

"What do you mean?"

"A few teachers tried to talk to him. He just bellowed at them. Another one emptied his bottle when they found it. I guess he emptied the coffee pot then, all over some of Mr. Smitt's test papers."

"Your kidding? He really did that?"

"That's what I heard, but I believe it. The fella's losin' it. He's plumb pickled out of his brain."

"No one can be that bad off that he'd change that much,.. and in just a few days."

"Hey, I just got out of his class." Here was an explosion of giggles. "Everytime he'd turn his back one of the guys would shoot a spit ball at him."

"That's elementary school stuff."

"Yeah but you should have seen his reaction. Each time he was hit he hollered, 'Hey' or 'Ouch' finally he asked one of the kids in the front desk if it was hailing outside." Another burst of laughter.

"What did the kid say?"

"Get this,.. he said no sir, but perhaps the sky is falling." The laughter continued. "You believe me, Old Man Johnson actually looked up." The two broke into peels of laughter until a voice at the front of room was cleared quite loudly.

"Are you through with your equations?" Mr. Harper asked.

"No sir." The two said sheepishly.

Pat was able to meet Suzanna for a few minutes before their third period classes. She flagged him down cheerfully outside her classroom.

"How's it been so far today?" He asked.

"Fine, I got a ninety on my exam in English. Thanks to Brady."

"You would have done the same without his help." Pat remarked sarcastically. "If not better."

"What's that supposed to mean?"

"It means you would have gotten the same grade if not a higher one if you would have stayed home last night to study."

"And not been out galavanting in mysterious dark alley's right?"

"You said it, I didn't."

"I thought you were on my side."

"I am, but I just don't think that Downing is."

"So what?"

"What do you mean 'So what?'"

"Well, what of it if Brady isn't on my side? The Lord is Pat, that's all that counts."

"No truer statement was ever made." Pat mumbled, then added. "You mean you doubt Brady too?"

"Well,.." Suzanna said slowly. "All I know is that I enjoy being with him, so .. why can't I?"

"I don't believe you!" Pat stated flatly. "The creep could very well have been behind your whole ordeal last night and you don't seem to care."

"But I do care. Pat I care about how I feel inside and I have to be honest. If I like someone I'll tell them. It's as simple as that. What harm can there be in it? Especially with the Lord watching over me?"

"The Lord may be with you now Sis but I doubt if he'll just wait around to pick you up everytime your ignorance get's you into scrapes."

"Ignorance, huh?" She laughed, "Maybe so. But Pat, I'm happy and I can't help but think that somehow, I'll be able to reach Brady with the Gospel."

"Now that is one miracle I'd really like to see."

"Then keep your eyes open." She remarked. "Because Peggy and I are both Praying and believing."

"Well, I have yet to see the evidence." He replied skeptically.

"I have." Suzanna smiled.

"Hey Pat!" Jeff called after him.

"Hi" Pat greeted.

"You got a minute?" Jeff asked.

"Sure, what's up?"

"I guess you've heard,.. the talks all over school. About my dad I mean."

"Uh huh."

"Well, you may not believe it but this has been the longest week in my life."

"I don't find that hard to believe at all."

"I don't know who to be upset with more. Mom for cheatin' on Dad, or Dad for taking it like this. Man is he ever acting out of line." Jeff let out a loud sigh. "Jenny's with Mom now, which is probably best. At least Mom is sober."

"How about you?" Pat asked.

"I don't know about me." Jeff paused. "The other day before class Denni mentioned something to me. He said that there was a time in his life when it seemed everything was falling apart, but the Lord changed all that, I don't understand."

"Well Jeff, what Denni is saying is that, like you, his life began to crumble and in many peoples eyes it did. But Jeff, Denni didn't crumble. He had Jesus and it was the Lord that gave him the strength, not to rid himself of his problems but to accept them and do what he could to see that his life got back in order. You can do that too. Although you're mother has done something that has hurt both you and your family, Jesus can comfort that hurt and give you peace. And although your father is reacting the way he is and submitting himself to the influence of alcohol, you can be above that by going to Jesus. He's got the answers Jeff."

"Oh Pat!" Jeff said exasperated. "I just don't know what to do. All my life I've scoffed at religion, and Sunday School. Just ask Den, he'll tell ya. Well, in the last few days it seems,.. well,.. ah.. that maybe there is something to it. I know mom hasn't got what you've got, and anyone can tell you that my father doesn't although up until last Friday he was one of the most stable men I'd ever met. You see I laughed at religion because I thought it was just that,.. religion. But I've found out that for some people,.. you.. Ben Daniels,.. Bill Winters,.. That friend of yours Mike.. and even Suzanna and Denni, that you don't have a religion like I'd known it but it's a way of life. It makes sense to me now."

"I'm glad to hear that." Pat said sincerely.

"I'm not ready yet to forsake all and follow him like the apostles did, but I am considering it." Jeff became silent.

"I'll be praying for you." Pat said.

Pat entered his third period class well after the last bell had rung. He hurried quickly to his seat, opened his psychology book then snapped to attention. Mr. Shuttlesworth sat behind his desk with a stern expression on his face. Pat smiled uncertainly at him.

"You're late Rhodes."

"I know sir."

"Is that all you have to say for yourself?"

"Not unless I lie sir." Pat answered quietly.

Shuttlesworth's eyebrows arched in amusement, and a few giggles could be heard among the class.

"Don't let it happen again."

"I'll try not to sir." Pat answered as the class proceeded with it's work.

Wheew, thought Pat, I'm a lucky one. I've known Mr. Shuttlesworth to give detentions for less than being late. Pat was sincerely relieved. He was one of the few who had gone through to their Senior year without a detention or mark of demerit against them.

But, he thought, I would have accepted ten detentions for the opportunity to relate the Love of God to Jeff. He was extremely pleased with what Jeff had to say and believed it would be only a matter of time before Jeff had joined them in the family of God.

The class period seemed to drag on. First of all Pat somehow failed to really get involved in the lesson and secondly, there would be no Phy Ed for him next period and he would be able to leave and go to the Hospital to help Michelle and Joanna, the baby, get settled.

After what seemed like weeks to Pat the bell rang. Once again he hurried from his class to meet Suzanna.

"Oh Pat!" Suzanna called when she saw him. "It's terrible, just terrible."

"What is?" Pat asked bewildered.

"What's happening to Mr. Johnson." Suzanna stated quietly. "I've been trying to ignore all the signs that others were pointing out to me,.. but I guess I can't anymore."

"What happened."

"Well a few of the other teachers had to come in and physically drag him out of class after he hit little Barney Flint."

"He hit Barney? In class?"

"Well it was kind of an accident, .. I think. At least it appeared to be. Barney had gone to sharpen his pencil so he could take better notes, when Mr. Johnson made one of his elaborate gestures and hit him smack dab in the kisser. He hit him so hard and fast that the force of the blow sent poor Barney sprawling. Then Mr. Johnson looked at him as if he hadn't done a thing. "Well Flint, isn't it about time you got up on your own two feet?" That was that, no apology, no remorse, just surprise."

"Did anyone say where he is now?"

"I *heard* they took him home; emptied his house of alcohol, and took his wallet and keys so it's almost impossible for him to get more. The other teachers are taking his classes."

"Do you think Jeff knows?"

"Oh Pat,.. I don't think so. You see, I only know because it happened while I was in his class. That was only about half an hour ago. Jeff wouldn't know unless someone specifically made a point to tell him."

"Do you know where I can find him?" Pat asked.

"No, but Brady would, you could ask him."

"Denni would know too though, right?" Pat asked, Suzanna nodded. "I'll find Denni." He stated.

"Boy aren't you the friendly one." Suzanna teased. "Brady doesn't bite you know."

"Maybe I do." Pat laughed as he left her at her class. He vaguely recalled where to find Denni and breathed a sigh of relief when he found him in his classroom a few minutes before the bell.

"Hey Den" Pat summoned from the hall.

"Hi" Denni replied as he came to the door.

"I want to talk to Jeff Johnson, you wouldn't by any chance know where to find him would you?"

"That would be tough. He and Brady both have a free period, they can be anywhere."

"You've no idea at all?"

"All I know, is that where they are I won't even consider going."

"Well, thanks anyway. By the way, are they driving?"

"I think Jeff takes his fathers truck."

"Thanks again. See you tonight." Pat hurried down the hall just as the final bell sounded.

Pat had no intention of wasting time on a fruitless search for two delinquent teenage boys. He left school after grabbing his jacket, sticking the note he thought from Mark into it's pocket, and headed home.

It was only a six block walk from school and Pat enjoyed it. He always felt guilty when he'd taken the car for it seemed such a waste, now as he hurried home his impatience caused him to reconsider.

Elizabeth Rhodes planned on accompanying Pat to the hospital. She had yet to see the baby herself. A few of the church ladies had come to her with special offerings for Michelle and the baby, these she placed in a card that she now had in her handbag.

"Are we ready to go?" She asked when Pat entered the house.

"We?" Pat asked then seeing her with her coat and handbag he continued. "Mom, that's great! Michelle would love to see you."

"Well" She began, "There's no prayer meeting, committee meeting, board meeting, bible study, class, car pool, or encyclopedia salesmen so it looks as if I'm free."

"Then let's hurry before something comes up."

Elizabeth allowed Pat to get behind the wheel as she got into the passenger side.

"I was wondering something." She began.

"What's that?"

"Well,.. you seem to have kind of paid special attention to Michelle. Is there a reason?"

"Oh, Mom." Pat said exasperated. "Not you too?"

"What do you mean, not me too?"

"It seems that everyone has been making a point today about the fact that I like Michelle. Well, I do like her, we're friends. I'd do the same for any others. My own mother wonders."

"Can I help but wonder son?"

"If you want to wonder Ma, wonder about that fella that's hanging around your daughter."

"I do Patrick, I do. But Suzanna is not denying her feelings any longer, I don't want you to fool yourself. I want you to be honest and know how you truly feel before you get involved. Suzanna is a problem I admit. But Pat you're not, you never were. It would just kill me to see you get hurt."

"I don't hurt easily Mom."

"Love hurts Pat, always remember that."

"I'm not in love with Michelle, Mom." Pat stated soberly.

"I'm glad."

Michelle was all packed and waiting when they entered her room.

"Oh Mrs. Rhodes, it's good to see you." She said excitedly. "Wait until you see my angel. She is so precious. Isn't she Pat?"

"She is beautiful Mom, I admit, I was surprised."

"Thanks a lot,. friend." Michelle answered flippantly.

"I held the firm belief that baby's were red, and wrinkled, and ugly. I changed that opinion now."

"Oh?" Michelle asked.

"Yea! I realize now that babies are red, and wrinkled, and beautiful." He smiled.

"Oh Pat, you oaf, I'll let you get by with just that one remark though. I'm too excited because I'm going,. I mean, we're going home."

"Where is the little one?" Elizabeth asked.

"Come on, I'll get her. I gave her a bath, and dressed her and I kept her in my room most of the morning. They rolled her bed right in."

Michelle led the way to the nursery where little Joanna slept peacefully. A young nurse lifted the tiny bundle and handed it to Michelle.

"Here you are mom."

"Thank you." Michelle stated. "Tell Penny and Judi I said thanks too."

"We'll miss her."

"I'll bring her back when she sees the doctor in six weeks, okay?"

"Sure, anytime."

They said goodbye again, and Michelle led the others back to her room. Pat grabbed her luggage, then looking at the roses that remained smiled.

"Well mom, I'm glad you came I never could have carried this in one trip." Elizabeth smiled as she lifted the large vase.

"These are just gorgeous." She stated.

"So is the thought." Michelle said quietly.

It was after his return home from bringing Michelle from the hospital that Pat found time to read his note. He was still sitting at the table in the Rhodes kitchen, his mother was busy doing up a few dishes, his father sat across from him reading a small monthly paper. Pat absently opened the note and scanned it's contents.

> Pat R.
> What happened to your sister
> was only the beginning.
> To bad it failed.
> You will be next,
> unless you BUTT OUT!

The note was unsigned.

Pat made a quizzical face. So his theory was true. Someone had planned the whole thing, but how far will they go? He glanced up at his father before quickly shoving the note into the envelope and placing it in his pocket. 'I've got to keep an eye on her constantly that's all.' He mused.

"I guess I'll be going now." He said to his parents. "Remember I'll be helping the crew out at Daniels' after school mom."

"That's right. I won't expect you until later then."

"Keepin' an eye on your sister?" His father asked.

"Kind of. I've seen her three or four times today. She seems to be doing real well."

"I'm glad." His father sighed. "I shudder when I think about what could have happened to her."

"Don't think about it dear." Sister Rhodes stated.

"I have to Liz, my daughter was in extreme danger last night and I want to do my best to see it doesn't happen again."

"But it just happened." She explained. "And Suzanna is fine. There is no one that's out to get her. Chances of it happening again are real slim."

"I'm not taking any chances."

"But you can't be with her all the time!"

"I know that, that's why I'm so frustrated about it. I'd like to keep her on a leash and not let her out of my sight but I can't. It's driving me nuts."

"Then don't think about it."

"That Liz is easier said than done."

"I'll see her once more before I leave school and if you'd like I'll see that she has an escort home."

"You do that son." His father answered. "And let us know if you have any idea's at all about who's responsible. I personally would like to know."

"So would I dad." Pat answered. "So would I."

Pat parked the old jalopy, and headed toward the west side of school where he knew his sister and a few friends gathered before their fifth period classes.

His thoughts were in quite an uproar. He was positive now that someone was out to harm his sister. He was sure also that they would try again. He was also sure that he would be a target for he had no intention of keeping still. But who were they?

A group of young people hailed him from under a cluster of birch trees.

"Hey Pat!" Mark Rankin called "Over here."

Pat walked over to the group. Mark and Matt were both there, along with a friend of theirs he didn't know. Peggy, Becky, and Angie Arnolds were there also. They greeted him.

"I thought I'd find my sister here." Pat stated as he looked the group over.

"So did we." Becky remarked. "I guess she deserted us though, because we haven't seen her."

Pat turned to Peggy, she just shrugged.

"She didn't say anything to you did she?" He asked her.

"Not a word. But she probably had to stay and work on some project of something."

"I don't think so." Pat stated. "I'd better find her."

"What's up? Are you some kind of chaperone or what?" Matt asked.

"I just need to see her, that's all." Pat answered as he hurried away.

Suzanna had left her fourth hour class and hadn't gone two steps when Brady was beside her.

"Let me take these." He said as he reached for her books. "Where are we having lunch today?"

"Here in the cafeteria of course."

"No way, I tried that mob yesterday. Today it's my choice and your coming along." Brady smiled as he looked at her and led her through the crowd to the exit.

"Jeff's got his dad's car now that the old man's home safe. We thought we'd take quick trip and get some burgers,.. come on."

"Let me tell Peggy first."

"No way. We'll have all those dudes swarmin' around again."

"They're my friends." Suzanna protested.

"So am I, right?"

"Sure,.. but."

"No buts. Come on. Look there's Jeffer, he's got Denni with him now. "Brady urged Suzanna into the backseat of Jeff's parents car. She paused slightly before she entered.

"Brady, I'd better stay here."

"I won't take no for an answer. Get in."

Reluctantly she did. Denni turned and smiled that old familiar smile that she'd seen most of her life.

"You're gonna have to get used to Brady ordering you around. He's got this secret ambition to be a drill sergeant and he's in training."

"Really." Jeff said with a grin. "I always thought he was gonna find a wife and get married, and have say,.. fifteen kids, and was taking courses on child rearing."

"Fifteen kids!" Brady gasped, "Get real."

Everyone laughed as the car headed toward the center of town.

"Oh no,.. Jeff, I just thought of something." Brady sputtered.

"What's that?"

"It's even now. These two Holy Joe's against us. We better be on our toes."

"No Brady, your outnumbered. You better be on your toes."

Brady was silent and an alarmed expression came on his face. "Don't tell me you're one of them?"

"No. At least not yet. But I'm not on your side either Brady."

"What's gotten into you Jeffer? I would believe it of anyone but not you."

"Things have changed Brady."

"Yea,.. I guess they have." He answered blandly. The car pulled in at Daves Delicious Drive-In, the town's old standy-by for burgers and fri's.

A few other car loads of kids from school were there. They greeted the others before placing their orders.

"How did your test go this morning." Suzanna asked Brady.

"Okay I guess. I suppose I passed,.. what about you?"

"I got a ninety."

"That's great! You know after last night I could take that test over myself and pass with flying colors."

Their food came and they joined the group outside. This was a different group of kids than what Suzanna was used to. Most were seniors, football players, and extremely good looking. The girls were mostly cheerleaders or in the pep club or athletes themselves. She noticed that although Denni was neither a football player, or involved in their activities he was good looking and quite friendly which allowed the others to accept him.

'That's funny' Suzanna thought. 'I've never thought of Denni as being good looking. Or of being friendly. He's always just been Denni to me.'

A few of the girls smiled at her, but she knew that her lifestyle was so far from theirs that she couldn't even hope to fit in. One girl, Sandra Marsh made it a point to speak to her.

"Hi Suzanna" She smiled encouragingly.

"Hi"

"Turn your head once, I want to get a good look at how you did your hair."

"Oh, sure." She said as she turned her head so Sandy could see.

"You know you have such beautiful hair. I heard that you've never cut it."

"No. I haven't" Suzanna said with a hint of pride.

"I've seen it when you wear it down. It's really long, and thick. It must take forever to dry after you wash it."

"I usually wash it at night and get most of the dampness out, then it's dry by morning."

"Now how did you get your hair like this?" Sandra asked and the girls continued talking as the others looked on curious and partly interested.

The boys on the other hand had disappeared under the hood of Jed Bently's old car. Jed pointing with one hand and holding a burger with another was giving a part by part description of what he'd done with his engine.

Time passed quickly.

"We have to be getting back for class." Denni stated glancing at his watch. Jeff turned toward his car.

"In a minute Jeffer." Brady said. He was in deep discussion with Jed. Jeff and Denni started toward Jeff's car. Suzanna turned to join them.

"It's not fair, you know." Sandra stated teasingly.

"What's not fair."

"Hogging those three to yourself."

"Oh," Suzanna laughed. "They're not interested in me." She motioned toward Jeff and Denni who were now getting into the front seat of the car.

"Don't kid yourself. Both Jeff and Denni have eyes for you, it's only Brady's interest that's stopping them."

"What do you mean?"

Sandra shrugged. "It's an unspoken rule around here. People kind of let Downing have what he wants. He can usually get them what they want,.. so it's even."

"It is?" Suzanna asked.

"Sure, well I'm heading back. I'll se ya. Take care." Sandi hurried away and piled into a car that was extremely over-loaded with girls. They tooted their horn as they left. Only the guys and Suzanna remained. She turned toward Jeff's car. Someone joined in step beside her. She glanced up expecting Brady but found someone she had never met. He was vaguely familiar. But then most of them were. He was tall and broad shouldered with gentle brown eyes and a kind smile.

"I didn't get a chance to introduce myself before." He stated. "I'm Chas Hagens"

"Hi, I'm Suzanna Rhodes."

"Yeah, I know. I've got a few classes with your brother. Smart kid."

"Too smart sometimes." Suzanna stated. Chas laughed. They had reached Jeffs car and he opened the door for her.

"Nice meeting you." He said then turned to Jeff. "Downing's going with us to check that car out, he said to go on without him."

"Okay." Jeff agreed. They pulled out and headed toward school. Suzanna was silent. Jeff and Denni shared and amused look before Jeff spoke.

"You can relax now, the big bad wolf isn't here."

"What's that mean?"

"We both know,.. Denni and I, I mean,.. that Brady tends to intimidate people. We seem to be his favorite toys. I doubt if he means it. It's just hard to say no to the guy."

"I quit trying." She stated honestly.

Both boys looked at each other, startled.

"Don't do that." Denni said soberly. "I'm just recovering myself now. Don't give in to him Suzanna if you know it's wrong.. It's not worth it."

"We'll help all we can." Jeff stated honestly. "Deep down he's a great guy. But if he want's something he usually gets it. Just watch your step."

Suzanna was bewildered. "I thought you were his friends."

"We are." Jeff insisted. "But things change."

"Only God is unchanging." Denni said quietly.

The first person to greet Suzanna when she returned to school with Jeff and Dennis, was her brother Pat. He was pacing anxiously outside her locker when she entered the building.

"Where in blue blazes were you?" He almost shouted.

"I went for lunch, why?"

"Why? You know very well why. We had an agreement with Dad that I'd keep an eye on you. How can I when you go traipsing off without telling anyone?"

"Oh, I'm sorry." Suzanna said sincerely. "I didn't realize you would be so worried."

"I have come to the conclusion in the last few days that you, little sister, are extremely daft."

"Oh my, You don't say." She teased.

"Actions speak louder than words I'm afraid."

"What's the big fuss anyway?"

"I was afraid something may have happened to you."

"But I was fine, Brady was with me."

"I was afraid of that."

"Well for your information, Denni was too." She reported. "And we met not one single fella wearing a blue ski mask or size 19 cowboy boots."

"Don't be funny." Pat interrupted. "This is serious." He reached into his pocket and pulled out the note.

"I wasn't going to show you this but if it will show you how serious this business is I'd better." He handed her the note.

Suzanna took the note from the envelope and glanced at it. A sober expression spread across her face.

"Now do you realize how serious this is?"

"I'm sorry,.. I really didn't realize... Why would someone be after me? What could I have done?"

"We might never know the answer to that, but we do know that last night was not an accident. They'll try again. We'll both need to keep alert."

"You're not kidding. Oh Pat what should I do?" Suzanna began to sound scared.

"First of all, you should stay as far away from that Downing as you can. He's involved here somehow but I just don't know how."

"I guess I could try." Suzanna stated. "But that's easier said than done."

"Secondly, I'm gonna show this note to Sergeant Williams. Maybe it will help him find whose behind this all."

"I hope so."

"So do I"

Pat turned to go but Suzanna stopped him.

"Pat, I'm sorry I acted so smart before. I'm not. I'm scared. I'm scared to death."

"Don't forget you're not alone and that someone who was with you last night is with you now."

Suzanna paused again. "I know that, I just don't have a lot of faith to believe it."

"It seemed like you had it this morning."

"After a forty-five minute prayer meeting I could have faith to move mountains. It just kind of dwindles when I attempt to face reality."

"Isn't it the truth." Pat responded. "But he will give us an everlasting faith if we ask him. A faith in him that won't be shaken, no matter what man might throw at us. We'll lose it all Suzanna in the midst of this if we lose faith in him."

Michelle Morrison sat contentedly rocking little Joanna. She was in the living room of her parents home south of town. Both her parents were at work. Her father at the local Paper Mill, and her mother at Gary's Good-buy's Groceries.

She glanced out the window at the beautiful afternoon. Colorful leaves were drifting softly on the breeze and landing quietly among others that covered the ground. A few squirrels ran among them searching for nuts to place in storage against the long winter ahead. The ribbon of asphalt and shadow, dotted with fallen leaves ran past her home on the way to Lincoln.

As she rocked, her thoughts drifted back, as they did so often these days,.. to Joe. Oh she knew where he was, she knew exactly where he was. He had joined the Marines immediately after hearing news of the baby. He hadn't sent her even a small note explaining why he'd left. His father had told her about Joe's enlistment, it was then from Michelle that he first heard about the baby. Joe had told his parents nothing. Mrs. Jamison refused to admit who the father was,.. but most knew.

Now as she sat rocking Joe's tiny daughter, her perfect child, all the thoughts that had plagued her these past months returned. Would she ever see Joe again? Would this little child that she held in her arms ever know her daddy. If Joe doesn't return, what should she do. She was only seventeen, and now she had a baby to take care of. She was both father, and mother as well as provider. This tiny baby was depending on her, she mustn't fail.

She glanced around the room. On the end table Elizabeth had placed the large vase of roses, the white, the red, the pink. They told Michelle a lot with just their presence. There was some who did care about her and they had hope that her and Joanna could be bound with a love that could withstand anything. The thought struck her that she had loved Joe that way. Why then had he hurt her so? Tears came to her eyes, she felt so alone. Never had she felt so alone.

The sound of racing engines caused her to glance out the window toward the street. Sure enough it was coming closer, two cars, both altered, came into view.

"Why that's Jed Bently." She smiled, both cars screamed past. Boys hung from the windows and shouted to each other as they raced on.

Michelle's smile faded. Those were her classmates, without a care in the world, and here she remained, a mother, a father, a provider,... alone.

Pat's last class was fifth hour. His schedule had allowed him to get the last few hours each day off for work. When the bell rang dismissing classes he hurried to meet Suzanna.

"I'm leaving." He stated. "But I talked to Denni. He'll bring you out to the farm after school,..okay?"

"Sure. You'll call ma and let her know won't you?"

"Yeah, I should be done working by five-thirty."

"If I get a few of the girls to come along would you mind driving them home?"

"Of course not. If you can talk Denni into taking them out. I'll drive them home."

"Thanks. That will be fun." She hurried to her class as Pat left school.

He was just leaving the parking lot when he saw Jed Bently's new car approach. He grinned and waved. Jed gave him a blast from his horn A-Ooo-Ga. Pat smiled to himself then turned toward the farm.

Brady had ridden with the others in their Hot cars up and down the road to Lincoln. After returning to school he sought out Suzanna who had just entered her sixth class.

"Did you sign that report at the station today?" He asked her.

"Oh! No!" She exclaimed "I forgot all about it."

"No problem. We'll run by there right after school, I've got to be here for practice at 4:00."

"No that won't work. I'm going right out to Daniels' farm after school. I'll have Pat stop before we go home.

"I'm sure he wouldn't mind you going right after school."

"You don't know my brother. He told me specifically to go out to the farm immediately after school. Denni's taking me. Peggy and Angie are coming too."

"Denni's taking you?" Brady was alarmed. "Since when does he start taking you places?"

"Since he's been a friend of the families for six years and is one of Pat's close friends."

"Oh sure." Brady said sarcastically. "Don't worry I'll take care of it."

"Brady." Suzanna said startled. "Just let it be. I'll be perfectly fine going out to the farm with Denni, and I'll stop later and sign the paper."

"I guess so" Brady said reluctantly. "By the way practice is over at 5:00, maybe I could wiz out to the farm for another riding lesson."

"Oh, I doubt if there will be time. My brother will be through working at 5:30. Maybe another day this week."

"Don't worry." Brady said dejectedly. "I can tell when someone is avoiding me. And we had such a good time last night together."

"You're right,.. we did." Suzanna admitted. "We will again too, it just doesn't work out right now. Okay?"

"Sure." Brady answered as he slumped away.

"Well" Suzanna thought to herself. "You'd think I'd spoiled his whole day."

Pat hadn't been the only one to come to Denni about a ride to the farm. Tom Van Dyke approached him after his fifth class.

"Hey Den." He called as he approached. "I've been looking for you."

"What's up?"

"Well, something turned up and my car's in the shop do you think I could get a lift off you after school?"

"Sure, No problem, that is if you don't mind female company. I'm bringing Suzanna out, and there's no telling who she'll drag along with her."

"Just as long as it's not that friend of your's..Downing."

"You two don't like each other do you?"

"We'd like each other to be on different planets I think." Tom laughed.

"Well, have no fear. He's got practice tonight so he won't be around."

"I'll see you after school then."

"Sure." Denni headed toward class but before he got there Brady pulled him aside.

"What's going on Den." He asked.

"What do you mean?"

"I heard you're driving Rhodes out to that stupid farm tonight."

"Yeah. Her brother asked me to. What of it?"

"I don't like my girl going with other guys anywhere."

"You didn't mind at noon when you deserted her to go hot rodding." Dennis pointed out.

"What's that supposed to mean?"

"Just what I said. Downing wake up will you. I'm not your puppet, I can do what I want."

"What's gotten into you?"

"I guess I'm beginning to see things I didn't realize before."

"Like what may I ask?"

"Like the fact that you seem to assume everyone will do everything your way. Well not anymore. Not me."

"Oh come off it Den. I'm only giving you a line."

"I don't mind with me as much as with Suzanna. You're playing some kind of a game with her and it's making me sick."

"So you thought you'd butt in and take over huh."

"This wasn't my idea Brady."

"Yeah, sure. I know better then to get too close to you Holy Joe's. You always stick up for each other. I'll just let you know one thing. You're not getting her without a fight. I mean it, and by the time you do get her chances are you won't want her anymore." He laughed.

"Brady, you've got me all wrong."

"I've heard that line before. She must have lots of friends around, boy did she fool me."

"She's done nothing but be honest with you. If only you would be the same with her."

"But you don't understand Denni. I don't have to be. I'm not the Christian. She is."

The bell rang for class and the two departed.

The work had progressed rapidly at the farm. The foundation had been poured earlier in the day and a few fundamental jobs remained to be done. Pat like the work, sure he felt sore and tired after a long day but it was a good feeling.

Ben had taken his new colt into the outdoor arena and he worked with him for a good share of the afternoon. The animal was gorgeous and when Mike saw him he wondered slightly if the horses Rich had spoken of the night before were indeed superior.

Mike had exchanged a few words with Pat when he came on the job. Pat in return had taken an envelope from his pocket and handed it over. Mike opened the envelope and read the note, his face grew sober, he quickly stuffed it back in the envelope and handed it back to Pat.

"What are you gonna do about the note?" Mike asked.

"Well, for starts I didn't show it to my folks. They don't need anymore to worry about. Secondly, I'm gonna run the thing over to the station tonight for Steve Williams."

"You shouldn't have to." Mike stated. "The fellow's around here somehwere. He's night shift,.. 9-5, I think."

"He's here?" Pat asked.

"Sure, he rode out a while back. They should be back soon."

"He's with Mrs. Johnson huh?"

"I don't know." Mike shrugged. "I've never met Mrs. Johnson, I only know Steve from last night. We talked a bit when he came around noon."

"Oh, Well you know Jeff of course."

"Yeah, the fella that was at youth service the other night."

"Well, Judy is his mother. Her and Williams have been getting together secretly for months. Everything kind of backfired late last week. It's all out now. So she's no longer sneaking around. But her husband took it pretty rough. I guess he's been drinking pretty hard, you know that though because you saw that fight last night."

"That was Jeff?" Mike asked "I didn't even recognize him. I had no idea! and the fist was really meant for Steve?"

"Uh huh, and here he comes." Pat nodded down the lane at the two riders approaching.

Steve drew up and dismounted as Judy riding Flasher continued toward the stables.

"Hi Pat. How's your sister today?"

"She seems fine, or anyway she was until I found this in my locker." He once again took the note from his jacket pocket.

Steve lost no time in reading the note, nodding his head all the while.

"You don't mind if I keep this do you?"

"Oh no, of course not."

"Who saw it besides you?"

"Just Mike here, .. and Suzanna."

"Don't mention it to anyone okay. I'll see what I can get from it."

"Do you have any idea at all?"

"Idea's don't hold water Pat, evidence does; Evidence I do not have. Idea's I do. Thanks for this note, it'll be a big help. I'll see if I can maybe have someone tail your sister for a while."

"Really?"

"Sure, the notes says it's only the beginning so they plan on trying something more, it would be nice to be prepared for them."

"I guess so."

"Thanks again, I'll see you around." He left them, leading his horse toward the stables.

Suzanna met both Peggy and Angie at her locker after seventh hour.

"Denni's waiting in the parking lot." She called, "Come on."

"You're sure he won't mind?" Angie asked quietly.

"We won't give him a chance to say no." Suzanna answered. "We'll just get in the car, he's too nice to ask you to leave."

"Suzanna Rhodes. I'm surprised at you." Peggy began. "You know very well that Denni wouldn't mind and you also know that if he did you won't be getting Angie and I to go along."

"I could give each of you my textbooks and when he asks I'll say that you are my official book couriers."

"That would unofficially fail." Peggy laughed. "But I don't think we have to worry. Denni knows you enough to assume that we'll be along."

"I don't think I like this." Angie put in.

"Why not? We do it all the time." Suzanna stated. "At least with my brother. This is the first we've ganged up on Den."

"There he is." Peggy whispered.

"I think I'll leave." Angie said turning away.

"Oh no you don't" Suzanna stated as she grabbed Angies arm and pulled her back. The three approached Denni who was waiting by his car.

"Denni's Dependable Taxi Service; at your disposal Ladies." He said in a formal tone as he opened the back door for them. "The name is Den, the man, and that gentleman in front is my co-pilot, Too Tall Tom. We're glad to have you aboard."

The three girls giggled as they entered the car. Angie was still slightly reluctant, but there was such an air of comradery that she soon relaxed.

"I will be giving you a guided tour of our fair city as we travel, so if you have any questions please ask." Denni continued. "As you may already know I began this tour from the parking lot of the esteemed and highly recommended John Fitzgerald Kennedy High School. The school noted for excellent student moral, excellent student participation, excellent student achievement and boring teachers. The only High School in the United States where every student graduates at the top of his class."

"You will notice as we are approaching this intersection many notable landmarks. On the far corner you will find the first and only public telephone booth to operate on a party line. Just put in a quarter and you are privileged to hear three conversation at one time. Very ingenious especially for the gossip columnist from the Junction Journal' which operates from that building to the right."

"Next we have on the corner as I hurry through the intersection is Roberts Junctions only working traffic light. Noted specifically for changing every half hour on the dot. Officer MaGillicudy used to stand in this intersection, but he's had to be replaced,.. God rest his soul."

"Denni! That's terrible." Suzanna stated between giggles.

"Thank you ma'am." He grinned. "Now continuing with our tour to the right we find Gary's Good-buy's Groceries. The store that causes you to say Good-bye to your pay check. Ahead we have the Capital building. Notice the great architectural structure. The pealing paint on the west side; the sets of twin double doors which, by the way, have been stuck permanently closed for forty years, and the official barred windows in the basement level. This building was named after the words CITY HALL were printed above the entrance in capital letters, Ladies and Gentlemen, the 'Capital' building.

"Yeah!" Suzanna cheered. "I traveled 3,000 miles to see this." She laughed.

"Wait!" Denni exclaimed "Ahead of us, as we leave town, if you look to the left you will find the VanDyke Mansion. Residence of my good friend, Too Tall."

"Good Day Senorita's" Tom spoke with an accent.

"In this magnificent home we find first of all a luxurious three and a half car garage, you will be amazed at how many of the neighbors borrowed tools can fit into this attached building."

"This home also features, the towns first trash compactor, it was installed five years ago, and worked one whole week before it was over loaded when Too-Tall here tried to compact his younger brother Soo-Slim."

The girls were giggling hysterically now as was Tom.

"Another feature of this fine mansion is the mail box, it is the biggest one in town so big it enables the telephone book delivery man from having to come to the door of their home, which was the idea. Now before we depart look again but this time at the door of that three and a half car garage. That Ladies is an original work of art. That garage door was painted ten years ago by the noted and accomplished artist Leanard O. Devil Inchi."

"Now I have concluded my tour for the day, you may relax and enjoy your ride for I will now proceed to watch the road."

"Please do." Suzanna stated. The whole group was laughing hysterically by the time they turned into the parking lot at Horsemen's Unlimited.

CHAPTER 13

A TIME TO MOURN

Wednesday, September 21st, 1983

Tom left the group immediately after arriving at the farm, but Denni waited around while the girls got out of the car.

"I've got the greatest news!" He whispered to Suzanna and Peggy after Tom was out of earshot.

"What's that?" Suzanna asked.

"Jeff talked to me today." Denni began "He wants me to pick him up for Bible Study tonight."

"Jeff! That's great!" Suzanna exclaimed.

"Excellent." Peggy responded.

"An answer to prayer." Denni added.

"Hey, were you this enthusiastic when I decided to come to church?" Angie wondered.

"Yes we were." Suzanna answered honestly. "You are an answer to prayer too."

"Thanks!" She said then paused. "I mean it. I've got a lot to learn I know, but I am pretty determined that I want to do things God's way."

"And we won't quit praying" Suzanna responded.

Denni left them to join Tom who he knew would be busy feeding the horses. The girls wandered over to Old Bill's workshop.

"Hi, Gramps." Peggy said as she joined him.

"Aye Missy, you don come out here to give an old man a hand?"

"No I didn't but if you need help, I'm here."

"No I'm just spoofin' ya. This is a man's job, even if it's a weak ol' man like me."

"I bet I could handle it." Suzanna commented boldly.

"I bet ye could too, but I ain't about to let ye." He retorted. "Now if ye's here to behave find ye a bale, but if ye's here to lip off, skedaddle."

"We're here to say Hi." Suzanna responded. "We're gonna take a few horses riding."

"Suzanna's taking Camalot, Angie's taking Denni's horse Prints, I really gave Gingersnap a workout last night, should I take Lady Jane, or do you plan on riding later?"

"Go ahead Missy, You take Lady. I'll be cuttin' out early as it is. Be back by 5:30 hear? I'll be pullin' out then."

"Sure,..Bye Gramps." Peggy called as she and the girls left him.

Pat was busy cleaning some tools he'd used when Sarah Daniels approached with little Nicolas.

"Hi Pat, I hate to bother you while your working."

"It's okay, in a way, I'm working for you."

"I guess you're right." Sarah laughed. "But I've got an idea and I want your opinion."

"Oh, oh,"

"It's okay, this idea's safe."

"Well okay, throw it by me."

"Suzanna's going to be fifteen a week from Saturday, what I'd like to do is get the young people together for a surprise party. Do you think it would work?"

"Oh, I don't know." Pat said thoughtfully. "Getting the guys together is no problem, but well, Suzanna's pretty sneaky she'll think something's up.. But you can try. Where would you have it?"

"That's just it. I'd like to have it here. Denni and Tom could load a wagon with hay, we could have a hay ride and stop for a bonfire cookout."

"That sounds like fun. Why don't you try it. If I can help let me know."

"I will, I'll give your mother a call right now, when I know Suzanna's not at home."

"You'd better before your plans collide with each other's."

"Thanks Pat, I'll let you know if I need your help."

"Do that."

Angie surprised both Suzanna and Peggy with her riding ability. It was clear that she had ridden a lot and enjoyed it. They had quite a time racing along the paths, playing follow the leader in the woods, and stopping in the orchard for juicy red apples.

"I really had fun." Peggy stated as they headed back toward the farm.

"This sure beats my last ride." Suzanna remarked.

"Why is that?" Angie wondered.

"Well, I'd gotten as far as the woods when I ran into the 'pain'."

"Who's the 'pain'?" Peggy wondered.

"Oh, that's just my new name for Brady Downing."

"I thought you liked him?" Angie reminded confused.

"I thought so too, until I realized something. Boy was I dumb."

"Well? What did you realize?"

"I realized that what I liked wasn't Brady but the attention he was paying me and when I realized that boy! did I feel stupid."

"You mean you don't really like him?" Angie asked.

"Let's say that I liked to have him carry my books, take me to lunch, get upset when I talk to other boys, even my brother, but I guess it was the things he said that I really liked."

"What did he say?" Angie wondered.

"Oh things like,.. how much he liked me, or my looks, or my personality. Compliments,.. stuff like that. It felt so good to think that someone thought that of me."

"But you don't really like him, huh."

"I don't like him manipulating people. I don't like him lying. I don't like him drinking, but above all he isn't a Christian."

"Does it make a difference?" Angie asked.

"I used to wonder that but I think now I know. I liked those things about Brady but still I was kinda afraid of him. But take someone who's a Christian. Well, that person would think hopefully like you, and even though you'd have different likes and dislikes at least they'd be clean and Holy."

"Suzanna?" Peggy interrupted. "Can I say something."

"Sure, anytime." Suzanna answered.

"You know this conversation we're having right now,.. I don't want you to get mad, but,.. it's an answer to prayer."

"I have a feeling you weren't the only one praying."

"I wasn't" Peggy admitted.

Suzanna's next problem was how to get rid of Brady. She'd allowed him to think things that weren't actually true, but then at the time they were. Oh,.. things were so mixed up. Her thoughts led her to venture toward the barn that was used to store hay, grain and other feed for the horses. She entered the building through an open door.

"Denni?" She called.

"Yup here" Came a muffled reply.

Suzanna looked up at the piles and piles of hay that lined the building. Denni was nowhere in sight.

"Where are you?" She called again.

"Over here." He returned and when Suzanna looked in his direction he waved, "What's up?"

"Are you busy?"

"Kinda. I've got a huge pile of these bales to stack, why?"

"Oh, it's nothing important."

"Don't give me that!" Denni said seriously. "What's up?"

"I just kinda wanted to talk."

"Oh,.. in that case, there's a ladder on the far wall right ahead of you. Come on up."

"Is it safe?"

"Of course silly." He laughed as he continued stacking bales of hay.

"This isn't what I had in mind." Suzanna mumbled to herself as she climbed the ladder. She soon found that climbing the ladder had been the easy part. She had quite a climb left, up and down uneven stacks before she perched on a stack beside where Denni worked.

"Wheew." She signed. "I'm tuckered out and I didn't even do anything."

"You get used to it." Denni responded as he kept up the work. "What's on your mind?" He asked.

"I think you know." She began. "A certain friend that the two of us have in common."

"Oh, that could be almost anyone." Denni remarked. "But his initials wouldn't by any chance be B.D.?"

"You said it."

"Well what's your problem? You seem to have him eating out of your hand?"

"Yeah, sure." She said sarcastically. "What do you think would be the best and safest way to tell him to get lost?"

"You don't understand something." Denni paused in his work. "No one, I mean no one, tells Brady Downing to get lost."

"Why not?"

"It's not safe. Believe me."

"Well, why not?"

"I don't want to get into it." He paused. "Okay so you want to tell him to get lost without getting him mad. The only time Brady drops anything is either when he's done with it or he finds something he likes better."

"He doesn't listen to reason huh?"

"Seldom, but I do admit he has at times."

"I guess I'm back to plan one."

"What's plan one?"

"Tell him to his face, that I was a fool and that I want nothing to do with him. I think it will work."

"Why's that."

"First off, I mean it, secondly, I'm gonna pray."

"That just might do it."

Pat joined Suzanna and Angie at the arena at five thirty.

"Ready to head home?" He asked.

"Yeah." Suzanna responded. "Just let me run up to the house to say good-bye to my buddy okay?"

"Be quick about it." He called as Suzanna headed toward the house. "Did you enjoy your ride?" Pat asked Angie after Suzanna had disappeared.

"Did I ever. It's been a long time since I've ridden."

"I'm glad it was such a nice day."

"Me too." She responded quietly.

The two just stood for a minute before Pat continued again.

"How's your brother Jim doing?"

"Not to good. My parents think he is but I know better. The work at college is really rough on him, and he's kind of involved with a few shady lookin' guys. They give me the creeps."

"That's too bad." Pat remarked, partly surprised at getting such a lengthy response from one so quiet. "Does he come home often."

"No, hardly at all. He left for summer school in the middle of June and we haven't seen him more than twice since."

"What about you? Do plan to go to college?"

"I did, but right now I've got three brothers in for their bachelors, one going for his Masters, and another for his Doctorate. When the family is together that's all I hear and I don't like a lot of the stuff I hear. Not the classes but some of the other stuff that's involved."

"I'm sure there's a college somewhere that would suit you."

"Well, I'm not sure of things anymore, I've got a lot to think about."

"Sunday was only a beginning." Pat remarked with a smile as Suzanna ran up.

"Yeah, the best beginning too."

When they had seen Angie safely home Suzanna recalled the statement she needed to sign from the night before.

"Oh Pat," She asked. "Could we run by City Hall, so I could run in and sign that report, it'll only take a minute."

"Are you sure? Ma's expecting us, and you know how rushed things are on Bible study nights."

"It shouldn't take anymore then that, oh by the way, do you still have that note?"

"No, I gave it to Steve Williams earlier. I saw him at Ben's"

"What did he say about it?"

"He said he'd try to get you a shadow."

"Huh?"

"A tail."

"A what?"

"Somebody to follow you to make sure something doesn't happen to you and to catch anyone who might try something."

"Like a body guard?"

"Not exactly, this guy won't be so obvious."

"Wow! and I can't even tell anybody. It's not fair."

"It's not a game" Pat responded soberly as he pulled up in front of the building.

It was a good forty-five minutes before Suzanna and Pat left City Hall.

"Well" Pat remarked, "There goes supper."

"And there goes Dad's good graces, which I'm seldom in anyway."

"He'll understand."

"What time is it?"

"Six thirty-two, do you want to stop at the drive-in for a bite, we'll have to rush to make service as it is."

"Yeah, let's. By the way, was ma concerned when you called?"

"She's worried about you."

"At least somebody is."

"What does that mean."

"I just wonder sometimes, if anyone really cares."

"You know better."

"I guess, but there are times I have to convince myself of it."

"Me too."

"You! My outgoing self-confident brother."

"Hold it Suez,.. I think everyone has thoughts or doubts about whether anyone cares. It's what we do with those thoughts that makes the difference."

"I guess I handle them wrong then."

"You said it, I didn't" He laughed as they pulled into the drive-in.

Daves food was indeed delicious and the two were both enjoying their hurried meal as they travelled home.

"I almost forgot to mention something to you."

"What's that?"

"Denni told us that Jeff Johnson had asked him to drop by and pick him up for church tonight."

"That's great!" Pat said enthusiastically. "I had suspected as much, though. Jeff's a neat guy. I really like him, too bad Dennis' other friend has to be such a slime."

"I agree."

"You do?"

"Absolutely."

"What changed your mind?"

"I guess I just kinda began to think things through a little more."

"Thank God." Pat sighed. "That's a relief."

Pat had just turned the car onto their street when Suzanna gasped. "Pat look!" She pointed to a teenage boy playing basketball with Luke in the Rhodes driveway.

"Speaking of the Slime." He said sarcastically.

"I wonder what he wants?"

"I don't."

Suzanna shot her brother a murderous glare as the car pulled into the driveway.

Brady smiled as they pulled in. He quickly walked over to Suzanna as she left the car. "Hey, that brother of yours is getting good for a pip-squeak." He winked at Luke.

"I'm sure he is." Suzanna responded "That's all he ever does, he gets a lot of practice." Luke stuck out his tongue at her.

"I was wondering if you'd ever get home." Brady stated.

"I got held up at the station, the questions they asked me were unreal. I can't stop to chat now I've got to hurry and get ready for Bible Study."

"Yes, I know. Your father invited me along with your family."

"He did?"

"Sure, you better hurry, we're leaving in half an hour." He gave her that enchanting smile of his, as she fled into the house.

"Dad! How could you." She demanded as she stormed into her fathers office.

"Oh," He responded obviously surprised at her outburst. "Did I do something wrong."

"It's terrible! How could you? You invited Brady along to Bible Study tonight."

"Of course dear." Her father said surprised. "I'd invite the president of the United States if I thought he'd come."

"But Dad! You don't understand."

"Obviously not."

"I can't believe this is happening to me!" She got up quickly to leave, but her father stopped her.

"Stay put." He demanded as he strode over and shut the office door. "Okay, what's this all about tell me everything."

Suzanna slumped down in a seat. Self consciously she put her head in her hands as she tried to control the sobs that wanted to escape from her. Her father wrapped his arms around her tenderly.

"Go ahead, don't be ashamed to cry. You've been through a lot, I've shed tears myself the past few days."

"You have?" she sniffed.

"Yes, I have, in fact I surprised even myself when I did."

Suzanna was crying uncontrollably now and her father left her and began pacing the room as he did he spoke quietly.

"Life can be mighty complicated Suzanna, there's decisions to make all the time. It's hard to make the right ones, and often the decisions you know you must make go against your better judgment."

"I have no idea what's going on between you and that young man out there, but I've a feeling you're very confused. Indeed you must have him confused too. At any rate he seems like a fine boy, he's intelligent, seems to be dependable, has a nice personality, and even you have to admit he is strikingly handsome. The only thing he lacks is God, and how else will he hear of the one who loves him unless he's told?"

"I know dad." Suzanna sniffed through her tears.

"It's my duty to see that he hears Suzanna, My whole purpose in life, even if it might hurt my daughter's feelings I owe it to God."

"Oh Dad, I'm sorry. I just don't know what to do anymore."

"Well, tell me about it?"

"Okay, but it all happened so fast." Suzanna began "It started last Thursday when I was out at Sarah's. I was gonna take Cam out and Brady was there with Denni. Well Denni let him borrow Prints and Brady asked if I'd go riding with him. I wasn't really sure if I should but I found it almost impossible to say no. And Dad we had so much fun, I really enjoyed it."

"I bet you did." Her father smiled.

"Well then Friday morning. He overtook me on the way to school and insisted on carrying my books. I couldn't get rid of him all day, although I did try. He was the one that told me the gossip about Ben Daniels. Boy did that shake me up."

"You know the truth now don't you?"

"Yes, dad, and I'm so glad" Suzanna said then continued. "Well the weekend was fairly quiet except for the call from Jeff about Brady's arrest Friday night. But Monday morning when I met Angie he was there, and he was really a jerk too. Imagine he thought Pat was my boy friend, it was kind of funny. Well he disrupted my whole day. Finding guys for each of my friends so we'd go to Charlies for lunch, and Dad some of these guys didn't have very good reputations; we were finally able to give them the slip outside Charlies. It was terrible."

"Then why did you still want to spend time with him?" Her father asked.

"That's the part I'm confused about. Most of the people I knew kept telling me to enjoy myself if I liked Brady, and you know Dad I actually began to think I did. But it wasn't him I liked."

"Oh, now I see." Her father smiled. "You don't like him in a special way, but you liked the attention and other things that went along with it."

"I'm afraid so. Oh Dad I'm so ashamed."

Edward Rhodes sighed loudly. "You are finding out right now that your fathers old fuddy-duddy rules are set for a reason." He said kindly. "I've gone into depths with all four of you children on how I wanted you to handle certain situations. In doing that you would have avoided being hurt as much as you are now." Silently he shook his head. "There are reasons I required you to be sixteen before you dated,.."

"We haven't been dating." Suzanna interrupted, her father ignored her.

"And there are reason's even your sister Cindi, at nineteen almost twenty, has had a chaperone. A heart is a very tender, and sensitive thing, and it can lead into dangerous predicaments that could have been avoided. There is nothing sinful in keeping company with Brady Downing, sweetheart. But as for what is going on inside you, when you allow his words to encourage thoughts and idea's that you know are wrong, you are tempting with something very dangerous that is better left alone."

"I know that now dad."

"I'm glad."

Neither Suzanna nor her father were quite ready when the Rhodes family left for the Bible Study so the rest were sent on ahead.

"We'll be along shortly." Reverend Rhodes stated.

"Are you sure dear?" His wife asked.

"Absolutely, you go ahead and take that young man with you."

"If that's what you want." She hesitated again before piling everyone into the car for the trip to church.

Cindi was in high form and all they heard on the short trip to church was Bob this, Bob that, and Bob does or Bob doesn't. It was after they had arrived at Church that Brady had to ask Pat quietly who Bob was.

The organist was just starting the first song when three young people greeted each other with smiles and waves before entering the building. One to hurry toward her family sitting near the front, the others to settle quietly in the back pew.

"Yea, though I walk through the Valley of the shadow of death I will fear no evil." Was the verse from Psalm 23 that was the topic for tonights bible study. As Brother Rhodes taught earnestly many agreed that sometime recently he'd seen perhaps a glimpse of that valley, just a glimpse of that shadow. Humbly he encouraged those that were present to place their trust and faith completely in him who was above all.

It was a simple message but many left uplifted by it, and many left changed.

Jeff Johnson, left in a different frame of mind. He felt he knew what the shadow of death might be like for his young mind found it hard to see beyond his present trials. Although they were great, he had chosen to allow them to burden him down in self pity. He left the sanctuary that night having taken the first step in releasing that burden and in return received a peaceable spirit and a great calm. He was overwhelmed.

"Boy" He said to Denni, "if I'd known I could get rid of my problems this easy I'd have done so years ago."

"Surprise Jeff. Your problems are still there. It's you that's different. Keep seeking him and you'll keep that peace."

"I will Den. I will." He stated through tears.

Another visitor didn't fair so well. Although it appeared to many that he did. Brady attempted to dissect most of what was said so he could repeat it for affect later, therefore anything that might have fallen on good ground got trampled first. He feigned interest, and in the end he assumed a false attitude of mild repentance. What he felt would make him look good to the preachers family but not go overboard.

Luke was the most deceived by Brady, for Brady proceeded to ask him simple questions that Luke felt so privileged to answer. Soon he found though that it might be best to have someone else speak with him so turning to Cindi he'd asked her to help explain the plan of salvation to this newly repentant and hungry heart. This pleased Brady quite well, and they spend quite a bit of time together discussing parts of the message. Bob was present and it wasn't long until they joined him.

"Oh Bob," Cindi smiled "This is Brady Downing, He's a friend of Suzie's."

"Hi"

"Hi, I've heard a lot about you."

"You have?" Bob asked. "From who?"

"Who do you think?" Brady smiled looking at Cindi.

"I had supposed you two were taking scripture but I guess it appears not." Bob stated obviously annoyed.

"But we were." Cindi stated calmly "Brady's just been around home a lot lately."

"Oh" Bob replied "The guys are waiting outside, we're going to Charlie's,.. you coming?"

"Sure," Cindi answered then after exchanging a few more words with Brady they left.

Brady had failed to see Suzanna after church, she was obviously avoiding him. He turned to look for her just as Brother Rhodes approached.

"Let me formally welcome you Brady, it was so good to have you with us." He held out his hand.

"And I really enjoyed it. Thank you, I hope I'm free to return."

"Anytime. The doors are open, so that whosoever will may come."

"I'm glad, I will return, and soon."

"I'm glad to hear that. You will always be welcome." Brother Rhodes answered. "By the way. Just to ease any doubts you might have about my young but very spirited daughter, she's obviously going to be giving you the cold shoulder. Don't let it bother you, take it like a man." At that he slapped Brady on the back and continued on to another couple he wished to greet.

Brady contemplated his words before leaving the Sanctuary. So Suzanna planned on giving him the cold shoulder treatment. What started that? She was the most impossible human being to understand. Well he would take it like a man, he had to, his standing in the preachers family depended on it. He left the Sanctuary to find a group of young people from school waiting outside.

Pat was there of course talking with Peggy and Angie who seemed to be taking in every word. The twins Matt and Mark Rankin were discussing music with Denni and Becky Franklin. Suzanna was nowhere around.

Luke soon appeared at his side.

"Pat wants to know if you'd like to stop at Charlies. They're kind of celebrating, Cindi and Bob you know. Some of their friends from Lincoln have come too."

"Not tonight kid. Okay. I've got a lot to think about." He stated.

"Oh sure, maybe some other time." Luke disappeared and Brady headed to the door, he'd only taken a step when Denni stopped him.

"Hey fella. After our spat this afternoon, I didn't know if I ever wanted to see your mug again, but I was so glad to see it. Thrilled to be exact."

"Thanks Den. I'm really sorry about this afternoon."

"You are?"

"Yea, you're surprised huh?"

"I've seldom heard you say you were sorry."

"This time I am. I've got a lot to be sorry for."

"We all do. But don't tell me tell him." And Denni pointed up. Brady automatically looked up but when he saw nothing but ceiling he realized his blunder and who he needed to apologize to. "It's called repentance" Denni whispered.

"I'll try it some time." Brady tried to act serious. "Where's Suzanna?"

"I think she walked outside a moment ago with Sister Chrys."

"Chrys? Do I know her?"

"I don't think so, she's our youth leader, she's kind of a wacko if you ask me but she's fun."

"Wacko?" Brady asked.

"Yea, crazy. Her brothers cool though."

"I'm gonna see if I can find Suzanna before I leave. I'll see you in school tomorrow."

"Sure" Denni responded "You going to Charlie's?"

"No not tonight."

"I'll see you tomorrow then."

"Bye Den." Brady stepped outside. A few people still stood around in groups talking. It was dark but Brady soon found Suzanna. She was in a small group of women and she held a tiny child in her arms. She noticed Brady approach and smiled.

"Brady, hi." She called.

"I thought I'd missed you?"

"No we're usually the last ones gone. It's kind of a tradition around here."

"Who's this fella?" Brady smiled down at the child.

"Oh, this is Nicki, he's my buddi and this is his mother Sarah Daniels, and Chrys Shephard."

"I've never met you Brady but I have seen you around. Your a friend of Denni's right." Sarah replied.

"Aha. Your farm came in handy last Monday when I ran out of gas and got a lift from Jeffer."

"Yes, I heard about your misfortune, I'm glad Jeff could help."

"Where is Jeff, by the way?" Suzanna asked.

"He's with my brother somewhere" Chrys replied.

"Jeff is here?" Brady was surprised.

"You didn't know?" Suzanna asked.

"No, he didn't tell me he was coming and I hadn't seen him."

"I think they're over by Mikes truck." Suzanna handed little Nick to his mother and led Brady away. "I need to talk to you anyway." She whispered.

"I thought so. But it's okay." He said softly.

"I need to apologize." Suzanna began "I led you to believe that you and I had a special relationship. Brady I was wrong. I was so confused about my feelings and stuff that because I enjoyed being with you I thought I liked you but it's not true. I liked the things you said, the compliments, the special attention,.. things like that but I was wrong to lead you to think anything more."

"We were both wrong." He spoke softly "Maybe through this whole confused relationship we can make just a vague passing acquaintance."

"It's not that bad, cheer up." Suzanna grinned. "I'm glad you understand but lets start again,.. as friends."

"Sure, and this looks like another friend." Brady stated as they met Jeff and Mike.

"Hey, Guy you'll never believe how surprised I am to see you." Jeff grinned.

"About as surprised as I am to see you." Brady answered.

The two began talking as Suzanna wandered away, Mike followed.

"How are you feeling today?" He asked politely.

"Oh Brother Mike, I'm fine, thanks to you. You and Chrys were and answer to prayer."

"But it was your prayer."

Another day was ending, more souls had been drawn nearer to God, yet at the same time what more could be up the sleeve of others. Perhaps if one could see into the hearts of those such as Brady Downing fewer would be rejoicing, for when guards are lowered, when resistance is down, that is when the enemy is most likely to strike. For some it was a time to mourn.

CHAPTER 14

A TIME TO DANCE

Thursday, September 22, 1983

Movement in the room disturbed Sarah's sleep Thursday morning.

"Ben?" She whispered without opening her eyes.

"What is it dear?" He asked.

"Are you leaving early again?" She asked.

"I'm just returning."

"You are? What time is it?"

"5:30, about time you got up."

"Yeah, right."

"Well if that's the way you feel about it go back to sleep, I'll wake Nick to show him what I've got." Ben left the room.

"Benjamin Daniels get back here!" Sarah demanded "Don't you dare wake that baby."

"If you don't quit yelling like that you'll be the one to wake the baby." Ben returned to the room and sat on the bed beside Sarah. She could tell he was trying hard to conceal something from her.

"Okay, what do you have?"

"Wouldn't you like to know?" He said sarcastically.

"Come on, let me see." She begged.

"It'll cost you a kiss."

She quickly gave him a kiss on the cheek.

"I said it would cost you a kiss" Ben repeated. "I didn't consider that a kiss."

"Maybe your idea of a kiss is different than mine."

"I don't think so." He grinned "Try again."

She did.

"Much better." Ben got up to leave.

"Hey! Turkey." Sarah called "You're supposed to show me what you've got!"

"Oh, that's right." Ben teased "Close your eyes until I say open them."

A moment later, with her eyes closed Sarah began to feel movement on the bed.

"Can I open my eyes?" She asked.

"Okay go ahead."

Sarah opened her eyes and squealed. There before her waddling around on the bedspread was the tiniest little German Shephard puppy she had ever seen.

"Ben, He's so cute. Is he ours?"

"Yup. I told you I wanted one. Someone dropped him by last night while we were in church and Rich left him in the barn with Alphi, this one, my dear; is guaranteed to bark."

The puppy took a playful bite out of Sarah's finger as she picked him up.

"Don't start that now." She reprimanded.

"This fella's gonna stay with me in the barn. Bring Nick out when he gets up, to see him."

"Sure, what's his name?"

"I haven't decided yet, got any idea's?"

"No, not really, but I'll think about it."

After Ben left, Sarah slowly prepared for the day. After her shower she sat for awhile and read her bible.

How she hated to wake up each morning but she always felt better after she'd prayed and talked to God. His word spoke to her heart in a new way each morning. God truly was good to her.

She quickly made the bed and headed to the kitchen. There was no sound coming from the baby's room and she was pleased. Her thoughts wondered back to the evening before, and the bible study. As she dusted the living room she began to think of the two young visitors that had joined them in service.

Jeff was a fine level headed boy, although she knew a little of his experimenting with alcohol and drugs, she liked him. She harbored secret hopes of his full salvation. It thrilled her to think of it.

Brady though, she had never met. Sure she'd seen him but last night was the first she'd spoken to him at all. He seemed like a very nice boy and if Br. Rhodes approved of him, she should too. He sure was nice looking. Sarah wondered vaguely if there was something serious in the making between him and Suzanna. The thought startled her for Suzanna was like a daughter to her, but then she would be fifteen soon.

'Time does fly doesn't it?' She said aloud.

Sarah had a long day planned so when Nicolas woke that morning Mom hurried to his side.

"Good morning little fellow." She sang. "Wait 'til you see what your daddy's got out in the barn."

"Da da Ba ba"

"Yes, Daddy's Bye bye, but we'll see him before we leave. Come now and have some yummy breakfast."

Nick was washed, dressed and finishing his yummy breakfast of cereal paste and watery fruit when a knock at the door startled Sarah.

"Come on in" She called as she continued feeding the baby. Sarah had gotten into the habit of calling out instead of going to the door for seldom did one come to their home that wasn't welcome. This morning it was Sylviah Martin, her presence always put Sarah on her guard but she knew the woman's word though often harsh were basically harmless.

"Hi honey!" Sylviah called as she entered "I just stopped by for a minute to chat, are you busy?"

"No, Nick's just finishing breakfast. Come on in. Sit down. Would you like a cup of coffee?"

"Just a small one Love if you have it." Sylviah requested as she seated herself at the table.

"Here you go" Sarah replied as she set the coffee in front of Sylviah. "What brings you out today?"

"Oh, nothing much. I needed to speak to Bill Winters about trimming Queenies hooves, as long as I was out here I thought I'd stop in."

"I'm glad you did." Sarah remarked. "How have you been?"

"Exhausted to tell the truth. We've been busy, busy, busy, and I just didn't seem to keep up like I usually did, I thought I was getting old and my years were telling on me."

"Don't say that Sylviah, your only in your thirties, you've got a whole life ahead of you."

"Well come to find out Love, I've more than a whole life ahead of me."

"Oh?" Sarah questioned, then seeing Sylviah's face she exclaimed. "NO!"

"You seem surprised."

"I just never considered it. Congratulations."

"Thank you, we just confirmed it yesterday and I couldn't wait to tell someone."

"I'm so happy for you." Impulsively Sarah went to her and gave her a hug, which Sylviah received rather coldly. "George must be pleased."

"Oh I don't know about that man!" Sylviah said exasperated. "He's acting like a little kid. He's already making plans to remodel one of the bedrooms for a nursery, we will of course."

"Oh of course." Sarah repeated. "Did you hear that Nick, there'll be another baby around here for you to play with soon."

In response Nick banged his sticky fist on his tray.

"When's the date,.. do you know?"

"Early March."

"That's the best time, the baby will have a whole summer to really grow before he's cooped up in the house for winter. Nick will be a year in April."

"When do you plan on having another one, or shouldn't I ask?"

"Oh, we plan on it. Soon hopefully."

"You make a good mother." Sylviah stated "I see plenty today I wonder about."

"I'm sure you'll be a good mother too." Sarah encouraged her.

"I am still in shock Sarah, believe me, at what I saw here the other night. Imagine a grown man beating on his own son like that. And the mother, she should have known better than to show her face around here."

"But Sylviah, both Judy and Ray are welcome here anytime. They're friends. Their horses are here. We have no reason to send them away."

"Even after the fight? Sarah surely even you can't allow that behavior."

"Your right we won't and Ben spoke to Ray about it."

"Well I hope he listens. I just don't understand men. Sometimes they overreact to such an extent it scares me."

"Some men do, and some women do." Sarah contradicted.

"Oh I'm aware of that too dear, but Men become so violent."

"Protective?" Sarah suggested.

"You think so?"

"Sure, but I know plenty of women who are that way too."

"Well, if Ray Johnson's protective he sure is going about protecting his son the wrong way."

"That was an accident."

"Don't be so sure Sarah, he hit another young boy yesterday in one of his classes. They had to get half the faculty to drag him from the room."

"I find that hard to believe." Sarah said honestly.

"I'll have you know I heard that from a very reliable source. But news will get back to you some other way I'm sure. It's just a shame that a man as deranged as that should be active in our education system."

"Come now Sylviah, it's not quite that bad."

"Oh, but it is dear, who knows what else will go on inside those classroom walls if we're not careful."

Sarah, left the table, unable to respond to Sylviah's words, she grabbed the rag and began to clear off her son's tray, and lifting him down returned to the table.

"Will you have the baby in town here?" Sarah wondered.

"Oh definitely, but George is pretty nervous. He's delivered umpteen number of babies but he's yet to deliver his own."

"That would make any man nervous."

"Oh by the way, I hear that Morrison girl had her baby."

"Yes she did. I plan on going to see her this morning. She's home alone most of the day now."

"It's such a shame but I expect things will be changing soon." Sylviah paused and when Sarah didn't inquire she continued. "I've heard that the oldest son of your Pastor has been spending a lot of time with the young lady."

"They've been friends for years."

"Oh Sarah, don't start that now. Young teen-age boys don't retain friendships with pregnant women."

"She's only seventeen Sylviah."

"You know what I mean. That boy is interested in something."

"Probably her soul Sylviah. Pat is a fine boy. He was one of the baby's fathers best friends. Such a friend that he wouldn't think of deserting Michelle now."

"Right, and where is that so called friend? Don't be so sure of that boys motive Sarah not all men are as trust worthy as that husband of yours appears to be."

Sarah wanted to say more, actually she wanted to choke the woman but she knew anything said or done would only bring on another torrent of gossip. She went on with a few simple chores ignoring Sylviah's chatter.

With little Nick bundled against the late September wind Sarah hurried from the house toward the stable and Ben's office.

"Want to see what daddy has? Want to see what daddy has?" She repeated over and over to her son.

"Da da da da" Nick babbled.

Sarah peeked into Ben's office and finding it empty went in search of the puppy. The first place to look of course, was by Old Bill.

"Ey Missy!" He called welcoming "This ere varmints been after me britches legs all mornin' he keeps this up and no one will get through dem doors even in broad daylight."

"I think that's the idea." Sarah responded "Alphie is just too passive."

"This fella here sure has fire in 'im."

The puppy was waddling around under Old Bill's feet, chewing on his boot laces and tugging at the cuffs of his overalls.

"He took a snooze a bit ago, which only gave him more energy to attack."

"Come,.. come,.. " Sarah called as she knelt on the saw-dust floor still holding Nick. The puppy waddled toward her. It's sharp teeth dug playfully into Sarah's hand.

"Ouch" She pulled her hand away. "Maybe it's not safe for Nick."

"Pup won't hurt 'im none" Bill answered positively.

Sarah held the puppy for Nick to see. He reached forward grabbed a paw and tried to put it in his mouth.

"You young man are more dangerous than that puppy." Sarah exclaimed. "Everything in the mouth. I don't know about you."

"You found him then" Ben said as he entered the barn. He was leading his new colt which he had been working with in the arena.

"Yes we did. We've also found that both him and your son have one thing in common."

"They do? What's that?"

"Everything goes in the mouth." Sarah explained.

"True" He smiled "But hopefully they'll both grow out of it."

Ben took the puppy from Sarah and held him fondly. "Your taking the car?" He asked.

"Yeah, I've tons of errands to run in town. You don't mind?"

"No not at all. Do you mind stopping at the bank for me, it'll save me a trip later."

"Okay. I'm gonna see a few people and have lunch with Chrys so don't plan on me being around."

"What time will you be back?"

"Hopefully before one so I can put Tiger to bed for his nap."

"He'll need one by then."

"Anything special you want from the store?"

"Let me think," Ben said as he led the way to his office leaving the Mark of Fortune for Bill to tend.

It had become chillier the past few days, becoming more and more like fall. Many of the trees had lost their leaves, and most farmers had gotten in the last crops. Men had been working since early yesterday in Ben's fields harvesting the last of his hay for the winter. Both Denni and Tom had helped once their daily chores were finished. Rich had joined the crew today and Sarah knew that Ben himself would join a bit later.

Autumn had always been one of Sarah's favorite times of the year. She loved the colors, the sounds, even the smells that accompanied it. Today as she drove into town her spirits soared. Life seemed so real and full and exciting to her. She was so thankful to be alive. Tuesday afternoon as she had looked on the scene of the accident and been told of the fatality that had occurred she had been shocked with the realization that it could have been her. She could so easily be wiped out. Life was too precious.

Once again the word Trust came to her mind. She had found it so hard to trust Ben when she didn't know the facts, yet so easy to trust him when she did. Here she was driving down a highway trusting that no one would hit her head on and cause her life to end. Wasn't she putting her trust in something superficial, man made, and yet it seemed so hard to trust God at times, and so hard to trust Ben whom she knew was following God.

Nick had complete trust in her. But what did he know, the only way he could distinguish anything was by putting it into his mouth to explore it. He knew nothing of values or ideas. All he knew was the mom was there and that she took care of him.

Why couldn't she become as that little child? Why couldn't she just realize that God was there and that he would take care of her. Oh she wanted to, how she really wanted to.

She entered town and drove toward the bank.

"Well Nick, your father is about to Trust the bank with his hard earned money and he thinks nothing of it. To tell the truth I never did either, 'til now. I think buddy that we take the idea of trust to lightly at times and at others are to serious about it."

The Roberts Junction Security Bank was on the main street in town, across from city hall. It was a modern building, with a small square in front containing a fountain and a few park benches.

Sarah parked the car beside the building and after gently gathering Nick from where he'd been secured in his car seat she entered the building. The lobby was quite large and each of the tellers windows were occupied, some had small lines forming before them. Sarah spotted Cindi at the far window and headed in that direction.

Cindi smiled pleasantly when she spotted Sarah and continued to help the elderly gentleman who was doing business.

"Look, Nick'l, Look who do you see?"

"Da da, da da!"

"No cereal brain, that's not Dada that's Cindi."

"DaDa" Nick insisted.

"Okay, have your way,.. but your wrong."

"Da Ba Da Ba" Nick continued.

Sarah prepared the papers that Ben had given her and waited as the man before her moved aside. He smiled at Nick as he left.

"Hi Cin" Sarah began "Time for Ben Daniel's weekly deposit."

"I was expecting it." She smiled as she went about recording the transaction. "I've been so excited all week. Imagine, me of all people getting married."

"That's not a surprise at all." Sarah said honestly.

"Well it was almost impossible for me to even meet any boys with Dad hovering around all the time. He must have learned that it wouldn't do any good because he seems to let Suzanna do as she pleases."

Sarah excepted the receipt and began putting it into her purse.

"What do you think of that boyfriend of Suzie's, Sarah? He sure is good looking."

"I really don't know him well. I've met him only once."

"Oh he is really nice, and considerate, he pays special attention to Luke too. Most teenagers wouldn't even think of it. Why he's wasting his time on my sister though, I'll never know."

"Maybe he likes her" Sarah suggested.

"Well" Cindi shrugged, "Somebody has too, she can be quaint sometimes and fun. I guess I'm around her so much I never see her good points."

"Remember that." Sarah said with a wink "After your married a few years. Don't ever let the little things Bob might do that irritate you fail to allow you to see the things about him that you love him for today."

Cindi looked puzzled, then smiled "I'm beginning to feel I should write a book. I'd title it 'Advice I received before marriage.'" She laughed, which Sarah was pleased to hear for Cindi seldom did. Maybe somewhere underneath her stony exterior there was a heart that only a certain young man could expose.

Michelle had just laid Joanna back down after her feeding when she heard a car pull into the driveway. Hurrying to the window she saw the Daniels' car and Sarah, retrieving Nick from his car seat. She hurried outside.

"Sarah! It's good to see you!"

"Michelle, you look great, but you should get inside it's chilly out here and look." Sarah pointed to Michelle's stockinged feet. "You don't have shoes on! What may I ask is the Baby gonna do if her mommy comes down with pneumonia?"

"Yes mom," Michelle said with a grin as she led the way to the house.

"I hope I didn't come at a bad time?"

"Yes, and no. The baby's asleep so you can't hold her, but you can take a peek if you want. But you will stay a bit and talk won't you?"

"Of course. Let's let baby sleep a bit, I'll take a peek before I leave. Now tell me how is everything?"

"Oh Sarah, it's just wonderful. That baby is so perfect, so tiny, I just marvel at her."

"But you'll be surprised how fast they grow. Nick was that small five months ago."

"That's right! He seems so big in comparison to Joanna, and yet he's so tiny himself."

"Joanna will grow too, Michelle. So cherish these days all you can."

"Oh, I am. She's all I have now. Sure I've got my parents, but although they've been great to me, Joanna is mine. My family."

There was such a tone of melancholy about Michelle's words that it startled Sarah, she had been so pleased to have the baby, still it seemed as if there was more to it.

"Pat has been a great friend." Michelle was saying. "He stops in every day if he can, I know with work, school, church and his family that it's rough but he finds time."

"Pat's always been that way." Sarah responded "I don't recall him ever doing a selfish thing in all the time I've known him."

"Really? And you've known him a long time?"

"Oh, not that long.. It's been seven years or so. Pat would have been lets see,..."

"Ten years old." Michelle supplied. "I'm surprised I didn't know him then, Roberts Junction being so small and all."

"Yea, it is pretty small. In fact some of the kids I baby-sat while in high school are in this years graduating class."

"They are?" Michelle seemed surprised.

"Hey, I'm not that old you know."

"Who did you baby-sit for?"

"Well the one I remember most is a year younger than you. My first baby-sitting job was for Bill and Ginny Little. Dennis parents. For him and his sister Connie."

"You baby-sat for Denni?"

"Sure, he was four and Connie was around one, that was twelve years ago."

"I guess it must be strange seeing him as much as you do?"

"No not at all, he's kinda like a kid brother to me, the good kind that never lived in the same home and fought with you."

Michelle laughed.

I also baby-sat for Jed Bently."

"Jed? I see him drive by here everyday in his hot car, what was he like twelve years ago?"

"I baby-sat him when he was eight. Only once or twice though. You'll never guess what he liked to play with."

"Your right I probably wouldn't."

"Hot wheels."

"Really? It's not hard to believe."

"He would take them apart. Paint them, put them together, race them. He had a lot of car models also."

"Boring, I bet he was a dud to baby-sit for."

"Jed? Oh I liked Jed. It was Denni that was the terror. Believe me." Sarah insisted.

"Denni? What did he do?"

"I really shouldn't say." Sarah said reluctantly.

"Now don't start getting me all curious and then refuse to tell me."

"Well, there was the time with the pail of water."

"Pail of water?"

"Sure. I had to put them to bed at 8:00 and he didn't want to go so I sent him to his room to change while I put Connie to bed. I put Connie to bed and walked into the kitchen and SPLASH! It was a perfect aim. I was drenched." Sarah and Michelle laughed.

"I have no idea how I finally cleaned the mess up but it was all over."

"What else did he do?" Michelle wanted to know.

"Well, I used to take my shoes off when I came. I'd leave them by the door. Well once one of my shoes was filled with shaving cream. The brat was sound asleep by the time I found it. I was so mad, more embarrassed really. His Dad couldn't quit laughing, Ginny at least tried." Sarah grinned.

"Boy am I glad he finally grew up and didn't need a sitter any more."

Sarah and Michelle had a nice talk about kids and sitting jobs while Nick explored the room, the furniture, and anything tiny he could fit in his mouth.

"Oh dear," Sarah exclaimed "I forgot Joanna's gift out in the car. Keep an eye on Nick, I'll be right back." She was out the door before Michelle could object.

"Well Nick, you should have told your mother that she didn't need to buy anything, she's already done plenty just by stopping by."

"Dada, Da da" Nick stated.

"Daddy huh?" Michelle said, then turned sober. "Your a lucky kid Nick, you've got a wonderful Daddy."

"Da da da da"

"I don't look much like a daddy do I?" Michelle asked. "But I guess I am."

Sarah returned carrying a gayly wrapped package.

"Sarah, you didn't have to do this you know that."

"But I wanted to," Sarah handed Michelle the box.

"The box is so pretty, I almost hate to open it."

"Oh, go ahead."

Michelle opened the package and after lifting the lid of the box she exclaimed.

"Oh Sarah, It's gorgeous. Did you make it?" She held up a small baby quilt, obviously hand made.

"It was fun, I'm glad you like it. Theres a note in there for you."

Tears came to Michelle's eyes as she read.

> Although this quilt is not perfect made,
> Although each square not perfect laid
> Although these hands that formed them
> may have failed in such a way
>
> When you look at every square
> think only of the love that's there
> a gift from me to you
> that's made with prayer,

And realize that in your life too
things may not fit like they should do
But there is one that's perfect
and he watches over you.

For on our lives he looks with pride,
and is not concerned with what we hide
so open your heart,...
and let him inside.

We Love you
Sarah, Ben, and Nick

Charlies Cafe' was quite full when Sarah, and Nick met Chrystal for lunch.

"Sarah Mae!" Chrys called when she entered. Sarah smiled.

"I almost didn't make it!" Chrys began. "I'm so booked with jobs right now I'm getting dizzy."

"Business is good then?" Sarah asked.

"It always gets tougher in fall because a lot of people make an early push for the end of the year."

"I'm glad. What are you working on right now?"

"Well,.. just this last week I signed contracts for, signs, ad's, a billboard, and can you believe it,.. I'm even working on a display in a store window."

"You won't get bored with that much of a variety." Sarah pointed out.

"Can you imagine if I would have taken a job in a firm of some type, I'd be doing the same thing over and over. I love it this way. In fact I've got a special meeting this afternoon."

"Oh really, another contract?"

"I hope so. The city is looking for a special display to put up in the town square. They can build it they're just looking for a designer."

"Well good luck with all of it."

"Thanks Sarah, I know you mean it." Chrys began "Oh look here's Charlie."

The two chatted with the gentleman who had seen them enter and had come to greet them. They both ordered their food, Sarah gave Nick some juice and a cracker.

"How is your day going. You've already heard about my whole week." Chrystal asked her friend.

"You wouldn't believe this hubby of mine."

"Your right, I wouldn't what did he do now?"

"He bought a puppy."

"Really? For the barn right?"

"Right, but that's where it's needed I wouldn't want a smelly dog in the house all the time."

"Only farm dogs smell."

"I live on a farm Chrys."

"Just teasing, what kind is it?"

"A shepherd, a black and tan one."

"Ah ha! he is getting a watch dog."

"His first suggestion was a pit bull."

"Be thankful he changed his mind."

"I am,... oh before I forget, guess who came to see me this morning."

"Who?"

"Sylviah"

"Ug, I still haven't gotten over that last conversation I had with her."

"She had some really surprising news."

"Don't be too quick to believe it."

"I doubt if she'll lie about this." Sarah began "Give her a few months and it will be obvious."

"What will?" Chrys was confused.

"She'll be having a baby in March."

Chrystal gasped "NO!"

"Yes"

"The poor thing. Oh my."

"I think they'd make fine parents."

"You do? Well like I said I haven't quite recovered from my last talk with her."

"It was a surprise to me also."

"Maybe it will improve her personality."

"It didn't improve mine." Sarah pointed out.

Charlie personally brought their food to the table. They enjoyed it immensely.

"I'm gonna have to quit eating here." Chrys began "I've worn a permanent path from here to my shop."

"Well at least you're eating well. I worry about you and Mike not bothering about meals, or taking the time, your both such work-aholic's. It can't be healthy."

"I was wondering why every time I stop at your place your trying to feed me."

"Just caring for the people I love, that's all."

"Well, you needn't worry. Mike and I manage fine. I admit sometimes he's late getting home, or I get busy on a project, but usually we enjoy our meals together. At least we have breakfast."

"Is it working out with the two of you?"

"Oh it's working just fine. Mike and I have always been close. It's funny lately I've been getting on his case because he's not interested in girls and he's been getting on my case because I'm not dating."

Sarah smiled. "I can just see the two of you going around and around about it."

"It gets funny at times. In fact you should have heard him the other night on the way home from your place. He was bragging up that friend of Bens,.. Rich,.. feeling me out to see if I was interested in him. Imagine."

"Are you?"

"Sarah Mae Daniels I hardly know him."

"I didn't ask if you knew him, I just wanted to know if you were interested in him."

"No I am not! and do you want to know what else?" Chrys said in jest. "I think you and my brother are both ready for the nut house."

"Chrystal he is not that bad."

"I didn't say he was bad. I said I wasn't interested. I'll use my brothers phrase,. if someone special comes along, I'll be interested."

Sarah laughed. "The both of you are chips off the same block I'm sure."

"Our parents were no spring chickens when they got married,.. and they were happy."

"Just look at their offspring,. right?" Sarah teased. The two laughed. It had already been a long day for Nick and he began dozing in his chair. "Oh no, I've still got groceries to get before I head home. You can't sleep now." She tapped on his tray to stir him awake.

"Are you heading home right now?"

"Well," Sarah began "I do have to see Sister Rhodes. I want to have a party at the house for Suzanna's fifteenth birthday. The morning just went too fast."

"Let me know if I can be of help with the party okay."

"Sure, I'll do that."

The two departed, the free-lance commercial artist to her meetings and drawings. The farmers wife to her birthday plans and grocery shopping.

Two so totally different lives.

Two such close friends.

Michelle sat on the rocking chair, her head in her hands tears flowing down her cheeks. She could barely keep up the charade any longer,.. seeing Nick had not helped. A knock on the door startled her. Quickly she wiped her eyes.

"It's Pat, Michelle, can I come in? Don't bother getting up."

She took a deep breath before answering. "The doors unlocked come in. I didn't expect you."

"I'm sure you didn't. I brought you lunch, something wholesome and nutritious,.. Ta da" He pulled it out of the sack "Chicken soup, guarantied to taste just like Mama's. The Lady at the Deli at Gary's assured me of it." They both laughed for it was Michelle's mother who worked in the Deli and had made the chicken soup.

"Oh Pat, I don't know what I'd do if people like you didn't care." She reverted back to her sulky mood.

"Now this doesn't sound like the mother I heard talk yesterday of how excited she was to be home with her baby."

"I am Pat, I really am, but it's harder than I thought." She broke down crying "Why don't you leave, I'll be okay in a little while."

"I have no intention of leaving until you tell me why you're so down."

"But it doesn't concern you."

"Anything that concerns a friend of mine is my business." Pat stated boldly. Then after a minute or two of her crying he continued. "I will leave Michelle if that is what you'd *really* like."

They were both sitting in the Morrison's living room, Michelle still in the rocker, Pat in the chair next to her. She reached out and took his hand, he held hers gently.

"You're a good friend Pat, I can trust you not to criticize me or judge me for the way I feel,.. please don't. I just feel so alone."

"But God's here Michelle and, he knows what you're going through."

"Sometimes that's hard to believe." She began "Sarah Daniels was here today. I guess I'm upset over her visit."

"She upset you?" Pat asked surprised.

"Oh Pat she was wonderful, we had such a great time. She brought Nick along but,..." Michelle broke into sobs again.

"What did she do? Did she say something that hurt you? I'm sure she didn't mean it."

"No, no, no, She did nothing. It's just that when she left, she had somewhere to go. She had a home, her little boy only five months older than Joanna has a father who calls him buddy and tickles him to make him smile, and Joanna has a father who doesn't even know she exists." Michelle cried some more but soon she stopped and said to Pat who still held her hand.

"All right, I'm done now. I'll go on from now, happy, patient, accepting my life, my role, my family. Do me a favor Pat, forget I ever said a word."

"I have no intention of forgetting what you said." Pat began "I'm your friend I want to help. I know someone who can heal all that is hurting inside you right now."

"I wish I could believe you, I wish I could believe Sarah, I wish I could believe Chrys. But Pat, if God loves me tell me, please tell me, why did he allow Joe to leave? Why?"

"God loves Joe too, and although I don't exactly know why God allowed this I know God will not force Joe to do his will, just like he is leaving you a choice also. Nothing could have kept Joe against his will."

"If things had only been different. If we had only not made that one stupid decision. If only we could go back all those months, and do it all over everything would be perfect."

"No it wouldn't."

"Yes it would Pat! I've learned my lesson I realize now."

"But you learned the lesson after you made the mistake. If you went back and did it all over the outcome would be the same. Nothing could change because it took this experience to make you wiser to make you understand."

"Don't talk like that, you make me sound like some idiot who wouldn't listen to reason."

"Well,.. you didn't. Many people tried to reason with you and Joe, it's too late to take advise now. It's time you took the responsibility and with or without Joe go on with your life. You owe it to that baby Michelle."

"You aren't sounding like much of a friend."

"Sometimes friends don't say what we want to hear."

Elizabeth Rhodes cut a generous piece of Coffee Cake for Sarah as they sat with cups of coffee at her kitchen table.

"This is what I have in mind." Sarah began "We can have a surprise hay ride. During the ride they can stop, have a bonfire and roast Hot Dog's and Marshmallows. When we return we can have cake and ice cream while sitting on bales of hay in arena."

"Sarah you don't have to do all that."

"I want to and I've already had several offers for help."

"You have mine also."

"Your helping right now." Sarah responded.

"Let me make my own daughters cake at least."

"Please do. That would take a lot off my shoulders." Sarah continued. "Now for the guest list. Who should we have?"

"Oh, the regulars,.." Elizabeth began "Peggie, Becki, that new friend of theirs Angie, Connie, Jeanie, Debbie, and well maybe Cindi."

"That's eight counting Suzanna. Pat will be there and Luke too probably,.. that's ten."

"That's quite a lot already."

"But I've only started. Denni's gotta be invited and the twins of course,.. Matt and Mark, Paul Bennet,.. can you think of any others?"

"Sarah, are you sure you want to have a hay ride with twenty some teenage boys and girls?"

"Of course, I trust them" Sarah said quickly then continued "We've got fourteen, fifteen if you include Cindi's shadow,.. Bob."

"What about Chrys and Mike and maybe that young girl Michelle."

"Great idea, that's eighteen already." Sarah wrote the suggestions on a small legal pad. Now what about those two friends of Denni's, Jeff Johnson, and Brady what's-is-name, should we include them?"

"Oh, I hadn't even thought of them. I can't see why not. They are her friends."

"Well that gives us twenty already. I'll have to have either Tom or Denni drive the team and Ben, Chrys and I will chaperone."

"You'll have your hands full."

"But I'll enjoy it."

"At least let me take Nick off your hands that night." Elizabeth offered.

"You are aware that one five month old can be more trouble then twenty teenagers." Sarah stated.

"You are aware that one teenager can be more frustrating than twenty five month olds." Elizabeth retorted.

"We'll see." Sarah agreed.

Sarah glanced at Nick sleeping contentedly in the seat beside her. It seemed such a shame to wake the poor kid just to get a few groceries. It was already past one and she was late.

"Well sport, it's now or never." She lifted the still form and carried him tenderly into the store.

Grocery shopping always frustrated Sarah. She hated making decisions, she hated the crowds, and she hated the fact that she was buying food and they'd eat it, and then she'd have to replace it in two weeks.

She had strapped Nick to her with a baby pouch and he was again resting contentedly.

"Looks as though you'll be up all afternoon." She sighed.

"Why Sarah Daniels, how are you?" A voice called. Sarah turned to find an old friend she hadn't seen in months coming toward her.

"Why Lynn. Hi" Sarah greeted. "I'm doing excellent and you?"

"Oh so, so,.. you know." Lynn shrugged. "And is this your little one?"

"Yes this is Nicholas."

"My how things change. Sometimes it seems like yesterday that you and Shep and I were sitting in the stands at the ball games drinking hot chocolate spiked with brandy."

"And sqeaking our clarinets" Sarah added. "I try to forget those days."

"Imagine, I've got a boy in first grade, and now here you are with yours. We used to joke about having kids and now you up and had your first without me even knowing it."

"Our lives have changed a lot." Sarah observed.

"What about Shep, She isn't hitched yet is she?"

"Well she wasn't when I last saw her,.. an hour ago."

"Who knows she might be one of those fast workers."

"I seriously doubt it."

"Why don't the three of us get together some time and talk, just like old times."

"That would be fine Lynn, except it won't be like old times."

"I suppose not, well I'll give you a call anyway."

"Do that, or stop by. Bring your boys, we've got barns full of horses, kittens and pups for them to torment."

"Hey, I'll do that." Lynn remarked as she moved on.

'I wonder what that will lead to.' Sarah wondered as she chose her groceries.

Pat left Michelle's house a little after twelve and headed to school for his fifth hour class.

"Life just doesn't seem fair." Pat mused "People find it so easy to blame problems of their own doing on God." Pat wasn't upset with Michelle. He pitied her, he felt that life had dealt her a rough blow. "Face it Rhodes" He said to himself "Things are not all rosy for that young lady."

He began to think of the other girls in school with him. He'd heard the stories, he'd been around the boys as they'd boasted. Why did Joe and Michelle's mistake have this result and not the others. If Pat had known the number of abortions performed on his classmates he'd have been shocked. Michelle had made a choice, Pat himself had encouraged it.

Pat joined the other students in his class, his thoughts far from his academic studies. Michelle's spirit had been crushed and Pat had compassion for her but what could he do? Nothing beyond what he'd already done. He knew that. Still he longed to see that bright spontaneous smile Michelle had always had return.

If Pat hadn't been a better student this past weeks work would have really suffered. But he was quick with his mind and well able to grasp enough to still do average work although far below his norm. He'd be glad when this class was over and he could return to the crew. No work was planned at Daniels until Monday but preliminary work would be done at the shop. Pat enjoyed anything that involved building. His thoughts were so involved he had failed to realize that the teacher had stopped beside his desk. Pat felt a hand on his shoulder that startled him.

"Yes Mr. Wiseman?" He asked.

"I'd like to see you after class Patrick, Okay."

"Um, ah sure." Pat stammered.

"Until then, try to keep your mind on your work."

"Yes, sir." Pat stated.

Class period was almost over and Pat did concentrate on his work until the sound of the bell reminded him of his talk with Mr. Wiseman. He knew he was about to be corrected for not being alert in class and it bothered him. He'd always been a star pupil. Cautiously he approached the teachers desk.

"I'm glad you waited Pat." Mr. Wiseman began as he pulled a chair next to his desk. "Sit down."

As Pat seated himself Mr. Wiseman prepared a few papers for the next class.

"I just wanted to ask you what plans you had after graduation."

Pat was relieved.

"I'd always thought I'd go on to college sir, but now I'm not sure."

"Your not?" Mr. Wiseman seemed surprised. "You are an excellent student, you'd benefit a lot from more schooling, what changed your decision?"

"I guess I like my job." Pat spoke honestly. "I work after school and during the summers for Frank Girard."

"Oh, I see." His teacher smiled "I'm glad you like the work, very few people find work they like and are therefore tormented all their lives with hatred for their jobs."

"I work with Mike Shephard, he's a great boss."

"Not all of them are though Pat. Don't put the thought of college aside. Think about it. It would be a shame if in ten years you wished you had done things differently."

Other students had begun to file into the class room for Mr. Wiseman's next class. He continued. "Let me know if you have any ideas, feel free to stop in and mention it. I'd like to help."

"Thank you sir. I'll keep it in mind." Pat stated as he left the room.

True to the nature of most babies Nick was wide eyed and chattering when Sarah finally returned home, well after 1:00.

"I guess there will be no afternoon nap for you fella." She commented "Well lets see if we can find a little shephard puppy somewhere."

She entered the dimly lit stables and walked quickly past the rows of stalls. She could hear Old Bill merrily whistling a tune in the work shop. She began to smile herself, Bill's moods were always contagious.

"Hi Bill," She greeted "We've come to see the puppy."

"Oh, that outlaw is finally sleepin' off his energy."

"Outlaw huh?"

"That's what he is missy, not a righteous bone in his body." Bill teased.

"Congratulations Bill, I think you've done it."

"Done what?"

"Well Ben asked me to think of a name for the little fella and you just have."

"I have?"

"Sure, we'll call him 'Outlaw'."

Bill laughed. "Quite a name to live up to missy."

"I think it fits." She smiled at the little bundle asleep on a small pile of straw. She glanced over at Bill as he continued his work, preparing shoes for 'the Queen's' hooves. Sarah patted the horses neck.

"Every Lady needs a new pair of shoes now and then Queenie, you just don't get a large selection to choose from."

"They're weren't anything wrong wit de last un's, cept that de Ms. Martin likes em new every couple la weeks."

"Did she tell you any news?"

"That's all that womans good fer is news missy, cept I don't abide by none of it though."

"I mean about the baby."

"No, she didn't mention any baby. What baby's that?"

"Her baby."

Bill dropped his tool, and it landed solidly on his foot. "Ouch!" He said as he quickly moved his booted foot. "Why'd ya have to go and alarm me with a story like that?"

"It's not a story Bill,.. it's true."

Bill was silent. Soon he spoke. "The Doc'll have a few pretty long months commin' up if'n ye ask me."

"Oh, I just know he's pleased."

"I suppose so Missy, He's a good man, the doc is."

"And his wife is fine too." Sarah persisted. "She just likes to stretch things a little far."

"A *little* far missy?" Bill asked with a grin.

"Well sometimes,.. too far. Who knows she may be a wonderful mother."

"Who might make a wonderful mother?" Ben asked as he entered the shop.

"Sylviah Martin."

Ben studied Sarah's face. "She is? Well great, the Doc'll be on cloud nine." Ben was pleased. "How was your morning."

"Wonderful, Michelle and I had a great time, I've got most of the plans settled for Suzanna's party and Nick slept for one hour and fifteen minutes."

Ben held out his hands to Nick who went to him willingly.

"Hey buddy, what do you think of the puppy?"

"His name is 'Outlaw'" Sarah interrupted.

"Outlaw?"

"Bill named him. Claims he doesn't have a righteous bone in his body."

"Well it is a unique name." Ben commented as he caressed the sleeping puppy with one hand.

"And how is the Mark of Fortune coming along."

"Oh Sarah" Ben began "I am so pleased with him. He's hearty and active, in excellent health. He's probably one of the most valuable assets I have right now."

"He ought to be." Sarah remarked.

"I know, I risked a lot Sarah, and had to sacrifice a few of my best mares but in a few years it will all pay off. In a few years Fortune will be one of the most sought after stallions in the area. Mark my word."

"I hope your right Ben. I really hope you're right."

Suzanna entered the library during her free period and sought an open table. Opening her text book she became so absorbed that she didn't notice Brady enter until he'd pulled out the chair opposite hers and was seating himself.

"Hi" She smiled. He gave her that enchanting smile of his.

"I see you've got a friend today."

"You noticed."

"I notice things like that."

"Where is he now?"

"Back in the patrol car outside, he'll be waiting outside the library when the period is over."

"It's really embarrassing."

"But why is he there?"

"You don't know?"

"No, I thought all you had to do was sign those papers. I didn't think you'd be under surveillance or anything."

"Well my brother received a note yesterday, warning him that Tuesday was only the start, and that they'd failed. He was also warned to stay out of it or he'd be next."

"But why would someone want to hurt you?" Brady asked her curiously.

"Who knows, maybe I've got bad breath or something." Suzanna suggested with a laugh.

"It's not funny" Brady sounded angry. "Someone's trying to hurt you, seriously hurt you and you think it's funny."

"I'm sorry Brady, I didn't know you were so concerned."

Brady sighed exasperatedly "Hey let me get this straight last night both of us were finally in agreement. Nothing can become of our friendship it just wouldn't work, but Suzanna that doesn't mean I ceased to care. I care an awful lot. Right now I'd like to ring a few necks if only I knew whose necks they were."

"But what would that solve?"

"It would give them what they deserve that's what."

"Settle down Brady, It's not that bad, I'm not hurt. I've been scared. Twice in fact, but God has had his hand on me,...I'll be fine."

"Twice? Did something happen since yesterday?"

"No I just had someone pester me while I was at the farm baby-sitting Saturday night. Sabatoged all the electricity by pulling the main switch down at the stables."

Brady appeared to look stunned.

"Do you have any idea who it was?" He asked.

"My bet is it was the guy with the size 19 cowboy boots."

"Who?" Brady asked quickly then recalled his description, "Oh, him."

"But don't worry Brady, I've put my trust in God, he'll take care of me."

"I wish I could believe that." He stated. "I really do."

Rich and Tom had worked side by side with the men from the harvesting crew that Ben had hired. For two days they'd hauled, baled, stacked, restocked, shuffled and counted bales of freshly cut hay. Thursday afternoon found the two of them stacking the last of it in Bens feed barn. Denni had taken a group out on the trails after school so by the time the haying was finished the two were bushed.

"I'm almost to tired to climb down." Tom commented.

"I'm tempted to slide down the whole works but then I'd have to restock each one."

"It's been a good year." Tom commented as he glanced at the full stacks. "Ben'll have quite a bit on hand when he needs it."

"mmmHmm" Rich commented "Say Tom, I've been meaning to ask you. What all did you find Saturday night when you searched the stables."

"Just the blown breaker." Tom began "I flipped it then came back to the house."

"Well, it seems someone was prowling around that night."

"I wouldn't be surprised." Tom said.

"You wouldn't?"

"No, you recall I was missing before you had me search the stables."

"Yea, but I didn't think nothing of it."

"Well, I was chasing someone."

"You were?" Rich asked alarmed. "Why didn't you say something?"

Tom was silent.

"Come on kid, something up. Someone was around here scaring the daylights out of Suzanna and you clam up. What gives?"

"She told she was being scared huh."

"That someone was out there yea, she was pretty shook."

"That's hard to believe Rich."

"Why, you just claimed you saw the guy. Too bad you didn't catch up to him."

"But I did."

"You did?" Rich was really upset now. "Okay Tom, come clean, your holding something back. What is it?"

Tom was silent for awhile before continuing.

"I didn't want to mention anything because, I guess I didn't want to believe it."

Rich nodded for him to continue.

"Well, I told you I chased the guy and caught him. Well Rich, he wasn't a prowler."

"He wasn't?"

"No, he'd been at the house."

"I know that, I saw his footprints."

"I mean Suzanna let him in the house."

"Are you sure?"

"Almost, but it all adds up."

"What adds up?"

"Let me explain." Tom began. "It'll be hard because I dislike this creep so much, but here goes,.. Theres this fella that Suzanna's been hanging around with, his name's Brady Downing."

"Oh, yes, Denni's friend." Rich acknowledged "I saved her from him once."

"Well, he was the prowler. I'd seen him and Suzanna together a few times before then but thought she was smart enough to get rid of him. Then that night when I found him sneaking around the house, when she's alone with a sleeping baby,.. I kinda had a rough time believing she'd pull something like that."

"But Tom, Suzanna doesn't like him,.. it's ridiculous."

"If she doesn't like him, why is she still seeing him? The two were pretty close the other day when I saw them on horse back,.. one horse may I add."

"It's probably nothing."

"They're together a lot at school too."

"I don't understand." Rich was puzzled. "If she's seeing him and likes him, why would she ask me to get rid of him for her, and tell me she doesn't like him?"

Tom just shrugged.

"Like I said" Tom began. "I didn't want to believe it. Suzanna's always been a straight kid, why she'd mess around with him I don't know. He's no good Rich, you can't trust him."

Rich thought about it more. He longed to tell Ben about the incident but knowing Ben's protective quality he felt he'd get upset with Suzanna and she'd be out of a babysitting job and Rich wasn't even certain of the facts.

"Well," Rich thought to himself. "Suzanna's going to babysit again tonight for a few hours. I'll keep an eye on her and see what happens."

Ben was quite weary when he entered the kitchen for supper that evening. With both Rich and Tom helping the crew and Denni off with a group on the trail, the majority of the daily chores had fallen on Ben. He was used to hard work, in fact he enjoyed it, but he also was planning ahead and began to consider the possibility of hiring new help.

Sarah passed him a heaping plate of beef stew as he sat at the table. Nick was busy smearing his face and tray before him with cracker, as the cat moved to and fro following close behind Sarah. Sarah seated herself and Ben led in a short prayer.

"Oh Lord, we thank you for your provision, for supplying our needs. We ask that you take this food, help it to strengthen and nourish our bodies, we ask in your name."

They began eating. After a few moments Ben began.

"There's quite a bit of work around here now."

"I can tell you've been working hard." Sarah commented.

"I didn't get near what I'd planned done for today, and the sad thing about it is that things don't look any better for the rest of this week and well into next."

"I could give you a hand on a few chores. Nick could play in his walker."

"No, No, not that. I don't want you're help, I just need to look at the fact that during the harvest and most weekends we're pretty swamped. Maybe it's time we did hire more help."

"But you just hired Rich?" Sarah was confused. "How come all of the sudden you need to hire two?"

"I had the boys all summer Sarah, and when they started back to school it dawned on me that I hadn't replaced my favorite helper." He gave her a warm smile. "Rich is taking over your work remember, now with the new stables and extra work with the stallions, also with such a demand for trail rides on weekends another person ought to fill the gap. I just don't know if I should advertise or if I should approach someone I'm familiar with."

"I'm not too keen on having a stranger, someone we barely know working with the animals." Sarah mentioned concern in her voice.

"That's how I hired Tom remember?"

"I guess so." Sarah remarked quietly.

"How about if I put a notice on the board by the tack room. Anyone coming in will see it. Perhaps we'll fill it that way."

"That sounds a lot better." Sarah commented.

"I'll have them fill out applications then, we'll look at them and decide."

"You want me to decide with you?"

"Don't I always?"

"Well, I guess so. But I kind of thought things were different now because you never even mentioned you'd be hiring someone when you hired Rich."

"Oh Honey, I'm sorry. Did it bother you that I hired Rich without talking to you first?"

"It did for a while." She said honestly.

"Don't you like Rich?"

"Of course I like Rich, silly." Sarah laughed, "I just felt left out. I saw you going about the business of the farm and felt it didn't concern me."

"Oh, but it does." Ben looked concerned. "I'm sorry I've been so preoccupied lately I haven't paid a lot of attention to some things."

"Ben, it's okay." Sarah soothed.

"No it's not Sarah, I've had way to much on my mind. You and Nick are more important to me then this place, then Cruiser or Fortune."

"I know that, and I'd like to help, Don't let Rich completely take over for me."

"But Sarah, What about Nick?"

"He'll be fine Ben, I don't intend on riding Bucking Bronco's or showing ponies."

They both laughed.

"We'll talk about it later, for the time being I'm going to post that opening on the board."

"Who knows the response you'll get with that."

Peggy waited patiently for her grandfather. He was usually so punctual, what was keeping him. She set the table, and once again checked the food she had prepared.

She wasn't one to worry but lately she'd been concerned about Gramp's. He didn't appear sick, he still ate most of what she put before him, but he seemed so old, so tired all the time.

The sound of his car brought her from her thoughts. Thank God. She whispered. He's home.

Bill entered the house slowly, seeing Peggy he smiled.

"Hi Missy, sorry I'm late, took a little bit longer on a few jobs today then I'd planned."

"It's okay Gramps. Come and have some supper."

"It sure looks good." He commented as he hung his jacket in the closet. After returning to the table they began the meal. Peggy well aware that Gramps was unusually quiet.

"How was school?" He asked.

"Great!" She said enthusiastically. "My geometry test was a cinch. I'm so glad, I thought I'd really be stumped."

"I haven't seen you stumped yet." Bill smiled.

"Then Mrs. Whitefield judged our sewing projects today. I managed to get a B+"

"That's great Missy, I know you worked hard at it."

"And hated every minute." She commented.

"Schoolin' can't be all math and science, Peg. you know thet."

"Oh sure, I'll fight my way through Home-ec and Phy-ed, and detest it. But I'll thrive on the others."

"And ye do I kin see thet."

They continued their meal in silence. Bill not eating quite as much as usual and Peggy keeping close tabs on his behavior, her concern showing.

"I'm a bit tired tonight Missy." Gramps responded, after the meal was through. "I'll just read the paper and then I'll turn in."

"But Gramps it's barely six-thirty!" She pointed out.

"I am a bit tired Missy." Bill repeated. Peggy realized sleep would probably be the best thing for him. Who knows he could wake up fine in the morning.

Rich was leading his mare from her stall when movement caused him to look toward the stable door. Ray Johnson stood there uneasily. He smiled and approached Rich.

"Evening Ray." Rich began.

"Hi Rich." The older man replied. "This is Spirit huh, I've heard about her."

"She was a gift from a friend."

"Nez Perc Indian I'm told."

"Uh huh."

"She's a beautiful horse."

"Thank you." Rich lead her to the hitching rail and tied her, so he could saddle her.

"That horse Ben received Tuesday is a beaut, too." Ray commented.

"Yeah, Reynolds Marksman has quite a line of horses at his place."

"Maybe I'll take the kids there someday so they can see the place." Ray considered.

"They'd enjoy it. Marksman is very business minded."

Ray paused a while before continuing.

"To tell the truth, Rich, I've considered looking for a new place to board my children's horses. I don't think I will find a place as convenient as this but it's too hard for me to come here and pretend things are okay."

"Why pretend Ray, we know what happened. And I'll let you know that at least one of us understand where you're coming from."

"You do?"

"You're right Ray, I would have responded the same way you have. I'm not proud of it but it's true."

"You think I'm a fool, don't you?"

"If your a fool Ray, I'm a bigger one."

"I hit my own son!"

"You didn't mean to."

"But who will it be next?"

"It doesn't have to be anyone."

"You don't understand Rich, I can't even trust myself anymore."

"You can trust yourself Ray, it's the alcohol you can't trust."

"Not a sermon from you too!"

"Don't worry. I'll be the last to preach being no better myself. But Ray I hope you learn that alcohol is not the solution before it's too late."

"What do you mean?"

"I guess some have to learn the hard way." Rich motioned Ray to the bale of hay next to him and proceeded to share his story, his disaster.

"I only hope that somehow you can wake up, before it's too late. Before you have memories that will never go away. Before you have feelings that plague you. Before you have to look at the consequences and say 'I did that, I chose of my own free will to take that life.' It's scary Ray, I won't ever be the same. I'd hate to see something like that happen to you."

And as Ray Johnson left the stable that evening his eyes seeing more clearly than they had in days. Rich McAllister silently turned toward home, there was a spring in his step that hadn't been there. You see he had seen beyond Ray's stony countenance and saw his words take effect. In his heart, he was dancing.

CHAPTER 15

A TIME TO CAST AWAY STONES

Friday September 23, 1983

The ringing of the alarm shattered the silence, Jeff pulled his pillow over his ears to block out the sound, he failed. Throwing the covers aside he stumbled from the bed, furious at himself for placing the alarm so far away but knowing it's placement was the only thing that roused him each morning.

After succeeding in eliminating the offensive buzzing he flopped wearily back on the bed, wide awake, yet desiring the peaceful limbo of sleep. Turning on his side he saw it, the bible Denni had given him just yesterday. Recalling his vow to read it daily he sat up. He took the book in his hands, his mind wondering what he was thinking. What difference could reading this make anyway? It was almost impossible to understand in the first place, tossing it back onto his bedside table he hurried into his clothes for his morning run. Jeff was an athlete, nothing inspired him more, or started his day like jogging. It was still dark when he left home but the sun was lighting the horizon. He headed east, taking the back roads, his usual route bringing him through the park and back toward home, a good two miles.

The air was chillier this morning. October was approaching. Many trees were already bare. It was his favorite time of day, being out among the world when the first rays of the sun opened each morning. His sneakered feet crushed the leaves as he ran on. Smoke drifted from many homes and lingered in the air. The park is usually empty that early, Jeff always enjoyed that, he had circled toward home when a lone figure on a park bench surprised him. He pulled up short.

"Morning." Ray said stiffly.

"Are you okay Dad?" Jeff asked.

"No, but don't be concerned."

"How long have you been here?" Jeff asked as he settled himself beside his father on the bench.

"Quite a while, it's hard to sleep son, knowing your wife is elsewhere."

"She's at work Dad."

Ray looked at his son seriously "That's not what I was referring to," He replied as he looked at his hands. Jeff was obviously embarrassed.

"I'm sorry Dad, I didn't understand."

"There's no way you could have son. After twenty years together,.. twenty years,.. I'm hurt that she left but I doubt if the loneliness will ever go away." Ray just remained seated staring at his hands."

"But Dad! Life goes on" Jeff tried to encourage him "You can find someone else." He spoke the words but the very thought of someone else with his father repulsed him.

Ray shook his head and sighed.

"I'm afraid not. Life is on the decline for me now, I've seen my years. I've no desire to start again, I've got no strength to,.. change,.. no wonder she left."

"Come on Dad, let's go home, I'll make breakfast, that'll cheer you."

"Thanks son, but nothing can cheer me now."

"Not even a plate of bacon and eggs?"

Ray smiled as he joined his son. They walked away in a silence broken only by the early morning sounds of Autumn.

"I made a decision last night." Jeff began. "And I guess you, being the football coach will be the first to hear it."

"Oh?" Ray asked. "I don't plan on being coach much longer."

"You don't?"

"I feel it's time, considering certain things that have happened this past week, that I resign."

"But Dad you love coaching the team, almost as much as I love to play,.." Jeffs voice stopped and he began to laugh.

"Well, what's so funny?"

"Us." Jeff continued "You may not be aware of this, but I am planning on dropping the team. This morning in fact. You're the first to know."

Ray smiled, "You are my son after all." He grinned.

"Did you ever wonder?" Jeff laughed, then seeing the serious expression on his father face his laughter was cut short.

"Your mind does crazy things to you at times like these." Ray assured him. "That wasn't the only one of my doubts."

"Would it have made a difference?" Jeff asked. "Would you have loved me less?"

Ray was startled. "Loved you? Nothing could change that don't worry."

"It wouldn't have changed my feelings either Dad, but if you'd look in the mirror your doubts would be dispelled."

"You are a chip off the old block aren't you?"

The Johnson's left for school after a hearty breakfast and a heartier talk. Ray spoke openly about Jeff's mother, and about his problem with alcohol.

"I haven't conquered the desire yet, but I will. Only a weak man would take that way out. I've been wrong, I'm thankful to Rich for telling me his story just have patience with me son, hopefully my drinking days are over."

"Same here Dad." Jeff said quietly.

"You? You're young Jeff what have you to rid yourself of."

"Alcohol same as you Dad." Ray looked surprised but Jeff concluded. "No Dad I never went overboard but I have drank, frequently too. I've seen something though, I saw a man who risked his family, friends, and his own self esteem, while intoxicated. I learned from your mistake.

"I'm glad to hear it." Ray began, then after a pause "What about the cocaine, Jeff?"

"Huh? You know about that?" Jeff was alarmed.

"I admit you're drinking was a surprise but I've known about the coke for some time."

Jeff remained silent.

"You say you've learned from my mistake, think about it son, don't make one of your own."

Jeff searched his fathers face. The face of a man at his weakest point. Probably at the lowest point he'd ever been in his life. Still he had waken to the magnitude of his problem, could Jeff admit his secret vice and change also? He remained silent.

Ray noted his sons silence and hopefully wished it reflected an earnest desire to consider the proposition of putting cocaine aside. He loved his son more than most men would admit, but he also knew that the fewer words spoken the better. Besides who was he to even mention the fact.

A lot lay before the two that day. Two resignations in one day would make quite a hot item against the football team. No one would allow that bit of news to just rest. Both Jeff and his father knew that much, both had tried to prepare themselves for the shower of questions and accusations. Ray also had many unpleasantries to respond to. Apologies he felt may not be sufficient. He was lucky he still held a job. Having to face his colleagues would be almost impossible but having to face the students was even worse. And it had only been a week since Jenny had packed her mothers bags. He'd lost his Jen now too, his sweetheart. Had he put his children in that much danger that Jenny would run to her mother for fear of what her own father might do to her. He shuddered.

John F. Kennedy High was just coming to life when the two entered the building. They stood together inside the double doors bound by their grief, almost afraid to part ways.

"See you Dad." Jeff nodded quietly.

"Good luck, son." Ray responded. "You know where to find me."

"Sure." Jeff answered then before his father turned away he spoke. "You know where to find me too." Jeff reminded him. Ray smiled back at him.

"A chip off the old block." He muttered as he shook his head.

Jeff joined the group of students that had gathered near his locker. Dennis and Brady were there of course, along with Jed Bently, Chas Hagens and Jim Townes. (All members of the football team). Jeff was nervous at first, his father had acknowledged the fact that he'd pulled off the team but his friends had no idea, and they needed an explanation.

"Hey Johnson, why so quiet?" Chas asked.

"No reason." Jeff lied. "You played so well without me last week, maybe you could manage again tonight."

"What!" Brady was shocked "Of course you're playing Jeffer, we're counting on you."

"I'm afraid not Brady, I'm off the team."

"They cut you?" Brady was stunned.

"No, I pulled out."

"Well you can pull right back in then, we need you." Brady stated.

"Yeah, Jeff, you're a good player, you can't quit now." Jim remarked.

"Sorry fella's, I already told the coach." He felt it wise not to mention his fathers plans. "Besides you played a fine game last week,.. without me."

"What are you?" Chas asked. "A quitter? A coward? Get us going on a great season and pull out, that's a rotten trick Johnson."

"Yeah" Jim replied. "We can't let you do that to us. We're a team, there's a lot at stake here."

"Calm down guys." Denni said "Jeffs got his reasons, do you really think it's fair to intimidate him with your accusations?"

"Let him be a quitter, see if we care, we're probably better off without the fiddle brain for all we know." Chas remarked.

"Yeah" Jim agreed.

Brady had remained quiet after Jeffs refusal to reconsider. 'This Holy Roller stuff has really gotten to him' Brady thought. 'Maybe if I put him on the spot.'

"Okay Jeffer, you're out. So tell us why, you loved playing."

"You're right Brady I do, I love the game, I love working with you guys. But right now I'm really mixed up. My family is what is the most important. We're broken now but I want to do my best to keep us as much together as possible, It's my main concern. Football doesn't seem important to me anymore. I hope you understand."

"That's not much of a reason Jeffer." Brady pointed out. "Your problems are simple compared to some of ours."

"Yeah." Jim replied.

"You're just using it as an excuse." Brady continued, "We want the real reason Jeff. Why are you dropping from the team?"

"I told you guys" Jeff stared at Brady hard. "I can't handle this mess with my family. Football just isn't important anymore. Do you want someone out there who isn't interested in the game?"

"We want you out there Jeffer." Brady replied.

"Yeah." Jim agreed. "You're a good player."

"Sorry guys. I made my decision. I'm off the team."

"It looks pretty convenient to me." Brady began, "That the coaches son would be the one that could pull something like this. I bet not a one of us could get away with it."

"Mr. Johnson is a very fair man, Brady." Denni put in.

"Huh." Brady laughed. "You haven't seen him lately have you? We call him the drunken professor." Brady, Jim, and Chas broke into riotous laughter. Jed was smiling too but was embarrassed by it.

"You won't reconsider?" Jed asked Jeff.

"No, I made my decision."

"Okay, but I want you to know it was a pretty lousy thing to do."

"I'm sorry you guys." Jeff said, he turned away, Denni joined him. No one made a move to stop them.

"Don't worry Jeff, It'll all blow over."

"But they don't know the half of it." Jeff responded.

"What's that?"

"The coach is resigning too."

Denni was quiet.

"We'd both made our decisions independently. Try to tell one of them that." He nodded toward the group they'd just left.

"It'll work out."

"That's easy for you to say, you never got real involved with those guys, winning those games is the most important thing to them. They don't care what it takes and with our Homecoming game next weekend, I can just imagine what they'll pull if they lose that."

"But they can't possibly believe that one person can make a difference."

"But one person does make a difference. That's one reason why I pulled out. One person out there whose heart isn't into winning could easily wipe out the game for everyone."

"Well, I hope you realize that not everyone is in total agreement with Brady and the team.

Jeff grinned at Denni, "I know Den, and I sometimes wonder if I deserve a friend like you."

"Maybe we deserve each other." Denni responded.

Jeff noticed Brady and Chas Hagens before him in the halls as he headed toward his second class. He hurried to join them.

"Notice the tail on Rhodes this week?" Brady remarked.

"Oh you mean the OFF FICE ER" Chas said the word mockingly.

"The PO LEECE" Brady responded.

"I guess they don't want more accidents huh." Chas asked.

"I guess some one sent big brother a little note."

"Don't look at me."

"Of course not, you're not getting credit for my good idea's."

Chas laughed.

"I hope to get even with her and that Williams at the same time."

"And get thrown in the slammer while you're at it?"

"Don't be stupid. I know what I'm doing, I was there remember. My memory just began coming back to me, I can describe a few of the fella's that were there quite well."

"No accents or cowboy boots?" Chas asked.

"No, but it'll be pretty clear when I'm through."

"Just then Jeff approached them.

"Hey guys." He called.

"Hey Jeffer!" Brady greeted. Chas just glared at him.

"Well if it isn't Benedict Johnson the traitor." Chas remarked sarcastically.

"Oh come off it Hagen's it's not the end of the world." Jeff responded.

"That's right." Brady agreed. "Jeff hasn't quite been himself lately." He gave Chas a knowing look.

"It's not that bad." Jeff remarked. "I'll be rooting for you, I only wish you understood that things are best this way. You wouldn't want a nin-com-poop out on the field with the ball would you?"

"I guess not." Chas agreed "Hey is the coach back today. I've got his class this hour."

"Oh he's here." Jeff assured. "And he's sober."

"Aww." Chas said in mock disappointment. "He was just starting to be fun."

"Well, fun's over." Jeff stated. "I hope it's over for good."

Although bodily occupying a seat in class Jeff's mind was elsewhere, back in the hallway before second period, overhearing the remarks made by Brady and Chas who'd been unaware of his approach. Brady had obviously continued with his plans to get even with Suzanna. What he had done Jeff had no idea, but the police had gotten involved. Jeff had gone to the bible study earlier in the week because he wanted to hear the word of God, he was curious, but he knew that Brady's presence there was part of some sinister plot of his. How did he ever fall for Brady's tactics in the first place?

Jeff considered Suzanna. She was an Okay kid, he thought, but why was Brady so intent on tormenting her? Chances are she knew nothing of Brady's deal last Friday and had nothing to do with his arrest. Why was Brady really after her? Maybe he should mention something to Suzanna about Brady's words and intentions. No! He couldn't do that. He wasn't a stooley. They may call him yellow for dropping the ball team but he refused to give them reason to call him a nark.

Jeff stared blankly at the math problems before him. All the good times he had shared with Brady came to mind. They'd really had fun together, but even as he sat contemplating their friendship Jeff already knew it was almost over. It seemed that the biggest things that had held their friendship together had been football,.. and cocaine. Without football, what did they have left,.. cocaine.

His fathers words of admonishment returned again. The choice was Jeffs, could he lick cocaine like his father chose to attempt to lick alcohol. Could they struggle together to conquer their faults? Jeff ran his hands roughly through his hair in exasperation. Could Jeff have the courage that his father had; could Jeff become a man and make a man's choice?

As Jeff stepped out of his second hour class Brady summoned him from across the hall.

"Hey,.. Jeffer." He said as Jeff approached. "I've got the wheels today, also the goods. I'm skippin' out after next hour, why don't you join me?"

"I don't know." Jeff began.

"Hey don't worry, I got the stuff."

"That's not it."

"Then you're coming?"

"I don't think so."

"Huh? You haven't got a class that hour, what's the problem?"

"No problem Brady, I'm just wondering if it would be wiser for me to lay off the stuff for awhile."

Brady looked at Jeff bewildered.

"Just awhile, huh?"

",.. a,.. I really don't know."

"What's gotten into you Jeffer. It's like you've changed overnight. You've never turned down a time like this. It's almost as if,.. Hey! You aren't turning Holy on me are you Jeffer?"

Jeff laughed, "No way, Denni's enough of a Holy roller for the both of us."

"Wheew." Brady responded "I thought I'd lost you for a minute there."

"Don't count me in on it. I'm putting the stuff aside for awhile."

"No kiddin?"

"No kiddin. In fact I've got some stashed at home right now, I'll probably destroy it."

"Destroy it!!" Brady almost hollered. "No way Jeffer, if you've got anything, I'll destroy it for you." Brady grinned, Jeff got his meaning and grinned also.

"Hey you want it?"

"Of course, don't waste the stuff."

"Maybe I will go with you next hour, as long as you realize I'm not using the stuff. We'll stop by my place and I'll get the stash."

"Sure Jeffer." Brady responded.

"Oh, by the way Brady. You're letting me drive... Okay?"

"Whatever you say." The two went their way. Jeff to his third class and Brady out the front door of school to his car.

"May I help you?" Asked the woman behind the desk.

"Yep. Is Cap'n Omaha Jordon free?"

"May I ask your name?"

"It's Brady Downing."

"I'll see if he's available. Please take a seat." Brady wandered over to the few chairs and settled into one. He'd had a great idea and hoped that he could pull it off without suspicion. He was glad that Williams worked the evening shift. He'd hate to have to contend with that dude.

"The Captain will see you now."

"Thank you." Brady responded as he followed the woman through to the captains office.

Captain Omaha sat behind his spacious desk. He was looking over a few papers that were before him.

"Come in Downing." He said gruffly without looking up. "You've been pretty busy this past week."

"No more than usual." Brady remarked.

"Oh? Does one week for you usually include, an arrest and a fight with suspicious hoods?" Omaha raised his eyebrows.

"No sir, but neither of them was my fault." Brady tried to appear sincere.

"Well as for this second instance let's hope not."

There was a pause before Omaha continued. "Don't waste my time Downing. What's on your mind?"

"Well sir, you see, Officer Williams asked us to come down here if we remember anything about Tuesday night."

"Yeah?"

"Well, I guess things started to come together."

"Oh?"

"Yeah, it's taken me quite awhile to get the courage to come here because I had considered these guys my friends."

"I guess you would."

"Hold it Cap'n. This is on the level. I can identify two of those guys that had me the other day."

"Okay,.. shoot."

"Well like I said it didn't add up until early yesterday and then I didn't want to say anything. They were supposed to be my friends."

"Anyway." Brady continued. "The fella with the cowboy boots and accent threw me off. Those boots looked so familiar but that voice didn't It was the accent. He faked it. He knew I'd recognize him and thought that if he disguised his voice I wouldn't know who he was."

"Who was he?" Omaha asked soberly.

"Dennis Little. He's a friend of mine who works at Horseman's Unlimited. I guess that's why he wears cowboy boots. The other guy was the left handed one, he's kind of like Dennis' best friend. I wouldn't have even suspected him if he hadn't mentioned something about it."

"He told you?"

"No not in actual words, but he let me know that he knew what had happened and no one but those that were there and the culprits knew right?"

"That's what we were hoping. What's his name?"

"Jeff Johnson."

"So what you're saying is that you think these two friends of yours were involved with the encounter you had Tuesday night."

"Yes sir."

"Dennis Little, and Jeff Johnson."

"Yes, that's them."

"Okay, we'll talk to them."

Brady was waiting when Jeff stepped from his class.

"Hey Jeffer, ya got a minute?" Brady called "I gotta tell ya something."

"Yeah, what is it?"

"Well, the other night Suzie and I got stopped by some creeps behind Charlies"

"You did?"

"Yeah, and I guess the cops are pretty concerned about it. They've got someone following her."

"What about you?"

"I don't know." Brady began. "That's why I thought I'd try to give who ever might be following me the slip. Here, you take my keys." Brady handed his car keys to Jeff. "Go pick up your stuff then drive over to 'Daves', I'll make sure no one sees me, Okay?"

"Sure." Jeff agreed but was still baffled. "Do you want me to go now?"

"Yeah, I'll get to Dave's, you get the stuff then pick me up!"

"Okay, see you in about fifteen, maybe twenty minutes."

"Yeah, right."

Jeff hurried from school to Brady's car. He didn't want to see Brady arrested again. Although he didn't fully understand what may have transpired Tuesday night.

No sooner had Jeff gone from view when Brady hurried into the lobby of the school to use the pay phone.

Jeff parked Brady's car in the Johnson's driveway and taking his keys he entered the house. He normally stashed his stuff with his football equipment but had moved it early this morning after making his decision about the team. Moving to his bed, he picked up the bible Denni had given him. The pages fell open. Taking the envelope from where he'd hidden it, he quickly shut the bible and left the room.

At that moment a squad car pulled up in front of the Johnson home. Two patrolmen stepped out and approached Jeff who now stood in the doorway.

"Are you Jefferson Raymond Johnson?" The first officer asked.

"Yes, that's me, what can I do for you?"

"We were originally asked to bring you to the station for questioning."

"Oh? What's up?"

"The Cap'n will talk with you about that."

"Now" The second officer began. "Does this vehicle belong to you?"

"No it belongs to a friend."

"What's your friends name?"

"Brady Downing."

"Well, it appears he reported his car stolen, about ten minutes ago."

"He did?" Jeff was shocked.

"Yes, I'm afraid you'll have to answer to that young man. Auto theft is a crime, you should be aware of that."

"Of course I'm aware of that but he told me to take his car!" Jeff pointed out.

"You tell that to the Captain."

The second officer nodded to the first one.

"What are you gonna do now?" Jeff asked.

"Well first we have to search you, who knows you could be carrying a gun." The officer attempted a smile.

Jeff's heart sank. Car theft indeed. How would he explain the cocaine. How did he get into this mess. What was Brady trying to do to him? He thought Brady was his friend.

Brady had hurried to Suzanna's class after reporting his car being stolen. She had already entered and the officer tailing her had returned to his vehicle in the parking lot when Brady arrived.

"Hey Rhodes." Brady hollered from the door of the room. "I have to talk to you."

Suzanna approached him. "What is it? The bell's gonna ring any minute."

"I needed to see you," Brady stated anxiously. "I guess two of the guys that surrounded us the other day will be taken in for questioning."

"Really? That's great!" Suzanna was pleased. "Do you know who they are?"

"No, but I guess they gave themselves away. They were the only ones but us that knew of the incident. They'll have to come up with some story if you ask me."

"Good, maybe then the police will tell their friend to go home."

"I'd enjoy his job." Brady smiled. "There's no one I'd rather follow around all day."

"Cool-it Brady." Suzanna insisted.

"And" Brady interrupted. "There's no other person I'd like to try to protect than you."

"I thought we had an understanding."

"We do." Brady began. "I just have a hard time ignoring my feelings. They haven't changed."

"Mine have." she responded.

"So that means we can't have lunch together?"

"Sure we can, in the cafeteria, with my friends."

"We don't even get to celebrate?"

"Celebrate?"

"Those two the cops are gonna question."

"We'll share a coke at lunch." Suzanna allowed.

"Oh boy, I can hardly wait." Brady mocked.

"Me either." Suzanna teased.

"Well have it your way...today."

"No, Brady, it'll be this way everyday, get that through your cranium will you?"

"I hear you, I hear you, I just wish it didn't need to be this way."

"It does though."

Jeff looked across the massive desk at Captain Omaha Jordon.

"Well, son, things aren't looking up for you. In possession of a stolen vehicle, and an eight of a gram of cocaine, that puts you in a pretty unusual predicament."

"I've explained it sir. That's exactly how it happened."

"This Brady Downing, gave you the keys to his car so you could run home to get the cocaine for him?"

"Yes, sir."

"That's almost as far fetched as the story he gave me Saturday."

"This one is true sir." Jeff responded.

"Even if it is. It is illegal to be in possession of any amount of cocaine, more illegal to supply it to people,.. like Brady."

"I'm not a supplier, sir." Jeff corrected.

"But you do agree you were getting this for him." Omaha lifted the bag of cocaine as he spoke.

"Yes, sir. I had decided to quit using the stuff and had planned on destroying it. Brady found out and asked if he could have it. So that's why I had it."

"That's really hard to believe."

"But it is the truth."

At that moment the secretary buzzed the Captain.

"Jeff Johnson's parents are both here sir."

"Thank you Miss Vale. Have them wait. We'll be through in a few minutes." He turned back to Jeff. "Now, about Tuesday night, may I ask what your involvement was?"

"Involvement in what sir?"

"This episode with Brady Downing."

"You think I was part of that gang that stopped him and Rhodes?"

"So, you know about it?"

"Very little sir, only what Brady told me."

"Only what Brady told you huh?"

"Yes sir, that's why he wasn't with me. He thought since you had someone following Suzanna you might have someone following him too. He didn't want to be caught with the coke."

"So the truth comes out." Omaha smiled. "You were purposely trying to avoid my men."

"Who wouldn't sir with an eighth of a gram of cocaine on them?"

"And a stolen car."

"I didn't steal the car."

"Okay, and a car that was reported stolen."

Jeff sighed exasperated. "You don't believe a word I say do you?"

"I base my belief on only one thing,.. fact. Fact has it that you were in possession of a car that was reported to be stolen and an eighth of a gram of cocaine. Both are crimes, both hold consequences. That's all I can go on. I can't take your word for anything."

"But you take Brady Downing's?"

Omaha laughed. "No, I don't take Downing's either, But he did report a missing vehicle."

Jeff sighed again and settled back in his chair. "What next?" He asked.

"Your parents are here. We can release you if someone will be accountable for your whereabouts and behavior."

"Then what?"

"We'll file charges of course, for the cocaine. Downing will have to decide about the car."

"What about Brady?"

"I'm sorry to say, we have got absolutely nothing on him as of right now."

"But he had all kinds of cocaine on him when you stopped him Friday."

"We can only except facts Jeff. I told you that and the fact is, Brady had nothing on him whatsoever when he was arrested."

"So, he's got nothing against him?"

"Nothing at all He's a pretty slippery fellow."

"I'll say."

A few minutes later Ray Johnson entered the room. He looked completely drained, his face was an ashen color, he could hardly look at his son. He seated himself closest to the door. Judy Johnson entered next, accompanied by Steve Williams."

"Sergeant Williams." Omaha exclaimed "What brings you here?"

"A special request. From Jeff's mother." He grinned "For support."

"Oh,.. I see."

"Can't you get him out of here! He's got nothing to do with this." Ray said bitterly.

"It's okay Dad." Jeff tried to soothe him. "If mom wants him here, I don't mind."

"But I mind." Ray returned.

"Steve, maybe if you wait outside." Omaha suggested. Steve looked at Judy for approval, she nodded.

"Sure Cap'n" He responded then turned to Judy, "I'll be right outside if you need me."

"Thanks Steve." Judy answered, she took the chair next to Jeffs and reached for his hand.

How long had it been Jeff wondered since his mother had held his hand like that. She seemed fine, not as distraught and lost as his father did. But then his father'd been so unpredictable lately.

Cap'n Omaha cleared his throat.

"I'm sorry to have to bring you here like this." Then turning to Ray "Especially taking you from work sir."

" 's Okay." Ray responded.

"Well it was necessary." Omaha continued. "I'll read what I have here. At 11:15 this morning your son Jefferson Raymond Johnson was stopped at your home on Elm Street in possession of a stolen car."

"Jeff!" His father exclaimed. "I can't believe this."

"I can't either dad."

"The car was a 1978 Ford Gran Torino two door sedan, License number FBD693 owned by Fred Robbins of 315 Trapline Road. It was reported missing by his step-son Brady Downing."

Ray let out an audible sigh. "That's a relief." He began, "They're friends. Jeff drives his car all the time, and likewise Brady had driven our truck a time or two."

"Yes, I realize that may be true, but Brady Downing called in and reported it missing. It is being handled as a stolen vehicle."

"Did you steal it Jeff?" Judy asked.

"Oh ma, of course not. What would I want to do that for. He told me to take it. I was going to pick him up later at Daves."

"See officer, that explains it."

"I'm sorry Ma'am, we only go by facts, like I've explained to Jeff he was in possession of a car that was reported stolen. That is a crime."

"Boy son, you really had me worried." Ray looked relieved. "I'm sure Brady must have forgotten he told you to take it."

Jeff remained silent.

"The report continues." Omaha interrupted. "He was stopped at 11:15 on routine business with a stolen car, and with an eighth of a gram of cocaine in his possession."

Judy's mouth gaped open as she stared at her son, but Jeff was more concerned about his fathers reaction. He wanted his father to know and understand fully what had transpired. Ray Johnson buried his face in his hands, after a few minutes his body began to shake. Jeff brushed his mothers hand aside and rushed to his dad.

"Dad, you don't understand." He began "I went to get the stuff because I didn't want to use it. I was gonna destroy it. But Brady talked me out of it, he wanted it, so he gave me the keys to run home and get the stuff for him."

"And then he called and reported his car missing, so you'd be stopped and found with the cocaine?" Ray finished angrily.

"Huh?" Jeff asked.

"Your gonna sit back and let a skunk like that Downing pull something like this on my son?" Ray asked Omaha.

"I'm sorry sir, but we can only go by the facts, and the fact is that Jeff had both the car and cocaine in his possession."

"And Downing's probably celebrating right now." Ray was furious. "If this department were run the way it should, cocaine wouldn't be available for seventeen year old boys!"

"We try our best sir," Omaha stated soberly, "But it would take more than just a well run Police force to lick the problem of cocaine."

"Well find out what it will take!" Ray stated. "And do it!" Ray got up from his chair abruptly and headed toward the door.

"Where are you going Dad?"

"To find a skunk by the name of Brady Downing and let him know what I think of him."

"That wouldn't be a very wise thing to do." Captain Omaha cautioned.

"Let me be the judge of that." Ray left the room quickly almost colliding with Steve who waited patiently outside the door.

Suzanna was pleased when Brady didn't meet her for lunch that day. So were her friends.

"I can't believe we've got you all to ourselves." Becky Franklin joked.

"Lunch hour's not over yet." Suzanna pointed out.

"That's right, he does tend to appear when least expected doesn't he." Peggy stated.

Angie joined them, the four had chosen a corner table in the cafeteria.

"Let's ignore him if he comes." Suzanna suggested.

"You should have done that a week ago." Peggy replied.

"Has it only been a week?"

"Uh huh"

"Wow. Has this ever been a long week!" Suzanna remarked.

Peggy laughed. "I never thought I'd see you with boy problems!"

"Boy problems? I don't have boy problems, I have Brady Downing problems." The others laughed.

"Just to encourage you." Becky started. "There's not one girl in his school who wouldn't mind being in your shoes."

"Oh YES there is." Peggy stated strongly.

"Make that two." Angie added.

"Well maybe you two are exceptions." Becky noted.

"But what about you?" Suzanna asked in surprise.

"Well, .. he is pretty good looking. And popular, he seems like a really nice guy."

"You sound like my father." Suzanna stated.

"I do?" Becky was flabbergasted.

"He said almost the exact same things about Brady himself."

"Your Dad did?" Peggy seemed surprised.

"Yeah, he did, I straightened him out on it though."

"I should hope so."

"Well," Angie began "He was in church Wednesday night, and he did look touched. Maybe he will change."

"That would be great!" Suzanna remarked. "Then Becky could date him, and he'd leave me alone." The others laughed again.

They continued their meal in silence for awhile, commenting only on a few test results and class work. They'd finished and cleared the table before Brady arrived.

"Hi!" He greeted them.

"Hi" Peggy and Angie said.

"You're behind schedule." Becky reported. "You usually start pestering Suzanna a good fifteen minutes before this. That is if you let her join us at all."

Brady enjoyed the teasing.

"I promise, it won't happen again."

Becky smiled but Suzanna seemed upset.

"Don't put yourself out."

"I'm not put out at all." He stated. "I was going nuts thinking I wouldn't be able to see you til after school."

"Brady, you have one to the thickest skulls I've ever known."

"Listen to her. All I offer is complements and what did I get in return,.. rebuffs, insults, and why do I continue?"

When the girls just shrugged he went on. "It must be true love."

Peggy made a choking noise, Angie blushed, and Becky grinned.

"I think I'm going to be sick."

"I hope it isn't serious." He said teasingly as he moved toward her. He felt her forehead as if to check for fever. He pulled his hand away in alarm.

"Ouch! I knew you were a hot item but I didn't expect this."

Suzanna rolled her eyes, as Brady continued. "A fever like that demands immediate attention."

"Sorry Brady, I'm not interested." Suzanna responded.

"Now, now, none of that now." He teased, he reached for her arm and began pulling her toward the door.

"Brady! I said I'm not interested." She responded angrily.

Brady whispered, "Shh, we have to talk. They arrested someone last hour and now anothers been taken in for questioning. Come on."

Suzanna willingly followed him from the cafeteria.

Brady had already retrieved his car and led Suzanna to it.

"Come on, get in we'll go for a ride."

"No way! We're staying right here."

"Okay, but at least we can sit inside."

"I'm not getting into that car Brady, unless you give me the keys." She stated firmly.

"Whatever you say." He remarked handing over his keys a second time that day.

After they were both seated Suzanna spoke "What's this all about?"

"You're not gonna believe this." Brady began "But, I must have misplaced my car keys. Someone swiped my car last hour. I just got the thing back or I'd have come for you sooner."

"Someone stole your car?"

"Uh huh."

"This old heap? It doesn't even look like it would run."

"This is a very reliable car, I'll have you know."

"Whatever you say, but who took it? Was it someone who was after us Tuesday? Is he the one that was arrested?"

"Well, I reported the car stolen and no sooner had I done it when they found the thing. They were pulling someone in for questioning about Tuesday, and here the dude had my car."

"You're kidding? Then he was one of them!"

"It looks that way. Although it's hard to believe."

"Why?"

"Because I thought he was my friend."

"Who was it?"

"Jeffer" Brady stated, "And not only did he steal my car but he had a package of cocaine on him. They've got him on those charges too."

"Jeff Johnson?" Suzanna asked quietly. "Jeff Johnson stole your car? He was one of the guys who pestered us Tuesday? He got caught with cocaine?"

"Yes, yes, and yes." Brady tried to sound hurt. "They've got Denni at the station right now for questioning."

"Not Dennis. Brady even You can't believe that Denni would be involved.

"I'm not the police, Suzanna. They've got a tip on him somehow. I hope they're wrong but after Jeff I think I could believe almost anything."

"I can't."

"Don't ignore facts." Brady said. He glanced over at Suzanna and saw that she was near tears. "Hey don't take it so hard."

"But Brady, they're your friends. Jeffs been arrested, already found guilty and Denni's a suspect. I can't believe it of either of them. And I won't." Tears formed in her eyes and silently slid down her cheeks. Embarrassed she closed her eyes and rested her head on the back of the seat. Brady could tell that she was forcing herself under control.

"It's okay to cry. I don't mind at all." He whispered.

Her tears began to flow freely. "Oh, Brady, why must everything go wrong? Why does it happen that everytime I learn to really like and trust people, they hurt me some how?"

Brady was silent a minute, then reaching up to her still closed eyes he brushed a few tears from them. "I won't ever hurt you Suzanna." He whispered quietly.

"I don't believe you Brady, and you know it." She answered "I have this gut feeling that you're behind this whole mess and that is what hurts most."

"Me? You must have been listening too much to that Williams. He has a very vivid imagination."

"You're the one with the vivid imagination. If you think I'll fall for your games. You've been in the role of king for too long already. It's time you realized life doesn't revolve around yours truly."

Brady remained silent. Suzanna looked at him. Surely one of the handsomest faces in school, the most enchanting eyes she'd ever seen, but beneath them... who knew what evil could be imagined. Suzanna chose that moment to make a final plea.

"What must I do Brady, to get you to leave me alone. To stay out of my life?"

Brady remained quiet for a few minutes.

"There's nothing you can do" He finally stated. "I always get what I want, and right now, I want you." He moved toward her, at the same time she opened the door and fled into the parking lot.

The parking lot seemed empty compared to the stiffling closeness of Brady's car as Suzanna sped across it's expanse toward the school. Behind her, cast in a heap,like a stone, rejected,.. sat Brady.

There was a smile on his face.

CHAPTER 16

A TIME TO GATHER STONES TOGETHER

Friday, September 23rd, 1983

It was early afternoon when Jeff Johnson left city hall accompanied by his mother and Steve Williams. He was quiet as they approached Steve's car.

"Well, where to?" Steve asked.

"That's in your hands." Jeff reminded him.

"True, you were put in my custody, but I don't feel I have much to worry about."

"You trust me?"

"Yes, and I believe your story about Brady Downing."

"At least someone does."

"So where to?" Steve repeated.

"Well, first on the list is finding Dad."

Steve was solemn. "I'm afraid my help wouldn't be too appreciated."

"Do you blame him?" Jeff responded quickly.

"I guess not."

"Why don't we just bring him home Steve. Maybe Ray will be therc."

"Is that what you want Jeff?"

"I guess so, if Dad's not there I'll wait for him."

They entered Steve's car, and as they were about to pull away from the curb, Dennis Little left the building.

"Hey Steve, Wait. There's my buddy Denni." Jeff announced as he rolled down the window and beckoned to Dennis.

"Hey Den. Over here!"

Dennis saw Jeff and approached.

"What brings you here?" Jeff asked.

"I have no idea?" Dennis began "I was questioned for something but still I have no idea what."

"What about Brady, where's he?"

"Probably in class." Denni answered innocently. "Did they question you too?"

"Yeah, but I knew nothing."

"How did we get involved then?"

"I can probably make a good guess." Jeff began "Hey, do you need a lift somewhere?"

"No, I've got my car here. But you're trying to change the subject, how do you think we got involved?"

"I can't say Denni because I'm not sure. But I assure you, I will get to the bottom of it."

"I hope so."

Denni waved as Steve pulled his car into traffic.

Denni had time to return to school for his last class and when he pulled into the parking lot the first person who greeted him was Suzanna Rhodes. She'd been watching for his return and when he pulled his car to a stop, she ran up to him.

"Denni, are you okay?"

"Yeah, sure. Why?"

"Brady said you had to go down to City Hall for questioning. I'm so sorry."

"Brady told you? How did he know?"

"Oh you know Brady Den, he just knows those things."

"Did he tell you Jeff was called in too?"

"And arrested,... yeah."

"He was arrested?"

"You didn't know?"

"He didn't say a word about an arrest, but he told me he knew nothing about what they were trying to get me on."

"That's a relief, I wouldn't have thought it of either one of you."

"Hold it. There's a few pieces of the puzzle missing, fill me in will you?"

Suzanna remained quiet for a moment.

"Well, I can't tell you what happened Tuesday night. I promised Officer Williams. But when Jeff was summoned to the station today I guess he had cocaine on him and they booked him for it."

"I just saw him leave the place with his mother." Denni informed her.

"Maybe he was released until they press charges in court."

"I've got to find out Suzanna, I've got to find Jeff."

"I thought you said he was with his mother."

"Yeah, I've got to find him and talk to him." Denni turned back to his car.

"Denni?" Suzanna asked. "Let me go with you."

"Sure, come on."

Suzanna climbed into the passenger side as Denni drove away.

"See that car over there?" Suzanna pointed.

"Yeah, what of it?"

"He's been following me all week."

"He has?"

"Yup, since Tuesday."

"What happened to start that?"

"Like I said,... I can't tell you."

"So,.. you're a suspect too," Denni said with understanding.

"No Den, I'm one of the victims."

Denni looked at her closely to see if she were pulling his leg, when he saw her serious expression he grew alarmed.

"They thought Jeff and I tried to harm you?"

"But you didn't Denni. I know that."

"Then who would give them that idea?"

"Who do you think was the other 'so called' victim, that got carted away from the scene right when I needed him most?" Denni looked at her questioningly. "Brady Downing, Den. Somehow he's got you two labeled as involved in this mess, and I'm sure he had more to do with Jeff's arrest than he let on."

"Why's that?"

"Can you believe it. Brady claims his car was stolen. When they found it Jeff had it and the cocaine. Now why would

Jeff take Brady's car? And why would Brady care even if he did? Things just don't add up."

"You're telling me." Denni answered as they approached the Johnson's home. "Well let's hope he's there."

"Let's pray this'll all turn out." Suzanna suggested.

Jeff sat dejectedly in the livingroom of the home now occupied by just him and his father. Soon maybe his father would be the sole occupant. Who knew what would be in store for Jeff in the weeks to come. His father had indeed been distraught when he left City Hall and Jeff secretly prayed that he wouldn't seek out Brady and cause him bodily harm. Although he did believe the jerk deserved it.

Hearing a car pull into the driveway Jeff hurried to the door thinking it was his father. He was met by Denni running onto the porch.

"Jeff. I just heard what happened. It's terrible."

"Hi Den. Come on in." Jeff turned back toward his chair. He never noticed Suzanna enter quietly behind Denni.

"You okay Jeff?" Denni asked his friend.

"I'll be okay Den."

"You want to talk about it?"

"I must have told the story fifteen times already."

"Then don't tell it again if you don't want to."

Suzanna moved toward Jeff.

"Brady gave you the keys to his car didn't he?"

Jeff was startled at hearing her voice. He glanced at her nervously before nodding.

"Was the cocaine his too?" She asked.

Jeff shook his head. "No, no." He began, "It was mine. I'd made a decision not to use the stuff. I was gonna destroy it but Brady wanted it."

"And he sent you to get it in his car?" Denni asked.

Jeff nodded.

"And after he knew you had his car he must have reported it stolen, knowing they'd search you and get the goods."

"It looks like it happened that way."

"And he's free?"

"Uh, huh." Jeff added.

"That's called Justice?"

"That's called facing facts, Den." Jeff stated soberly.

"To bad the facts don't always portray what is really happening." Suzanna responded.

"What is happening?" Jeff wondered.

"Good question." Denni commented, and managed a weak smile.

"It's a marvel to me how one person can cause this much of a disaster." Suzanna put in.

"Well, he can if that one person is Brady Downing." Jeff said. "I'm sorry guys, I know what he's like and if you get in his bad graces nothing at all will stop him from getting even with you."

"I guess you're right." Denni was still skeptical.

"Well look what he's been doing to Suzanna, he's not gonna quit 'til he has his way."

"What do you mean Jeff?" Denni asked again.

Jeff looked at Suzanna. "I'm sorry, I really should have said something sooner but until now, I always left his business alone."

Suzanna nodded, she understood.

"You had problems Saturday night?"

"Yea, while I was babysitting,..hey was he behind that?"

"Uh huh, I'm surprised you didn't find out. Van Dyke caught him."

"Tom did?"

"Uh huh, but instead of being a prowler, I guess he got Tom to believe he was welcome."

"Oh Yeck." Suzanna remarked.

"Well he told me he had to get even with you, he thought you had narced about his deal last Friday, he was really upset. People don't do things like that to him."

"What about Tuesday?"

"He told me about that, but only to explain why someone might be following him."

"But what about those guys, were they friends of his or what?"

"I don't know, I can't answer for sure but I did hear him talking to Chas Hagens about your tail too."

"Chas Hagens?" Suzanna was surprised but not completely, Chas was a good friend of Brady's.

Denni moved toward the window and was looking out. "Cops just parked outside. He doesn't even look worried."

"He probably knows the truth."

"Steve does." Jeff commented.

"That's great" Suzanna said excitedly "At least one adult is on our side."

"My Pa believes me too." Jeff smiled. "In fact he left City Hall in a rage, he wanted to find Brady and choke him I guess."

Dennis and Suzanna exchanged glances.

"Let's hope he doesn't succeed."

"Brady's not worth risking life imprisonment for." Denni commented.

"But,.." Jeff began, "He thinks, I am. He wants to get even."

"Where is he now?"

"I have no idea."

"Do you think we should go look?"

"You'd go with me?"

"Sure."

"Hey, that would be great. Steve couldn't because every time he gets close enough to my Dad, Dad starts swinging at him."

"He does?" Suzanna asked.

"And sometimes Jeff gets in between the two." Denni remarked nodding at Jeffs still evident scars.

"The police asked when I did this. I told them it happened Tuesday evening. Boy did they enjoy that 'til they called the Doc and got the truth." Jeff filled in.

"Well,.. where should we look first?"

"The school." Jeff responded.

"I hope you realize that you and I are both missing class." Suzanna pointed out.

"We'll make it up. They'll understand."

"I'm not so sure."

"Dad will talk to them."

Denni hesitated. "That just might make things worse."

"The most important thing" Suzanna spoke up, "Is to find Mr. Johnson before someone get's hurt."

"Let's go then." Dennis agreed.

Ray Johnson had returned to school. He was upset that was true, but just as upset with Steve Williams as with Brady Downing. He actually got a hold of himself enough to return to his classroom. Somehow, the word had spread about Jeff and a few came to him asking about his son. He just looked at them and made no comment. They knew better than to press the issue.

It was after class period and Chas Hagens had remained behind.

"I heard your son's off the team coach."

"That's right."

"Wouldn't have to do with the cocaine would it?"

"If it did Chas, you and half the other guys would be off the team as well."

Chas grinned. "Come on coach, you know us guys better than that. Why would we mess with the stuff?"

"Listen Chas. I know more than you'd think and if I had my way the team would be a clean one. But there is no way I can prove anything. Now we've got no practice today because of the game, a few of the guys are gonna come to the game after using the stuff. I'm the coach Chas, I can tell. And yes, I know Jeff used it too. We talked about it this morning."

"I hope you know you're wrong coach. Most of us are clean. Jeff was an exception."

Ray just smiled knowingly. Chas headed toward the door.

"See you tonight coach."

"Stay in shape Chas. We need a clean team tonight." Ray called after him. He'd gathered a few of his belongings and was reaching for his coat when Brady Downing entered.

"Hi Coach." He began. Ray glared at him and he froze in his tracks. "... what's wrong?"

"You know very well what's wrong Downing. You're not fooling me like you fooled the Police."

"Police? I don't follow you."

"It would be wise of you to stay as far from me as possible Downing. Do you understand?"

"No I don't, But I'll leave if that's what you want."

"Please do." Ray stated soberly.

Brady quickly left the room.

Ray sat back at his desk and stared at the room before him. He was still there five minutes later when Jeff entered.

"Dad?" He whispered from the door.

"Come in son." Ray remarked. Jeff entered, Dennis and Suzanna remained in the hall.

"I'm sorry about all this." Jeff began.

"I know son, don't say anymore. I understand what happened. I also admire the fact that you were honest about the cocaine."

"I had to be Dad."

Ray nodded. He rose from his chair and once again reached for his coat.

"Should we go home, I need to be back by five thirty,..as of this morning I'm still coach of the team."

"They deserve the best."

The two left the room together. Denni and Suzanna were nowhere around.

Suzanna climbed into the passenger side of Denni's car. He joined her and both of them let out a sigh of relief.

"I'm so glad we found him before,.." Suzanna began.

"So am I" Denni interrupted. "This whole thing is so unreal to me. Right when Jeff was making steps toward God, this happens. Why did God let this happen?"

"The Lord's not gonna stop Brady from doing what ever he wants, you know that. It's our choice to do God's will."

"But what about Jeff? Who knows what will happen now."

"But Denni, Jeff did have cocaine on him."

"But he wasn't gonna use it!"

"The police don't know that."

"But God does. He knows, he knows what's in the heart of all men. How could he allow this to happen to Jeff?"

"For the same reason he allowed me to be cornered in a back alley by four hoods, and allowed you to be suckered into your share of Brady's enterprises. We've got our own will Den. We've got to accept the consequences."

"Yeah, sure." Denni said dejectedly. "My best friend is going to be charged for possession of a stolen vehicle and an eighth of a gram of cocaine and Brady Downing is sitting at the sidelines crowing about it. Where was God Suzanna? Where was he?"

"Right here Den. He was with us all along."

Denni remained quiet for awhile just staring into space.

"Don't blame this on God Den, He knows what he's doing. He's still in control."

"I guess you're right. But why Jeff?" Denni turned away from Suzanna. The tears of anger that had welled up in his eyes against Brady Downing flowed freely.

Beside him, Suzanna was in tears too. For Jeff, and for Denni, even for herself. After a few minutes Dennis composed himself.

"Should I take you home?"

"Thanks Den, I'd like that."

He started the car. "We must really be a sight." He commented. "red eyed and sniffling."

"It's the inside of me that's the bigger mess." Suzanna responded.

"I'm sorry Suzanna, I was really being selfish. Here I was blaming God for all Jeff's problems and look what you've been through and never once complained."

Suzanna was silent.

"What happened Tuesday night?" He finally asked.

Suzanna reluctantly told him, completely to her rescue by Mike and Chrys and also the admonition of Officer Williams. Denni already knew the complete story, she just filled in the details.

After hearing the story Denni was quiet for a while, Suzanna knew he was upset.

"Hagens, huh?" He finally spoke.

"That's what Jeff said."

"You telling the Police?"

"I might, I'm not sure."

"You better."

"Why?"

"Listen, I know Brady. He's not through. I also know that Hagens won't take the whole rap. He'll sing like a canary. It might be the only way we have of learning the whole truth."

"I never thought of that."

"If you don't want to say anything, I'll mention something to Jeff."

"No Denni, he's involved enough already."

"Yeah, you're right." Denni responded as he stopped at the Rhodes home. Luke was playing basketball. Brady Downing was with him.

"Well look who's here." Denni whispered.

"Just my luck." Suzanna returned. "He's got my family eating out of his hand."

"Not Pat."

"Thank the Lord for that. Well, here goes nothing." She opened the car door.

"Hey, thanks." Denni said sincerely "For everything I mean."

Suzanna smiled back. "You're the one who deserves the Thanks. But then that's what friends are for." They smiled at one another as Suzanna closed the car door and waved Denni on his way.

Brady was beside her in a minute. "You left in quite a huff at noon, I thought I'd see if you were upset." Brady began.

"Oh I'm not upset. I just don't care to ever lay eyes on you again in my entire life." She turned and marched into the house.

Youth service that night got off to a rough start. It was the boys turn to have a skit and one of their main characters Professor Perfection, was being absent minded. Actually Denni couldn't help it. He tried but he just didn't have anything left to put into the part. He was drained.

Although Denni did have a few problems the overall skit went fine. Even Luke the only young person who had the advantage of being in both skits played his part well.

The subject of the skit was the simplicity of the Gospel. Of the simple fact that there is one God and his name is Jesus.

After the skit and a short song service led by Peggy Winters, Chrystal Shephard spoke about the Love of God. The Unconditional, unchanging love.

Jeff was there.

And in the hour of need, Jeff, Denni, Suzanna, had begun to gather together, to bind together, to go to God together for the strength they needed against their adversary.

CHAPTER 17

A TIME TO EMBRACE

Saturday, September 24th, 1983

"Oh boy, Cheerio's for breakfast." Denni responded sarcastically "Again."

His mother gave him a disgusted look from where she was ironing her blouse for work.

"You know where everything is Den."

"Try this." Connie mentioned between bites of a thick sandwich.

"What is it?" Denni looked at it skeptically.

"Peanut butter, Jelly, Banana, and Raisin." She stated.

"Yuck."

"Well if you prefer Cheerio's"

"I'll find my own breakfast if you don't mind."

Denni opened the refrigerator and began removing items.

"There's plenty of lunchmeat for your lunch, You'll be working all day?" His mother wondered.

"Mnn Hmm." Dennie mumbled. I'll be home around six."

"Connie and I are going shopping in Lincoln we'll plan supper for Six-thirty."

"Mom, can I get a jean jacket for school?" Connie began. "All the kids have them, they look really cool."

"With dresses?" Her mother asked skeptically.

"With denim skirts, and stuff,...sure."

"Well,..'

"Denni has one, why can't I?"

"Denni needs his for work Connie; Your fall jacket is good enough for school."

"But mom,.. all my friends have them."

"All your friends? Does Jeani?"

"Um, no, but..."

"Does Becky?"
"No,.."
"Does Debbie?"
"No,.."
Suzanna?"
"No,.."
"But all your friends do?"
"Peggy does mom. And all the kids at school."
"Peggy wears hers when she's working with her horse right?"
"She wears it other places too mom."
Denni was laughing.
"It's an old one of her Grandpa's." He laughed.
"M-O-M"
"I'm sorry dear, but it's just not practical. You have a nice jacket you don't need a new one. Next fall when you need a new one we'll see."
"But mom,.." Connie wailed.
"Wait right there." Denni said as he ran from the room. He returned a few minutes later with his old discarded jean jacket. "Here you go."
"Oh yeck, you can't be serious. I'd be the laughing stock of my whole class."
"Why?"
"It smells like a barn."
"Wash it."
"It's all faded."
"They sell them that way."
"But,.. but,." Connie turned the disgusting item over a few times.
"Well, what's wrong?"
"It was yours." She said quietly.
"Who's gonna know it was mine?"
"Everybody." Connie remarked seriously.
"I don't think so."
"I know so. They'll know exactly who's it was. I just can't wear it."

"Settle down dear." Virginia remarked. "Dennis is being very kind to offer it to you. If Peggy's not to proud to wear her grandfather's, you shouldn't be too proud to wear Denni's."

"Well I suppose I can at least try it on and see what it's like."

"Do that." Denni said as he left the house. He hurried to the car shaking his head at his fickle sisters strange demands.

Denni was the first to arrive at the farm. Tom came in later, and worked into the evening. Rich was always on hand, but Bill was seldom around on weekends.

Denni checked the tack that Rich had prepared the night before, he then proceeded to the stalls where Ben kept his rental horses. He enjoyed the work but today his mind was preoccupied with other things. Mainly Jeff.

They'd had a nice talk last night after Youth Service, Jeff seemed in good spirits considering the up coming charges in court. He'd even joined the others at Charlies afterward. He did have an awkward time when some young people entered after the game. The team lost.

"Why couldn't things go right just once?" Denni wondered. "First Jeff's mother, then his father, then the team against him, and the cocaine, all that in just one week. Why?"

Denni saddled the horses that he'd be using for the first few hours. As he worked Outlaw ran around his legs.

"You'll get kicked one of these days and then you'll know enough to stay away." Denni commented.

The puppy tugged playfully at his jeans. Denni continued working. It was another beautiful day, although much chillier than the past few had been. He vaguely wondered what the day had in store for him.

Yesterday. Denni was amazed at what had transpired the day before. "How could I have been so blind?" He wondered "Just look at how Brady managed to manipulate even the police to arrest Jeff. How could I have been so blind that I hadn't seen through Brady before now?" Dennis kicked at Outlaw in frustration. The tiny puppy skidded across the dirt and landed in a heap. It yelped. Denni shook himself from his thoughts and approached him. The puppy cowered from him, away from his grasp.

"You're a smart dog, Outlaw." Denni commented playfully, he let the dog wander away as he finished his work.

"Morning Den." Rich greeted when he joined Dennis a few minutes later.

"Hi"

"Looks like you're all set, should be a nice day."

"I hope so."

Rich looked over the row of horses that Deni had saddled and tied to the hitching rail outside the entrance to the stable.

"Okay, let's see if I've got these names right." Rich began. "That's Smokey, Bonanza, Whiskers, hmm, that is either Ranger, or Star."

"That's Star."

"Okay, Star, Jinx, Beauty, Lady Jane and Freckles. But I don't recall this last one at all."

"That's my horse Prints." Denni laughed. "I'm gonna bring another horse out and use it myself later today before Ben adds it to the line."

"Which one is that?"

Denni turned toward the horses in the nearby field. "Let's see,.. Oh he's over there."

"That big Chestnut?"

"Uh, huh, that's Ten Gallon. Ben bought him a few weeks ago. I've ridden him a few times. He's gentle enough."

"Sure is a big fella."

"Over sixteen hands. Not much of a bloodline though, couldn't tell you what he was myself."

Rich took another look at the horses, then checked his watch. "Should be arriving anytime, the first group is scheduled to leave at 9:30."

"I think I'll grab a lead rope and bring Ten Gallon in. I'll put him in one of the empty stalls."

"Fine, go ahead."

It was after Denni had returned with the first group, and had wandered into the lounge for a break that he saw the note that Ben had posted.

POSITION OPEN

PART - TIME WEEKENDS

CONTACT: BEN DANIELS

It wasn't much of a notice but Denni immediately thought of Jeff. Jeff would really be interested, he'd told Denni often enough how lucky he was that Ben and Sarah had hired him, now was Jeff's opportunity. Denni could hardly wait to see him.

The notice had only been up since last evening. Ben had tacked it up before he'd left for Youth Service with his family. Already there had been some response. Rich had handled a few inquiries in Bens absence, given them applications and told them they'd be considered. Ben wanted the position filled as soon as possible.

"Wheew," Ben exclaimed when he saw the applications. "It seems this is going to be harder than I thought."

"I hate to tell you this." Rich began, "But I think a lot of those applicants think the job will be a piece of cake."

"I can see that, I've never heard of most of these people. I thought tacking that notice up here where all the owners would see it, one of them, or their children would be interested." Ben leafed through a few more. "Here's one to consider. "She's pretty young for the job I want now but I'll hang on to it." Ben tossed an application to Rich who read it.

"Jenny Johnson - sure, she was here with her mother last night. She's twelve?... yes that's pretty young."

"Uh, huh." Ben was leafing through the remainder. "A few of these look promising but I haven't taken the time to really read through them." He had separated the stack into two piles. One he placed in a folder in his file. The other he left on his desk awaiting further thought. "How busy are we today?"

"Well, eight horses went out at both nine-thirty, and eleven. A group of fifteen is scheduled for twelve-thirty, and another group of five for one. Tom will take the first group out, Denni the second."

"You've got the horses?"

"Yeah, but we're using all of them,.. except the two Bill shoed yesterday."

"When do the next ones go out?" Ben asked.

Rich checked a note pad that he pulled from his pocket. "There's a group of ten scheduled for 2:00, all the horses should be in by then."

"Use Tom's horses, they'll be fresher, and try to keep track of how long some are on the trail. I don't want to see the same horses used all day."

"Okay. Anything else?"

"No, no, I'll be here if anyone needs me."

"I'll tell them."

After Dennis had helped the last rider dismount at twelve he joined Tom in loosening cinches and leading the horses to water.

"It's such a cool day, they're hardly winded." Tom remarked.

"The breeze is excellent. Oh I noticed the grape vines out along the south fence are just chuck full and ripe."

"Remind me, I'll ride out there later, bring some back for Sarah."

"Maybe she'd like to go too?"

"Yeah, I'll mention it."

The two were quiet for a minute, breathing in the cool, crisp, autumn air and the smell of freshly bailed hay.

"I heard about Jeff Johnson." Tom said.

"Yeah, I suppose they'll throw the book at him." Dennis commented.

"It's really too bad." Tom began. "Jeff's okay. It's that other friend of yours that gives me the creeps."

"Me too." Denni admitted.

Tom was startled.

"Surprised you didn't I?" Denni began. "Well I surprised myself more. I just can't believe I didn't see through that phoney mask of his before now."

"What happened?" Tom wondered. Denni told him as much as he could about Jeff's arrest and what they had agreed was Brady's part in it.

"Brady's always given me the creeps but I never thought he'd stoop that low. Jeff was his best friend."

"Uh huh."

"Does Suzanna Rhodes know how it happened?"

"She's the one that figured it out and told me."

"She did?"

"Yeah, then Jeff confirmed a few more things."

"I'm glad she knows. It made me sick watching the two of them together."

"Who's that?"

"Brady and Suzanna. I admit I was beginning to wonder about her. Am I glad she's wise to what he's like."

"They were together a lot then?" Dennis wondered. He had assumed that their relationship had existed of Brady making advances and she warding them off.

"I guess so. They were together Saturday night while she was baby sitting. Alone, in a dark house. Then I saw them riding together, on one horse. It really made me sick. I'm glad she knows better."

"Yeah, I am too." Denni responded quietly, "What was it Jeff had said to Suzanna about Saturday night." Denni wondered as he turned back to his work.

"Alright!" Denni exclaimed as he recognized the Johnsons truck parked before the stables. He was just returning with a group of riders and was excited at the prospect of seeing Jeff.

He found him with Misty and Faleene.

"Hey, Jeff!" Dennie called.

"Den Hi."

"You alone?"

"Yeah, Pa's not comin' back. He thought of pulling our horses out and putting them somewhere else. He left it up to us. Jenny and I both decided to stay here."

"That's great! But then,.. he's not coming back huh?"

"It doesn't look like it."

"That's too bad."

"Yeah, I know. I miss him already."

"How did he manage the game last night?"

"There was a reason they lost." Jeff smiled. "Pa refused to allow certain individuals to play."

"Really?"

"Uh huh, and they were steaming mad."

"Can they do anything about it?"

"No I guess Pa talked to the other coaches and advisors and told them before hand."

"Yep, and he told them I'd be off the team for good,.. they assumed it was for the same reason."

"The cocaine?"

"Yeah, I don't mind. They're believing that Pa kicked me off the team and the others are under suspicion."

"Who'd he pull out?"

"Brady of course, and Chas Hagens and Jim Townes."

"Wheew, no wonder they lost! Those are our best players."

"You might say my Dad's not very popular this morning."

"Is he at home?"

"No I dropped him off at school. He decided to remain coach."

"He did? Why?"

"I really don't know. It's funny, all of the sudden he sticks to it right when he becomes so unpopular."

"It might be his only way of getting back at Brady." Dennis suggested.

"Hey, I hadn't thought of that." Jeff remarked. "That could be it." The two of them left Misty and Faleene and walked toward where Denni's next group of riders was gathering.

"Well, it's back to work for me." He commented.

"Be thankful."

"Hey, did you see the notice Ben put up?"

"Uh huh."

"Why don't you apply. You're here most of the weekend anyway."

"I don't think so."

"Why not?"

"I just don't think I'd get the job."

"What are you talking about? You have as much of a chance as anyone."

"I doubt it.

"It won't hurt to try, you've ridden Ben's horses,.. you know he trusts you."

"Not anymore Den."

"Why not?"

"Denni, things have changed."

"What do you mean?"

"I've got charges against me now Den. Things will be different."

"Not with Ben, Jeff."

"I just don't know."

"Will it hurt to try?"

"Well it won't hurt to think about it."

"He could give the job to someone else while your thinking too."

"Well, let him."

"You mean you're gonna let this opportunity go by and not take advantage of it?"

"Uh huh."

Jeff saddled Jen's horse and joined Denni's next trail ride. They enjoyed riding together; Faleen was left asleep with her mother in her stall.

"Just think Jeff, you could be getting paid for doing this." Denni remarked as they returned.

"Yeah, sure."

"I mean it, it won't hurt to talk to Ben."

"I'd rather not Den,.. Okay?"

"Suit yourself."

Dennis helped the riders dismount and cared for the horses, while Jeff took care of Poncho. Both were so involved that they didn't notice a girl arrive. She watched them for awhile, then approached Denni.

"Hi," She said.

Denni looked up startled.

"Uh,..Hi, Can I help you?"

"Not really, I'm just wondering around 'til my daddy get's through talking to Mr. Daniels."

Denni looked at her more closely. She was about his age, and wore designer jeans, and a tailored Denim Jacket, on her feet were tiny cowboy boots. Her thick blonde hair was cut and fell in curls around her shoulders. She wore a red bandana in her hair that contrasted with her deep blue eyes. She smiled encouragingly and Denni realized that she was one of the prettiest girls he'd ever seen. He tried to return to work, but she continued watching.

"Does it bother you if I watch you work?" She asked.

"Um,.. uh,.. Not really," He lied then thought better of it. "I mean,.. it shouldn't."

"It does though, then let me help. I do this all the time at home." She expertly loosened the straps on the saddle of one of the horses nearest Denni, then removing the bridle she clipped the lead rope onto the halter and hung the bridle on the saddle horn. She spoke to the horse all the while, and patted it fondly.

Denni couldn't help but be impressed, they worked together in silence for a while. Jeff looked on thoughtfully as he groomed Poncho.

"You've been around horses before." Jeff remarked.

"Oh is it obvious?" She replied seeming to see Jeff for the first time. "I kind of grew up with them. My name is Julie Marksman, I live near Abraham, my father raises horses there."

"I've heard of him." Jeff smiled "Ben just bought a young colt from him."

"That's right. Daddy wanted to come and see how he had adapted to his new home. My brother and I both rode along, Joel is talking to that one tall guy."

"Rich"

"Yeah, I couldn't stand their boring conversation so I thought I'd wander around and see what I could find,.. and look what I found. It must be my lucky day." She smiled.

"Or ours." Jeff responded. Denni shook his head in amazement.

"I'll tell you what. Den is working here but I'm not, I'll show you around a bit."

"Would you really?"

"Sure, my pleasure." He began to lead Poncho toward the barn. "We'll start at the nursery, come on, it's not everyday I get to show off Misty's new filly."

Julie began to follow, then turned back toward Denni.

"I'll look for you later." She whispered as she ran off.

Denni smiled to himself, she would probably forget all about him, after Jeff started pouring on his charm.

Brady Downing also visited the farm that afternoon. He found Denni putting grain in the stalls for the horses.

"Hey, Den Old Boy, what are you up too?" He asked as he joined him. Denni gritted his teeth and didn't speak.

"Workin' huh?" Brady remarked after a few minutes.

"What's on your mind, Brady?"

"Oh, nothing." He shrugged.

"I'm not surprised." Denni said sarcastically.

"What's with you?"

Denni turned and just looked at his former buddy.

"Well if you want her that bad Den you can have her." Brady remarked dramatically.

"Huh?"

"Suzanna, I noticed the two of you together, and don't worry. I'll step aside. She was right all along, nothing could work between us."

"I don't like,.." Denni tried to defend himself.

"Don't give me that line. I can tell. Even if you might be able to hide it, the fact that she adores you is obvious."

"It is?" Denni fell for it.

"Why sure. And I apologize for what I said about her the other day, I was being selfish, it's obvious for the two of you to be together."

"Brady, I'm not interested in Suzanna." Denni stated.

"Sure you are."

"Sorry, your wrong. You've been wrong about a lot of things lately."

"Like what?"

"Like thinking you can fool Jeff, Suzanna and I indefinitely."

"Fool you?"

"We've got your number Downing."

"Come off it Den."

"No you come off it. We know what you pulled on Jeff. I admit he wasn't being very bright to fall for it like he did but he's wise to you now."

"I don't get it." Brady said with false sincerity.

"I think you do." Denni began. "What you've pulled on Jeff was really low. Also putting Suzanna in danger like you did, you can't be human."

"Suzanna in danger? You must really be jealous to think that, I suppose you're the one who got her to believe the story about my involvement Tuesday night. It's a story Den, there's no fact to it. And I haven't seen Jeff since yesterday morning." Brady defended himself. Jeff returned at that time with Julie.

"Well if it isn't Mr. Nice Guy." Jeff remarked sarcastically. "Did you get your stolen car back?"

"Hey Jeff, I'm really sorry about that. I forgot all about giving you the keys."

"But I was to meet you in twenty minutes. How could you forget that?"

"It just slipped my mind. When I found out you had it everything just clicked, I couldn't believe what I'd done."

"I couldn't either."

"I'm really sorry Jeff."

"I doubt it." Jeff just stared at him.

"Hey Jeff." Julie interrupted the tension. "I already met Dennis, aren't you gonna introduce me to your other friend."

"He's not a friend, and no I'm not." Jeff responded sharply. Brady smiled at Julie.

"I'm Brady Downing, I thought I was a friend of Jeffs,.. and Denni's" He looked at the two. "Obviously I was wrong."

"We still could be friends," Denni remarked "We're just through playing your games. If you be honest and straight, we can be friends. But if you're gonna use us and try to manipulate us you can forget it."

"I haven't done anything." Brady demanded. Jeff and Dennis just stared at him as if challenging his statement. Julie became uneasy.

"I guess I've seen enough of the farm for today." She turned to go.

"Wait." Denni called. "I'm really sorry you had to hear what was said. I should have known better. I brought my personal feelings to work with me today. I can't do that. I hope you forgive me."

"Oh I'll forgive you Den, anytime." She smiled encouragingly as she turned to leave. Peggy entered the stable at that moment.

"Julie! Hi." She said brightly. "I saw your brother, he told me you were on the farm somewhere."

"How did you find me here?"

"I knew where to look." Peggy said knowingly. Both girls laughed.

"I guess you would, you've had a lot of practice."

"I'd like to forget that." Peggy began. "Did Dennis show you around."

"Denni has work to do." Julie frowned. "But Jeff was kind enough to show me his little filly; I'm sure Brady would have accompanied me but he just arrived."

All three boys looked at her admiringly. Denni tickled by her encouragement but rejecting even the thought of responding. Jeff secretly hoping, and Brady determining in his heart to win this new prize. Denni returned to work, but the others followed the girls from the stable. There seemed less friction between the two so consumed where they in impressing Julie.

"Cindi, your Honey's here." Suzanna remarked in a sing song voice when Bob Morris' car pulled into their driveway that afternoon.

"Oh no! Bob's here." Cindi flew off the couch where she had been reading, and headed toward the stairs. "He can't see me like this! If he did he'd never marry me. Stall him will you." She ran up the stairs taking curlers from her hair as she went.

Suzanna shrugged, then called out.

"This will cost you something."

"Anything,.. just stall him." Cindi called desperately.

Suzanna smiled to herself and went to answer the door.

Bob Morris was not a striking looking man, neither was he homely, he had a unique look about him that was appealing. He smiled when Suzanna answered the door.

"Oh Bob." She gushed, imitating her sister. "Did you come all the way over here to see little old me?"

Bob broke into a laugh. "Actually, I came to see your sister."

"You can't blame me for trying, it's not often that I get to open the door and find a guy standing there,.. and smiling."

"I've got a lot to smile about."

"I hope you know what you're getting into."

"I think I do." Bob responded. "Is Cindi home?"

"Yup, but she looks like a witch right now, she asked me to stall you."

"She didn't have to do that."

"Oh yes she did. She's trying to hide her true nature from you, I'm surprised you didn't feel the breeze from her broomstick when you came in the door."

"There must be something in that thick potion she makes me drink each time I'm with her that keeps bringing me back." He said with a thoughtful attitude.

"You took 'THE POTION'?" Suzanna said dramatically. "Don't you know it has drastic side effects?"

"It does?" Bob appeared to be looking all over his body.

"That last fellow who took it had his hair turn green, and grew feathers on his legs."

"No, You're kidding. She should market the stuff, she'd make a fortune."

Both were laughing by then and Cindi was quite surprised to see them in such a state when she came downstairs.

"It's good to see you." Bob said lovingly. "I was in the area and I thought I'd stop by."

"What brings you around here?"

"I'm gonna stop at Ben's and take a look at his truck, he's gonna bring it to the shop as soon as I can fit it in."

"Let me go out there with you."

"I was hoping you'd want to." The two were anticipating a nice ride together, when Luke arrived.

"Hi Bob, where ya going?"

"Out to Ben's."

"Really, can I come. Ben bought a new puppy and I really want to see it."

"I don't think so Luke" Cindi remarked "Bob's going to look at Ben's truck and you'll be in the way."

"You will too." He said seriously.

"I'm gonna go talk to Sarah."

"Then I'll go talk to Nick."

"I said no Luke" Cindi responded seriously.

"Oh Cindi, it's okay. I don't mind if he's along at all."

"Are you sure?"

"Absolutely."

"Yea!" Luke said enthusiastically.

"If he's going, I'm going too." Suzanna informed them.

"Oh sure," Cindi said sarcastically. "Why don't we just make it a family outing."

"You could pretend we didn't exist. You're good at that. Besides you owe me one."

"Well Okay." Cindi said disappointed.

"Thanks sis. Thanks a million."

"I think I'll stay in the car if you don't mind." Suzanna mumbled when she recognized Brady's car in the parking lot of Horseman's Unlimited.

"I knew it! You just begged to go along so you could torment me." Cindi announced. "Can you believe her? She pleads to come and now that we're here she's gonna sit in the car."

"No she's not." Bob remarked as he opened the door. Suzanna didn't trust him one bit and was out of the car before he could force her.

"I was just kidding." She said. "I'll just sit here next to the car on the fence and wait."

"Go ahead." Bob remarked "Dennis is working right? And Tom? I can go drop the hint that you're playing hard to get."

"Bob if you say one word about me I'll..."

"What'll you do? Punch me in the nose?"

"I'll try." She threatened.

"I'm glad to see you two get along so well." Cindi commented dryly.

"It's not hard to handle infants." Bob remarked.

"You handle your own life, I'll handle mine."

"Face it Suzanna, the sooner I find a sweetheart for you, the sooner you quit pestering us." He pulled Cindi close.

"Yuck." Luke responded.

"I'll find my own sweetheart,..please." Suzanna said with a grin.

"I won't hold my breath." Cindi remarked as she joined Luke and headed toward the Daniels home.

Suzanna made a face behind her back. Bob grinned.

"You really won't say anything, will you?" She asked desperately.

"Of course not silly. I'm gonna have to put up with you as an In-Law for the rest of my life, why should I give you something to attack me with."

"Thanks." Suzanna replied in appreciation, although she still didn't want to see Brady. "Hey Bob, I was wondering,.. You'll be looking at Ben's truck right?"

"Yup."

"Well, there's someone here I don't particularly care for. If I want to get rid of him could you give me a hand."

"No way, Hosea', you're on your own,.. fight your own battles."

"Some Brother-in-Law you're gonna make."
"All in the name of sanity." Bob responded as he left her.

Suzanna thought awhile, then taking a deep breath she approached the stables. It was indeed a busy evening. Reynolds Marksman had stayed much longer than he had intended, Tom was returning with another group of riders, and many owners were doing various tasks with their horses. Suzanna shuffled her way over the dusty path. Laughter came from the arena, she glanced in that direction. From where she stood Suzanna could make out four teenagers perched on the arena fence. The center of attention was obviously the young lady who was laughing loudest, while reaching for support every now and then from the two boys that surrounded her. The second girl was Peggy, she sat next to Jeff slightly apart from the others, it was obvious that the conversation didn't please her. Suzanna was relieved to see that the second boy was Brady and that he seemed to be currently occupied.
"It looks like your friend found a new source of entertainment." Said a voice behind her. Startled Suzanna turned.
"Actually, I'm glad,.. it's a relief." She spoke as Denni approached.
"Are you?"
"Uh huh." Suzanna began. "I guess I've got a lot to learn."
"You too huh."
"Yup."
"Have you met Julie before?"
"That's JULIE?" Suzanna was surprised. "No wonder Peggy had such a rough time with her, she sure moves fast."
"Your not kidding, either."
"Well she can have him if she wants him."
"She does." Denni remarked "She'd take anything."
"How did you manage to escape her clutches?"
"I've got work to do." Denni stated seriously.
"Don't let me hold you up either." Suzanna apologized. "I won't be here long and I wanted to see Outlaw."
"Did you?,.. He's back here."

Denni led the way to the back of the barn as he spoke. "He's kind of adopted an old rag bag of Bills for a bed."

Suzanna scooped the wiggly bundle of fuzz up into her arms. She buried her face in his soft fur.

"You smell like a puppy." She remarked as she seated herself on a bale of hay nearby.

"What did you expect him to smell like? Perfume?" Denni asked teasingly as he joined her on a bale nearby.

"He could have smelled like Moo Cow." Suzanna said dramatically.

"What Cow's?"

"Horses then."

"An altogether different smell."

"Is it really?"

"I'm not sure, but I'd like to get people to believe it."

Suzanna smiled as she laid Outlaw in her lap, he soon scampered away to chase the kittens who had also chosen Old Bill's work shop as home. Denni made no move to get back to work.

"How's Jeff today?" Suzanna asked presently.

"You saw him. He seems in good spirits."

"I can't believe that after what Brady did to him, that Jeff and he would still be friends."

"They aren't."

"But they're out there together. I saw them."

"Oh they're out there all right. They're rivals."

"Julie?"

"Uh huh. I've never seen Jeff so stuck before."

"What's she like?"

"Okay I guess. I didn't spend much time with her."

"Is she pretty?"

"Uh huh." Denni agreed embarrassed.

"Good, then maybe Brady will leave me alone."

"Remember Brady doesn't give up easily."

"I'm praying that he'll make an exception."

"So am I."

And once again as another day is closing we see change come upon our friends in Roberts Junction. Some looking with anticipation, embracing a new day, a new hope; While others in their ignorance seek out their own desires and longings. Where will it all lead?

CHAPTER 18

A TIME TO REFRAIN FROM EMBRACING

Sunday, September 25th, 1983

Early Sunday morning, while Sarah Daniels scrambled eggs in her large country kitchen, and the Reverend Edward Rhodes sat in his office going over a few last minute notes for this mornings lesson, Richard McAllister stood in a circle of birch trees and drank in the fresh September air. He'd dismounted long ago and journeyed forth on foot. A blanket of crisp gold leaves covered the ground and announced his arrival to the squirrels and chipmunks who abandoned their search for food to gain shelter. The sun that had barely risen over the horizon shown through the now almost bare branches casting spider web shadows. Still no matter how far Rich wandered he could never wander from the guilt that plagued him. That guilt that worked as a vice grasping, squeezing, holding his own heart in it's grip. The sun could never shine bright enough to penetrate the shadow of pain that enveloped him. The air could never be fresh enough to revive the life that had left him.

Soberly he walked, among cherished friends, who seemed to understand his very thoughts. Friends that stood firm, not cowering from his presence. Not rushing forth to soothe, what they had no comprehension of, but there, his friends. He'd walked here before of late and although he remained bound in fetters of guilt, each time he came, he left something more and the burden grew lighter.

Returning to his mare, he spoke to her soothingly as he mounted. The fields were bare now. The harvest was in. The stubble that remained had become the home of a family of pheasants. As he travelled the bordering path, Rich marvelled at the fact that year after year without fail rain and sunlight could produce growth. Life went on.

But somewhere in Aspen Colorado was a man who'd been cheated. Robbed of his wife and children. How could life possibly go on. How could life possibly go on for one man who'd had to accept such senseless deaths. Was it really fair that Rich's life went on?

Wild geese arrowed the sky, crashing the silence with their trumpeting. They appeared to slice it in half as they instinctively journeyed south. Rich journeyed also. His journey returned him to the stables where he knew his job awaited him.

Ben, looking unnatural in a dark three piece suit in comparison to the jeans and flannel shirt which was his normal attire, was just coming from his office. He paused as Rich approached.

"There you are. I left some more applications for the job opening they're on my desk if you need them. I'll be back before twelve. Both Denni and Tom are off today so you're on your own." He began to turn away.

"Good Morning." Rich said.

"Huh?" Ben looked back, then laughed. "I guess I did kind of bombard you didn't I?"

"I think buried me would be a more fitting word."

"Well don't take it to heart, I always get in a tiff on Sunday mornings."

"I'll remember that."

"Well I'm in a hurry, I'll see you around twelve."

"Sure."

Midmorning found Rich alone in the loft of the big barn, grasping bales of brittle hay that thudded to the floor below creating a cloud of dust. The smell of harvest, the sound of the crisp hay breaking beneath his boots, the sensation of the yellow barbs that clawed his hands, the fragments of hay that lingered in the air all led to a strange sense of peacefulness. Strange in the aspect that peace had become so foreign to him.

He worked in silence, his only companion the kittens that had made homes there and the pigeons perched on the rafters above him. From below came the sounds that had become so familiar. The thud of hooves, the gentle whinnies, the snort of a muzzle in the bottom of an empty grain bucket. Maybe he did belong here after all.

He backed slowly down the ladder, breathing in the lingering smells; sensing that peace was about to be shattered.

Outlaw appeared and attacked him playfully. Rich smiled, yet shoved him aside for his playfulness could be very disturbing. Especially when there was work to be done.

A car door slammed nearby, and voices became mingled with the peaceful sounds of the farm. Rich continued to work.

Doc Martin had been a busy man this past week, there had been Michelle's baby Sunday night, another late Monday, two patients had scheduled surgery for Thursday morning and among other things his mind was on the future, and the child that his wife now carried.

Doc was a good man, with a heart of Gold, he'd left his mark on society by being a friend as well as a physician to many of his patients. He wasn't the type to waste hours on a manicured lawn tapping balls with the end of a long stick but preferred to spend his time at Horseman's Unlimited.

Sylvia accompanied him again this morning. Such an oddly matched pair, but then who else but Doc would willingly suffer the consequences of her energetic tongue. As Rich continued the chores they prepared their Saddlebreds for a ride. Rich was forking clean straw into a stall when Sylviah approached.

"Excuse me, Richard, when do you think Ben will be returning from church?"

"He'll be back before noon, can I help you with something?"

"It's Queenie."

"What seems to be the trouble?"

"She's favoring her left hind hoof, I was hoping Ben could take a look at her."

"I'll take a peek, where is she?"

"I've got her tied in the arena."

Rich followed her from the barn to the indoor arena situated near Bens office.

"Lead her about for a minute first." He asked.

Sylvia led Queenie a few yards and she did indeed have an obvious problem, favoring one of her legs.

"Let me see." Sylviah held the mare while Rich lifted the hoof. "New shoes, huh?" He commented.

"Bill Winters put them on Thursday afternoon."

"That could easily be disturbing her, but I can't say for sure."

"She's never had problems before."

"I can't tell you that it is the problem. But it is a possibility."

"Would Ben know?"

"He'd know more than I do, but Bill's the expert."

"You think Bill's competent then?"

"Why of course,.. why wouldn't he be?"

"Well, he is getting up there in years."

"We all are."

"I know that. But some elderly people do loose it a bit."

"So do some of the younger ones I know."

"Richard, I don't like what you are implying. I asked Bill three days ago to fix Queenie new shoes, at the time he looked at me as if I didn't know what was best for my own horse... And now look at her. All because one old man who thinks he knows more than the horse's owners tampers with her. I should have known better."

"Excuse me Ma'am, but there is absolutely nothing wrong with Bill Winters' mind. It may be just coincidence that Queenie is coming lame now."

"Coincidence? I should say not. I'll have someone come out and look at her the first thing tomorrow. And in the mean time try to keep that senile old Gentleman away from Queenie."

"Ms. Martin, there may be nothing wrong with Queenie, at least have Ben take a look at her."

"Oh I'll see that Ben sees her, and that he hears what I have to say about Bill Winters."

"Bill was just doing his job Ma'am."

"And I was fool enough to pay him for it."

"I'm sorry you feel that way."

Rich was quite upset after his conversation with Sylvia Martin. Returning to work he felt both furious and guilty. Had he handled the situation wrong? He was supposed to be in charge of the woman's horse, she'd put it in his care. Couldn't he have at least held a decent conversation with her. Couldn't he at least have acknowledged the possibility that Bill could have been negligent. Could Bill have been negligent? Rich hardly knew him. What if Bill had done an insufficient job and Queenie would have to suffer. Rich tried to erase the thoughts from his mind. The fact that Sylvia had spoken against Bill had made him furious yet it also made him doubt the quality of Bills work.

He was deep in thought when Steve Williams approached him.

"Hi Rich." Steve greeted "Isn't it a beautiful day?"

"Sure is."

"Judy and I are taking the horses to Bulletin this morning. They have excellent trails there through the National Forest."

"I've heard that, have you been there before."

"No, but friends of ours have."

"Let me know what you think of it." Rich asked. "It sounds like something I'd enjoy myself."

"I'll do that, oh by the way, I was wondering something."

"What's that?"

"Well Judy told me that her daughter Jenny insisted on applying for that job here. I hope Ben doesn't seriously consider her old enough."

"I really can't tell you what Ben thinks." Rich said, "you'll have to ask him, but I do know he was hoping to hire someone older."

"Has Jeff applied?"

"I really don't know. I only handled Jenny because Ben was away, he would have handled any of the others."

"I'd like to see Jeff apply, he's good with horses, and loves hard work. He also needs something constructive and solid he can put his energies into right now."

"I heard about his arrest. I'm truly sorry. How did Ray take it?"

"I'm not sure, he was fighting mad when he first found out but I think that was because I was present. He settled down some and even returned to work."

"Drinking?"

"Surprisingly no." Steve went on "It would be to my advantage if he licked the habit completely."

"Before he licks you completely?"

"Something like that."

"I doubt if you have to worry any more. I heard that he refuses to return here so you're safe for awhile anyway."

"I feel as though I'm being stalked by a wild cat."

"And he feels like that stallion who's lost his mares to one much stronger and comely then himself."

Steve was quiet.

"How Ray is reacting is wrong Steve, but is what you pulled on him month after month justified?"

"I love Judy, Rich. Should I deny the fact and allow her to remain in a marriage where she's unhappy?"

"And should Ray refrain from using the bottle if it is what makes him happy?"

"I have no objection to drinking at all. In fact I enjoy it myself." Steve laughed. "Let's just say that Ray Johnson and I are not good buddies and leave it at that."

Ben returned to the farm at 11:45 that morning. Doc and Sylviah had gone riding after renting a horse of Ben's for Sylviah. Rich was helping Steve load Flasher into his trailer, Judy was loading their tack. After parking the car in the garage under Rich's apartment, Ben walked the well worn trail to the stables and joined them.

"Heading out for the day?" Ben asked.

"If we can get this fool loaded we are." Steve remarked.

"Problems?"

"This critter is as stubborn as a mule."

"That's funny I can't recall having problems with him before."

"He's always loaded okay?" Steve asked.

Ben paused in thought. "I really don't recall ever loading him."

"Well it's a fine time to mention that now." Steve said frustrated.

"He's probably just spooked." Ben remarked as he walked confidently toward the gelding. Patting the animal fondly on the neck he reached for the lead rope and began to lead him around, talking to him all the while, after making a wide circle around the truck he led the horse undisturbed into the trailer."

"I can see why you own this place and I don't" Steve laughed. "I'll remember that little trick."

"Where are you headed?"

"Bulletin?"

"The National Forest?"

"Yup"

"You'll really like it. It's a nice spot."

"I'm looking forward to it."

Rich returned to work leaving Ben and Steve talking. Judy waited in Steves truck.

"I was asking Rich before about that job opening you have."

"Your not considering applying are you?" Ben teased.

"No but I was thinking of Jeff."

"So was I as a matter of fact. He'd come to my mind as a possibility a week or so ago."

"Did he apply?"

"Not that I know of."

"You'll consider him then if he does?"

"Of course Steve, I'm pretty fond of Jeff, I trust him with my horses."

"Even after his arrest?"

"Arrest? I hadn't heard."

"He was arrested Friday afternoon, He had in his possession not only a stolen vehicle but an eighth of a gram of cocaine also."

"A stolen vehicle?"

"I guess it was a buddies. Their stories didn't jive."

"I see."

"You're not surprised about the cocaine."

"No Steve, I'm not. I knew he used the stuff."

"And you did nothing to help him?"

"I tried to be his friend Steve."

"But you never approached him?"

"I may have, if it had continued."

"I guess his father knew also."

"How'd Ray take it?"

"Like everything else these past few days."

"He got violent huh."

"Yeah, but I heard he settled down later."

"I hope you know this doesn't change how I feel about Jeff."

"I'm glad Ben, that will mean a lot to him."

"If you talk to him, encourage him to apply for the job. I'm gonna make a decision about it tomorrow."

"I will, thanks for considering him." Steve turned to his truck.

"Have a nice ride."

"I will."

Ben continued to his office where a stack of applications awaited him. One particular one had been set aside for serious consideration. Peggy Winters had filled one out the night before while she'd been visiting, Brady Downing had also. His was placed for consideration but Ben had his doubts. Peggy he trusted, as he also trusted Jeff. Suzanna had been in a tiff for she wanted to apply but her father had proclaimed her too young. She tried to sweet talk him into letting her, but she was never good at sweet talk, especially when she knew it was a hopeless case. So she had hung up the phone in disappointment.

Ben looked at a few of the applications then glanced once again at Peggy's. He knew he'd contacting her in the morning.

A sharp knock on the door disturbed his thoughts.

"Come in." He called.

Sylviah Martin entered the room.

"Ben I'm glad you're back,.."

"Hi Sylviah."

"I'm very upset over Queenie and I want something done about it." She insisted.

"What seems to,.."

"That man you have working for you has ruined her hooves."

"Bill?"

"Why of course it's Mr. Winters. I took Queenie to him Thursday morning for new shoes. He made some ignorant remark about her not needing shoes, as if I didn't know what was best for my Queenie."

"Maybe you were mistaken."

"I'm never mistaken Ben, I've been working with horses all my life I should know when one needs new shoes."

"Bill is usually pretty careful in his work Sylviah."

"But he is getting rather old, and in my opinion the quality of his work is deteriorating."

"I haven't seen any evidence of that." Ben remarked.

"Have you been watching him Ben? or are you becoming too interested in your Stallions to be concerned about the quality of carc our horses get."

"I feel the horses are getting superb care." Ben said soberly.

"With Bill Winters, and Richard McAllister as you chief employees?"

"They are both very knowledgeable individuals, Bill in his work shoeing, and other hoof care, Rich is doing well maintaining the place as it should be."

"But yet most of us know nothing about Rich."

"I have known Rich for the majority of my life."

"So you know of his wereabouts the last few years."

"Yes Sylviah I do."

"And yet you continue to retain him after you know of his prison record."

"Yes I do, He is a fine young man."

"I'm sorry I don't agree, about either him or Bill Winters. Rich treated me totally wrong today, as if I didn't know what was best for my own horse."

"I'm sure he was only doing his job. I'll talk to both of them, we'll see if we can straighten this out."

"I hope so. I like this place. I like you and your wife but I want Queenie to have quality care and if I feel she's not getting it, I'll bring my mare elsewhere."

"I hope you won't find it necessary to do that, but I do understand your concerns."

"I'm glad someone does." She turned to go.

"Oh by the way." Ben stopped her. "Congratulations."

"Thanks, Ben."

Ben was exercising Fortune in the outdoor arena, when Ray Johnson dropped his children off before the Stable. The rancher beckoned to him but Ray continued on his way. Ben was unaware of the turmoil that raged in the mans soul, that jealously that leaped out violently without his control. He chose to stay away because he could no longer face Steve Williams and maintain his composure. Maybe if Judy and Steve had been more open he could have accepted it. But after months of deception, who did they think he was anyway? The very thought of them together turned his stomach into knots, the very sight of her car, now theirs; brought him to the boiling point. The sight of them together could prove disastrous.

Jenny had chosen to remain with her mother, the shock of her parents separation was far less than the fear that had gripped her when Ray had struck out blindly the other evening and hit Jeff. Although together this morning she usually accompanied Steve and her mother when they came. Jenny was a timid girl of twelve, her long blond hair was permed into waves that billowed thickly down her back. Her blue eyes were clear, she smiled freely. Although the past week had been rough on all involved she had fared better than her older brother who was the more sensitive of the two.

Her innocence had done much to protect her from the bitterness that so easily could have corrupted her soul. Today she wore faded levi's over pink hightop sneakers, a grey pullover sweatshirt of her brothers completed her attire. A strange combination, but then not for horse back riding. She climbed the fence into the pasture to look for Poncho.

Jeff had gone directly to Misty's stall, an apple and sugar cube for a treat were hidden in the large pockets of his jacket. Misty knew exactly where to find them and soon was nosing him playfully. Faleene cared little for treats or Jeff's attention, being by mommy was all that seemed important to her. Jeff taking the lead rope he'd brought with him, clipped it to Misty's halter, and led her from the stall. Eagerly the filly followed. Jeff swung aboard Misty before he ever left the stable and going slow enough to allow the filly to follow he began to walk Misty slowly down the trail. Faleene soon grew weary and Jeff was forced to return.

Rich who had just put Fortune in his stall joined him when he dismounted outside the stable.

"Misty's itchin for a workout huh?" Rich asked.

"She should be fine, I had her out yesterday a bit."

"I'm glad to see that. Even Faleene looks the picture of health."

"She's tuckered right now but nothing serious."

There was a pause before Rich continued. "Steve talked to me this morning."

"Yeah?" Jeff asked.

"He told me a little of your trouble."

"I wish he hadn't done that."

"I know it's embarrassing. But Jeff it doesn't have to be the end of the world."

"That's easy for you to say."

"You're right it is. The most you can get right now is correctional school, I'm acquainted with a young boy who was imprisoned when he was eighteen. He had a rough time for a while but I'm glad to say he went on with life."

"Where'd you meet him?"

"In prison, He wanted to end his life. I tried to help him all I could and am thankful that he's still alive today."

"Really? He's out of jail now?"

"Uh huh, and he returned home to work with his family."

"What does he do?"

"His family raises Appaloosa horses. My horse is one of their rejects."

"I don't think your horse is a reject."

"They do." Rich smiled. "Don't let this destroy your life Jeff, go on with living. That's what everyone tells me."

Chrystal breathed deeply the crisp fall air. Once again on her way to the farm she was happy. Mike accompanied her.

"It's a shame that fall doesn't last forever." she sighed.

"It's a shame that spring doesn't come twice a year." Mike returned.

"You'd like that wouldn't you?"

"I guess I really like it just the way it is, by the time I'm tired of raking leaves, it starts to snow, by the time the thrill of shoveling wears off, it's time to till the garden, and then it's time to pull weeds, and mow lawns."

"Is that all you think about,.. work?"

"Most of time, yeah." He stated honestly.

"No wonder no girl wants anything to do with you."

"Actually it's you that scares them off." He teased.

"I'm serious. All work and no play makes Mike a dull boy."

"So I'm a dull boy,.. what of it?"

"You know what I'm aiming at. There is no reason why you couldn't be dating some nice young girl."

"Sure there is."

"What may I ask is that."

"I don't like any of them."

"Well then do something to meet more of them."

"Is it that important to you?"

"Yes it is, I want to see you happy."

"I'm happy."

"How long do you think you'll stay that way?"

"Probably as long as I'm single."

"I didn't ask you to get married. I asked you to date someone, get out, have fun, do things."

"Like you huh?"

"We're not talking about me."

"I am."

"Just because you don't want to be put on the spot."

"You're the one who brought up the subject. You've been bringing it up a lot lately, what's the matter are you trying to get rid of me or something?"

"Actually I don't know what I'd do if you did get married." She stated, "At least I don't have to go home to an empty house."

"I'll consider that a compliment. Although I'm aware it wasn't meant as one."

"Okay, so suppose I find a date for you, would you go?" Chrys asked.

Mike paused a minute. "Suppose I found a date for YOU, would YOU go?"

"I guess it was a stupid question."

"Absolutely."

"Well back to square one."

"What's that?"

"We still have to find you a girl friend."

"Correction, I'll find my own. When I'm ready."

"But it might be too late."

"Believe me it won't be too late." Mike said. "Now about you."

"What about mc?"

"Well where are all these nice boyfriends you should be having?"

"That's what I'd like to know." Chrys smiled. "They're probably at home somewhere raking leaves, shovelling snow, tilling gardens, pulling weeds, and mowing lawns."

"Hey, sounds like my kind of people."

"I'm trying to make a point Michael."

"Oh, I'm sorry. I missed it."

"Well listen close, you may want to wait before considering marriage Mike, but the girls are not."

"Meaning."

"You're not gonna have much to choose from."
"I don't seem to have much to choose from now."
"Do you know you have a very thick skull?"
"It's hereditary." Mike smiled.

Neither of the Shephards owned their own horses but their friendship with the Daniels was such as would allow them a horse anytime they so desired. No one would question it. Both were anxious for a ride that day. Ben and Sarah decided to join them.

Jenny had just finished releasing her horse to pasture when Sarah approached.
"Jenny I was wondering."
"Yes." Jenny asked.
"Are you gonna be on the farm for awhile?"
"Oh yes. Daddy won't be picking us up until after four."
"Do you have plans right now?"
"Well,.. not really. I was gonna go by Jeff we were hoping ma would be back soon."
"The reason I asked is that I want to take a ride with Ben and was hoping you'd be able to watch Nick for me."
"Really?" Jenny said enthusiastically "I'd really like to."
"That's good, come on up to the house, I'll get you settled."

As Sarah was securing a sitter, Ben and Mike were saddling horses for their ride.
"My wife mentioned that grapes were ripe so be prepared for a detour on the way. She'll probably want to stop and check them out."
"I won't be the one to stop her. I've tasted her grape jelly and I think it's worth it."
"You do have a point there."
"How is Rich working out?" Mike asked.
"Real good; I'm pleased, I just wish Sylviah Martin was. She can make life miserable for the best of us."
"I've been lucky enough to escape her rough tongue."
"You're young yet."

"What's she got on Rich?"

"He's not hiding the fact, but it seems he served a prison term a year or so back."

"Really, what for?"

"It's a touchy subject, he'd been drinking, he was in an accident, the people in the other car were killed."

Mike was quiet for a minute.

"Wow, That's rough."

"You bet, there's a lot more to that man then most are aware of."

"I'd hate to be in his shoes."

"He did quit drinking, and using drugs." Ben acknowledged.

"Maybe I won't be so quick to hint around that him and Chrystal get together."

Ben stopped his work abruptly. "You would do that?"

"I thought of it."

"Rich is a nice guy, but Mike, he's not a Christian."

"I know that, but what's stopping him from changing?"

"He is. He's got it into his head that Jesus won't forgive him. When he can get over that barrier maybe we can get somewhere with him."

"I guess I really wasn't being fair. When you mentioned his prison record, I right away wanted to keep him and Chrystal apart, why don't I just keep my nose out of it, If they're meant for each other it'll work out. I guess I just...."

"She gets pretty lonely huh?"

"She does have me, but that's not the same. It's been years since she's dated. It's such a shame too, Chrys has her problems, I can tell you everyone but otherwise she'd make a wonderful wife and companion."

"What would You do if she married." Ben asked.

"I hate to say this but I'd probably do the same thing." Mike laughed.

"Okay. Who is she?"

"I have no idea. As far as I know I haven't met her yet."

"You will, don't rush it. And don't rush Chrys either. God's got his hand in it. Things will work out."

"I just hope my life can be as happy as yours and Sarah's."

"So do I." Ben replied.

Sarah and Chrys followed by an excited Alphie joined them. They mounted and left the cheerful setting, the red buildings, the white picket fences, the golden blanket of leaves beneath the dark skeleton of trees, the deep evergreens that lined the path to the house, and the blue of the sky. They journeyed the border of the pasture, in search of a relaxing ride in the changing weather, in search of a rest from the weeks work, in search of late September grapes. In the process they found more then they had bargained for.

Rich was busy replacing boards for one of the stalls so he didn't hear anyone approach. He was startled therefore when he heard someone gasp.

"I can't believe it. It's Rich McAllister."

He turned quickly, upsetting the tools he was using. Nails scattered into the hay at his feet.

"Ooops, I'm sorry. You startled me." Rich said absently. Looking up he saw a woman with three young boys in tow.

"Hey boys" She said "Let's see which one of you can pick up the most nails." the boys flew forward and started digging through the hay.

"Can I help you?" Rich asked.

"You don't remember me do you?"

Rich looked closely at her. She had short Auburn hair, and beautiful brown eyes, her smile was welcoming. She seemed vaguely familiar.

"Lynn?" He asked. "Lynn Deems?"

"You do remember me." She smiled pleased. The boys had made quick business of the task before them and come charging back to Mama with their hands full. The oldest in his rush to get the most had lost half of what he had, and the youngest had but four in each hand.

"Well congratulations Danny." She spoke to the four year old. "You're the winner." Rich took the nails and replaced them. Lynn reached into her purse and handed fifty cents to Danny.

"Well" Rich asked. "What brings you here?"

"I told Sarah I would bring the boys out sometime to see the animals. These are my boys, David, Danny, and Doug."

"Hi fella's" Rich greeted. "Sarah's out riding now, she should be back before long, would you like me to show you around?"

"Would you?"

"Let me just get this last board in place first." Rich went back to his work, while Lynn continued.

"I'd heard you were back in town but I didn't expect to find you here."

"I guess not."

"Well what have you been doing with yourself? It's been years."

"Oh the normal. I keep pretty busy."

"Are you gonna settle around here?"

"I'm not sure yet."

"We've missed you." She smiled. "Things just aren't the same. I hope your not a,.." She paused. "Well I guess I want to say I hope your not 'Into Religion' like Ben and Sarah. That would really be a bummer. We barely see them anymore."

"No, but I doubt if you'll see much of me either."

"Well we'd like to. Tim will be so glad to hear you're back. Scott and Gail would too."

"So Scott and Gail finally got married I hear."

"Oh yeah. It was funny, when she first told me they were getting married I couldn't believe it. They'd been together so long I'd forgotten they were never married." She laughed.

"What about you?" Rich asked "How are you doing?"

"Real well. The kids and the job keep my busy. But I still find time to enjoy life."

"I'm glad." Rich answered "Tim's okay."

"Oh he's the same."

Rich finished his work then stood to leave. The boys gathered around him.

"Are you a Cowboy?" Three year old Doug asked.

"No, I'm too friendly with the Indians." Rich replied.

"Do you have a cowboy hat?" Danny asked.

"No, but I do have a baseball cap."

"Will we see a bucking bronco?"

"I hope not!" Rich said seriously.

"Aww I thought this would be fun." Complained David.

"Well David, have you ever seen a horse that was only one week old?"

"No. Can I see one?"

"Sure, she's this way." Rich led the way to Faleenes stall. Jeff had gone his way by that time and Rich allowed the boys to climb the gate and peek in. There were many ohh's and ahh's. Then a lot of explanation by their mother as to what the little one was doing with her head under mama's belly.

"I don't seem to be able to win. I try to show them something and it always leads into a major explanation." Lynn sighed.

"Well kids are curious. I know just what they'd like to see next."

"What's that." Danny asked excited.

"It's a secret."

"Come on, tell us."

"I just found it this morning."

"Is it alive?"

"Yes it is."

"Is it big?"

"No, it's very tiny."

"Can I touch it?"

"I don't think you should."

"Why not we'll be careful."

"Follow me, but remember,.. No touching." Rich walked to the ladder that led to the loft. After climbing it he waited for the boys and led them to a far corner. As he approached a small field mouse scampered across the hay."

"She's got a family right over here." Rich began.

"Really? Was that a rat."

"No it was a mouse."

"You're sure it wasn't a rat."

"Yes I am."

"That's too bad."

"Why."

"My friends would think baby rats so much neater than baby mice."

"These are mice." Rich began.

"Your friends don't know that Davey," Lynn stated as she joined the four looking at the small nest of baby mice.

"Hey that's right. I could tell them they were rats."

"Hold it." Rich began. "If you tell them that they're rats don't tell them they're in Ben Daniels' barn."

"Okay, I'll just say we saw a nest of baby rats."

"Can we climb on the hay, Mister, can we?" Dough asked.

"Go ahead, but keep all the stacks like they are."

"Okay, this is great!" The three boys ran off to climb the towering stacks of bales. Rich and Lynn found a place to sit.

"Those three certainly do have energy."

"You're not kidding," Lynn began. "Thanks for bringing them up here, they seem to really like you."

"Someone has too." Rich laughed.

"You've got lots of friends Rich. You should look them up sometime."

"Maybe."

"Well, I for one am going to tell everyone that you're home. I'll tell them where to find you too."

"You don't have to do that." Rich said becoming uneasy.

"But I will. We'll all celebrate."

"No Lynn, No celebration."

"Why not?"

"I don't drink any longer."

"You don't."

"And no drugs."

"None?"

"None."

"Well no wonder no one knew that you were home."

"Things are different now."

"I'll still come see you, even if you won't come see me." Lynn gave him a long look. Rick felt uncomfortable.

"I'm usually pretty busy."

"I'm sure you'll find time for me."

"Maybe not." Rich rose, but Lynn reached for his arm and summoned him back down.

"What's the hurry? The boys are enjoying themselves." She spoke quietly. "I am too."

"I've got a bit of mending to do on a few of the stalls." Rich spoke. "I'll talk to you another time." He hurried to the ladder and disappeared below.

Ben lead the small group of riders from the woods and headed toward the marsh where he knew the grapes grew along the fence line. Berries grew also there through the year, in the thickness of the dense woods nearby. It had been a very relaxing afternoon and Ben was in good spirits. Work on the new stable would begin in the morning and if everything went as planned would be completed by Friday. Mike had assured him that there should be no problems.

Chrys and Sarah had acted like giddy teen-agers during the whole ride, laughing and giggling over the simplest things, finally settling down to planning the path of the hay wagon during the party next Saturday.

Mike was thrilled to see his sister in such a mood, she was usually so composed. A few times, only with Sarah, he had seen her like this. The horses grew agitated as Ben led them toward the marsh. Ben noticed it, Sarah did also. Mike and Chrys unaccustomed to riding as they were noticed nothing. Still, Ben continued, as they were nearing the marsh Bens horse stubbornly refused to go further.

"Well if that don't beat all." He mumbled. "I just don't understand."

"Maybe there's something ahead that they sense." Sarah supplied.

"Horses usually aren't afraid of things unless they are a threat to them."

"Do you think we should force them on and see what's up?" Sarah asked.

"I'd hate to put us all in danger."

"What's up?" Mike asked at the delay.

"The horses won't go any farther, we figure there must be something ahead that has them spooked."

"Didn't you say Denni rode by there yesterday?"

"He probably rode by a dozen times." Ben commented. "I'm curious."

"Are you going ahead?"

"No, but I'm coming back another time and checking it out."

Nick had been asleep when Jenny had come. Sarah, had shown her what to do if he awoke, still Jenny was quite unprepared for Nicks reaction upon seeing her instead of Mama looking down on him in his crib.

Nick had always seemed a happy child so Jenny wasn't prepared for tears at all. But when He set to crying nothing could silence him. She checked his diaper, and changed it while he kicked and screamed. She tried to give him a bottle of milk, he refused it, and juice, and crackers. In desperation Jenny tried to comfort him by rocking. When that didn't succeed she rose from the chair and began pacing back and forth as she bounced him. He cried louder.

Jenny also was now near tears. She'd been so happy and excited to be baby-sitting, she wanted it to be perfect. She wondered what Sarah would do, or even Suzanna Rhodes Nicks regular sitter. Surely they wouldn't lose their cool over it. Jenny looked around the room, she tried to interest him in various stuffed animals, then in rattles. Nothing helped. She wondered if she called for Jeff if he would know what to do. Finally she settled back in the rocker. Beside her on the table was a tape player.

Music.

Perhaps, this was the answer. Struggling with the weeping baby in one arm, she turned on the tape player. Soft music filled the room. Nick continued to cry but it was noticeably less fervent as before. Jenny was pleased and as she rocked she felt him relax more and more.

In a few minutes Nick was quiet, looking up at her with red eyes, his cheeks bearing the marks of the tears that had poured across them. The music had done what she couldn't. As it played she began to recall the same songs from her childhood.

All night, all day,
Angels watching over me, my Lord
All night, all day,
Angels watching over me,

Her mother had sung that to her when she'd been sick many times. The memory was clear, her room with her mother nearby, her fathers shadow in the doorway. That was long ago. Had it only been a week since her mother had left?

It was a little after four when Ray stopped his truck before the stables. He slowly left the cab and went in search of Jeff. True he'd told his children both that he wouldn't return but the farm had become such a part of him in the past years he couldn't stay away.

Jeff had Misty out a second time she was tethered to the hitching rail, Jeff was grooming her.

"Where's your sister?" Ray asked.

"She's around. She watched Nick for awhile when Sarah went riding. I haven't seen her since they got back."

"You're mother's not back then?"

"No but Rich told me that they'd had a late start, he doesn't expect them back for a few hours."

Ray stood awkwardly.

"Dad." Jeff began. "Ben's got a job opening. It starts next week, both Dennis and Rich have encouraged me to apply for it. What do you think?"

"It really doesn't matter what I think does it? You need to make that decision on your own."

"Well your not much help."

"The decision is yours."

"I was afraid of that."

"Well, what did you decide?"

"I guess I'll let it go." Jeff said dejectedly.

"That's really the only fair thing to do son. A month or so from now you may be unable to work, you know that. It wouldn't be wise to make a job commitment knowing you can't keep it."

"I guess not. But Dad. I was waiting for an opportunity like this for months."

"I know son, but I don't see how it would work."

"I guess not, but Denni's been really begging me."

"Did you tell him how you felt."

"I tried but I don't think he understood."

"He will, eventually, if he's as good of a friend as I think he is."

"There is something else."

"What's that?"

"Brady Downing was here last night. He put in an application. I don't think I could stand seeing him with the job I wanted so badly."

"Hiring Brady would be to Ben's disadvantage, I hope he realizes that."

"If he's as fair of a man as Denni said, he'd give Brady the same chance that he would give me."

The two walked in silence toward the stable, leading Misty between them as another day ended in Roberts Junction. A day in which seemingly nothing had transpired, but in essence great steps were made toward change. It was a time of refraining, Rich felt it when he left Lynn and her children alone in the loft, Ben felt it when he put aside both Brady's application, and the decision to ride into the marsh, perhaps even Ray felt it as he watched Jeff refrain from the job he had long desired. Yes, there are times when it becomes necessary to refrain.

CHAPTER 19

A TIME TO GET

Monday, September 26, 1983

The sun had barely risen when Suzanna started out to meet Angie for school Monday morning. It was chilly, frost still covered the leaves that blanketed the lawns. She walked quickly to keep the chill from penetrating her clothes. Angie was waiting when Suzanna approached the corner.

"Let's hurry." Suzanna called. "I'm gonna need at least ten minutes to thaw before class."

"I've got a test first period and I think my brain is froze." Angie giggled.

"Is brain froze anything like brain dead?"

"I don't know, but you've heard the phrase Air Head, well today I'm an Icehead." They continued giggling as they hurried toward school.

"Hey" Angie teased. "Now would be a good time for that 'boyfriend' of yours to come past and offer us a ride."

"You'd take it too I bet."

"Only if you did."

"I think he's finally out of the picture."

"Really? Why is that?"

"Have you ever met Julie Marksman?"

"No, but I guess Peggy knows her."

"Well so does Brady."

"He's pestering her now?"

"I think it's a little of both."

"Well, they ought to get along good then."

"I hate to say this but I hope so. I think they deserve each other."

"I hope you never say anything like that about me." Angie teased.

"I will if you give me reason to." Suzanna smiled. "I'm not worried though."

The two approached the school, Peggy was waiting for them at the east entrance, Becky Franklin was with her.

"Hi!" She called as they approached.

"Hi Peg, Beck, ready for another day at the grind?" Suzanna asked.

"As ready as I'll ever be." Becky remarked.

"You'll do better than we will, I'm brain froze and Angie is an Ice head." They giggled. "You bus students don't know how lucky you are."

"Oh no," Becky said sarcastically. "We've really got the life. The bus comes right to our corner,.. which in my case is a quarter of a mile away, where we board it. It's okay if it's on time, other times I wait in the rain, snow, sleet you name it for up to ten minutes. Then after getting on the bus I usually have to share a seat with these Junior high boys who are really obnoxious. I step in a wad of gum almost everyday, I get hollered at if I talk, walked on if I'm quiet, the whole trip lasts forty-five minutes. I wouldn't trade it for the world."

"She's got the good route." Peggy agreed. "I had a kid throw-up in my hair once, another kid poured glue on my shoe, and once when I was younger they tied my shoe laces to the seat and when I went to get off the bus I fell flat on my face."

Angie looked at Suzanna, they both looked relieved to be able to walk to school in peace. Well almost.

Peggy fell in step beside Suzanna on the way to their first class.

"Ben stopped by our house after church last night."

"Oh?"

"Yeah, he wanted to let me know that he'd accepted my application and wants me to start work as soon as possible."

"Peggy, that's great! If it couldn't have been me, I'm glad it was you." She laughed.

"Thanks, I thought maybe you'd feel bad. I could tell you wanted the job."

"My father is the one that kept me from applying not you."

"Ben said that I had the most experience with horses of all the applicants."

"See that's already a mark against me, you would have gotten it fair and square even if I'd applied."

"I told him that being practically raised on the farm has it's advantages."

"I bet your grandpa was pleased."

"He seemed pleased, but I couldn't really tell. I guess it's going to be hard for him to see me working, I've always been his baby."

"It'll be like a family tradition."

"Yeah, my father was raised on that farm, and gramps, and my great grandpa."

"I'm happy for you, really I am." The two exchanged smiles as they parted for their classes.

Suzanna had much that plagued at her mind that day at school. She was sure about one thing and that was Brady Downing was a lying skunk. He'd had the nerve to return to service last night as if nothing had happened, as if he hadn't rigged the arrest of his best friend, as if he hadn't been behind the danger Suzanna had been in the Tuesday before. The fact that he had sat with her own family during service the evening before, and they had welcomed him made her skin crawl. Couldn't they see what he really was? Couldn't they see through the false front? She longed to expose the deceit and lies so all would understand how she felt.

Her father had talked with him long after the family had gone home. Suzanna wondered what games he was trying to involve her father in, yet at the same time felt slightly guilty. If anyone needed to be in Church to hear the Gospel it was Brady Downing. Why then did his presence there upset her. Probably because she knew him and had learned to read him like a book, she alone could see through his false sincerity. But the question that wouldn't give her peace was,.. why?

Why was he really there? What did he want? Had he been using her to get after her father, or was he now using her family to plague her? None of it made any sense at all.

She stared vacantly at the problems before her, why wouldn't he just get out of her life? The thought made her feel dirty inside. She absently doodled on the paper before her, she had done her best to avoid a confrontation with Brady last night and thanks to her father she had. She knew however that she would have to confront him sometime. The thought made her nervous. Nevertheless she didn't have long to wait, for upon leaving class after the bell, he joined her. He reached for her books.

"Let me take those." He stated.

"No thanks, I'm doing fine."

"Uh oh, that doesn't sound to good."

"It wasn't meant to."

"What do I have to do to get in your good graces?" He asked frustrated.

"Get out of my life." She said loudly. A few students turned and looked at them curiously as they passed.

"Excuse me." Brady said dramatically "But I find that almost impossible to do."

"I can see that." She said honestly. "Look Downing, I don't want to make a scene, I think you're a skunk, a liar, a self-centered ego maniac, and a creep. Now please leave me alone, I have plenty of friends, I don't need any enemies to mingle with them."

"That's not much of a Christian attitude."

"You're not a Christian."

Brady glared at her hard, she could feel his wall of self assurance crumble.

"I'll have you know Ms Goodie Two shoes, that I ALWAYS get what I want, the harder it is to get, the more I enjoy it so watch it sister my eyes are on you. I'll get you yet." He turned and fled, Suzanna stood rooted to the spot, unable to shake the doom that hung over her. How long she stood there with her fellow students swarming around her she didn't know.

"Suzanna are you alright?" A voice asked, Suzanna looked up into the eyes of Dennis Little. She shook her head hard.

"Are you sick?" He asked.

"No, no,.." She was near tears.

"Let's get you some fresh air," He led her out the side door of the school. Suzanna sat exhausted on the top step.

"Feeling better?"

"Denni,..I.. thanks." She stammered.

"Are you sure you're fine?"

"Sure." She took a deep breath, she'd been able to control the tears until then. Suddenly the dam that had been holding back a flood for many days released, leaving her sobbing.

Denni was baffled. Class would start any minute, yet he couldn't just leave her out here crying.

"Tell me what's wrong."

"Denni." She began slowly "Brady's determined to destroy my life. I told him off a few minutes ago, and he vowed to get even with me."

Denni understood her fears. Anger began to well in him toward Brady.

"It's time you talked to someone. He'll destroy you if you don't."

"He'll destroy me anyway Denni. I've been lucky, can you imagine what could have happened to me this past week. I'm not prepared to fight against him and all his buddies."

"Greater is he that is in you than that is in the world."

"Yeah, thanks, but it doesn't always jive."

"God's on you're side, so am I. Don't worry things will work out."

"I wish I could believe that."

"You can."

The final bell to begin second period shattered the silence that followed.

"Let's get you to class." Denni stated.

The two walked back toward the entrance together. As they entered the school who should confront them but Brady Downing.

"I see," He said wickedly "Just go off crying to little Denni, He'll protect you." Brady blocked the hallway.

"What do you want Brady?"

"What do you think? The two of you have been plotting against me for a week. You both know what I want." He smiled at Suzanna. "And you both know I'll get her too. It's a shame no one will believe your wicked tales of the now repentant Brady Downing."

"More have seen through you're deceit then you think Downing." Denni remarked.

"What? Star football player, Honor Roll Student, Sports editor of the school paper, would even think to make threats like that? And after his great dramatic conversion last night? I'm sorry not even your own father will believe you now." He smiled again at Suzanna "It's such a shame you two are late for class. Especially after I tell the coach, where and how I came upon the two of you. It's gonna be pretty hard to answer to that."

"We're not playing your game Brady." Suzanna said.

"You don't have too." He grinned. "Everyone else is."

Suzanna dreaded third period. She had 'Coach' Johnson for a teacher and didn't put it past Brady to already have spread delicious rumors about her and Den. What was with him anyway, who did he really think he was fooling? She secretly hoped that the coach hadn't been taken in with Brady's charm.

She moved slowly through the hallway in an attempt to stall the moment when she'd have to face him. Fellow students rushed past her hurrying to class. She managed to slip in to her seat just as the bell rang. She glanced up half expecting Mr. Johnson's eyes on her, but found only a vacant spot behind the teachers desk.

He entered presently and his first glance was indeed in her direction. She tried to shrink lower in her chair but failed. He smiled at her discomfort, then proceeded on with the class. Suzanna was miserable, it was obvious that the 'coach' had been told something. Brady probably went to him immediately. But what kind of a fabricated story he had told she could only guess.

Absently she went through the motions of the proper student, inwardly dreading what lay ahead. It was nearly the end of the class period when Mr. Johnson called her forward. He smiled as she nervously approached it.

"You can relax." He stated. "I had a talk with Denni, he told me the truth."

"I hope sir, you didn't think?" She began uneasily.

He laughed. "That Brady Downing was telling the truth? If it had been anyone else I may have."

"Thank you sir."

"But, he continued. There is no telling who Brady has given his story to."

"You mean?"

"Your not completely in the clear, I know Brady's story is a bunch of hoey, but I'm not Mr. Bradly, or any of the other members of the faculty."

"So, What should I do?"

"Tell the truth." He stated.

"Of course. But what else?"

"Stay as far away from Brady Downing as you can. I think I recall saying those very words to you before."

"Yes, sir."

"I hope you listen this time."

"It's not as easy to do as you may think."

"I'm finding that out." He remarked. "If you need me, I'll be here."

"Thanks again sir."

Just as Brady had suspected there were plenty willing to play his game. Both among the students and the faculty. By early afternoon it was a well known fact that Suzanna Rhodes and Dennis Little had been caught in the act. Suzanna was shocked at the reaction the news had on her classmates. Girls who had never spoken to her went out of their way to say "hi" and yet those who should have known better turned up their noses at her in disgust. The hardest to take was Angie.

Angie had defended Suzanna to the end. Telling everyone that there must be some mistake, Suzanna wasn't like that. Over and over she argued until her fifth hour teacher had stopped a heated discussion of the incident with her report of the supposed facts. Angie was stunned and humiliated thinking she had put so much trust in one, like Suzanna, who was so hypocritical. She refused to even speak to her.

Peggy, however, was furious. Mild tempered Peggy who always looked for the best in people had her share of words for Brady Downing that afternoon.

"That sawdust brain's got an iceberg for a heart." She declared. "He's the greasiest, most foul smelling deteriorating, human centipede that ever set foot on this earth. His brain is so small that an ant once mistook it for a flea and wiped it out. His heart is so hard you could drive a fleet of Mack Trucks over it and never crack the surface."

"Yup we're talking about the same guy." Suzanna remarked.

"I can't believe a human being could do that to anyone. Especially to those who had been his friends. Talk about callous."

"Yea, I guess so."

"What'll you do now?"

"I guess just wait until it all blows over."

"And let the whole world go around believing that you're some kind of loose floozie who will hop in the sack with anyone?"

"Denni isn't just anyone." Suzanna defended.

"You know what I mean, you'll let people believe that."

"People will believe what they want. What am I gonna do, have Denni and I go forward publicly and deny it? Boy would that look cute."

"Well you can't just let it go."

"Why not?"

"Because it's a lie. It's false. You know it! I know it! Half the people in this school know it, but are just going along with popular opinion."

"What do you suggest?"

"I don't know, but believe me, if you don't do something about it, I will. I can't let people believe this kind of garbage about my best friend."

Suzanna lay across her bed that evening totally disgusted with life. Not a word had been spoken to her about Denni when she got home from school, yet she sensed that all had heard. She felt like an alien amid her own family. Pat had left for the farm from school and later taken supper with Mike, so he hadn't yet returned. She was alone in her misery.

The faint voices that drifted up the stairs and into he room couldn't soothe her, couldn't bring her back, couldn't include her. Not today, now when all thought of her as,..easy? How could she ever, face another day at school? How could she ever even look at Denni again?

Tears welled up in her eyes, tears of frustration and pity. Her whole world seemed to have crumbled before her, she held nothing back. Quietly she soaked her pillow with tears until it hurt even to breath. How could such a fabricated accusation pass such a profound judgment upon her? Where was justice?

She had no idea how long she lay there, It seemed like decades. Firm footsteps mounted the stairs and stopped before her door. There was a soft knock. She remained quiet.

"Can I come in?" Pat asked as he opened the door a crack. "I thought maybe you'd want to talk."

She remained silent, burying her head once again in her pillow.

"Well even if you don't want to,.. I do." He quietly entered the room. After throwing a few garments off the rocker onto the floor he sat down. Slowly he began to rock. The quiet squeek of the rocker mingled with the other sounds of the evening, reminding Suzanna of his presence although he remained silent.

"I have a few classes with Jed Bently,.. do you know him?"

Suzanna nodded.

"Well he seems to know you also." Pat was quiet for a moment. "He never knew what hit him."

"You hit him!" Suzanna sat up suddenly.

"I had to after hearing the things he was saying about you. I had to shut him up somehow."

"But Pat everybody's saying those things."

"Not to me they aren't."

"Oh Pat! what'll I do?"

"Act like Suzanna Rhodes and come up fighting. Not moping around like a weak kneed sissy."

"Fighting? You want me to fight?"

Pat laughed. "Not literally, but the majority of fighting is defense, Get that shield over there." Pat motioned toward her bible, "And wrap so much of it inside your heart that no matter what curves man throws at you, you're protected."

"It sounds easy." She said doubtfully.

"It's not. It'll be the hardest thing you've ever done. But he'll be your strength. Your friends are behind you too. So is Dennis."

Suzanna buried her face in her pillow again and wept. She'd been so selfish. Thinking only of herself when Denni must be going through the same ridicule if not worse.

"I talked to Denni, he's pretty upset. Here he was trying to help you and instead gets you involved in such a scandalizing lie."

"It's not his fault."

"The both of you trusted that weasel with far too much. You're both paying the price now. Jeff is too."

"I feel so all alone." She replied.

"You're far from that, God's on your side. Peggy and I both will stand behind you. You're not alone."

"Does dad know."

"I doubt it, this is the kind of thing he wouldn't keep quiet about."

"Brady told me that Dad wouldn't believe my story."

"Dad doesn't believe stories. He waits til he has fact then he makes his judgments."

"But he likes Brady."

"He loves his soul, just like he does the soul of useless Larry the old Railroad bum that comes around each winter.

He's a man of God first Suzanna, don't forget that. He'll welcome anyone that comes with a repentant heart."

"But Brady Downing is far from having a repentant heart."

"He's a good actor."

The two were silent for awhile, both lost in thought. Outside the sky had grown quite dark the stars shown brightly in the clear sky. The moon cast a shadow on the bare branches of the apple tree outside Suzanna's window.

"I told you Denni's pretty upset." Pat went on.

"He needn't be."

"Yes he does."

"Why?"

"He's afraid this will ruin your friendship. That you'll avoid him, not want to be seen together."

"Oh." Suzanna's heart fell. She dreaded facing him after what everyone had said.

"Consider him too, he's pretty shook up."

"I don't know if I could face him."

"Why, what has he ever done to you, but be your friend? Now you avoid him over one lousy rotten stinking lie?"

"Pat,.."

"Listen to me. Friendships are made of thicker stuff than that. What has happened today will be only a drop in the bucket to Denni. If you desert his friendship now you'll hurt him even more. He needs you."

"Huh?"

Pat looked at her soberly. "Don't disappoint me. I know you're made of the true stuff,.. after all, You are a Rhodes."

Yes, another day, another change, a time for all to think. What will become of Suzanna? of Denni? Will Brady ever get what he truly deserves?

CHAPTER 20

A TIME TO LOSE

Thursday September 27, 1983

Ben had started out early Thursday morning to survey his property. The late September sun was reflected in the leaves that mirrored it's glow. The paths were dry for there hadn't been rain for two weeks, a fire at this time of year could prove disastrous. The brittle leaves crunched beneath the horses hooves, twigs snapped, a tiny vapor of dust rose from the trail.

Nearing the marsh he recalled his horses hesitation Sunday afternoon, and although he normally didn't ride through there each morning he headed in that direction. Even the marsh was dry. The ground that would originally be soft and hard to travel was solid. The pools of water that usually formed had disappeared, only a small trickle of water remained. It had been a dry year.

The berries hadn't faired well either, they seemed small and sparse compared to previous years. Ben dismounted and approached a path of Black Berry bushes. They hung ripe on the vines, their aroma sweetened the air. He picked a few, they fell freely into his hands staining them with their purple juice. The taste of blackberries ripe from the vine had always brought with it memories. Memories of Ben's childhood digging among the thickets at the side of the tracks for such a harvest as this. Ben looked about him, the marsh was a changing place, each time he entered he marvelled at the difference, at the growth.

If he hadn't dropped a few berries he may never have seen it. But as he stopped to retrieve a few berries he had a closer look at the ground around the bushes. Tracks had been left there. Not ordinary tracks, not human tracks, but large round tracks of an animal with sharp claws.

"What's this?" He whispered to himself as he investigated them. "Bear." He announced with dread. "A hungry one too."

He glanced around more closely 'No wonder the horses hesitated, no wonder the berries seemed so sparse.' Evidence that the bear had been there in the past was pretty clear. He could only hope the bear would find what it wanted in the confines of the swamp. He'd give the D.N.R. a call when he returned to his office. Bears were pretty scarce in this area.

Later as he rode back toward the stables he couldn't shake the thought that a bear could be dangerous. He'd have to see that the gates to the woods and the marsh were secured. He'd have to tell Denni and Peggy to keep the riders on the open trail. He couldn't risk an accident.

Work had continued on the new building that would stable both 'Cruiser's Buck' and 'Mark of Fortune'. The framework had been completed yesterday, today's progress was pretty rapid. Mike stopped his work when Ben approached.

"How is it going?" Ben asked.

"As well as I'd hoped, this weather is really an advantage."

"Let's hope it holds off for a few days then. I'm looking forward to some rain."

"It does seem pretty dry."

"Risky weather, especially this time of year." Ben replied. "Oh speaking of risks, I took a ride into the marsh just now."

"Yeah?"

"Remember our horses put up a fuss the other day? Well they had good reason to. There's a bear in that marsh."

"A bear?"

"That's right, I'm just hoping it finds what it wants and doesn't come any closer to the farm."

"Did you see it?"

"No but it's tracks were huge. I plan on calling the D.N.R. as soon as possible and let them know what I found."

"Imagine that,.. a bear."

"Would you have been as willing to go riding if you knew it was there?"

"I'd rather know it's there then be surprised by it."

"I guess you've got a point there."

"I'd hate to tangle with him."

"I don't intend to, or have anyone else for that matter. I'm gonna have Rich go out and lock the entrance to the woods and the marsh this afternoon. Hopefully it will stay put."

Rich was in the tack room cleaning a saddle when Ben found him.

"I've got a job for you."

"What's that?"

"Take these padlocks, and put them on the gates to the woods and the marsh."

"Sure, I'll get after it right away, although I will admit that I'll miss taking rides in that woods."

"It won't be permanent, just until the threat of the bear is gone."

"Bear!"

"I found bear tracks today in the swamp. I doubt if it will come out in the open fields but I want to keep everyone out of it's vicinity."

"I can see why." Rich rose to go.

"Oh, by the way, how did Peggy work out on the job yesterday?"

"Give her a few days, then I'll let you know. She does seem to be a very competent girl though."

"She is, Bill's pleased too, I can tell. It broke his heart to sell this place eight years ago, but I think seeing her among the horses will really please him."

"So do I." Rich began. "I wasn't aware though, that you'd bought this place from Bill."

"Yeah, I did. Remember, I went to work for him during my Junior year of school, I'd had my own horse out here before then. When it came time to sell he gave me the first crack at it. He knew I had big plans for the place; I guess

I was as close to family to him and his wife as you could get. He gave me quite a deal on the place. I felt like I was cheating him. He refused to acknowledge the fact that he was asking way below market value, all he wanted was a corner of the property to build a retirement home."

"It's a shame that his wife passed on so soon afterward."

"You're right, but do you know I could never have made this place go without him. There's over a century's worth of experience in his family. That means a lot."

"Peggy's inherited it too, huh?"

"Looks like it. But it stops with Bill. Peggy has other plans."

"It's a shame he didn't have someone to carry on the tradition."

"His son would have."

"He's been through a lot that old codger."

"And after all these years he still has to tangle with Sylviah Martin."

When Ben came into the kitchen at noon Sarah was overflowing with plans for Suzanna's party.

"You can have a hay wagon ready for us?"

"Of course," He answered.

"Pulled by horses,.. not a hunk of machinery."

"Two teams if you'd like."

Sarah thought a moment. "One should be enough. We don't want to go overboard."

"No, of course not." Ben replied sarcastically.

"Now where should we have the bon fire?"

"Bon Fire?" Ben asked.

"Yes, Bon fire, I thought we'd stop in the woods and have a bonfire. I can almost picture it, the glow of the fire, the sparks shooting high in the air. The young people sitting on fallen logs,..singing songs, and roasting marshmallows."

"Ahem" Ben cleared his throat. "There will be no hay ride into the woods, and there will be no bonfire."

Sarah looked astonished. "But Ben, I've been planning this for a week. The party's in four days and now you tell me I can't have a bonfire, or a hay ride! What did you think I wanted the haywagon for anyway?"

"You can have a hayride." He replied. "Just not in the woods."

"And a bonfire?"

"No, no bonfire."

"But Ben, I have my heart set on this. Why can't we have a bonfire?"

"Sarah, listen to me. It's as dry as a desert out there, one loose spark could destroy acres of woods and fields. There is no way I will approve of a bonfire."

"Please." She begged. Ben thought a moment.

"Okay, you can have one."

"Alright!"

"On one condition."

"Oh, anything."

"That it rains steady for the next three days."

"Benjamin Daniels you are an A-1 jerk sometimes, you know that?"

"Of course."

"What do you suggest we do then?"

"You can have the hay ride."

"I mean after that, for refreshments."

"Oh, I trust you'll think of something."

"Ben where are we going to put twenty to twenty-five teen-agers?"

"We've got room."

"Where?"

"Why not the garage? Or even the back yard? I'll pull the equipment out of the shed if you want to use that."

"I guess the garage will be fine."

"You want a suggestion?"

"From you? Not really." She teased.

"How about an old fashioned taffy pull?"

"Hey,.. that's a pretty good idea. I'll have Chrys help me with some games too, now that I'm thinking of it it'll be a whole lot more fun then setting on a picky log in the dark while smoke from a blazing bonfire penetrates your clothes and stings your eyes."

"I'm glad you see it my way." He continued. "Now, let me tell you what I found. I went to check out the marsh where the horses had spooked the other day, and I found some pretty big tracks in the blackberry bog."

"Really, what was it?"

"A Bear."

"You're kidding!" She exclaimed alarmed.

"I'm hoping he stays put, but you never know. I had Rich lock all the gates this morning, we don't want anyone wandering too near."

"I guess we must have been pretty close Sunday."

"I imagine the bear was in the bog when we drew near, that is why the horses refused to go closer."

"Think about it." Sarah began "I'd hate to get that dude mad."

"I tried to get a hold of Marty Jones with the D.N.R. he won't be back in his office until one. I hope he'll be able to give me some advice."

"He'd better."

Marty Jones didn't have advice, but he did have authority. He judged that a bear living within' three miles from town and on property boarding a public recreational facility such as 'Horseman's Unlimited' was a possible threat. He planned to get a crew out there as soon as possible to locate the critter and remove him to a nearby National Forest. Ben was relieved that the threat of the bear would soon be over. Marty had assured him that he'd come by the end of the week. If all went well, the gates could be opened and the hayride could go as planned,.. through the woods.

Suzanna had made an attempt to avoid Dennis all day. She was so shook by the accusations that had arisen that she didn't think she could maintain her composure if she saw him. She was indeed lucky not to have him in any of her classes. Peggy had been great about the whole thing, attempting to cover the absence of Angie Arnolds friendship, but the loss was evident. Suzanna was crushed. She felt dirty inside, although she knew she was innocent. The talk had hurt her deeply. She barely spoke to anyone all morning. It was Jeff Johnson who finally spoke. She couldn't avoid him.

"I didn't recognize you without a smile on your face." He stated.

"I don't have much to smile about."

"I'm smiling."

The fact that Jeff indeed was smiling did something to encourage her. Here was one who had reason to be down, especially after all Brady had pulled on him.

"I'm sorry Jeff. I should take your example."

"Actually it was you who was my example last Friday, when I needed one, I figured if you could smile after Brady had used you like he did I could too."

"Thanks Jeff." Suzanna actually smiled.

"Now." Jeff began. "Not as many believe Brady's story as you may think."

"It doesn't matter anyway, the damage is already done."

"I hope there's not more damage done than necessary."

"What do you mean?"

"You and Denni. I hope this doesn't ruin the start of a good friendship."

"Did he ask you to talk to me?" She wondered.

"Denni? Are you kidding? He'd murder me if he knew I said a word. He hasn't said anything about it. But I've seen his face, and yours isn't any better."

"I don't think I can face him."

"Because of a stupid rumor?"

"Because people are believing it."

"He obviously knows the truth." Jeff said teasingly.

"Still Jeff, I don't think I could handle seeing him."

"I'm sorry to hear that, I think it would mean a lot to him. You've avoided him all day."

"It's best this way." She stated.

"I don't agree."

"Listen Jeff." Suzanna said shortly. "I don't want things to be like this any more than you do. But because of me, Denni's reputation is shot as well as mine."

"Sure." Jeff said sarcastically. "The only way you would have avoided that is by going along with Brady's game. Then more than just your reputation would have been shot!"

Suzanna was quiet.

"I'm right aren't I?" Jeff asked.

"I guess so."

"So you'll talk to Denni?"

"I'm afraid not."

Jeff looked at her in frustration. "Suit yourself." He shrugged.

So lost in her own misery Suzanna was barely aware of what was going on around her. Although she was more sensitive to things that were said to or supposedly about her, she neglected to notice the sympathy and understanding others attempted to show her. The rumor which had caused such a dramatic commotion just yesterday, was now having a more lasting impact on the student body, for circling among them was a petition which many were more than willing to accept.

Suzanna choose not to meet with her friends at lunch but wandered off to the far corner of the property alone. Beneath the branches of a maple tree she rested in a nest of red and gold. The fact that no one sought her company depressed her even more. Desperately she tried to sort out her confused feelings. The humiliation at what others might think of her, the anger she had toward Brady, but most of all the dread she had of facing Denni.

Pat had been right. Den had done nothing but be a friend, he'd tried to help her and he'd taken the humiliation of the same rumors. Why then didn't she want to face him? She herself didn't know.

She tried to rid her mind of thoughts concerning the whole mess, but each time she did, thoughts of Denni would invade her mind again. Visions of him kept reappearing. The things he'd said kept echoing, she tried to shake them from her mind but it was useless. In the midst of her anxiety her brothers words came to her loud and clear,.. Denni needs you.

Tears began to form in her eyes, what had Pat meant? She had resolved never to speak to Denni again because it was his friendship with her that had brought him such misery. If she just drifted out of his life maybe he could restore some semblance of order to it. Still, every time she turned around it seemed someone or something was attempting to put them back together, urging a confrontation.

The first bell for fifth hour rang. Vainly she attempted to compose herself before returning to classes. Slowly she approached the school. She halted. Before her stood a group of Junior and Senior boys. She recognized Brady immediately. Anger blinded her and turning from the group she slowly left the school yard.

The sound of metal against metal filled the workshop as Bill Winters pounded into shape the iron that lay on the anvil before him. He worked quickly yet precisely, for years of experience had taught him to the best advantage. His sporadic whistling accompanied his work, his old patched boots kept time on the rough unpainted floor boards. Coils of leather hung from the wall behind him like neglected garden hoses, and a row of tools in various sizes gave the impression of a disappearing fenceline. All was still save for the echo of his hammer, and the lingering notes of melody. It was early afternoon, the kittens had departed to their attic homes after a generous helping of warm milk from the saucer Bill had placed in the corner. Outlaw lay curled in a ball on his now familiar rag bag. Bill breathed in deeply the warm smell of horses and hay, a tinge of sawdust filled the air drifting in from the direction of the site of the new stables. Placing his hammer down slowly Bill shuffled to the door.

Time changed things. He recalled the first nails of this very building. As a five year old child he had followed in his fathers seemingly gigantic footprints across the vast expanse of lawn to the mountain of lumber. He'd stood obediently by his side, day after day, nail after nail, He'd watched the lumber change from a mountain to a platform to a walled enclosure until it had assumed the shape it now had. That was over seventy years ago. He's lost count of the coats of paint he'd applied over the years, or new shingles, window panes, and hinges. He'd stood in this spot nearly every day of his life, as time went by as change took place. But something's never change.

Above him the sun shone as it had for his seventy some years. There was still work to be done, although today the hands that once strongly gripped the hammer, now were gnarled and tired early. These legs that once would run head long after stampeding cattle, now found it hard to manage the simplest flight of stairs. Time was leaving him behind.

A screen door slammed behind him and Bill knew it would only be moments before Ben would join him. He remained at the door watching the changing shapes of the clouds as they drifted across the sky. It seemed nothing remained the same. The sound of Ben's footsteps approached behind him. Outlaw roused and stretched, a long pink tongue escaped, curling at the tip, only to be snapped back. Bill turned, and made his way to the bench placed beneath the window. He sat amid the beams of sunlight that wafted through the dusty pane, reaching beside him he lifted the tangle of leather that was the halter he was repairing. Ben entered the room, he walked to the far wall and reached for the longeline that hung there.

"Did you take a look at Queenies hooves this morning?" Ben asked.

"I had the old gal in here a while back. If she's kept off her feet she should be okay."

"Any rotting or disease?"

"Not that I seen. Mighty sore feet though, it's those shoes she's got."

"Ms. Martin will be sending the vet out to take a look."

"Whatever for?"

"She thinks that there may be a serious injury. She wanted the Doc to stop yesterday, but he was out of town."

"Would that be Doc. Prentice from Roberts Junction?"

"No, they always brought their animals to Riley in Lincoln."

"That man gives me the jitters." Bill commented.

"I'm not to comfortable with him myself."

"Let's hope the critters fine so he can give Ms. Martin a good report."

"I think that's what we all want."

"Well Doc. What do you make of it?"

"I really don't know Mr. Daniels, doesn't seem to be nothing amiss,.. physically that is."

"Soreness from being shod?"

"I think that's it. Have your fella adjust them a bit til they fit a tad better, although the limp is almost gone, she may be tender. I'll have Mrs. Martin rest her for a week at least until the limp is completely gone."

"How are the shoes?"

"Huh?" Ben's question caught him off guard.

"Mrs. Martin seems to feel that the work on the shoes was of poor quality."

"This is Bill Winters work isn't it?" The Doc continued without waiting for an answer. "Bill's one of the best farriers in these parts, there is nothing except expert workmanship in those shoes."

"I'm glad to hear that."

"That man may be getting on in years but it does not affect his work."

"That's how I've felt. He's slowed down some in the past month or so. It'll be hard to see him go when the time comes."

"Well, he's put on a lot of miles, that man has. I only know him vaguely, heard much though, most good."

"Well," Ben continued."Thanks for the report, I'll put this record in her files; You'll be getting in touch with Mrs. Martin?"

"Oh yes, she insisted on hearing from me right away."

Suzanna walked slowly through town. She had two more classes that day but somehow she knew she couldn't face going. It was wrong, but she was too desperate for answers to consider the consequences. Passing the street that led toward home where she knew her mother would be busy with a group of ladies, cutting patches for quilts they were making; she rounded the next corner, toward the church. There was a ministers meeting in Lincoln early this afternoon, so she knew her father would be out of town.

She locked the door behind her and quickly entered one of the back pews. This place had become a second home to her. She had been here the day that they had accepted her father as Pastor. He had held her in his arms as the church had given thanks to God for his provision. She had watched the church grow from that first handful of saints to close to one hundred. True it was still a small congregation but what they lacked in numbers they gained in faith, for God had blessed them.

Sitting quietly alone in the darkened sanctuary Suzanna tried to get a grip on her feelings. Her true feelings. Brady had gone way too far in his game playing - Jeff, Denni, and herself were suffering because of it. If she had just avoided him that first day nearly two weeks ago, maybe things would be different. But that was in the past, Jeff had a future ahead which he alone must answer for. She hoped and prayed that his sentencing would not be too severe, for he had taken some dynamic steps toward God the past week and it thrilled her. Denni however was innocent. He'd done absolutely nothing to merit the ridicule of the lies that Brady had fabricated. It didn't seem fair. The fact that she herself was innocent never entered her mind. She considered this the punishment for being involved with Brady Downing at all.

Silently she hoped that her father was not being taken in by Brady's ways for hc could be courteous and polite in the midst of acting a complete lie. She had witnessed it. She knew Luke thought the sun rose and fell on the personage of Brady Downing, but he was but twelve and his opinions tended to lean in the wrong direction anyway. Cindi, however seemed to like Brady and had encouraged Suzanna to date him. Her mother, Suzanna felt, had seen through Brady immediately. Pat had always been her biggest supporter, even when she herself had begun to be taken in he had held firm to his belief of Brady's true nature. These thoughts and more drifted through her mind as she sat in the back of that silent church house, with the rays of the sun shining into the windows creating patches of gold contrasting the present shadows. If she could have seen into the hearts of others she would have realized that she need not feel so alone. Peggy of course had declared spiritual warfare on Brady. Jeff also had seen the light as had both his parents and Steve Williams. Ben had not the knowledge of Brady's nature but was wary of him anyway, as was Rich. Surprisingly enough Mike Shephard and Tom VanDyke both held him in some degree of contempt.

As Suzanna fought with her true feelings, sorting them, analyzing them, bringing them to God in prayer the one 'feeling' that she couldn't acknowledge was her feeling toward Denni. She had desperately wanted to avoid him the past day and a half yet even in doing so she had longed to see him. That familiar smile, that laughter that was so quick and spontaneous, mostly his understanding nature. In the depth of her despair reality was dawning on her, when it had happened she couldn't say, but in searching her heart she found that she was falling in love with Denni and was angry at herself for doing it.

Peggy had searched in vain for Suzanna all afternoon, she grew anxious, unsure of whether Suzanna had wondered off to be alone or if some certain demented seventeen years old member of the football team had enticed her into playing another round of his game. 'The snake'. She thought to herself.

Denni had spoke very little to her yesterday, although they had worked side by side, she had felt more in the way than anything. Tom had been in much better spirits which wasn't a surprise. He'd offered to drive her to work after school knowing she could get a ride home with her grandfather. She had agreed to meet him at the main entrance near the phones. As she hurried to meet him she hoped to catch a glimpse of Suzanna, or even Brady that would assure her that Suzanna was safe.

Tom met her as agreed and they hurried toward his car. Tom had been given a brand new 83 Pontiac Grand Am for his eighteenth birthday. He'd had a stereo put in the week before. Peggy found it hard to believe that one so young could have something others never attain in their lifetime, but that had always been the way with Tom's family. They seemed to thrive on the struggles of others. Tom was excited as they left the parkinglot.

"I received my letter of acceptance for 'Mount Garrison' School of Veterinary science last night. I can't wait to tell Ben. He wrote a great letter of introduction. I know he'll be pleased." Tom said enthusiastically.

"You're going to Garrison?" Peggy was surprised.

"I'd planned to. It's an excellent school. They only take a select few students, I'm lucky to be one." He paused. "I suppose my father had something to do with that."

"I hope to go to Garrison too." Peggy began, "To their school of nursing."

"Really? I hope it works out that way."

"So do I, it's something I've wanted for a long time."

"Me too, I have an advantage working with animals now, and hearing what people like Old Bill,.. I mean your Grandfather have to say."

Peggy laughed. "I'm glad that I am not the only one who appreciates gramps."

"Far from it. I'm sure Ben feels he's indispensable."

"I hope he can keep at his job for a while then."

"He thinking of quitting?"

"No, but he is slowing down some, I'm worried about him."

"It'll take a lot to slow him down."

"He's nearing eighty." She stated.

"Wow." Tom gasped. "I guess I never considered his age until now."

"He doesn't have much time left."

"I hate to think of anything happening to him."

"Me either."

"What would you do?"

"Don't know, I don't really belong in New York although I'd make sure I wasn't a burden on anyone."

"What's in New York?"

"My mother and her family."

"Your mother?" Tom was surprised. "I'd assumed your parents were dead. I figured that was why you lived with Bill all these years."

"No, my mother is very much alive. She and my step-father live in New York. I visit during the summer but I really don't fit in."

"That's rough."

"Not really." Peggy said surprisingly "I don't know any different life then what I've always had with Gramps. Granny was an excellent mother for me although she was older, I could have gone with mother when Granny died but I chose not to."

"You wanted to stay here."

"This has always been home to me." She stated "Besides if I left who would stay with gramps?"

Suzanna had arrived home at the same time that her older brother pulled into the driveway, Bob's car was also out front.

"It looks like the goon is here for supper." Suzanna remarked as Pat joined her.

"At least you're here. You were missed at school today."

"Did they call home? already?"

"No, but your friends are worried."

"I didn't think I had any friends."

"Think again will you." Pat said sternly. "I hope you realize that you are over reacting."

"I just needed to be alone, I'll be in school tomorrow."

"Where were you?"

"Church."

"No kidding? We thought maybe you were with Brady."

"After what he pulled on me? It would take an army to fight me first!"

"He's got an army." Pat answered soberly. "We didn't know what to think."

"Who's we?"

"Your friends."

"I asked who."

"Mike and I, and of course Peggy," Pat paused. "And Denni."

"I suppose I was a major topic of conversation."

"You were a major topic of concern."

"Yeah, sure. It seems everyone is concerned about Suzanna Rhodes and here whereabouts." She said sarcastically.

"Don't get so upset about it. We only talked because we care."

"I guess so, I'm sorry Pat. I've had a really rough afternoon try to ignore my vicious comments."

"A few people would welcome any comment, even vicious from you."

"I think you and Denni both talk too much."

"Did I mention Denni?"

"You and about half the state."

Pat just looked at her.

"Okay, so I exaggerated. Jeff gave me an earful too. I'll talk to Denni when I'm ready."

"Promise?" Pat asked.

Suzanna remained quiet a moment before answering. "I can't promise anything, I hope you understand that."

"No I don't understand, but I'm getting tired of the whole mess." Pat said critically.

"Don't you think I'm tired of it?"

"Then snap out of it! You're causing more problems by moping around than anything else."

"I just had to get some things straight, at least for myself. Okay?"

"So you'll talk to Denni?"

"I'm afraid not."

"Why not, give me one good reason."

"I told you, I had to get some things straight, I didn't tell you I'd talk to Dennis." She broke into tears. Confused she apologized. "I've been doing this a lot lately, maybe it's best if I just gave up living."

"Oh that would really prove something." Pat remarked "Maybe you should just *START* living."

The smell of new wood and sawdust filled the air as Ben wandered over the site of his new stable. The walls that had consisted this morning of only vague framework were now paneled, the windows and doors all in place. The roof boards were secure awaiting the shingles that were now stacked neatly with the siding beside the building. Ben's dreams were becoming a reality.

Walking to the location of Cruisers stall Ben halted. Although he had placed a lot on his new colt, Cruiser was his first, his pride. He recalled the ridicule, and skepticism he had met on his first venture. No one believed he would succeed. He had been alone when Cruiser was born, a turning point in his life. He'd made a success out of his first stallion, it's a wonder no one doubted his ability with Marksman's colt. Marking the stalls in his minds eye, he walked among the remains of sawdust, wood shavings, nails, blocks of wood and insulation. His dream was becoming a reality. His horses would be noted through out the state for their excellent breeding. His name would become synonymous with others like Reynolds Marksman. He had thought it would take a lifetime to succeed, but he had yet to turn thirty.

He climbed upon a discarded workman's horse, and sat down. Looking about him he was filled with awe. He had longed for an establishment as a child where anyone could experience the thrill of riding, here he had created that place. Also creating a class of horses with the strength and stamina, mingled with speed that many people longed for. Satisfied he breathed in deeply, savoring the smell of the new wood. Things had gone excellent for him the last few weeks. Even amid the tangle of accusations against him concerning Judy Johnson, Ben was well pleased.

The sun had begun to set when Ben returned to the barn. Both Tom and Rich had gone home, but Denni was bedding down the last of the horses for the evening.

"Another day's work over huh?" Ben smiled.

"I enjoy it." Denni returned.

"Has Peggy been any help?"

"I'll say. She's pretty handy with horses."

"I'm glad to hear that. I'd thought as much." Ben began, "She's just in training remember so don't be afraid to repeat things to her."

"I haven't needed to. She knows this place like the back of her hand."

"That's a relief. You know I was really disappointed in the response I received when I listed the job. Peggy was the only one besides Jenny Johnson who applied that had any experience. I'd been hoping to see Jeff's application."

"I was hoping he's apply. I encouraged him too. But he seemed to feel that you wouldn't want him. Also he has kind of an unstable future and didn't want to make a commitment to you."

"He couldn't have been farther from the truth. I should have come right out and asked him like I had considered doing. I give him the opportunity to come to me and he thinks I wouldn't want him." Ben was confused.

"Jeff is going through a lot right now, but in a way I'm rejoicing. I know that his problems are bringing him to the realization that he's not in control and that there is someone who is."

"Has he said much about God to you?"

"He doesn't have to. I can feel it. And I think that says a lot more than any words could."

"You're absolutely right." Ben agreed.

So we find that in the midst of Jeff facing one of the biggest trials in life he loses out on an opportunity that he'd been waiting for. Would life continue to deal him such heavy blows?

CHAPTER 21

A TIME TO KEEP

Wednesday September 28th, 1983

Suzanna was still home when Pat joined the family the next morning. Luke had already gone to meet his friends and Cindi was just gathering the last of her things.

"Are you still here?" He asked when he saw Suzanna.

"I'm waiting for a ride." She grinned.

"Oh? From anyone special?"

"Uh huh."

"Who's the lucky fella."

"You" She laughed. Pat joined her.

"Okay, what's the deal. Haven't you and Angie Arnolds been walking together."

"Not since Monday." Suzanna put in.

Pat was surprised.

"She apparently wants nothing to do with me." Suzanna continued. Her mother hearing that remark grew concerned.

"You two aren't fighting are you?"

"I'm not ma, but Angie is quiet. I waited, and waited yesterday. Then after I saw her at school, she wouldn't even speak to me."

"Have you done anything that would upset her?" Her mother asked.

Suzanna looked at Pat before answering.

"I haven't done anything; but that doesn't keep her from thinking I might have."

"She doesn't seem like the kind who would make false judgments like that."

"I really don't know her that well." Suzanna put in.

"No wonder you've been moping around so much lately. I thought maybe you were coming down with something."

"No mom, I'm fine."

"Well it'll do you good to have a ride to school today, it's pretty chilly."

"Thanks mom."

"Yeah, thanks a lot." Pat said teasingly. "All my friends come to school with gorgeous girls beside them and who do I have? Miss Mud Puddle Queen herself."

"And you're the luckiest one of them all." His mother answered as she winked at her daughter.

"At least it's safe." He grinned

.

After she was settled into the car for the ride to school Pat questioned her.

"Okay, out with it. Why isn't Angie walking to school with you?"

"She doesn't want to."

"Why not."

"I wish I knew."

"She believed the rumors huh?"

"I think so."

"Well what are you gonna do about it?"

"Nothing."

"Wrong."

"Wrong?"

"You're gonna have to talk to her."

"But why?"

"So she realizes the truth."

"She's not gonna believe me."

"But you owe it to her to tell her. She deserves to hear the truth."

"I'm tired of forcing myself on people, trying to prove to them what I am."

"As far as I can see you've proven nothing. You've hid yourself in a corner since this whole thing started. It makes you look pretty guilty if you ask me."

"It does?"

"If you're not guilty, what are you afraid of?"

"I just don't want to see people."

"Why?"

"Because they might have believed the rumors."

"So you're going to do nothing to prove otherwise?"

"What can I do?"

"Get on with life! Don't let Brady destroy the only thing he couldn't control without your help.. Your spirit. He's done that, you've let him. He's taken an outgoing sensitive fourteen year old girl and changed her into a week kneed, wishi washi, fearful; Mess. Don't let him get away with it. He told Denni that once he got through with you no one would want anything to do with you- not even Denni. Don't make that statement come true by deserting the very ones who care about you."

"I haven't deserted Angie, she didn't want anything to do with me."

"But you've deserted Denni."

Suzanna remained quiet. Denni was all she had thought about lately.

They were pulling into a stall in the parkinglot at school, when Suzanna first saw them. Dennis had parked his car near the entrance and she noticed that as he got out someone also opened the passenger door. Suzanna stared in surprise. It was Angie.

Pat followed her glance and noticed the two also.

"Hey talk about killing two birds with one stone here's your chance to talk to them."

"Pat,.. I can't." She faltered.

"You'd better get ready to, they already saw you. They're coming this way."

Suzanna looked up. Sure enough Dennis and Angie Arnolds were walking toward her. Embarrassed to see Denni after the rumors had been spread and equally uneasy about talking to Angie who believe the rumors, Suzanna was in a state of shock. Unable to run she stood transfixed to the spot. Pat stood with her, knowing it would be hard for her and wishing to provide any support that he could.

Suzanna stood as one waiting upon the firing squad. Nothing she thought, could be harder than this. She could feel her heart beat faster, her face became hot with embarrassment. The two walked on together, toward her. Not as one, but as a seeming multitude both making demands on her just by their presence. She watched them as they approached but as they drew near the face of Denni held her. That familiar face that had laughed with her over the years, had shared with her, had grown up with her, and had cried with her just last Friday at this same place. Why did she have to go and spoil it all by having feeling toward him. Angie was the first to speak although Suzanna never took her eyes from Denni's kind face.

"Suzanna." Angie began. "I need to say I'm sorry. I was wrong to believe the lies that Brady started. I didn't at first, but when it seemed everybody was confirming it, .. I was hurt that you had led me to believe that you were different, that your God was different. I'm sorry I didn't come to you right away, but I felt you had wronged me. Denni just told me the truth, I had to apologize to him also. I hope we can still be friends.

Suzanna smiled slowly but still said nothing. Pat placed his arm around her and whispered in her ear. 'Be a Rhodes' the very words that had always brought out her true spirit of honesty. She smiled at him. Taking a step toward Angie she held our her hands, without words the two fell into an embrace and wept tears of joy. Neither saw the silent shake of Pat's head but when the tears were dried,.. Denni was gone.

Class had just started and all were busy working when Pat was called to the front.

"I've got more work for Michelle, Pat. I hope you don't mind bringing it to her."

"I don't mind at all. I'll be seeing her anyway."

"How is she?"

"Fine I guess." Pat began. "She's getting pretty depressed though."

"That's a shame. It must be tough knowing that you'll be off school that long."

"I think it's more raising the baby alone."

"She kept the baby?" He asked flabbergasted.

"Yes she did."

"Why would she do a fool thing like that? There are hundreds of families willing to adopt babies, why would an intelligent girl like Michelle choose to keep hers, when she knows it will tie her down the rest of her life?

"It's a tie to Joe." Pat answered.

"Joe?"

"The babies father. Joe Jamison."

"Oh, I see." He paused. "I hope she'll be able to return to classes soon."

"So do I sir." Pat began "I'll see that she has every opportunity."

"Oh?" The teacher smiled.

"Someone has to." Pat said simply.

"And you think it's you."

"Me and other friends that care about her." Pat said testily.

"Then she's actually not as alone as she thinks."

"No, she's not. She's got a father in heaven that loves her and a family on earth that will do their best to show that love."

"It's not the same Pat, you know that."

"It's all we can offer."

"Is it?" The teacher asked.

Pat was frustrated. It seemed who ever he spoke to felt that him and Michelle were dating or at least assumed something of the sort. Why couldn't a fella innocently be nice to a girl without everyone assuming that he loved her. True there was nothing wrong with Michelle, she was a nice girl, polite, and fun. But she was also wrapped up in Joe Jamison. Pat wouldn't even consider the thought. It appalled him that others, including his very mother would think that of him.

He returned to his desk heavy hearted, a weight pressed upon his soul, crushing his feelings leaving them in bits and fragments. Vainly he tried to concentrate. The teacher's words droned in his ears, he fought for comprehension but gained only jumbled thoughts and idea's. Time slowly passed, a wasted class period, nothing gained.

The shrill sound of the dismissal bell had barely started when Pat fled the classroom.

Mark Rankin approached him in the hall.

"Cheer up dude, there's life after High School."

Pat grinned.

"But I agree this is a disgusting place."

"It's not only the place, it's the people."

"That sounds pretty harsh coming from you." Mark said seriously "You're always so outgoing and love being with people."

"I do, but I don't like people making false assumptions, especially about me."

"Hey, speaking of false assumptions, have you seen the school paper?"

"No, I haven't."

"There's a letter in it you'll be interested in. I was pleased."

"Anything special."

"It concerns your sister."

"Oh no! She's just stepping back into reality, this could set her back."

"It never mentions her name. - or Denni's."

"Who wrote it?"

"A few teachers signed it. Only Mr. Johnson's name was mentioned in the letter itself. It was in response to the petition Peggy instigated."

"Peggy started a petition?"

"You didn't know?" Mark asked surprised "She sent it to all the teachers urging them to obtain facts about Suzanna and Dennis' guilt before making comments concerning it."

"I'll have to read it." Pat said.

"Here take my copy." Mark pulled his copy of J.F.K. High's paper 'The Adress' from his folder. "I'll get another."

"Thanks Mark, I appreciate it."

After Pat was seated for his next class he opened the school paper. He found the letter quickly. It was on the front page.

To the student body-
We as members of this schools faculty would like to publicly apologize to certain individuals for relating false accusations as truth. Nothing of this sort has ever happened before in the history of this establishment. In repeating certain items of interest many teachers have placed themselves in the capacity of spreading unfounded rumors. Thanks to members of the student body who have asked that we provide evidence, and to Mr. Ray Johnson who assured us that there was none; we now stand corrected. Please accept this apology and be assured that the situation will not be repeated in the future.

Pat sat back in his seat with a sigh. Nothing more need be said. Those who had heard the rumors now knew they were unfounded. Pat was relieved, only a vague shadow remained over his heart. Why couldn't he just be friends with Michelle without everyone thinking otherwise?

Only the faint squeak of the rocker disturbed the silence of the Morrison's living room. Michelle sat wrapped in a quilt, teeth catering, to weary to arise to turn up the heat. Not really caring anyway. Joanna slept soundly warm as toast beneath mountains of comfort. Michelle rocked absently.

It was cold for September. But it was not the cold that chilled Michelle, causing her to shake, it was the loneliness. Plenty had come to see her, and she'd been cheered at their presence. But each had left, leaving her once again alone. A mother, a father, a provider, at seventeen.

Time stood still, endless hours, longing to be about; returning to classes; to games; for pizza at 'Charlies'. It was over for her now. All she could vision was an endless highway and a heavy burden. She pulled the quilt closer about her, the warmth it provided did nothing to cheer her. The rocking continued.

She closed her eyes to the world about her. It was her only escape from the loneliness, for then Joe consumed her thoughts. She had traced the outline of his face so many times she could almost see him. The way he looked when they first dated. Michelle was barely fifteen, Joe sixteen awkwardly holding hands beneath the table at 'Charlies'. Passing between classes, notes that said nothing but meant so much at the time. She'd worn his letter jacket, his favorite baseball hat, and his Wisconsin Badger sweatshirt. He'd actually worn the sweater she'd knitted him for Christmas. There was a poster of her tacked in his locker, five photo's of him in hers. He had called her Shel, she had called him Bear. It seemed like centuries ago. When he walked out on her he'd taken life with him. Michelle had hoped that Joanna could replace that life, that love, but still it fell short. Michelle was alone.

Slowly she rose from the rocker, taking the quilt with her; she wandered to the door, opening it. She leaned against the frame. The chill in the air seemed to revive her, she breathed in deeply. It felt so good. If she couldn't go on in life with Joe, she didn't want to live at all. But now Joanna needed her, his daughter, their child. Vaguely she wondered if he even knew Joanna existed.

Pat searched for Peggy after his third class. He had no idea where to find her, but was in luck for she had chosen to stop at her locker as Pat was passing through.

"Hi!" He smiled as he approached.

"Hi Pat."

"I came to say thanks."

"Whatever for?"

"For fighting for Suzanna, I really appreciate it."

"The fights not over."

"I'm aware of that, but you did what you could."

"Her and Angie are speaking again, but things aren't the same."

"They never will be. Peggy, what she has experienced the last two weeks will leave scars for life. Things won't ever be the same again."

"It's something else."

"What do you mean?"

"She's happy, almost too happy."

"Really, she was pretty shot when I last saw her."

"I guess what I mean is; she's accepted the apology from Angie, and acknowledged the apology from the faculty, but she seems too ecstatic about it,.. like she's acting out a role in a play or something."

"That's strange; Suzanna had done silly things in her life but she detests pretence. Well, all we can do is keep praying."

"I am."

"Others are too."

"Have you seen Dennis"

"No I haven't, I bet he's thrilled about the letter also."

"He seemed to look a little more relieved, but something is still bothering him."

"Peggy Winters insight again."

"I'm seldom wrong Pat." She stated with mock seriousness.

"I'm sure things will return to normal." He paused. "I'll have a talk with Den after school, we'll be finishing the shingling and siding on the stables today."

"Really? That's great. That building went up so fast, it seemed like overnight."

"Mike is a good man when it comes to most construction work. I'd like to see what he could do on his own once."

"He does seem to know his work, I hope I can be as competent as he's been. Or you, even Dennis and Tom. I've got this fear of making a serious mistake and wiping out Ben's whole stock, leaving him bankrupt."

Pat laughed. "Dream on, but please no more, nightmares." He began to leave. "I'll see you tonight."

"Yes, I heard there's a special speaker."

"Br. Rankin is going to talk a little about the Mission work in Brazil."

"I'll enjoy that."

"I've gotta run." Pat stated as he hurried down the hall.

"Bye."

"Thanks, I mean it." And he was gone.

Michelle was looking for Pat's arrival. He'd come nearly every afternoon. He'd been so kind. Bringing treats, news, homework and just his friendship. She began to look forward to his visits.

Today Joanna was awake, Michelle held her close, caressing the soft skin. A tiny fist closed on her finger, the other grasped at a lock of her hair. Joanna's eyes blinked at the light. She was indeed beautiful.

Pat tapped lightly on the door before entering. Smiling at the two, he approached carrying a folder with homework, and a large paper sack from Dave's Delicious Drive-in.

"I brought you some lunch." He smiled.

"I expected it." She answered with a grin. "I quit arguing with you long ago. I can't get it through your thick skull that it's not necessary, so I'll just wait until you get bored, then I'll go on with life."

"I don't get bored easy." He remarked.

"Let's trade places then."

"I wish I could." He said honestly.

Michelle paused a moment. "Joanna's awake, do you want to hold her?"

"Does she bite?" Pat asked..

"Only if she doesn't like you."

"Maybe I'll pass." He responded, yet he held out his arms. Michelle placed tiny Joanna in them. Joanna seemed to get lost in his strong arms, Pat felt awkward. True he'd come to see Michelle often, but he'd paid little attention to Joanna, this was the first time he'd actually held her. He looked down at the tiny form squiggling in his arms. Only a little over a week old. So perfect, so beautiful, and so dependant on others. Pat's heart grew heavy, this baby would have to go on without a father. It didn't seem fair.

"She must like you." Michelle began "She hasn't bitten you yet."

"Maybe she knows I won't taste good."

Michelle smiled, Pat was pleased to see it.

"I brought some work for you, also a copy of the School Paper. I thought you would enjoy it."

"Really. I'd like to see the paper. The work will keep, for a few hours anyway." She picked up J.F.K. High School's paper and began to skim the front page.

"What's this all about?" She asked. "I've never known any of the teachers to apologize publicly before."

"It was necessary." Pat stated.

"Really? What happened?" She asked.

"It isn't important." He tried to avoid the discussion.

"Oh,.. it's about someone I know huh."

"Kind of." Pat paused. "I might as well tell you. You'll probably hear it from some else anyway."

"Not necessarily."

"I'll tell you anyway." He began. "It seems that Monday afternoon, a member of the football team claims to have come upon a couple together in the football equipment closet. According to his story he had opened the door earlier and was returning to lock it after he remembered he'd forgotten to."

"A story like that is pretty easy to believe." Michelle remarked. She nodded at Joanna. "Most kid's at school are quite active."

"Not the ones that were named."

"Oh? Who were they."

"Well the fella was Dennis Little."

"No! how did his name get involved with something... like this?" She nodded at the paper.

"It seems him and the girl had been detained at the same time, and the story kind of spread from there."

"Who was the girl?"

"My sister." Pat said soberly.

"Oh, Pat. I'm so sorry. This is terrible. The story would have been easy to believe. But not about Suzanna, and Not about Dennis."

"Not everyone knows Denni and Suzanna."

"I can see that." Michelle began "She must have taken it pretty hard."

"She was miserable, but she is a Rhodes and she'll pop right back in place."

"She's lucky to have you to encourage her."

"She doesn't always feel that way."

"I guess sisters wouldn't." Michelle smiled.

Pat approached Mr. Wiseman's desk after class.

"What's on your mind?" The teacher wondered.

"Well I've done a lot of thinking." Pat began "About what we talked about last week."

"Oh, Good, You've decided to continue school then."

"Well, I'm reconsidering it. I really like the work I do, I thought that was the most important thing."

"It is Pat." Mr. Wiseman responded. "But it's just a shame that someone as bright as you would want to do manual labor all his life."

Pat smiled at the remark.

"Like I said I'm reconsidering. I looked at the work I was doing and the part I like best about it. Then I had a talk with my friend Mike Shephard."

"I remember Mike, Fine boy, hard worker."

"I work for him. He shared a lot of his dreams with me, and in the process let me know that at times he regrets not going on to school."

"So he encouraged you to continue schooling?"

"Yes, he did. I was beginning to wonder what kind of friend he was. Discouraging me from doing the work I enjoy. Then he pulled out a blue print, and showed it to me."

"Ah ha! The builders layout."

"Yeah, he started explaining how complicated some of the dimensions, figures and angles were. That it all needed to be figured out to perfection before a building is even planned. He told me he wouldn't even know where to begin. Gerard took care of any changes on a blueprint. Mike just follows orders."

"So?"

"Well, he thought that if I was serious in building, and in the structure of buildings that I should consider taking classes in Drafting and Architecture. Even if I didn't get a full degree the knowledge would be valuable."

Mr. Wiseman smiled. "If I know you, you'll be getting a degree and pass with flying colors. Do you have any schools in mind?"

"No, but I intend to look into it."

"Let me get some information for you. There are a lot of schools that offer such."

"Thank you sir."

It was indeed cold that afternoon, the crew working on the stable felt it more than most. Mike worked alongside Pat shingling the roof. Another group worked on the opposite side of the peak, while another worker finished putting on the molding and siding to the building.

"How are things with you today?" Mike asked.

"Fine I guess." Pat began, "That sister of mine is sure a trouble maker though."

Mike laughed "I could have told you that.

"I was concerned when I found out that Angie Arnolds wasn't speaking to her."

"Angie believed those rumors huh?"

"Lock stock and barrel. Denni talked to her early this morning and straightened it all out. Angie apologized."

"That must have been hard for her, she seems so quiet of a girl."

"She is, but she's opening up a lot more." Pat continued. "Suzanna still isn't willing to talk to Den though."

"Any idea why?"

"I'd rather not say, I don't want to start something else for her."

"You know, I don't create stories." Mike said slightly offended. Then after a pause continued. "So you think she likes Denni more than she lets on?"

"I didn't say that!" Pat defended himself.

"But you think that."

"Let's just say it seems that way."

"Well between you and me," Mike began "I think he likes her more than he lets on."

"I know he does." Pat stated. "We talked about it. He feels so rotten about the fact that he just sat back and watched Brady walk all over her. He feels it's his fault this happened."

"And she feels..."

"That it was because of her that Brady started this mess and involved Denni."

"And neither one knows how the other thinks."

"No they don't, and I won't interfere. I may encourage Suzanna to talk to Denni, but I refuse to tell her how he really feels."

"They need to do that on their own."

"I think I'd be opening a can of worms if I say too much."

Mike nodded, they continued working for awhile, the sound of their hammers echoing in the distance.

"So," Mike broke the silence. "Who's your latest sweetheart?"

"Me?" Pat smiled. "I'm not serious about anyone, never have been."

"That doesn't keep you from dating?"

"No, but I do try to pick girls who won't get serious and assume things on me."

"I don't think I could do that."

"You don't?"

"It seems like such a waste of time."

"But it's fun." Pat remarked, "As long as no one gets the wrong idea."

"What do you mean?"

Pat was thinking of Michelle, he had never even considered dating her, and here people were assuming things about them.

"Well." Pat began, "Do you remember Michelle Morrison?"

"Yeah, sure, she just had a baby right?"

"Uh huh. Well it seems I can't even talk to her, where people don't get the wrong idea."

"Really?" Mike seemed surprised. "I didn't think people were that nosey."

"Oh they are. My own mother was concerned. Claimed she didn't want me to be hurt." Pat scoffed.

"That's hard to believe."

"You have to remember, I'm her eldest son."

Mike paused a minute.

"Tell me Pat, how often do you see Michelle?"

"I usually stop, or try to during my lunch hour,.. she's alone you know."

"Did you ever make an effort like that for any of the girls you dated?"

"No, I told you I wasn't serious about them."

"But your not even interested in Michelle?" Mike asked pointedly. "Yet you make an effort to see her everyday."

Pat put down the hammer he was using and stared at Mike.

"I never looked at it that way." He hesitated. "But if I don't go see her, I'm afraid no one will and she's not doing well at all."

"Maybe if you mentioned it to the ladies at church."

"I thought of that, but when Sarah Daniels went to see her, she was more depressed then ever."

"Why?"

"Because, Nick had a father and Joanna doesn't."

"Oh, well maybe the kids from school could stop by."

"I'll see what they say. That might work." Pat didn't sound too enthusiastic.

"You'll miss seeing her won't you." Mike asked.

"It doesn't matter one way or the other." Pat shrugged.

"Don't kid yourself." Mike stated.

Brother David Rankin arrived at church early that evening to prepare for the service. He'd hung a flag of Brazil in the foyer beside a map of the Amazon. A table before them held samples of clothing, toys, utensils, and text books that differed drastically from what was found in Roberts Junction. The table also included a scrap book containing newspaper articles and Photo's of the work there.

In the center of the table stood a family portrait of the Rankins before their last mission building. It had been taken after the farewell service a little over a year ago. Brother Rankin, a sturdy man of fifty, with a thick head of greying hair and equally thick glasses, held an open bible. His wife Jane stood beside him. She was a tiny woman, yet stood straight, almost challenging in her stature. She was fine featured, and at forty eight her hair was as blonde and full as it had been at twenty. Their oldest daughter Esther, now twenty-five stood with her husband Roger Ongers, beside her father. Roger took over the mission work when Br. Rankin left. Their two sons Aaron and Levi were pictured with them. Ruth Honover was the Rankins younger daughter, she had married an American doctor that was working in a local hospital she was twenty, he twenty eight. The Rankins three sons sat on the ground before them. The twins Matthew and Mark both sixteen flanking their older brother Daniel, twenty-eight. It was a happy Christian family that shone from the photo, a family that would eventually cause drastic changes in the church at Roberts Junction.

Pat was pleased to see that Jeff Johnson had chosen once again to join them, he was equally surprised and a little anxious at seeing Brady Downing also, and although they had not come together, Jeff joined Ginny Little and her children Dennis and Connie in their pew. Brady, boldly sat with the Rhodes family beside Luke. He was playing his game well.

Glancing over at Suzanna Pat could sense her uneasiness, their mother sat between them. Pat whispered.

"Mom, could Suez and I go and sit with Mike and Chrys tonight?"

"Of course but don't make a habit of it. Your father would like to see us together in church."

"Thanks Mom." He smiled. Suzanna gave him a relieved glance.

"Can I press my luck mom." She asked. "And sit with Gramps and Peggy instead?"

"Only if I don't hear any whispering." Her mother stated. "Understand?"

"Perfectly." Suzanna smiled and fled to the safety of her friend.

Having worked along the Amazon river missions for twenty-five years Brother Rankin had much to share. He told of the people and their ways. At times the congregation shook with laughter, at other times, with fear. There indeed was a work to be done, and not just in Brazil. There were souls everywhere that had yet to have the full gospel preached unto them. Story after story came forth that night, telling of people who hadn't heard, who couldn't read it for themselves, who had yet to see the revelation of the one true God. Many hearts were stirred, lives changed that evening. In conclusion Brother Rankin put an offering plate on the alter, the offering would be sent to his Son-In-Law Roger Ongers for use at the mission.

One by one people drifted to the front, others to the foyer to look over the scrap book. There was a sense of urgency in the air, a balmy silence existed. Ben Daniels approached Br. David. After shaking hands he smiled uneasily.

"Almost thou persuadest me to be a missionary." He spoke.

"I would to God, that not only thou, but also all that hear me this day, were both almost and altogether such as I am, except these,.." Brother Rankin held up his hands. "Old decrepit bones." He concluded.

The Reverend Rhodes sat again in his office. He wasn't studying, or praying, just sitting back in an old swivel rocker that had been placed before the window. The night was black, only a few stars were visible. Slowly he opened the window, a chill blew in, the scent of autumn leaves. Somewhere crickets chirped, an owl hooted. A muffled howl came from the direction of Hambones coop. Brother Rhodes closed his eyes, and leaned back in the chair. An abrupt knock on the door startled him.

"Dad?"

"Come on in son."

Pat slowly entered the room and took a chair beside his father. Br. Rhodes smiled at his eldest son.

"I was wondering something." Pat began.

"What's that?"

"Well, you know Michelle had her baby."

"Uh, huh."

"Well, I've gone to see her a few times."

"Your mother told me."

"She did?"

"Yes, she thought you might get yourself involved and be hurt."

"I'm not like that Dad."

"That's what I tried to tell your mother." His father stated. "I trust you son, but that doesn't mean you should go traipsing over there all the time."

"Someone has to, Dad."

"Someone should yes, but it needn't be you."

"I know that, but I'm worried about her."

"I understand that but it's not your concern."

"But it is."

"Because you make it so. She would probably do just as fine without you."

"But she needs somebody."

"So, let someone else help her, I'm sure your sister would."

"Yeah, I guess Suez would if I asked her."

"I was thinking of Cynthia. Suzanna is a bit immature yet to relate well with someone going through what Michelle is experiencing."

Pat groaned inwardly.

"What's the problem."

"It's all my fault." Pat sounded frustrated.

"What's your fault."

"Michelle's situation. I felt I was doing the right thing at the time, but now when I see how depressed she gets, I want to hang my head. Why couldn't I have minded my own business. She would be sitting in class with the rest of us, instead of being tied at home with a baby."

Brother Rhodes face began to turn white as he tried to decipher his sons words. Pat's fault? Pat responsible? Was Pat trying to tell him that it was he that had fathered that baby and not Joe Jamison as everyone had assumed. That would of course explain Joe's immediate departure, for it had been obvious that he loved Michelle, but how could Pat have kept this quiet so long. Brother Rhodes fought desperately for composure.

"Run that by me again son. Your saying you are responsible?" His voice cracked.

Pat looked up and studied his fathers face. Realization dawned on him that his father had misunderstood.

"No Dad, It's Joe's baby, her name is Joanna Jamison. But after Joe left Michelle considered abortion. I was the only one that knew at the time that she was pregnant. I talked her out of it somehow. Now she's got a little one to be both father and mother to and she's only seventeen. I feel like I can't desert her now."

"You can't get emotionally involved either. His father said, much relieved to find his son innocent.

"I'm just doing what I feel Jesus would do. Is that wrong?"

"Your intentions are right Pat. But it's the church as a whole that is an extension of God's love, there are others here that would also be willing to help. You needn't feel obligated."

"Maybe you're right."

"I think I am, I'll talk to Cindi we'll see what she says."

"Sure Pa." Pat said quietly.

CHAPTER 22

A TIME TO KEEP

Thursday, September 29th, 1983

Warmer weather returned Thursday, Sarah hoped it would continue, at least until Sunday. The weather had held to see the stable completed; now if it could only hold until after Suzanna's party Saturday everything would be perfect.

Sarah was pleased at the response she'd gotten from the young people. All planned to attend. It would be a surprise, she only hoped that Suzanna hadn't caught on. Liz Rhodes was stopping for lunch with her husband, they would discuss plans then. Sarah dressed hurriedly, Nick was already tossing in his crib, soon he'd be demanding her attention again.

Descending the stairs a few minutes later she was surprised to see her husband still at home. He was seated in an easy chair, his bible was open before him.

"You're still home." She stated.

"Uh huh." He mumbled.

"Not busy today?"

"About the same." He continued reading.

Sarah entered the kitchen and began preparations for her and Nick's breakfast. Ben rarely dragged his feet in the morning. She wondered if he felt alright. She contemplated asking him but didn't want to disturb his reading.

Later as she passed the room to retrieve a now wide eyed Nick, she heard the faint mumble of prayer. She smiled, pleased that Ben had chosen once again to put aside his job to talk to the creator.

Lynn Deems chose that morning to stop for another visit. True, she missed seeing Sarah when she'd stopped Sunday, but there was something else that brought her back.

"You never mentioned that Rich McAllister was working for Ben." She mentioned to Sarah accusingly.

"I didn't think you knew Rich."

"Of course I know Rich, everyone remembers him."

"I don't."

"You don't?" Lynn was puzzled. "Are you sure."

"Uh huh."

"Hold it, do you remember the night that you and I got stranded at that party in Lincoln."

"Do I ever," Sarah remarked. "That is one night I'd like to forget."

"You forgot some of it already."

"Oh?"

"Don't you remember how we finally got home?"

"Sure, you hocked somebodies car keys, and said you wouldn't give them back if he didn't agree to drive us home."

"That was Rich."

"It was?"

"I don't forget things like that."

Sarah was quiet. She hadn't remembered Rich from that night at all. Chances are he didn't remember her either. She hoped he didn't anyway.

"I told Tim that I'd seen Rich and he sent me out here to make sure Rich knew he's welcome to stop by any time. We've got a continual party going."

"You can mention it to him." Sarah remarked. It amazed her that in seven years Tim and Lynn's life style hadn't changed. They were doing the same things as in High School. It was almost as if they'd never grown up and here they were with children of their own.

Both David and Danny were in school, David in kindergarten, Danny in preschool. Doug was on the floor making faces at Nick, who giggled back at him.

Lynn was still talking about Rich, about the days when Tim, Rich, Scott Marks, and Ben had been friends. Lynn had dated Tim since she was sixteen, Sarah and Chrys weren't along on the dates so they never were real acquainted with Tim's friends. It wasn't until after Ben and Sarah were married that they'd made efforts to reestablish the friendship. It hadn't worked well, their lifestyles were too different. Ben and Sarah wouldn't share in the favorite pastime. They never regretted the fact that the friendship had been severed. Every few years or so Lynn would reappear and make a friendly attempt to return things to what she felt was normal but it was futile. The fact remained,.. Ben and Sarah were no longer part of the crowd. Lynn suggested that they find Rich so she could talk to him. Sarah bundled Nick and they left for the stables.

Rich was in the midst of a pretty demeaning job. Working around horses was always enjoyable, but not as much so when it came time for the clean-up. Rich bore a shovel into each of the stalls to retrieve the old bedding, he'd been working all morning, emptying the stalls, hosing them out, leaving them to dry. He would replace the bedding later.

Sarah took Nick and Doug to see Outlaw. Lynn alone was present when Rich looked up from his work.

"Don't you ever quit working?" She teased.

"Oh sure. All the time, watch." He put the shovel beside a pitchfork and walked over to join her. "Well what brings you around?"

"I missed Sarah the other day. She's showing Doug the new puppy." Lynn began. "I also came to see you."

"Why's that?"

"I mentioned to Tim that I'd seen you Sunday. He asked me to come out and invite you to the house sometime."

"I'm pretty busy." Rich made excuse.

"I won't take no for an answer." Lynn began. "Come out some evening for a barbecue. Tim and the boys would love it. I'll invite Scott and Gail too."

"I guess that would be fine."

"You don't sound too enthused."

"I've changed a lot in ten years."

"You couldn't have changed that much."

"Ben has."

"That's true. But you told me that you hadn't joined Ben and Sarah."

"I also told you that I no longer drink."

"It won't matter. We want you to come."

"Okay, name a time."

"How about Saturday evening?"

"Sounds fine."

"Around five?"

"I'll be there."

"Tim's really looking forward to it. Scott too." Lynn responded. "Oh and Bring your girlfriend too."

"I'm afraid I can't oblige there either."

"What. No girl. Well I can fix that."

"Please Lynn, don't bother."

"No bother at all. You just come planning on having a good time."

Rich sighed. "Sure." He said exasperated.

Edward and Elizabeth Rhodes left for Horseman's Unlimited late that morning. He was in a good mood, enthusiastically whistling a tune, occasionally breaking in with the lyrics. His wife was much more quiet, thoughtful. They were just leaving town when she disturbed his concert.

"Pat talked to you last night?"

"Huh? Oh yeah. It's all taken care of."

"What do you mean?"

"He's not gonna see her again."

"He's not?"

"No. I told you that you had nothing to worry about."

"But he can't just up and leave her now. With no one."

"I thought that was what you wanted."

"It was but,.. I guess not really." His wife shrugged.

"Well, I'm having Cynthia visit her every few days."

"Oh, that's good."

"Maybe a few of the others will take her example."

"They didn't follow Pat's example." Elizabeth pointed out.

"Pat had very excellent motives. He was just mistaken on how they should be handled."

"He understands now?"

"Of course, He did come to me didn't he?" Her husband reminded her.

"I'd like so much to see Michelle living for God."

"A lot of us would dear, but as of right now she's not, she needs our prayers."

"She's had them."

He smiled at her a moment.

"That other teenager of ours worries me more." He began.

"Suzanna? She's so young, she doesn't know yet what she wants out of life half the time. But she has been moody lately. I thought I'd see her and Brady together more but I'm wrong."

"She never mentions him does she?"

"No, and frankly I'm surprised. I'd assumed they liked each other."

"I guess he treated her pretty shady awhile back, she's probably having a rough time forgetting."

"He didn't hurt her did he?" Sister Rhodes asked.

"I'd tan his hide if he did." Brother Rhodes stated. "No, he lied a few times, and pulled a few games on her. She can't tolerate that kind of stuff. You know that."

"Do I ever. What kind of a boy is Brady anyway?"

"It's a little early to judge. But he spoke honestly to me, really let go. He was a very confused boy, yet I like the lad. If he keeps attending church we may see a mighty work of God in his life."

"I'd like to see that." She began. "What about that other young boy, Denni's friend."

"Jeff Johnson. I haven't really been able to talk to him much. He's not very open with me, although it seems he's spoken often to Dennis."

"Pat spoke to him also. I guess the boy is really going through a rough time."

"Oh?"

"Isn't it his family that made that trouble for Ben a few weeks back."

"Could be."

"A few of the women mentioned that his father began drinking heavily and was taken out of classes."

"Oh, he's the teacher I met a week or so ago. Luke and I almost got caught in the middle of a confrontation between him and his wife."

"I hate to see families break up. Too many people suffer because of it."

"No one puts any serious emphasis on marriage these days. They enter marriage with the assumption that if it doesn't work they'll get a divorce. Just like that." He snapped his fingers.

"You know at the rate this world is going we will soon become a minority."

"We are already."

After lunch the women gathered the dishes together while the men went out to the new stables.

"How are plans coming for my daughters party?"

"There's been a few changes." Sarah explained.

"You know you didn't have to do this Sarah."

"But I wanted to."

"I know she'll be pleased." Elizabeth began. "Now what do you have planned?"

"Well we're having the hayride, like I planned. Although Ben refuses to allow a bonfire because of how dry it is. Then we'll meet back in our garage for an old fashioned taffy pull, my husbands idea."

"Of course. It involves food."

Sarah smiled. "Chrys said she'd prepare a few games. I think it will be fun."

"I've already planned the cake, I plan on making the layers into a Victorian mansion, she'll love it."

"Sounds great. Chrys mentioned that the young people pooled their money for a gift. I can't imagine what it is."

"We bought her a portable stereo, boom box. She's been wanting one of her own." Elizabeth continued. "Believe it or not, Cynthia is probably giving her the best gift. It's not an actual gift but a number of months from now Suzanna will be in her own room."

"Any definite plans."

"Just that they definitely want to get married, and they definitely don't want to wait long."

"How long have they dated?"

"Six months or more, I forget. I forsee a wedding in June, although they haven't said much."

"They make a fine couple."

"We hope so, She is our first daughter remember. It'll be hard to see her go."

"A few more years and it'll be Pat's turn. Think of it, in ten years you could have them all married and a slew of grand children running around."

Elizabeth smiled. "I only want them to be happy."

"I'm sure they will be."

"Cindi knows her own mind, it's my younger one that is so inconsistent."

"I don't think so." Sarah pointed out.

"One day she's moping, the next we have to tie her down. It's such a contrast."

"Maybe when she gets a nice fellow she'll settle down. Give her a few years."

"I was afraid she'd be taken with this Downing boy, Especially after his steps toward God."

"Don't rush her, she's got plenty of time. You don't care much for Brady huh?"

"My husband likes him, but I feel uncasy around him. Neither of us would like to see our daughter with him at the time."

"He is coming Friday night, I'll keep an eye on them." Sarah smiled slyly.

"You'll have a lot more to keep your eyes on. All of my children will be here. Cindi and Bob, Pat is bringing Michelle Morrison, just out of courtesy he insists. Suzanna will have her hands full if she tries to avoid Brady, then there's Luke."

"Oh the blessing of innocence." Sarah began.

"Luke has a one track mind, I don't have to tell you what it is."

"Oh, I know. Horses."

They laughed.

"Well it's a safe subject." Elizabeth continued.

"Not if he tries to make a living from it." Sarah remarked.

"But he'd be happy." Elizabeth continued.

"That is important to you isn't it."

"It's something that has recently become important. That they be happy and living for God. We had such high hopes for Cynthia, she was our first, we've had nineteen years to dream about what she could become in life. I myself imagined her married to a prominent man, living in a modest house with adorable children, having everything she ever wanted. Now reality is causing me to look at her, married to what we refer to as a 'body' man. Putzing around in an old garage with other peoples dented cars. It's hard to picture, an apartment instead of a house, old vehicles instead of the sedans. I wholly approve of Bob, I just wish they could be better off. It's funny how parents want so much more for their children then they had themselves."

"I'll remember you said that, when it's time for Nick to leave. I know it's different with sons, but I'd so like to see him marry someone better than myself."

"We all do." Elizabeth said.

Early afternoon found Horseman's Unlimited quite active. Steve Williams, alone today, was exercising 'Special Export' in the outdoor arena. Bill, in his workshop was grooming one of Ben's mares. Rich was now applying fresh layers of bedding to the clean stalls. Ben stood with his Pastor in the shell of the new stable.

"Looks impressive." Br. Rhodes began "Mike ran the job huh?"

"Yes, and he did an excellent job. So did your son, he's a good worker."

"I think so too, I'm rather proud of the boy myself."

"He's got a lot going for him."

"I wish I could be as pleased with that second daughter of mine."

Ben laughed. "Give her time, she'll come around."

"Sometimes I'd like to turn her over my knee and give her a good paddling, and just when I'm about to she does something that makes sense and it throws me off." Br. Rhodes laughed.

"I heard teenagers are like that."

"I've got four, my last one barely twelve and I already feel as if I've aged ten years in the past week." The two laughed as they left the building. Marty Jones had just arrived and the two joined them.

The trucks had pulled up before the stables, the first a Ford F350 crew cab, short box pick-up. The second another Ford, had an enclosed box for transporting wildlife. Both trucks were brown and bore the logo of the State department of Natural Resources in off white.

Jones was a short man, with a quick gait. He bounced with each step, in a haphazard attempt to gain stature. His grey eyes were piercing, his voice rumbled from deep in his throat. He was a small man, with a big responsibility. Beside him stood his crew, a vague collection of graduates from a local school of forestry. All rugged in looks, disciplined in dress, and bearing some semblance of courage. Rich and Bill had come from the stables and Steve wandered over from the arena when they arrived.

"I hope you know what you're doing." Ben teased.

"I don't carry this badge for nothing." Jones replied seriously "I just hope we find the critter and remove her before there are problems."

"Haven't been any so far." Ben commented. "I've kept the riders in the open fields, hoping that there would be no need for it to leave the woods."

"Good, good," He looked around. "I see you've got a few strong hands around, could use 'em do you mind?"

"Oh, no. Not at all." Ben began. "Rich McAllister and Bill Winters both work for me. The other fella is Steve Williams, and this is Edward Rhodes."

"If you're willing to lend a hand," Jones began addressing the group. "We could use the help."

"I'm with you." Rich answered.

"McAllister,..right?"

"Yes sir,"

"I've heard of you."

"You have?"

"Old Colleague of mine was wondering if I knew of your whereabouts. You might want to get in touch with him. Names Emmet Carlson, I guess you took a few courses from him at Bridgeway."

"Carlson, yeah. Is he still teaching there?"

"He's sort of a permanent fixture around the place."

"Well, I'll make sure that I look the guy up."

"Fine,.. anyone else."

"Is they any age limit? If no include me." Bill commented. Jones nodded approval.

"I'll join you too." Steve replied.

Ben and Brother Rhodes also chose to join the crew. Soon all were on their way. Rich and Bill in Rich's Datsun pick-up, and Ben and Br. Rhodes with Steve. They led the way between the stables down the lane toward the swamp.

When Brother Rhodes had left home that morning he hadn't anticipated going bear hunting. True they had no intention of killing the bear but still they must locate, and capture it. He was not a timid man, he'd been raised on a farm, had done a mans work since he was ten, still as they led the way down the path towards the swamp he felt un-easy. God alone knew what lay ahead for them. And only God could protect them now.

Ben seemed immune to fear. The immense danger he was entering never came to mind. He just knew that he wanted this bear controlled and hoped that Marty Jones knew his job well enough. He was excited about the prospect of being part of the capture.

Like all officers of the law, Steve Williams had been trained not to be affected by his own fears, but to overcome them and move forward to complete the job. Danger was not something new to him. He looked death in the face nearly everyday. He could recognize it now and something com-pelled him to do what he could to see that the farm was a safe place for himself and Judy, also for Judy's children.

Following close behind Steve in Rich's old Datsun Pick-up Bill was in high form.

"Had an old she bear here 'bout thirty years back. Must a been in fifty four or so. She was an ornery old Monster too. Had two of the pertiest little cubs with her. Made havoc of the woods, lookin' for honey and berries. Entered the fields a few times also."

"What did you do about her?" Rich asked.

"Right now what's left of her is a laying before me fireplace at home. That's how we did things back then. No one would dream of trying to let the fool thing live, even if she were pertected by the state."

Rich smiled. "They'll find an ideal spot for this one, where there is plenty of food and shelter. Room to roam free of highways, homes, and humans."

"I think I myself would enjoy a place like that." Bill remarked to referring to heaven.

"I would too." Rich agreed, yet desiring the secluded life of a recluse. Two different lives, to different thoughts two different destinies.

It was after four when the group returned from the swamp with the bear. She wasn't very large, only a few years old, and hadn't caused any problems. Tom, Dennis, and Peggy were all present to see her before they transported her to the National Forest nearby.

"I don't think I've been this close to a bear before." Dennis commented as he looked through the bars of the cage. The animal had been sedated and seemed quite inactive.

"I know I've never been as close as I was today." Ben remarked. Rhodes agreed.

"Ye should-a been around in fifty four." Bill began again. "I'd a been hamburger meat if the Good Lord hadn't seen fit to confuse everything and let me get a good aim at the thing."

"I'll call you next time instead of having Marty come all this way." Ben teased.

"I'm a hopin' there ain't another for thirty more years or so, I'll only be little over a hundred then, I'll have plenty of spunk to drop the fellow."

Rich smiled. "It'll be the first bear shot from a wheel chair."

Bill laughed. "No way sonnie, I'll be a leavin' this world before these legs leave me. Count on it."

"I'd rather have you around awhile."

Sarah and Elizabeth joined the group around the trucks.

"So." Sarah began, "You're the one who attempted to put a damper on Suzanna's birthday plans?" She spoke to the bear.

"You'll be able to use the woods. Rich saw that both the gate to the woods and the marsh were open."

"Good, I'm glad. Now who do you have driving the horses Saturday?"

"It doesn't matter to me." Ben began. "I could do it myself; or Denni, Tom and Rich will both be off early."

"You'll have a wagon ready?"

"Yes ma'am. In fact it's in the feed shed right now, full of hay. All I'll have to do is have the horses hitched and drive it on out."

"Good, now I can quit worrying about that and start worrying about other things."

"Don't worry about the cake." Elizabeth returned. "I'll see that it's here. I'll bring it out at four, and I'll pick up Nick."

"Thanks, I appreciate it."

"I'll remove the car from the garage for the night. Bob's got my truck so it's not going to be in the way."

"I believe he'll be bringing it that night." Brother Rhodes began. "Pat will be driving Cynthia out to Lincoln, she'll be taking his car."

"Good, I've only been without the truck since Monday but I'm kinda lost without it."

"I know how you feel." Brother Rhodes added. "My son's assumed the right to our second car so we always have to check with one another to see who gets to have the wagon."

"I usually win." Sister Rhodes smiled.

"I'm afraid the neighbors are gonna start calling me the 10-speed preacher because when Pat inherited the car for work I inherited his bike."

"Well it is more convenient for making rounds than it would be for doing the family shopping."

"It was fine until my son Luke put a sign on it that said 'CLERGY'. up until that time I could give the impression of going for a bike ride instead of using it as a necessity."

"I could loan you a horse and buggy if you'd like to go in style." Ben offered.

"Now that would really start the tongues waggin."

The crows began to disperse, Jones and his crew finished preparing the bear for transport and had gone their way. The Rhodes left for home, promising to remind Suzanna that she'd be baby-sitting that night at 6:30 for Nick.

Suzanna had become, to most, the old Suzanna. After Angie had apologized she'd regained her energetic, outgoing, nature. Only those that were close to her saw the scars of the ordeal. Her brother saw, Peggy also. But more important Dennis saw and it concerned him, for although Suzanna no longer avoided him she hadn't actually spoken to him either. He'd made a few attempts to single her out but it was usually met with shrugs and silence, for Suzanna could not bear to speak. It hurt to much."

Pat offered to drive her to the farm that evening.

It was not yet dusk when they left for the farm. The sky; orange in the distance, contrasted with the dark outlines of the trees and buildings they passed. Rolling down the windows of the car they allowed the brisk air to slap at their faces, wisking their hair and giving them an invigorating breath of late September. Neither spoke, too lost in their own selves. Suzanna arming herself against an accidental brush with Dennis, Pat trying to put aside the guilt of not giving Michelle a reason for his absence today. He knew that she had waited. She knew him too well. Pat only hoped that she knew him well enough not to hold his actions against him. They'd meant nothing to each other, or had they?"

Sarah was waiting when Suzanna entered the kitchen.

"Look Nicki, Suzanna's here." Sarah encouraged her son who smiled a broad toothless smile. "We haven't seen much of you lately. I bet you've been busy?"

"I would have stopped in Saturday night but Cindi was here and I don't think I could have stood one more Bob conversation."

Sarah laughed. "Give her a few years She'll be talking about Bib in a different light."

"It hardly seems possible. She sounds like a broken record."

"Remember that when you're in love."

"I don't intend on ever being in love." Suzanna said.

"Oh?"

"I lied." Suzanna grinned. "I found out that falling in love was something that I have absolutely no control over."

"You'd better get some control, I'd hate to see you in love with some MOBSTER."

"Oh Darling." Suzanna remarked. "You have the most gorgeous Automatic Machine Gun, I've ever seen. And your Bullet proof vest is the height of fashion. Won't you please take me for another spin in your armored car?"

Sarah laughed. "I must admit, who ever you do fall in love with had better have a sense of humor."

"He does." Suzanna thought to herself as Sarah left. Sarah had agreed to begin giving riding lessons to a few Junior High girls. Jenny Johnson and two of her friends from school. They would work in the indoor arena today. Suzanna was welcome to bring Nick down to see Mommy but she chose to remain at the house. The chances of meeting Dennis at the stables was too high.

Nick seemed tired so picking up a childrens story book she carried him to the rocker. Rocking slowly she began to read in a soft voice and point to the pictures. Nick nodded sleepily, content in loving arms with a quiet voice to soothe him.

Suzanna's mind raced as she felt Nicks body go limp in slumber, she thought once again of Dennis. Dennis had done more than the average friend. He'd seen Angie's desertion and had explained the situation. It must have been terribly hard for him, especially when he himself was an object of the same rejection. So why had he done it?

She'd taken note of every word he'd said all day and attempted to resurrect his words from the past. She had fond memories of Den from early childhood even before his family had become Christians. Pat and him had played together, she'd tried to tag along but being the youngest they often abandoned her. She'd cry then until Mommy looking for her Baby would dry her tears on her ever present apron and kissing her wounded head carry her home to cookies and milk. Later, as they grew the boys found her good enough to play with, only if they needed someone to be catcher, or to keep score, or set up targets, or any multitude of jobs that might be required of the common slave. She'd never minded, she had always adored her big brother and gloried just in being in his presence.

So lost in thought was she that a sound from the kitchen nearly caused her to jump through the ceiling. Looking up she saw Dennis in the doorway.

"Sorry to startle you." He apologized. "I didn't think anyone was in the house or I would have knocked." He walked over toward the cabinet and pulling out a drawer, lifted out a camera case. "Ben asked me to run up and get his camera, he's going to take a few pictures of 'Fortune' and also the new stables." Denni explained his presence. Then nodding good-bye he left the house.

Suzanna had not spoken at all. Just his presence had caused her to clam up. Why? Just because she,.. liked him? No. Not because she liked him, but because she was afraid he didn't like her back. She would rather have her memories be pleasant ones, then have cruel reality. If anyone were to be a fool, she would, and not another soul would know.

When Sarah returned she wasn't alone.

"You're in luck." She stated. "Denni's offered to give you a lift back to town. Ben's still out there braggin about his 'Fortune' it'll take a bit of pleading to get him away. You may have been stranded here a while."

"I wouldn't have minded." Suzanna stated.

"I hope not but Denni is on his way out anyway. He's waiting outside for you."

"Sarah," Suzanna began. "..I don't want to ride home with Denni."

"Why not?" Sarah asked bewildered.

Suzanna just looked at her wearily. "You'd never understand."

"I could try." She responded.

Suzanna sighed deeply. "I don't think I'm ready to explain. But thanks anyway." She moved toward the door. Denni's car was parked outside.

"You like him huh?" Sarah asked.

Suzanna nodded.

"Good for you. He's not a Mobster, and he does have a sense of humor."

Suzanna still said nothing, she could barely see the outline of his car through the dampness in her eyes.

"Does he know?"

Suzanna shook her head.

"Wait on it. If he likes you he'll let you know." Sarah continued. "Somehow. Now you'd better get out there, and be yourself."

Suzanna moved mechanically to open the door.

"I'll say a prayer for you." Sarah began. "I know it's important to you."

Suzanna turned and smiled. Then quickly she was out the door, across the lawn, and into the passenger side of Denni's car.

He forced a smile when he saw her.

"I'm sorry to put you on the spot." He began "I know you'd rather not be with me. I understand."

"You do?" Suzanna said surprised.

"After what I allowed happen to you. I wouldn't blame you for never speaking to me again."

"Huh? What are you talking about?"

"Brady of course. You realize that I could have stood up to him months ago and you wouldn't have had to go through these past few weeks of horror."

"It wasn't your fault."

"Sure it was. I knew exactly what he was like, I could have warned you."

"I probably wouldn't have listened, I had to go through what I did to know some of the things I know now."

"Yeah, you had to go through ridicule, humiliation, possibly bodily injury to know that Brady Downing is a complete jerk." Denni said sarcastically.

"That's not what I learned."

"Oh?"

"I learned who my real friends were. Thanks Den. It's hard for me to say it but thanks, I couldn't have gone through it without you."

"Me?"

"And Peggy, My brother, and surprisingly enough Jeff Johnson." She paused, "But mostly you."

"Then I have a question."

"What's that?"

"Why won't you talk to me?"

"Aren't I talking right now?"

"You know what I mean."

Suzanna laughed awkwardly.

"I guess I was really embarrassed about what happened. I didn't know what you thought of me. I was afraid you'd hate me for getting you involved. I guess I thought if I ignored you enough you'd go away and then I'd never have to face you."

"I don't plan on going away." Dennis responded. "We've been through too much together to just forget about one another. We've been to good of friends for too long."

Suzanna was quiet. She had managed to speak to Denni, but yet couldn't manage to speak her true heart. Neither could he.

Thus we find in the midst of steps toward one another that there is always something more that must give,.. something more that must go,.. whether it be pride, or stubbornness or whether it be just plain insecurities,.. something must go.

CHAPTER 23

A TIME TO CAST AWAY

Friday September 30, 1983

It had been agreed that Suzanna could have a few friends for the night. They'd been anticipating it all week. Peggy was coming of course, so was Angie, and Becky Franklin. Suzanna had conned her mother into allowing them to sleep in the guest room rather then send Cindi there for the night. The guest room was a special place reserved for visiting preachers. It was a large room, containing a full sized bed, dressing table, and night stand. It also had an area which included a sofa sleeper, coffee table and a comfortable arm chair. There was plenty of shelves and closet space. Suzanna had spent the night here only when Cindi had chosen to have friends over.

At breakfast Suzanna was still making plans.

"Could I have the tape player tonight in the guest room."

Elizabeth paused, a plan began forming in her mind. "I don't see why not. I just don't want to hear music playing half the night."

"Speaking of music mom, could I invite the guys over for an hour or so after Youth Service to go through a few songs." Pat asked.

"Fine. I had planned on having pizza for the girls. Should I pick up a few for your group too?"

"Thanks mom that would be swell."

"I can't believe this!" Suzanna stammered. "My birthday comes only once a year and my brother plans on ruining it with his presence and his useless friends." She sounded upset. "And my own mother okay's it."

"They will be in the family room Suzanna. You will be elsewhere. You may not even see each other." Her mother responded.

"Don't bet on it mom. Watch Luke bring his friends home and Cindi bring that creepy Bob."

"Bob is not Creepy!" Cindi defended. "And I should think you girls would enjoy having the boys around." She smiled. "Maybe I will bring Bob home for awhile."

"Yeah, sure. Invite the whole town." Suzanna said sarcastically.

Pat was laughing. "Remind me not to mention that the girls will be here. It might scare the fella's away."

"I'll make sure they know." Suzanna stated bluntly. "I'll let them know they're not welcome."

"But they are welcome dear. Just as much as your friends are." Her mother stated.

"Mom, you just don't understand." Suzanna was frustrated.

It seemed that more then her mother didn't understand. Her friends didn't seem to mind at all.

"I don't mind." Angie stated on the way to school. "You remember I have nine brothers. I'm used to having boys around."

"Well, I think it's rotten of Pat to pull it on a day that I already had planned something."

Angie shrugged but said nothing. Becky's response was different.

"Hey, we'll have a blast! They think they're coming to practice, well we'll just give them an audience to play for." She smiled. "That'll really wipe out their concentration. Especially when they see the faces we make and hear our remarks."

Peggy couldn't help but laugh, although she added.

"They're really serious about working this group out, but I can't see anything wrong with giving them a lesson in audience control."

Even Suzanna was pacified with the turn of ideas.

"I really feel terrible." Peggy began. "Tomorrow is your fifteenth birthday and I'll be working all day."

"You can't help that." Suzanna remarked.

"But I'd love to spend the day with you guys."

"I know you would."

"What do you plan on doing?"

"We're gonna go shopping in Lincoln. I've got some baby-sitting money; so do Angie and Beck we're gonna shop at McCurruthers and Barnes, then have lunch at the 'Palace' in one of the gardens. After that we'll stop at the Christian bookstore, I haven't read a decent book in ages."

"You don't have to, you've got a big enough imagination to make up for it."

"I'll have to agree with that." Suzanna began. "Too bad I can't channel that imagination into concrete idea's."

"I have concrete idea's,.. but no imagination. Let's share." Peggy suggested. The two laughed.

"Maybe we'll stop at the farm to see you on our way back from Lincoln." Suzanna suggested.

"Who's your chauffeur?"

"Sister Chrys is driving us in. She's got to get some supplies and offered to give us a lift. My mother arranged for 'Bob the creep' to bring us home. He'll do anything to please her, it's kind of sickening."

"He's not that bad." Peggy stated.

"I thought you were the one who didn't like him."

"I don't, not to go out with anyway,.. I think him and Cindi make a fine couple."

"She sure could use help." Suzanna stated.

"Be thankful you've got her. My sisters are strangers to me. I don't mind, but sometimes I miss having someone to share with all the time."

"I don't share much with Cindi." Suzanna stated honestly. "I usually go to Pat."

"My brother is only ten, but I admit he is easier to go to then the twins."

"It must be strange having a mother that lives so far away."

"This is the only life I've ever known." Peggy responded. "I admit I sometimes feel lonely without someone who could understand about how I feel, but there are others like you own mother who have kind of taken me under their wing."

"I'll share her with you anytime." Suzanna agreed.

All was still dark when Jeff and his father left home that morning, the streetlights created little oasis' of illumination in the dim world. Their feet pounded rhythmically upon the hard pavement. Together they ran, the younger setting the pace, his father maintaining the speed, like the seasoned athlete that he was. Running was not tearing them apart but creating a bond between father and son which was so necessary at this crucial time.

They were alone now; in running, in living, but they were together. Mere circumstances could never sever the tie that held them. They circled the familiar park, the trees, silent witness', appeared to nod as they filed past. Overhead the last of the stars blinked, dawn was approaching.

Their home had seemed so barren in the past week. Lingering memories of a wife, a sister, were always there to welcome them, shutting them into it's cold grip of abandonment. They fought daily against the force that would invade their memories to no avail. Life was not always pretty.

Jeff had never hurt so. Each day seemed to bring new misery. His only strength had been not in his father,.. but his friends Dennis, and Pat. He had clung to their words, desiring that peace they talked so freely about, that strength that had held Denni's life together when his father had left. Could he ever obtain that peace, or that strength for himself?

Entering their home once again they returned to their private worlds in silence. Jeff a confused, frustrated seventeen year old boy. Ray his father, a brokenhearted, helpless, individual both preparing for a day that would force them once again to face what life had dealt them.

In the seclusion of his room Jeff stood before his mirror. Tossing his head, holding it at different angles. Smiling, frowning. He was studying his profile. He had never been given to much vanity but today was special. It was Homecoming. Julie Marksman had eagerly excepted his invitation to the game tonight. There would be a dance following it. Jeff harbored secret hopes that Julie would turn out to be the girl for him.

Hurrying into the guest room, Suzanna carelessly dumped a stack of cassette tapes, a trivia game and her Cabbage Patch doll onto the coffee table. She scanned the room for the tape player her mother had mentioned was there. Not finding it she was about to call to her mother when she noticed a gayly wrapped present lying on the bed.

She eyed the gift thoughtfully. Of course she wanted to rush over and tear off the wrappings, but is that what fifteen year old girls do? She should wait so her mother could be there when she opened it. Slowly she lifted it from the bed. It was heavy. She shook it, nothing rattled. Silently she set it back on the bed. Then, her curiosity getting the best of her she lifted it again, turning it slowly. Looking at it from all angles.

"I see you found it." Her mothers voice startled her. She jumped, then laughed.

"It's okay dear." Her mother urged. "It's for you. Open it."

Suzanna slowly removed the wrapping. As she did, she became aware of the familiarity of the package. It's weight, it's size. She worked more quickly.

"Is it,..?" She couldn't bear to express her desire. "Yes it is! Oh mom, this is super, just super. Thank you." She gave her mother a warm hug.

"Where's Pa?" She asked.

"Right here." He said from the doorway.

Suzanna went to him also. "Thanks Pa, I love you."

"Now maybe someone else can use the tape player around here." He teased, then soberly he looked at her. "Fifteen already and it seems like only last week that I held you on my knee. Don't grow up too fast, I don't want to miss one minute of having my baby girl around."

"I don't intend on leaving for a long, long time." She grinned.

"I should hope not dear." Her mother declared. "Don't mind your father, he's been an emotional mess since Cindi announced her engagement. You'd think he was losing his right arm."

"In a way I am." He began. "She's part of the family and when we separate there is always sorrow."

"But there is joy in knowing that she's happy." Elizabeth responded. "And just think you're gaining a son-in-law."

"Bob the creep." Suzanna commented.

"I'd rather you not refer to him as that." Her mother reprimanded. "Your sister might be hurt."

"She doesn't mind when he calls me Suzanna Banana, or that everytime I answer the phone when he calls he starts singing 'O Suzanna', and he's always threatening to do horrid things to me."

"Has he done any of them?"

"I told him I'd bite him if he tried."

"Suzanna!" Her mother was surprised.

"Well, I will." Suzanna insisted. Her father laughed.

"Well if your sister can't handle her future husband she can always send him to you."

"Don't even mention it. Just the sight of him makes me nauseous."

"Is he that bad?" Her mother asked soberly.

"No, not at all. But if he's gonna be part of the family I better treat him like one,.. right?"

Her mother shook her head in exasperation.

The game started at six. Five thirty found Jeff Johnson driving into the impressive yard of Marksman's Stables. He was uneasy, this was his first date with Julie and he wanted to impress her. She hurried from the house when she saw him pull up.

He had thought her strinkingly beautiful when he'd met her last Saturday. Today was different. No longer dressed in denim jeans and cowboy boots, Julie seemed a goddess, the express image of beauty. Gold curls surrounded her head, blue eyes sparkled like diamonds, her skin as smooth as silk. She wore a short skirt under a large oversized sweater that still revealed her trim figure. Dark stockings ended in short black high heeled boots. She climbed into the car before Jeff could offer his help.

"Whew." She exclaimed "Get me away from this nut house."

Jeff laughed.

"Another minute and I would have been climbing the walls. You're a life saver you know that."

She didn't wait for a response.

"This is great." She continued. "I've been thinking about tonight all week."

"You like football then?" Jeff asked.

"Are you kidding? Can't stand it." She stated. "I'm not going for the game Jeff."

"Oh?" He remarked.

"You should be used to it by now." Julie continued. "As good looking as you are, I bet I'll make a whole flock of girls jealous tonight."

"Don't count on it."

"All I can say is I like what I see, and that's always been enough for me." She smiled teasingly at him.

Jeff remained quiet. In all his years he had never felt quite like he did at the moment. It was as if he and Julie existed alone on an endless highway, no ballgame, no dance, no parents, nothing seemed to be separating them, but the steering wheel of the car he was driving. In his silence Julie had moved closer to him. Each breath he took brought the frangrance of a delightful garden in full bloom, the nearness of her sent tingling barbs shooting through his body. Casually she looked for a station on the radio, deliberately brushing him in her pursuit. Jeff took his arm and placed it around her, she snuggled close. Jeff was ecstatic. A whole evening with Julie would seem like heaven to him. Maybe his choice not to attend the Youth meeting that night was a good one.

In the days lengthening shadows red, white, and blue prevailed. Streamers, banners, and floats all bearing the school colors gathered at the ballpark. The marching band stood like wooden soldiers at attention, the team looking like overstuffed turkeys in American flags gathered on the field. The air was growing cooler now, the smell of freshly popped corn settled thickly through the bleachers slowly filling with dark shapes in various sizes.

Jeff parked and led Julie toward the bench. His father greeted him, smiling at Julie although he didn't speak.

"Well I got a smile out of that grouch." Julie stated.

"Only because you're with his son." Jeff grinned.

"That's your father?"

"Sure is."

"But I was led to believe your father was a delirious, old, alcoholic that couldn't even keep a steady job."

"False stories travel fast." Jeff remarked.

"I wonder what else I've been told about you is false."

"Does it matter?" Jeff asked.

"Actually,.. no." She seemed pleased.

They found a seat near the team. Jeff feeling vaguely guilty for quitting the team so soon in the season. He loved football, and half wished he could be playing tonight.

A figure ran in from the field, it was hard to distinguish who it was under the uniform, but Jeff knew. It seemed that Julie knew also. She gave him a smile and waved. Brady approached them.

"Don't the two of you look nice and cozy?" He smiled.

"There's room for one more." Julie encouraged. "But no, you're gonna spend your evening chasing a lopsided ball."

"And doing a good job of it." He admitted proudly as he took the seat next to her. "I've got a few minutes before the game starts."

She smiled encouragingly at him. "That uniform doesn't do you justice you know."

"It comes with the job." He remarked. "But I must say, your uniform is sure doing you justice."

"Oh this." She spoke of her clothes. "I just threw these on at the last minute."

"I'd like to see you when you tried to look smashing." He informed her.

"Would you?" She asked.

"Of course."

"I'll show you then, if you give me a good reason to."

"Maybe dinner sometime? And a movie?"

"I'd love it." She smiled again.

"Monday? Five o'clock?"

"I'll be ready." She stated.

Jeff had heard every word, yet appeared unconcerned. In reality he was very much concerned. Brady Downing had managed once again to humiliate him. He should be getting used to it. Julie didn't seem the slightest bit uneasy about the whole thing.

The entire evening went that way. Jeff slowly gaining confidence in his relationship with Julie. Brady destroying it with his presence. The fact that Brady made a few plays that enabled his team to win didn't help matters. Julie rushed to greet him as he ran off the field after their victory. They joyfully embraced each other, Jeff came up behind them, his father also.

"You did a fine job, Brady. I'm proud of you." Johnson spoke.

"Thank you sir. They played a hard game."

"Not hard enough though." The coach responded.

"You do have a few of your better players back tonight."

"Straight ones, Brady, that's all we ask."

A few others had gathered around and as the coach encouraged each one, Jeff led Julie back to the car.

"I think I'm gonna like football after all." She commented.

"I don't think it's the game you like." Jeff said soberly.

She laughed.

They had returned to Jeffs car and were seated, yet Jeff hadn't turned on the ignition.

"Jeff?" Julie began.

"Huh."

"You're stalling."

"I'm thinking."

"I think I know what." She moved closer to him. "I only accepted the date from Brady to humor him, it's you I like."

"Or is it me your gonna humor tonight?"

"Jeff, you are all I've thought about all week, how could you think I wasn't serious about you?"

"You hugged Brady." Jeff responded simply.

Julie laughed. "But Jeff, he made the first move, it meant nothing to me, but maybe coming from someone,.. like you for instance,.." She paused.

Jeff got her message and pulled her close. What Brady did Monday didn't matter to Jeff. All that mattered was that tonight he and Juile were together, alone. He kissed her passionately, she received it invitingly. Nothing Jeff thought could go wrong now.

The homecoming dance was in the High School Cafeteria. Red, white and blue streamers hung from the ceiling, wrapped each pole, bordered each doorway. Red, white, and blue lights flashed onto the dance floor. The members of the band also wore the school colors.

While Julie spoke with a few girls she knew Jeff joined his friends.

"Where's the party?" Chas asked.

"They ain't one." Jim answered.

"Where do you want one?" Brady asked. "This place is the pits. It's so clean around here even the air squeaks."

"We could take a ride out to founders park."

"And leave the girls? We'd never hear the end of it."

"Of course we'll take the girls. That's the best part."

"You're gonna have to do some pretty swift talking to get them to agree," Chas stated. "They came to dance."

"Well." Brady began, "You can just offer them better surroundings and better music to dance to."

"We'll try," Jed began. "Let's meet out front in about ten minutes,.. okay?"

"Gotcha."

Jeff had stood in the midst of the group feeling defeated. He knew what they meant when they said Party, and he wanted nothing to do with it.

He waited patiently for Julie to return. They'd just do the dance alone with the dead beats. He failed to notice that Brady had gone to seek Julie out. They were deep in conversation when Jeff looked their way.

"What the,.." He mumbled as he hurried to her side. She saw him approach.

"Jeff! There you are. It's about time to leave if we want to meet for the party."

"We're not going." He stated.

"Of course we are." She announced.

"No Julie, we'll stay here."

"But why Jeff? It'll be a blast."

Jeff remained silent, determined not to get dragged into Brady's games another time.

"Please, Jeff. It is so horribly bland here. There's no life. Brady's got the stuff to put life into a party."

"That's why we're not going."

"But Jeff, I want to go. Please,.."

Jeff wanted so to relent, he wanted to join the others, if only to please Julie. A warning bell sounded inside him, he'd made a choice to quit the stuff, why put himself in the midst of it.

"Jeff?" She asked again.

"I'm afraid we're not going."

Her face fell, Jeff instantly regretted his decision, but also knew it was the right one.

"You might as well bring me home then because I'm not going to stay another minute in this hideous place with all these immature babies."

"Okay, Julie. I'll take you home." Jeff agreed, they began to turn away but Brady stopped them.

"I'll take you to the party Julie."

She turned.

"You would? What a life saver."

"Hold it Brady." Jeff began. "She's with me."

"But Jeffer, you were bringing her home, why not let me take her from here if that's what she wants."

"Oh please Brady. I'd never be able to thank you."

"I think you will." He smiled at her as the two walked off leaving Jeff alone, defeated, his perfect world a perfect failure.

The flashing shadows around him seemed to blend into nothingness, only the sight of Julie with Brady remained. Anger boiled within him. Yet he stood immobile. A rock amid swaying marsh grass, rejected among his peers. Cringing inwardly at the stark reality of life, he left the place more colder than he had ever felt before.

Youth Service was fairly low key that evening. Chrys had put together a few bible games. Teams were picked for quizzing. Matthew and Mark Rankin were chosen as captains. Suzanna found herself on Matt's team, beside Denni.

At first it seemed awkward, feeling the way she now did toward Den, but his outgoing personality, and warm smile seemed to cause that uneasiness to slip silently away. It was as if they were children again, laughing giggling, conspiring against the other team. All the inhibitions of peer pressure left them, all the conflicts of the past week were forgotten. They rejoiced together with each added point, and groaned at the seemingly stupid errors of their team. Suzanna hadn't realized it but the healing process was working overtime in her heart. Recreating that innocent joy that had once radiated from it.

True, their team lost, but neither really cared. They were friends again. True friends. As the young people departed after the services Suzanna and Denni remained together enjoying each others company, and fellowship. Others soon joined them, and after piling suitcases, sleeping bags, trombone, saxophone, trumpet, and other paraphernalia into a few over crowded vehicles they left for the preachers house.

They arrived just as Elizabeth Rhodes was taking the first pizza out of the oven.

"Hands off, all of you." She declared "If you'll just hold your guns a bit we'll have them all hot and waiting in a jiffy. Don't even think of snitchin' before then." Turning to Cindi and Bob who had also returned home she stated. "You two can be kitchen help."

"Us?" Cindi was stunned.

"You're gonna have to learn to work together sometime, may as well be now."

Bob grabbed for an apron. "I'm game but I admit, I'm all thumbs."

"I can use thumbs too." She answered.

Suzanna led the way to the guest room. The girls exclaimed excitedly over her tape player. It wasn't until Angie first saw the cabbage patch doll plopped securely on the bed that she spoke?

"Is she your's?" She asked.

"Uh, huh. Someone special gave her to me."

"Really? Do you sleep with her?"

"She kinda stays on my bed."

"This is great." Angie laughed.

"What is?" Suzanna asked.

"I've got a doll I've kept on my bed for years, I started to become embarrassed by it, but I can't seem to put her away. She's the sister that I never had."

"Did you bring her?"

"No, I couldn't. I was afraid you'd laugh if you knew."

"Well I know that at least Peggy wouldn't laugh at me." Suzanna grinned. Peggy was reaching into her suitcase and she brought out a second Cabbage Patch doll not much unlike Suzanna's.

"Someone very special gave her to me." Peggy grinned.

Becky looked at the two and then at Angie.

"I think you two had better explain, Angie's bound to be curious."

"They were given to us last Christmas, right before Becky began coming to church. We were the only two girls at Kennedy." Peggy began "I was a sophomore, Suzanna a freshman. We felt really lost and alone."

"One day." Suzanna added. "Sister Chrys told us to start praying for souls. That there were babies out there that were ready to be born." They laughed.

"We had no idea how to go about it. So she began by telling us that when a mother is pregnant they have to take such good care of their bodies, eat the right thing, get exercise. Then she told us that spiritually we needed to feast on the word of God and exercise our faith. Sarah Daniels helped a lot because she was pregnant with Nick. People laughed because we began acting just like we were expecting too." Peggy paused as she spoke. "We even began eating pickles and ice cream to get on everyone's nerves."

"We never had morning sickness though." Suzanna added. "Thank God for that."

"Well, at Christmas we both had gifts underneath our trees no one would explain where they came from. Well we knew they were from sister Chrys when we opened them and found our 'babies'."

"She had taken the Adoption papers and rewritten them, the names were blank but Jesus was the one who was adopting the children. She asked us to name the babies after the first new babies from our spiritual efforts were born."

Suzanna held up her baby. "Angie, I'd like you to meet Rabekah Marie Franklin JESUS."

Becky smiled at Angie, there were tears forming in both their eyes.

Peggy held up her baby. "This one is being introduced for the first time. Guys meet Angela Rose Arnolds JESUS."

When the girls entered the family room for their share of pizza all was chaos. Instruments had been opened, music distributed, shoes had been tossed off with the sweaters and jackets and were in disorderly heaps around the room. A folding table had the remains of a few pizza's. Bob garbed in an apron approached balancing a fresh pizza high in the air on his finger tips.

"La de da de da." He sang as he placed the pizza elegantly on the table before the girls. "Bet you never knew I was so talented."

Suzanna studied him a minute before retorting. "You must want to marry my sister awfully bad."

"Yes, Ma'am I do." He agreed. The girls laughed. Taking paper plates they chose pizza for themselves and looked for a place to sit.

All the chairs seemed occupied. Matt Rankin and Luke sat in a corner on lounge chairs by the bookcase obviously talking about basketball, Mark and Pat were into a heated discussion about cars by the inactive fireplace. Mike Shephard and Dennis looked up from their conversation on the couch. Mike rose first.

"Have a seat ladies."

"No Mike, don't bother getting up. We can sit on the floor." Suzanna began.

"Then we'll join you and it will be a shame that no one takes the couch." He responded as Dennis joined him at the table for another slice of pizza. They returned to the girls when their plates were full.

"Give Chrys a message for Peggy and I." Suzanna spoke to Mike. "Tell her we have officially announced the name of our second Baby."

Mike smiled, having been in on the project from the start. "That's wonderful. I'll tell her." He looked at Angie. "I was adopted years ago but I can always use another sister."

"Sister" She said confused then it dawned on her. "Sister." She repeated. She looked at the girls around her. "Sisters! All my life I've wanted a sister now I've gained three in one day."

The girls smiled with her.

"Maybe now I can get rid of my baby."

"Don't you dare." Suzanna stated "She's a symbol of your sisters just as ours is a symbol of our children."

"I guess so. But do I get to change her name?"

"Of course."

"She get's three names though. 'Margaret Suzanna Rabehak Arnolds."

"I love it." Becky exclaimed.

The others nodded. Mike and Denni looked at each other and grinned.

Jeff Johnson joined them at a little past ten. He had wandered around like a fugitive for awhile before deciding that what he really needed to do was to see Denni, or Pat.

Bob opened the door still wearing his apron and holding a dish towel, Suzanna had added to his apparel by tying a scarf around his head. He smiled when he saw Jeff.

"Rhodes Raving Nut house, May I help you sir?"

"Yes Ma'am." Jeff smiled back. They both grinned.

"Don't stand out there come on in." Bob insisted.

"Is it safe?" Jeff wondered.

"It is now. They ate all the dangerous stuff." Bob answered as he led Jeff to the back room where the group was slowly trying a few tunes.

"Hey Johnson." Denni greeted enthusiastically. "Have a seat our audience needs some improvement."

He joined the girls.

"Are they any good?"

"I've heard worse." Becky began. "Ever hear a cat fight?"

"Fingernails squeaking on a blackboard." Peggy asked.

"Someone dropping a box of pots and pans down three flights of stairs." Suzanna added.

"50 preschoolers and a ten by ten room." Angie concluded after a pause.

"That bad huh?" Jeff asked.

"Well,.." Becky began. "I wouldn't necessarily say bad. It's hard to tell."

"It is? Why's that?"

"They haven't played anything yet." Becky responded.

At that moment Mike counted to three and they began to play for the first time that evening as a group. It was a simple tune familiar to all, 'The Battle Hymn of the Republic' True, the horns still squeaked, and the trombonist came in at the wrong time but all in all they did a fair job. The girls were surprised. Half way through the song Suzanna got the idea to get her tape player and try it out for the first time. She rose quickly and left the room.

Denni had seen her leave so when they took a break and Pat joined Jeff, Denni went to find Suzanna. Suzanna was on the floor with her tape player before her. She was glancing through the pamphlet of directions that had come with it.

Denni waited for a moment in the doorway. She turned and smiled.

"Hi, I didn't think anyone missed me."

"I did." He answered. "Can I come in?"

"Sure, I'm gonna want you guys to play some more so we can get it on tape."

"We're just taking a break."

There was an awkward pause. Suzanna opened the tape player and inserted one of the new cassettes her mother had included with the gift. She couldn't bear to look at Denni afraid she might not find what she wanted so much to find. Someone who no longer regarded her as some punk, Pat's little sister, or one of the preachers kids. She wanted so much for him to become a closer friend than any she had ever had. They'd shared so much in life was it wrong for her to hope that they could share more? His voice penetrated her thoughts.

"Suzanna?" He asked. "She turned to look at him. That familiar face, that smile so full of fun and honestly. "Things are different now." He began. "I tried to explain a little yesterday but I guess I'm not too good with words."

She was silent. Hope began to stir within her preparing to blossom.

"I guess I should just be honest with you. This past week or so woke me up to a lot of things. The most important was you, and how much I really care about you. I couldn't get you off my mind all week, almost declared insanity when you refused to talk to me. It's all so new to me. I've never felt like this before. I know how much you liked Brady and were hurt by him, but I couldn't live with myself if I didn't tell you how I felt."

Suzanna was so overwhelmed that she was close to tears. Someday Denni would fully understand how she felt about Brady 'the slime', but for now he needed to know how she felt about him.

"Den, I don't know what to say?" She finally said honestly.

"Don't say anything right now." He began. "Just tell me. Can the two of us go on from where I'm at."

"Yes,.. yes, we can." She said immediately.

He sighed deeply before he spoke. "I hope you know what this means to me."

"You, yourself have no idea what it means to me." She returned honestly.

"I think I do." He responded.

And in that moment, all the feelings of uneasiness, the days of indecision, of uncertainty were cast away. With that bold statement of 'yes' more was gained than a mere end to a conversation. Life is like that.

Darkness had settled quietly on the town of Roberts Junction. The clear sky shown bright with stars that blinked sporadically at each other. A slight breeze still blew, grasping a few golden leaves from the trees, casting them to and fro before depositing them in gentle heaps. All was at peace, all the world was at rest.

At the home of Rev. Edward Rhodes peace had given way to pandemonium. The tune of 'The Battle Hymn' could be heard played enthusiastically. Pat at the piano, Denni with his trumpet, Matt and Mark with their sax, and trombone, Jeff with a tambourine, Peggy the spoons, Angie a washboard, Becky two pan lids for cymbals, Suzanna an old harmonica, all in unison while Mike Shephard joined them playing his face.

Cindi and Bob, in the next room were thankful that they had grown up. But not too thankful.

CHAPTER 24

A TIME TO KEEP, AND A TIME TO CAST AWAY

Saturday, October 1, 1983

The sun had already risen halfway up the eastern sky when the girls entered the Rhodes Kitchen, bleary eyed, and weary. Peggy, much more chipper than the others, was dressed in a full demin skirt and one of her grandpa's old flannel shirts, prepared for a days work on the farm. The others were still in robes and nightgowns. Their feet made a peculiar sound on the linoleum floor, for Peggy wore boots, Angie fluffy pink slippers, and Becky colorful argyle socks. Suzanna was barefoot.

A stack of dirty breakfast dishes covered the countertop. Bits of crust from toast, drops of juice and a tub of butter invaded with breadcrumbs, littered the table. Elizabeth Rhodes was at the stove, artfully turning pieces of french toast.

"I heard you ladies coming and started breakfast for you." She began. "I hope you like french toast."

"Love it." Becky responded.

"Good, it's Suzanna's favorite." Then turning to her daughter she remarked. "Happy Birthday dear."

"Thanks mom."

"Something came for you already."

"Huh?" Suzanna replied, her mother nodded toward a vase containing a small pink rose and a spray of babies breath.

"Suzanna it's gorgeous." Becky exclaimed.

"Who's it from?" Angie wondered.

"Yeah, who is he?" Peggy grinned.

Suzanna lifted the small pink vase and gently touched the fragile flower. A tiny card was attached, slowly she opened it.

Suzanna,
Happy Birthday
-- a good friend

That's all it stated, no name. Suzanna supplied the name herself, although not aloud. The girls were indeed curious. It wasn't fair that whoever sent it hadn't signed it. Now they would have to wonder about it until they could successfully pry the truth from Suzanna.

"I bet it was from Brady." Becky suggested.

"I don't think so," Peggy remarked. "She hasn't thrown it across the room yet."

"Maybe it's not from a boy?" Angie added.

"No girl would send another girl a rose." Becky stated.

"Didn't you all went Michelle Morrison roses?"

"That was different."

"Maybe this is different too?" Angie suggested, then turned to Suzanna. "Do you know who it's from?"

"Uh huh, at least I think so."

"How will you find out?"

Suzanna shrugged. "Ask him I guess."

"Ask who?"

"Den,.." Suzanna realized her blunder and groaned. She covered her face with her hands."

"Dennis?" Becky asked. "Well it's about time."

"We thought he'd never get the nerve to talk to you about how he felt." Peggy added.

"You knew."

"Of course." Becky continued. "It was pretty obvious."

"How come I didn't see it then?"

"Maybe because you didn't want to." Peggy suggested.

Suzanna was quiet. It seemed that her friends had known all along that Denni liked her. Even Becky who had dated him just a few weeks before seemed pleased.

"This is just the beginning, think of the fun we'll have." Becky was saying. "Dating I mean."

"What?" Suzanna asked.

"Well, Matt Rankin asked me out last night." Becky continued. "And I have a feeling Angie will be next. I noticed more than one pair of eyes on her lately."

"You did?" Angie asked.

"Sure, I'm not telling who's they are but I do think the brown ones are so much nicer than the hazel ones."

"Jeff Johnson?" Angie asked.

"See, you knew all along. You're just pretending you don't notice those things."

"I, umm I never considered it." She stammered. "Do you really think he likes me?"

"He could." Peggy said honestly. "Just be yourself Angie, and even if Jeff doesn't notice, someone will."

"Just as long as it's not Brady Downing." Suzanna remarked. "You'd be better off with a Water Buffalo."

Everyone laughed.

After adding her dishes to the ones stacked by the sink, Peggy moved toward the window.

"I hate to leave you with the dishes Sister Rhodes, but my ride will be here any minute."

"Don't even think of it dear, just do the best you can today." Then whispering she continued. "You're nervous aren't you?"

"I guess so. I was training all week with either Den, Rich, or Tom. Now I'll be on my own."

"Ben chose you because he felt you would be best for the job."

"And I don't want to let him down."

"Then don't. If you go and strive to do your best, he'll know and understand."

"I hope so." Peggy responded.

As they were speaking Tom pulled up in front of the Rhodes home. He signalled to Peggy with a sharp toot of his horn.

"Peggy Winters" Suzanna began. "Since when did you start getting rides from Tom VanDyke."

"Since him and I work the same shift at the farm, Suzanna Rhodes." She replied teasingly as she fled from the house.

The sun shone brighter that day, the air was fresher, the skies bluer. At least it appeared that way to Dennis. Arriving at work he did his chores enthusiastically, there was an eagerness in his steps that hadn't been there before. The baffled pigeons flew from their perches as he tossed bail after bail of hay from the stacks, the kittens held him aloof for invading the privacy of their homes. He had sailed through a good portion of the chores before Rich arrived.

"It looks like someone's been busy." Rich smiled.

"Morning," Dennis said cheerfully. "I'll have the horses ready in a jiffy."

Rich looked at him curiously. "Are you okay?" He teased.

"Sure."

"I guess I'm not used to seeing so much energy so early in the morning."

Denni grinned.

"We'll need ten horses at nine-thirty." Rich informed him. "Did Ten Gallon work alright for you last Saturday?"

"Yeah, I took him out with a group on Tuesday also. He'll do fine."

"Good then use him. We'll need all the horses we can get today. If the groups are larger than 6, Ben wants to put two of you with it, so see that either Peggy or Tom are with you." He checked his notebook. "There is only one real large one today, that's twelve riders at 1:30. Have Peggy go with you."

"Sure." Dennis responded.

"Now, let's get those horses ready." Rich spoke as he departed for the tack room for saddles and bridles.

Denni's heart felt light. It was as if he were walking three feet off the ground, all because Suzanna had chosen to share her feelings. How had he ever neglected to realize what he truly thought of her? But now he knew. This past week had been torture, he'd known his true feelings since Monday as he stood outside the school building trying to get her to compose herself. She'd shunned him since then.

Thursday he had forced her to talk, but last night she'd been willing, not only to talk but to be honest about how she felt. It was worth the wait. He thought.

He hadn't thought about the rose until he had left her home the night before. He wanted to surprise her in the morning. It was late so nothing in town had been open. He felt defeated but recalled a store in Lincoln that was open twenty-four hours and always had a display of flowers on hand. He had found the rose with it's spray of babies breath looking simple amid a collection of large plants and silk flowers. It seemed so simple, so small, yet Dennis knew it was perfect.

He'd delivered it himself that morning, only Pat knew. Suzanna would guess of course, but he'd meant for her to. He hoped that she could read in that simple gesture that feeble cry of his heart.

A blacktopped highway ribboned it's way through the countryside toward the town of Lincoln, where storefronts lined the main road like stacked up dominoes. A kaleidoscope of colors erupted from within them, shading the street into an artificial rainbow. McCurruthers and Barnes was a favorite stop for the young people from Roberts Junction, for although it carried good quality merchandise the prices were reasonable and within range. Only a few, such as Sylviah Martin, or Cindi, would turn their noses up at items from Mc and B's.

Standing in the halo of color that fell from the display window the girls made their plans.

"What do you guys want to shop for?" Becky asked.

"Sweaters" Suzanna and Angie said in unison. They grinned at one another.

"Sounds good to me."

"And skirts." Suzanna added.

"Definitely." Becky agreed.

"Nothing practical." Suzanna added.

"Sweaters and skirts sound practical." Angie commented.

"Not the ones I want to buy."

The girls laughed as they entered the building. Minutes later they entered the Junior Department where racks of bright bold color and large exotic prints greeted them. Angie scanned the department quickly.

"There are plenty of impractical clothes here." She stated.

"You're telling me." Suzanna commented.

"The sweaters are over here." Becky said as she led the way through the crowded aisles.

As Suzanna looked through the racks of sweaters she had mixed feelings. Until last night she had been determined to buy the most impractical outfit she could imagine. Practical was her mothers favorite word. Sweaters in bright blue, green, and bold prints were definitely not as practical as drab solids in grey or tan. White was even impractical because it stained so easy and Suzanna tended to be a slob. So, as she stood before the rows of clothes and contemplated what she wanted, she realized that impracticality was not what she desired. Nor was her mothers original choice. What Suzanna wanted most was to please Dennis. Becky, whose choice in clothing tended to be a bit trendy, was already exclaiming over a rack of new arrivals. Angie much more conservative was sorting through a rack of delicate sweaters with crocheted lace collars. Suzanna stood awhile contemplating her choices. Dennis won. Hands down.

Suzanna had never been much of a feminine dresser, aside from wearing skirts and dresses, she had shunned all forms of lace, ruffles, ribbons and had refused to wear pink.

Angie held up a teal blue sweater. Suzanna was slightly surprised that she found it pretty. She joined her.

"That's really pretty." She responded. Glancing up she realized it was a perfect color for Angie. "It looks as though it were made with you in mind. You really have good taste in clothes."

"I have a house full of critics at home." She smiled shyly.

"I'm gonna need your help. I have to find something that's perfect."

When they left Mac and B's an hour later each carried parcels under their arms. Angie the teal sweater and a pleated skirt to match, Becky a large black oversized sweater with designs of green and purple, she'd also bought black tights and a black and green bow for her hair, Suzanna had bought a practical light grey sweater, with embroidered pink roses and a beautiful crocheted lace collar. There was a single pink rose waiting for her at home, he had chosen it for her, she would choose this for him.

Tim and Lynn Deems lived in a rather new section of town, most of the homes had not been built when Rich left town ten years ago. Theirs was a nice sensible ranch home, a replica of the others on the street. David was out front on his bicycle when Rich arrived.

"Hi cowboy!" He called.

"Hi big fella." Rich answered.

"I'm pretending this is a horse." He stated.

"Oh? Is it a bucking bronco?"

"No way, I can't ride a bucking bronco until I'm eight."

"Oh."

"This is an apple-oosa" David continued. "That's what mommy told me that you had. Are all Apple-oos'a polka-dotted?"

"Only the good ones." Rich teased.

"Then mine's polka-dotted, because it's the best one."

"What's it's name?"

"Lassie."

"Lassie? Isn't that a dogs name?"

"It's a horses name too."

"I see." Rich stated although he didn't see at all.

Tim and Scott were already in the back-yard. Tim busy with a few steaks on the grill, Scott digging in an open cooler for a second can of suds.

"Hey, Look who's here!" Tim declared when he saw Rich. "It's been years."

"It's really good to see you guys." Rich stated honestly. "I should have looked you up sooner but things have been pretty busy."

"Hey, no sweat." Scott began. "Lynn told us that Benny's been workin' you like a slave."

"I expect to work hard." Rich responded.

"Ben doesn't." Tim laughed.

"He was always so quick at giving orders." Scott observed.

"That's because he was the only one of us who ever had any common sense." Rich stated loyally.

The others laughed in agreement.

"Well how does it feel to be back." Scott wanted to know.

"Everything's changed."

"We haven't." Tim responded quickly and slugged Scott on the shoulder.

"But I have." Rich reminded.

"You couldn't have changed too much. Lynn assured us that you hadn't gone Holy on us like Benny did." Tim remarked.

"That's true."

"But you're straight?" Tim questioned.

"Uh huh."

"Whatever for?" Scott asked curiously.

"It was just a decision I had to make a few years back."

"I hope I never have to make a decision like that one." Scott remarked.

Rich found himself a can of coke in the cooler and joined the fellas in the yard talking of old times. Memories flowed easily for the threesome had done much together. Often Rich's sides ached from laughter. The delicious aroma of the steak mingled with others wafting from the open kitchen window seemed to trigger their appetites, and by the time the steaks were done and Lynn had assured them that all was ready Rich was ravenous with hunger.

True to her word, Lynn had found a date for Rich. Jennifer Schultz had moved to Roberts Junction less than a year ago. She worked as a secretary with Lynn at the clinic. At twenty-six she was rather heavyset with a cheerful round face and hazel eyes that were framed with glasses. She smiled easily and laughed heartily, Rich sensed almost immediately that she could easily be the life of the party. He decided to make the best of it, although he preferred to be aloof in her presence.

"The meal was great." Rich remarked, after finishing a large piece of Apple pie. "You two make a good team."

"Join us anytime." Lynn extended the invitation. "It must be unhandy for someone who works as hard as you to return home and fix your own meals."

"I agree I'm not much of a cook but I manage. I stop at 'Charlies' a few times a week and Sarah is always insisting I come to the house or sending something over."

"If you had to eat Sarah's cooking all the time you'd starve." Lynn commented. "Chrys and I used to go into fits of hilarity over Sarah's culinary efforts."

"They're not that bad." Rich commented quietly.

"Well promise to stop by sometime we'll enjoy it."

"I'll do that."

"Good."

After the meal Scott suggested that they all go over to 'Monty's' for a few games of pool. There was to be an excellent band playing that night.

Reluctantly Rich agreed, he hadn't been inside a bar since his release from prison, but felt he couldn't avoid the experience indefinitely. As he entered with the others painful memories invaded his mind. The dim lighting gave the illusion of familiarity to the place. This could have been 'The Outhouse' in Aspen Colorado for all he cared. The feeling was the same. That crushing sense of guilt that he could never shake became seemingly unbearable. He ordered a coke and joined Tim at the table.

"I'm hoping that your pool playing has changed too." Tim remarked. "For the worse."

"I'm kind of out of practice."

"Excellent, in all the years I've know you I've never licked you in a game of pool."

"Well" Rich responded. "Today may be a first then."

The band arrived during the game, trip after trip was made to their truck for speakers and equipment. Tim seemed not to notice. Although out of practice Rich still managed to win the game, it was a close one. Scott insisted on a challenge so the balls were stacked again. Scott had been drinking heavily all night, although he could handle the alcohol fairly well it did have an affect on both his reflexes and his language. Rich began to feel more and more uncomfortable. Hoping to slip out unnoticed after the game he played silently. Scott was a sharp player and managed to gain the advantage early in the game, but as the game progressed Rich's clear shooting brought him the victory. Scott was about to make a scene about his defeat, when the band began it's first number. Rich was relieved, quickly he headed toward the door. But not quick enough, Jennifer had seen him.

"Leaving?" She asked.

"Yup."

"Do you mind if I beg a ride home?"

"No problem, but don't you want to stay?"

"Not necessarily. I've been around after they've all gotten waisted before. I'd rather not repeat the experience if I can help it."

Rich understood and held the door for her as they left. Outside the streets of town were lined with cars. It was Saturday evening and 'Montys' was not the only tavern on the street. Loud music filled the air, voices rose above it, laughter. As he drove her home through the darkened streets he felt uneasy. Lynn had arranged for her to be his date, and he had succeeded in avoiding her the entire while. It wasn't fair to her, she deserved better treatment then that. He didn't like making excuses for himself but shouldn't she have some kind of explanation?"

"Rich?" She began.

"Huh?"

"Thanks for the ride, I know you would have preferred to leave without anyone seeing."

"I don't mind at all."

"Well I want you to know something." She began. "When Lynn asked me over the other day and mentioned your name, I had no idea who you were so I asked around. I know you spent the last three years in prison,.. and I know why."

"And you're still dumb enough to get into this truck with me?"

"I don't think I was dumb. I could have stayed at 'Montys' I've done it before. But I kinda wanted you to know that I admire what you're doing."

"Admire! Listen, don't ever admire anyone unless you know what makes them tick. Unless you can admire the hours they spend in total darkness trying to forget. Day after day with shadows of their past lingering behind them, demanding attention. It's not pretty. I wouldn't wish it on my best friend, and I wouldn't admire it."

"I'm sorry Rich, I didn't understand."

"No you couldn't. I didn't quit drugs and drinking because I chose to. I did because I couldn't have continued and still lived with myself. But I did it too late." His voice drifted off.

"It's to late for them, but it's not to late for you." She added quickly.

"So you think I should go on with life as if nothing had happened."

"No, but instead of letting it rule you, learn from it, accept it. Don't let it hinder your own future."

"I don't deserve a future. Don't you understand that?"

"No I don't understand. I don't intend to."

The Daniels had a three car garage but even it seemed small. Tables were made by placing plywood over carpenters horses. Old chairs lined the walls, a few picnic benches also. Sarah and Chrys had spent the afternoon blowing up balloons and hanging streamers. A gorgeous mansion in pink decorated the center of the main table, colorful gifts had been placed around it.

At five o'clock guests had begun to arrive. Peggy was first, bearing the gift. Angie and Becky arrived with her. Denni remained at the barn until the last minute, he'd loaded the wagon and hitched the horses to it.

He watched as the young people parked at the stables and walked toward the back of the garage. Fiddling over the harness, polishing the brass on the bridles and checking the horses hooves, he stalled. He wasn't interested in talking to the others. He just wanted to be there, to see her. Something cringed within him when Brady Downing's car stopped at the stables. Inwardly he fumed. Brady could easily destroy everything between him and Suzanna, he'd tried before and almost succeeded. Frustrated he watched as Brady entered the path that led to the garage. His presence was a challenge to Denni to actively take his place in Suzanna's life. Brady had previously tried to intimidate him, but not anymore. Denni was determined to take a stand for what he felt was true.

Standing at the entrance to the feed shed, Denni could see the lights in the garage and hear the chatter of young people, Pat would be arriving soon and Denni wanted to be one of the first to see Suzanna. Ben would drive the wagon over as soon as things settled down a bit.

"Hey fella" Ben startled him. "I thought you were already up at the garage."

"No, I was just making sure everything was alright."

"Of course it's alright, but are you?"

Denni looked at his employer gravely. "I'm not sure, all I know is that if Downing acts up tonight I'm libel to deck him."

Ben laughed.

"I'm serious. Suzanna's been through too much these past weeks, I'm not gonna sit back and let it happen anymore."

"Oh, so that's it." Ben smiled.

"I might as well let the whole world know before Downing makes a shambles of it."

"I doubt if she'd allow him to do that."

"I'm not that sure,.. yet." Denni spoke.

"You really like her don't you." Ben remarked casually.

"Yeah."

"Then don't put off letting her know. If she's sure of where you're coming from Brady can't sway her."

"I certainly hope he can't."

"I know he can't."

Denni smiled. "Thanks Ben, You're a friend."

"And you friend," Ben began. "Are a fine Christian, and don't you ever doubt it."

Suzanna was surprised when her mother returned from an errand and had Nick Daniels with her.

"That Sarah," Her mother had started. "Trying to do a million things at once. If I hadn't taken Nick, she'd probably have passed over him."

"Now mom, Sarah would never do that."

"That's right, but I did need an excuse to take the dear fellow off her hands."

"That will give you two babies to watch this evening." Suzanna remarked. "Are you sure you don't want me to stay home. Pat and Michelle can go out to the farm alone."

"No dear, I'm afraid we need you to go with them, Michelle is comfortable with you, besides your father is home, He'll help me with the babies."

"Are you sure?"

"Positive, have fun, I must say your brother is looking forward to it."

"You don't seem to like Michelle much mom, Why?"

"Oh, I like Michelle fine, I just do not want Michelle and Pat together. Not right now."

"But why?"

"I don't want him to be hurt."

"Pat?"

"Ycs. Your older brother is not infallible dear."

"I know that."

"I need you to be his chaperon."

Suzanna laughed, "Mom won't you ever learn?"

"I hope not. Now get on with you. Your brother will be here any minute."

Suzanna was supposedly going along on a visit to the Daniels. Michelle had barely left the house since Joanna was born, and Elizabeth had offered to keep the baby a few hours.

The Garage door was closed when Pat parked the Rhodes old 'clunker' in the Daniels driveway. Suzanna opened the back door to step out at the same time that the garage door was opened. She thought nothing of it, so she was indeed surprised when a massive shout of HAPPY BIRTHDAY SUZANNA was heard.

Flabbergasted, she stood there, rooted to the spot. Embarrassed yet at the same time pleased. Smiling at the crowd only one face held hers; Denni's. No words needed to be spoken, she took a step forward, he met her.

"Happy Birthday." He whispered.

"Thanks Den." She smiled shyly.

Suddenly everything erupted around them. Young people gathered around her to wish her a Happy Birthday. But Suzanna and Den had shared enough, they both knew. Life would never be the same again.

In the midst of the well wishers and hugs the sound of sleigh bells could be heard, Suzanna turned once more to find Ben sitting on the massive seat of the hay wagon. Two of his horses were harnessed to it and stood stomping the ground impatiently, clouds of dust rose with each step.

"Happy Fifteenth Birthday Suzanna." Ben grinned.

"What will you guys think of next."

"Pile on troops." Ben shouted. "We'll take a spin through the woods, and then come back and devour that handsome mansion there and all those goodies."

Ben jumped from the seat and held the horses, as the young people climbed aboard. Suzanna however stood, looking at the cake, it was gorgeous.

"Your mother made the cake for you." Sarah spoke as she joined her. "Did we surprise you?"

"Yes, absolutely. I should have guessed when mom came home with Nick this afternoon, though. I guess my mind was elsewhere."

"I don't think I have to ask where." Sarah stated as she nodded at Denni who stood with Ben by the horses. Suzanna just smiled, there were some things that were to obvious to hide.

"Uh hem." Ben disturbed Denni's thoughts.

"Huh?" Denni asked.

"Perhaps you'd like to be the chauffeur tonight, I think a certain someone would enjoy a ride in front with you."

"Thanks Ben," Den returned. "But I'm not sure you offered because you want her with me, or because you want to keep her from Downing."

"I don't know of any finer young man I'd like to see her with Den, and I'm sure others would say the same thing."

"Thanks" Den said quietly. Ben held the horses while Denni approached Suzanna. "There is a throne awaiting the guest of honor tonight." He smiled. "Allow me." Carefully he helped her onto the high seat, then joined her. Lifting the reigns he nodded to Ben, who quickly joined the group in back. Suzanna was silent as Dennis encouraged the horses forward toward the path leading to the stables and beyond.

"Thanks." Denni said presently.

"What for?"

"For being you, and choosing to be with me rather than in back with the crowd." There was much laughter and merry making accompanied by song coming from behind them.

"I'm just trying to decide if I'm dreaming or not."

"Your not." Denni answered. "If you are, I must be too."

There was an awkward pause.

"Thanks for the rose." Suzanna began. "It meant a lot."

"I wanted it to." he smiled. "I do admit the sales lady thought I was nuts when I bought it."

Suzanna looked at him curiously.

"Last night at eleven forty-five at Zellipo's in Lincoln."

"No!" Suzanna remarked with a laugh "You are crazy you know that."

"I hope I get crazier."

"I kinda hope you do to, then I'll know for sure that we belong together." She stated boldly.

Denni searched her face. "I'm glad you said that, we do belong don't we."

She nodded.

The moon rose and cast a warm glow upon the nearby countryside, as the wagon full of laughter, song, young people, unspoken promises, and hay; journeyed toward the woods. They were just nearing the trees when Pat spoke up.

"Hey Brother Daniels, My father told me that you trapped a bear here the other afternoon."

"Sure did, he was raiding all my wifes berries so I was glad I got rid of the thing. I don't think I could have gone a full year without Sarah's homemade preserves."

"Well I hope that there was only one bear, and that it's brother isn't lurking around here somewhere."

"Couldn't be, the D.N.R. were here and they checked it out."

"Well I just hope we don't meet with one anyway."

"I've got my gun stashed behind the seat just in case. Hey Den, if you see anything that is big and black and growls make sure you let me know in time to get a shot at it."

"Sure thing." Denni agreed.

Suzanna was enjoying herself, just being with Denni, and her friends was enough to make the day perfect. She settled back in the seat completely at peace. Brady Downing was less than ten feet away, but he could be a million miles away for all she cared. She watched the lengthening shadows of the woods as they traveled, everything seemed so peaceful. Suddenly a shadow moved. She sat up straight. Sure enough it moved again.

"Den" She said uncertainly "There's something up ahead, by those bushes." Denni looked closely.

"Sure, I see it, It's pretty big." Denni began, then called "Ben there is the presence of a living object ahead. It looks big and black but I haven't heard it growl yet."

Suddenly the air was pierced by a savage growl.

"Now I heard it." He declared as he pulled the horses to a stop.

Ben hurried to the front of the wagon and reached for his rifle. The young people were terrified, Suzanna among them.

"Is it a bear?" She whispered.

"Looks like it, see it's coming this way."

"Stop or I'll shoot." Ben called.

Suzanna was a trifle baffled that Ben would address the bear. The bear growled and took a step forward. A shot rang out, crashing the silence, smoke rose from Ben's gun barrel. The bear lay in a heap on the ground.

"Good shot, Brother Daniels." Pat remarked.

"Good shot?" Cindi stated, "He may well have saved our hides."

"Oh, Thanks Ben." Pat corrected.

"I don't believe this is happening." Cindi remarked. "Ben Daniels killed a bear on his first shot."

"Okay Den." Ben spoke "Bring the horses closer, We'll have to take the carcass home with us."

"WHAT!" Cindi sounded incredulous. "You're gonna put that foul smelling thing in here?"

"Of course, I can't leave it lay there. What do you want me to do, let the varmints get it?"

"Why not?" Brady asked from the darkness.

"That's the first bear I've ever shot. I'm taking it home for a trophy." Ben stated.

Den urged the horses forward glancing at Suzanna he gave her a sly smile. She was confused. This whole night seemed so bazaar. Almost like a dream. In back of her she heard Sarah remark.

"You had better not bring tics into my house Benjamin Daniels."

Closer and closer they came to the fallen creature.

"Come Pat, give me a hand." Ben stated as they pulled up as near as possible to the still form. Together Pat and Ben descended from the wagon and approached the bear. Silence, had reigned among the young people since the bear had first been sighted. The younger girls Connie, Jeanni and Debbie were terrified; Sarah and Chrys tried to reassure them. Brady, the Ladies man, couldn't do a thing his own fear had him at a disadvantage.

Suzanna shuddered as the two approached the bear. Denni's arm slipped silently along the back of the seat behind her. She glanced at him, he was trying his hardest not to break down. Not from fear, but from laughter.

"Is this a dream?" She asked.

"A pretty well planned one." He responded quietly.

Suzanna looked at him again, his eyes danced mischievously. She glanced once again at where her brother and Ben were now trying to carry an uncooperative furry creature from the path before them.

"Okay," She asked after a minute. "Who is it?"

"Who's what?"

"Who's wearing the bear costume."

"Bear costume?"

"Uh huh." She nodded catching his grin. "Out with it."

"No way." He stated.

Without thinking Suzanna jumped from the wagon and approached her brother and Ben as they struggled with the bear.

"Suzanna! Get back here." Cindi called.

When Suzanna didn't stop she addressed Dennis.

"Don't just sit there, Denni do something." She begged.

"I am." He stated. "I'm holding the horses."

"I give up on you guys." Cindi stated exasperated.

Suzanna joined Pat and Ben in their struggle.

"Thank you." She stated.

"Huh?" Ben remarked.

"I love it. I just love it. You've got a whole wagon load of terrified young people and I just love it."

Pat began laughing. "We thought you would."

"But who's the bear?" She asked.

"Me." Said a voice.

"Mike?"

"Yup, will you tell these guys to take it easy on me, I'm only human."

"Mike if you were my brother I'd give you a big hug, This is great!"

"You'd better not. Bears are known to have ticks."

"This is excellent. But when are you gonna let others know."

"Ben's gonna skin the bear when we get it to the wagon." Her brother answered.

"Which will be in about three minutes." Suzanna stated.

Suzanna led the way, and with Ben lifting the shoulders and Pat the feet they lifted the bear onto the back of the wagon. Ben made a big show of pulling out his knife.

"What. May I ask, are you going to do with that?" Cindi stated.

"I'm gonna skin it. I have to gut it immediately, or it will ruin the taste of the meat. Have you ever eaten bear steak? It's excellent." He appeared to attack the bear with his knife.

"This is crude." Brady stated. "How did I get here anyway?"

"The same way you do everything else, through hypocrisy and lies." Jeff Johnson spoke honestly.

"Amen." Suzanna remarked.

Cindi frowned at her sister as Ben began to tear the bear costume off and revealed Mike.

"Hey Brother Daniels am I glad to see you."

"Mike! How did you get inside that bear?"

"It's a long story. I was out for a drive and I passed Old Bill Winters house. He was outside climbing a ladder into his apple tree. Well I opened my window and hollered out, 'Go up thou Bald head!' and this bear jumped out of the bushes and gobbled me up. Am I glad you came in time."

The young people were roaring with laughter. Partly at the story Mike had told and partly from relief that the whole thing had been a hoax.

"Imagine, it was Mike all the time." Cindi mused.

"Boy," Brady remarked. "This is one day I am bound to remember for the rest of my days."

"Me too." Suzanna whispered to Denni, who had silently laid the reigns in her hands and was instructing her on how to drive the horses.

Suzanna was ecstatic. Today had been perfect. Now she sat with Denni's hands gently guiding hers. It was perfect. Nothing could spoil it now.

It was quite late when the wagon pulled up a second time before the Daniels garage. The young people quickly jumped from the hay and hurried inside.

Suzanna had begged to be allowed to drive the horses back to the feed shed where Denni would unstrap their harnesses'.

"Hurry back, you've got candles to blow out and presents to unwrap." Sarah called as Suzanna drove off with Denni into the darkness.

The young people had casually fallen into groups. Sarah served punch, while Chrys prepared the mixture for the oncoming taffy-pull. Michelle had made herself at home and was freely discussing classes with Peggy, as if she hadn't missed a day at school. The older boys had gathered around the stereo and were looking at Mikes tapes with Angie and Becky. The younger boys however, Luke and Paul Bennet were having a wrestling match on the front lawn. Ben stood with Mike, and surveyed the scene as Cindi and Bob helped Pat carry a few items from the trunk of his car.

"Someone's missing." Ben commented soberly.

Mike glanced around. Everyone seemed accounted for.

"Brady Downing." Ben remarked.

Mike looked serious. "I'll go look for him."

"Just take a quick trip through the stables, Tom should still be around. I'm gonna check the house."

When Suzanna and Denni left the garage they assumed they were alone. Neither bothered to glance back to see if anyone was hiding in the hay. That is why they missed seeing Brady. Suzanna drove the horses slowly. It felt so wonderful to be alive, with Denni. He smiled at her.

"Happy?" He asked.

"Do you need to ask?"

"Okay, are you unhappy?"

"Of course not silly." She grinned. "Denni in case you didn't realize it. This is the most wonderful day of my whole life."

"I hope there are a million more like it for us to share together." Denni said seriously.

"There will be, if you're there."

They had reached the feed shed and after Denni had taken the reins from her he carefully led the horses through the wide open doors into the darkness. Suzanna was about to climb down when she first smelled smoke. Thinking that Ben had started a fire she swung down from the wagon and joined Denni. He smiled again, that friendly familiar warm smile. Suzanna was at peace.

However the smell of smoke grew stronger, one of the horses began snorting uneasily. Suzanna glanced up and was amazed to see smoke illuminated in the light from the moon. She hurried to the back of the wagon. It was already engulfed in flames.

"Den." She called. "The hay in the wagon is on fire!"

"Quick" He returned "Run for Ben, I'll drive the horses through the door on this side. I'll unhitch them when I'm through."

Suzanna was out the entrance in seconds. It was darker outside then she had thought. Ben was at the garage, she would have to hurry past all the barns and up the path, it seemed like miles. A shadow approached her, stopping her as she ran past.

"Hey, slow down. What's up." It was Mike.

"A fire! The wagon." Was all she could say before she gasped for breath. Mike quickly released her and hurried to the feed shed, she collapsed in a heap on the ground. Suzanna attempted to rise, but by that time, others were approaching. The fire spread quickly, their unified efforts kept it from spreading to the fields, but their prayers could not produce the miracle that was needed. The shed burned out of control. In minutes it became a scalding inferno. Suzanna remained where she had fallen, clutching her face. Refusing to look.

Rich saw the flames half a mile away. He drove his small Datsun pick-up as close to the fire as he dared and prepared to help. As he rushed past Suzanna he heard her gasp Denni's name.

Stopping Jeff he asked.

"Anyone in there?"

"We're not sure."

"Where's Dennis?"

"He was bringing the horses in with Suzanna, Ben thinks he's still inside."

"Anyone gone in there?"

"Mike did at first, but he didn't get far, there's a wall of fire in there. Anyone would be a fool to try now."

"I guess I'm a fool then." He mumbled to himself as he rushed to the opposite side of the building. Most of the fire was in the center. Mike was busy at the door, beating away flames with a wet burlap bag. Rich paused a moment.

"I'm going in." He said.

"Rich don't." Mike began, but found it futile. "Lord" He prayed. "Keep your hand on that man. I want to see him alive and worshipping you someday." Mike could hardly see as he beat at the flames, then dipped the sack in a bucket of water and repeated the process. His eyes hurt from the smoke, his throat burned, but somewhere inside that building two souls lives were at stake. Someone began working beside him. Glancing up he saw Suzanna.

"Go up to the garage." He stated hoarsely. "Ben wants you up there with the girls."

"Nothings gonna keep me from doing my part." She declared. "Denni's in there somewhere."

The sound of sirens could be heard in the distance as the trucks from Roberts Junction left town. Suzanna barely heard them. It seemed like ages before she noticed a figure emerging from the flaming building.

"Denni?" She spoke. Then seeing it was Rich something crushed within her, for he was not alone. He carried the still, silent, form of seventeen year old Dennis Little.

CHAPTER 25

A TIME TO REND, AND A TIME TO SEW

Sunday, October 2nd, 1983

Miles away along Highway 63, in Southern California, nestled among culverts, billboards, and overpasses, was D.D.'s Truck Stop. It was a low block building not very inviting by any means, but the food was edible, so the business flourished. The waitresses, in grubby white skirts and blue blouses, worked from behind a lunch counter in one corner of the smoke filled dining room. Cheap vinyl, cracked and patched with grey duct tape covered the seats of the swivel stools that held a wide assortment of lower-class customers. Chipped platters held heaping portions of deeply fried foods, heavy mugs held thick, black coffee, and the silver rarely matched. Each of these added to the atmosphere that some of the regulars had come to call home.

A middle-aged man, wearing a long gray overcoat, sat at the far end of the counter. His face was creased with age, his graying hair unkempt. A piece of slightly charred apple pie was before him. Slowly and methodically he forked a tasteless piece into his mouth. He seemed unaware of his surroundings. Ignoring the bits of conversation that others aimed in his direction, he ate silently. The bell over the entrance jingled twice, the place grew still.

Never looking up from his pie the man continued eating. The hollow sound of booted feet on the hardwood floor approached and stopped near him. Slowly a tall figure, in the dark blue uniform of the Sheriffs department took the stool beside him.

"Is your name William Little?" The deputy asked. The man nodded.

"I'm from the Sheriffs department. I've got bad news. Your wife has notified us. Your son, Dennis, died last night."

The sound of a fork falling to the counter-top shattered the silence. Something else shattered also, the memories that had kept the man living day after day, vanished into nothingness.

Rich stared silently out his living room window, had been standing there for hours. He'd watched the last star grow dim, the sun attempt to spear it's way through the layer of clouds that began to gather, still he stood. The trauma of the night before paralyzed him. He could still feel the intense heat, that had surrounded him; the thick smoke that had attempted to choke him. He groaned.

A figure approached.

"You've been standing here for awhile. Why don't you go get some rest?" Mike asked.

"Why don't you?"

Mike didn't respond.

"Tell me I imagined it." Rich continued.

"I can't lie to you Rich, Dennis is dead. Nothing can change that."

"But it was such a freak accident. It happened so fast."

"There was nothing anyone could have done."

"I can't believe that. If I hadn't been gone, I would have been here."

"And the fire would still have occurred."

"But I would have got to him in time."

"I couldn't Rich." Mike stated bluntly. "I tried, Ben tried, You risked your life Rich. I didn't expect to see you come back alive."

Rich was silent.

"But the fact that you did was an answer to prayer."

"Prayer? What good does prayer do? Dennis was only seventeen. He had his whole life ahead of him. If prayer worked why weren't you praying for Dennis? And why isn't he alive today?"

"I can't answer that but I can say this. I know Denni, he's happier now then he's ever been. I don't know why God allowed this to happen, but I thank God that he spared your life. Denni was ready to die, are you Rich?"

"Who cares if I'm ready to die? I don't deserve to live!" He turned and faced Mike. "I've seen too many innocent people die Mike. Women, children, teen-agers like Dennis. Three of them killed by my own hand." He paused as he glanced angrily at Mike. "You didn't know you were in the same room with a murderer did you?"

"It doesn't matter to me."

"But it does! Three lives were lost because of me, yet I stand here this morning and Dennis Little, seventeen year old Dennis Little, who only desired to help others, and live a clean life, lies cold and stiff in the mortuary. Don't tell me it doesn't matter. It does! It matters a lot."

"Not to God." Mike continued. "I can accept Denni's death. I loved Dennis very much, but he is in God's hands. He chose to be there himself, you haven't made that choice."

"Spare me the sermon will you!" Rich responded angrily.

"No Rich, listen to me." Mike continued. "God doesn't care where you've been or what you've done. He loves you, he can take that guilt that you've allowed to crush you and replace it with peace. It isn't important how good or how bad we've been all our lives. What matters is that we place our lives in his hands and turn it all over to him."

"So he can allow us to die an unnecessary death?"

"No, so that in both our lives and our deaths, he might be glorified."

"I fail to see God's glory in the death of Dennis Little." Rich spoke. "If there is a God out there Mike, He is either asleep, or he doesn't care."

Later that morning while Ben and his family were at church, Rich left the seclusion of his small apartment. Silently, he stepped out onto the landing, the screen door slammed loudly behind him. Deliberately he descended the steps and followed the path toward the stables. He felt empty inside,.. alone. All that remained was an ugly gray mass of inadequacies and guilt. His feet felt as anchors, yet he forced them, one after the other, toward his destination. The lingering smell of burned timbers engulfed him once again in recurring memories of that lifeless body he had held and carried through the flames. Even the familiar red buildings seemed shadowed by the tragedy.

His mind could still picture Dennis, working beside him while they harvested the hay. A young boy doing a man's job. "He was a far better person than I will ever be." Rich mused dejectedly. Shuffling along, deep in thought, his head hung forlornly, watching the path before him. Beyond the barns lay the former site of the feed shed, now just black masses of charred timbers. Fine broken lines of smoke still rose from the dampened remains.

Rich found his truck parked where he had left it the night before. The battered, weather beaten vehicle was the only object that seemed familiar. He rested his weary body against the front hood, his life seemed like such a waste.

Movement at the far side of the clearing caught his attention. A middle-aged man sat huddled on an old fallen tree, a battered hat lay on the ground beside him. Rich could barely make out his features, buried in his hands, beneath a long gray overcoat. Rich took a step toward him. The man glanced up. He acknowledged Rich's presence with a slow nod, yet stared unseeingly at the blackened ground.

Rich awkwardly joined him on the fallen tree, two strangers silently keeping vigil at the ruins of a young boys death. Leaves from the trees overhead were slowly covering the dampened ground. In a few months a blanket of snow would completely conceal the tragic scene. Ben would clear the debris away and probably replace the building in spring. Nothing however could replace the life that had so quickly been snubbed out.

The older man rose slowly, taking a few steps forward, he spoke.

"Where did they find him?"

"On the north side, less than ten feet from the door. One of the horses had collapsed on him. It took all the strength I had to get him out."

Slowly the man walked toward the spot. He kicked absently at the remains of the door frames, never taking his eyes from where Denni had breathed his last breath. Rich waited silently, minutes passed. The man didn't move.

"Is there anything I can do?" Rich asked wanting to share the man's grief.

"No." He said vaguely. "The fact that you are here shows that you were a friend of his."

"Yeah, we worked together."

The man remained silent for a moment, then quietly added, "I was supposed to be his father." Tears came to his eyes then, large, silent, tears. Rich rose and joined him.

"I'm sorry Mr. Little."

"Not any more sorry than I am!" He spoke wearily. "But it's too late to be sorry now. Where have I been? My son dead and where have I been the past eighteen months?" Desperately he buried his face in his hands. "Oh Lord," He cried. "Forgive me."

The Reverend Rhodes stood soberly before an equally sober congregation that morning. The tragic death of one of their young people had disturbed them all. Ben had cancelled his class that morning so distraught was he over the events of the night before. Chrys had been equally shaken, but Mike had been able to restore her composure with the hope of a happier home for Denni. Suzanna hadn't spoken since she had regained consciousness. She had collapsed upon seeing Rich carry Denni still and life-less, from the building only seconds before the roof collapsed. Few knew of the torment her young mind was in, she stared vacantly ahead. Pat was beside her as she held his hand firmly, attempting to overcome the despair that tried to settle upon her. In the pew before them Ginny Little sat straight and composed beside the crumbling form of her daughter Connie. Ginny had found accepting Denni's death far easier than accepting the loss of her husband over a year earlier. Denni was happy now. Maybe only a mother could take comfort in that fact.

The church doors opened quietly, two figures entered unseen, and quickly found a seat in the back of the small sanctuary. The older a middle-aged man, with fading grey hair wearing a long overcoat. The second, a tall young man of twenty-eight feeling out of place in his patched jeans and flannel shirt.

Brother Rhodes spoke clearly and certainly of a place, not made with hands, a promise of an eternal home. Denni had gone before them, but someday all would bow before the maker of heaven and earth. In dismissing he had his son stand and read from John the fourteenth chapter, verses 1-4.

> Let not your heart be troubled,
> Ye believe in God, believe also in me,
> In my fathers house are many mansions
> If it were not so I would have told you
> I go to prepare a place for you
> And if I go to prepare a place for you
> I will come again,
> and receive you unto myself
> That where I am, ye may be also
> An whither I go ye know,
> And the way ye know.

Not far from the small church, on a side street lined with Maples, a small gold ranch house stood emptier than it had ever seemed before. In a back bedroom, it's walls lined with colorful football posters, Jeff Johnson sat Indian style upon his bed. In his open hand he held a small black bible. The crushing events of the past few weeks had left him on the border of despair. He had watched as his supposed friend, Brady had lied, cheated and used him. The false accusations that had faced both him and Denni seemed to echo over and over in his mind, but the recurring sound was nothing compared to the actual truth. His only TRUE friend,

Dennis, now lay still and cold. Dead. The only friend he had ever had that didn't criticize and ridicule him. The friend who had gone out of his way to encourage him, support him. The very one who had believed in him, that he could make a go of it despite the facts against him. The one he had sought out Friday evening when Julie had left him so hastily to join Brady. He had been one of the last to see Dennis alive.

The bible lay closed. Jeff studied the gold lettering on the soft leather cover. He had promised Denni that he would read it. Why had he broke that promise? It had seemed so important to Denni at the time, Why hadn't Jeff taken it seriously? Opening to the first page, he read the inscription writtin in bold blue ink.

JEFF
I pray that as you read this
that you may come to know and
love the author as much as he
knows and loves you.
your friend always
DENNI

Jeff stared for a long time at the words Denni his friend had written. It had only been in these last few weeks that Jeff had come to rely on Dennis' strength. Where would he go for strength now? Who would believe in him now? Who would care?

Slowly he opened the book and paged through. Chapter after chapter; book after book; of a story, a beautiful story. But Denni had found his strength in these pages, his peace and joy in the one who had formed each word. Jeff had promised to read it, he hoped it wasn't too late to keep that promise. He hoped it wasn't too late to find that peace and strength that Dennis had.

"Tonight." He resolved. "I'll be able to face the people at his church. Not because I'm anything, but because I know that Denni believed."

And as centuries ago when Elisha received the prophets mantle and a double portion, Jeff beheld the same as he opened the word and began to read.

The tiny Datsun pickup sped swiftly over the winding highway leading to Horseman's Unlimited. Rich had offered earlier to drive the distraught William Little into town to be reunited with his wife and daughter for the next few days. When they had pulled up before the white clapboard church house, he saw that Bill Little was in no way prepared to enter the building alone. So Rich had accompanied him.

Grief stricken as he was, Rich's heart remained cold toward the very thought of God. He cringed at the idea of religion. Entering the building, he expected to be presented with burning candles, expensive statues, memorized prayers, and a previously fabricated sermon. Alas, he was surprised, for it was not the pious multitude he'd expected in a church, but a group of warm friendly people gathering together, not in some ritual, but in unity to worship God.

As hard as his heart was, God's word was stronger and a tiny seed was able to penetrate that stony heart of his. In the midst of the sermon, Rich began to consider the possibility that maybe, just maybe there was a God. He rejected the very thought and now heading back toward home, it returned.

God.

It was hard to deny God. Spending the amount of time which he had during his life among the trees and animals, it was hard to reject that fact that somewhere, someone or something, had created it all.

Rich considered Dennis; a young teen-ager, doing a man's work, making a man's decisions, living a man's life. What had made him different? Where did he receive that strength? It all came back to the same thing,..

God.

Rich brought his old bucket of rust and bolts to a stop before the Daniels' garage. He noticed Tom's car at the stables and decided to seek him out.

Tom was in the loft of the main barn, sitting on a stack of new hay, staring at his hands. Denni had helped him stack these bales only a week ago. A small kitten rubbed against Tom's leg. Absently he picked it up and lifted it onto his lap. The rumbling purr within increased as he stroked the animals silky fur.

Rich joined him. Neither spoke, so lost were they in their own thoughts, that neither were willing to speak the words that would span the gap between them. The awkward silence brought inner turmoil for both. Tom, wanting so much out of life and seeing the sudden and unavoidable presence of death, was seeking to free himself from it's oppression. Rich, on the other hand, was willing the world to stop so that he could get off, he'd ridden long enough.

Two more kittens joined their brother in Tom's lap, each desiring a little added attention. Tom had all he could do to dissuade them, so bent they were on disturbing him.

"Too bad Dennis didn't have nine lives." Tom commented.

"I'd give him mine if I could." Rich stated dejectedly.

"The whole thing is so unreal, I half expected to see him when I came into work today."

"It'll take a while getting used to."

"A mighty long while." Tom declared "Why couldn't it have been some creep like Downing who'd died instead of Denni?"

"Why couldn't it have been me?" Rich whispered.

Tom didn't seem to hear him. "You know, Denni's always had to struggle. He stood pretty firm when his father left, but it wasn't easy. And here I sit, I have everything handed to me on a silver platter, money, opportunities, you name it. But yet Denni, the one who struggled day in and day out just to be pleasing to God, suffers a death meant as torture. I don't understand."

"No one understands Tom, you don't, I don't. I guess we just have to learn to accept it, not understand it."

"But death is so,..so..."

"Final?" Rich finished bluntly.

"Exactly. I can't avoid accepting it. It's there, it happened. But yet at the same time, I hope vainly that, like these kittens, if I ignore it enough it'll go away."

Slowly Ben ascended the few wooden stairs to the main porch of the 'Heritage Inn' the only overnight accommodations in town. A heavy oak door, framed in elaborately carved rosettes marked the main entrance. He crossed the wide expanse of porch and hesitated slightly before entering.

A massive staircase rose from the entrance hall to a balcony overlooking where he stood. Above him a crystal chandelier hung suspended. At the far end of the long hall a door opened and Maud Perkin's head appeared.

"Ay? Oh Hi Ben. Bill's upstairs, I put him in the blue room. It's really a shame about his son isn't it?"

"Sure is. Thanks Maud." He quickly crossed to the staircase. A large parlor was to the right of the entrance, with a drawing room behind it. It was decorated in colonial and early American furniture, with added contrasts such as numerous throw pillows and giant vases of freshly cut flowers. A huge stone fireplace separated the two rooms, also allowing for a warm cozy atmosphere. To the left a long trestle table spanned the dining room. Tall ladder back chairs bordered it giving it the appearance of an infants crib. Hutches containing priceless heirloom china, lined the walls. A crisp white muslin runner topped the center of the table, bowls of fresh fruit were placed at intervals.

Ben entered the upstairs hall, the dark mahogany woodwork contrasted drastically with the delicate tones in the tapestries that lined the walls. Following the hall past large oak doors painted in different hue's of yellow's, pink's, and green's, he stopped at the blue door. Knocking lightly, he waited.

"Cmin"

Ben entered the room, Bill Little was seated at a chair before an antique roll-top desk. He smiled when he saw Ben.

"Sorry I didn't say hi this morning." Bill apologized. "It's been a rough day."

Ben hesitated again. "How are you doing?"

"Oh, just fine, work gets pretty tiresome at times. Can't seem to stay long in one place."

"I'm sorry about Dennis, Bill."

It was Bill's turn to be silent.

"Is there anything I can do?"

"Ben, you've already done more than expected." Bill began. "You took that boy under your wing the minute I left. I mourn for the boy, but why? I wanted nothing to do with him for the past months."

"You loved him Bill." Ben stated

"I guess love is one thing you can't run from."

"Maybe you should quit running."

"It's too late, he's gone now."

"But Connie's not."

"Neither is Ginny. Ben, I left because I couldn't hack it any longer. I still can't. I'm not going to raise false hopes by trying to put back a marriage that is over and done with."

Both men were quiet for a few minutes before Bill continued.

"You're my friend Ben, one of the few I have. If you don't think that I miss my wife you're wrong. I miss her every minute of every day. You were right about Dennis, I loved him Ben, I love Connie, and I love my wife."

Agitated he rose from the chair and paced the floor.

"It was the hardest thing I ever did when I left them. I don't want my life to be this way. I put her through nearly eighteen years of misery before I finally left. Eighteen years in which she wondered constantly where I was, or who I was with. I guess I was just never meant to be a husband or father. I've failed them so desperately."

He seated himself once more and turning to Ben continued.

"Now that I've eased my conscience maybe I can put up a decent front the next two days."

"Bill" Ben began soberly. "You realize that I'm the one responsible for Denni's death."

"It was an accident."

"One that could have been avoided." Ben continued. "I know what a danger fire at this time of year can be. I thought I had exhausted all avenues of precaution. I'm still baffled over the whole episode. Besides I was the chaperone, negligent as anything. I'm half tempted to shut the farm down to avoid another accident."

"That doesn't sound like the Ben Daniels I know."

"Forgive me Bill. That boy of yours was far too fine of a person to pay the price he did. There are a lot of empty hearts today, he's touched a lot of lives. I feel like such an utter failure. In my sporadic attempt to help the boy, I create the very incident that causes his death.

"No Ben, you're wrong. When I left, Denni was still in braces, his voice was changing, and we couldn't get him to clean his room, much less the stalls of fifty to sixty horses. I wasn't the example that created the boy that I've been hearing about all day. You were."

The common room at the Gold Abode opened out onto the patio that ran along the back of the Manor, along the Flint River. It was the second of October, and a colorful array of leaves carpeted the ground. Many of the trees still clung to their castaways as if willing to clothe themselves against the winter chill. There had been frost on the ground that morning, a brittle sheet covered the grass, shattering at the slightest pressure.

A handful of residents, with their wheel chairs, walkers and hearing-aides; had met for the afternoon bible study. Bill, grayer and more tired looking then Peggy had ever remembered, stood unsteadily before them. Supporting himself at the small podium he began to speak in clear, simple, language, news of the creator. Words that never failed to comfort her fell softly from his feeble lips. Peggy sat inattentive through the entire meeting, thinking about death.

Death had become her personal enemy. It had deprived her of a father, taken her grandmother, and now, tragically, had come again and claimed a friend. Last night as the men had worked at controlling the flames, Peggy had paced the length of the Daniels garage in prayer. Silent, fervent prayer for Denni's safety had gone forth long into the night. She had sought for peace, yet found none, until in desperation, she had requested, not Denni's life, but God's will. Peace prevailed. With her prayer answered Peggy knew that once again Death had touched her life.

Her thoughts carried her back to that evening, over five years ago. To a small bed, in a dimly lit room, of the intensive care unit at the Good Samaratin Hospital. Her Grandmother lay before her, her thin gray hair, flattened from the pressure on the crisp white pillowcases. Her eyes seemed hollow, her skin transparent, aged creases attempted to conceal the familiar face. Her body was overcome with pain, yet at her last breath peace had prevailed. God had visited them.

Why was death such an object of fear? Wasn't it just the passing from this life into a perfect and more glorious one? That's what it had been for her Grandmother, for Denni, and she believed, for her father. Yet, what about others that didn't have that hope of eternity? She glanced around the room, each man and woman that was gathered here would someday have to face death. Would it be an object of fear? Of peace? Would facing death herself be as natural as it had seemed to her Grandmother?

Peggy glanced through the open window, at the colorful landscape. Catching a slight breeze, leaves swayed to their death. The trees stood, clutching their last form of life, attempting to hang on against the process of nature, making a last feeble effort to survive.

After the last of the congregation went home that evening, Reverend Rhodes sat silently in the darkened sanctuary staring at the pulpit. Alone with this thoughts and with his God the man wept. He wept for Virginia Little whom life had dealt with so brutally to have taken such a life. He wept for Bill, Den's father who had stepped so purposely out of his son's life, never contemplating the finality of his actions.

He wept for the young people, Den's friends, who had shared his life. For Pat, and for Suzanna, even he had seen the seed of love begin to bud and tragically get crushed. He wept that night for Ben, strong unwavering Ben, whose very life projected rock hard stability. Beneath the tough exterior, was a very tender heart. He wept tears for the young lad who had sat that evening, in the back pew, clutching a black bible to his heart. A changed heart. A changed life.

In the darkness that surrounded him, the Reverend Rhodes fought against all inhibitions that would break communication between him and his savior. Staring at the empty pulpit he felt more alone than he had ever felt. Tomorrow he would once again stand behind the same pulpit. Before him would be placed a closed casket. Was he prepared as a man, called of God, to encourage God's people in the midst of such a tragedy?

Alone with God that night, Edward Rhodes wept. For Ginny, Bill, Pat, Suzanna, Ben, and Jeff; but mostly for himself.

CHAPTER 26

A TIME TO KEEP SILENCE, AND A TIME TO SPEAK

Monday, October 3rd, 1983

It has often occurred that gloom prevails on the days that loved ones are buried, but that wasn't so on the day of Dennis Little's funeral. The sun shone with all it's glory on a town still wrapped in grief. On Broad street, at the home of the Reverend Edward Rhodes, the gloom of the previous day had given way to acceptance.

Suzanna, alone in her room, studied the small pink rose that rested in a vase on her bedside table. Dry eyed she touched the tender bud, the symbol of something so precious and so beautiful that had been destroyed so soon. She had cried her way through the past thirty-six hours, now exhausted and drained, she was able to maintain her composure. She had been beside herself with grief but had found comfort in those around her, Pat, her parents, Sarah Daniels, and Mike Shephard had all encouraged her by the strength in which they had accepted Denni's death.

She rose quickly, her mother would be leaving for the church soon, to prepare for a slight luncheon after the funeral. Opening her closet her eyes rested instantly on a gray sweater that hung there. He had never seen it. The pink roses so much a symbol of their love, now seemed so faded and cheap to her. She gently touched the sleeve, the softness was the same as when she had first held it, it hadn't changed, she had. Deliberately Suzanna removed it from her closet, she had bought the sweater with thoughts of Denni, those thoughts were all she had left.

Minutes later she entered the kitchen to join her mother. Bob was already there, a cup of coffee in his hands. Slowly he lowered the paper he was reading. Without speaking he folded back the page and handed it to Suzanna. It was open to the obituaries, Denni's was in the middle of the page.

LITTLE, Dennis William - age 17

Died unexpectedly Saturday October 1, 1983 at approximately 8:15 PM. He was born on August 28, 1966, in Roberts Junction. He is survived by his father, William J. Little of Sacramento California, his mother Virginia (Sells) Little and sister Constance both of 225 Oak Street, Roberts Junction.

Dennis was a junior at John F. Kennedy High School, and an active member of the Youth in Action program at the Apostolic Holiness Chapel.

Services will be held on Monday October 3, 1983 at 11:30 AM at the Apostolic Holiness Chapel. Visitation is at McMillan Funeral Home preceding the services.

A memorial fund will be established for the Blessed Hope Mission in northern Brazil.

Suzanna stared silently at the paper for the longest time after reading the obituary. It seemed so impersonal, so cold. Not like Denni at all, Nothing was mentioned of his kindness or his humor; Nothing was said of his patience or good nature; just bold bare facts.

"Well at least they have the facts right." She spoke soberly.

"What did you expect dear?" Her mother asked.

"I'm not sure, something more personal maybe."

"The paper isn't the place for being personal." Her mother answered equally sober.

"It tells all about his birth and his death but almost nothing about his life. Isn't that the most important?"

"Yes it is dear, and for those of us that knew him we've got the memories of him that will help us."

"I wish I had more memories."

"You're forming more right now." Her mother assured her.

Elizabeth Rhodes, accompanied by both her daughters and Bob Morris had been of the first to visit the funeral home. Suzanna wearing the rose sweater and a gray corduroy skirt, kept herself behind the rest. The casket would be closed but she had yet to close the chapter of her life that included Denni.

As her mother comforted Ginny Little, Suzanna watched as Cindi and Bob approached the casket, side by side, his strong arm around her. Her heart sank, she could almost feel the presence of Denni's arm around her as it had been Saturday night while he was teaching her to guide the horses. Suzanna noticed Connie coming toward her, she attempted to smile but it was hopeless, tears came instead. Unspoken words choked at her throat as her and Connie embraced and held each other a moment.

"I'm glad you came." Connie finally managed to whisper. "I need to tell you something."

Suzanna just nodded.

"I need to thank you." Connie began. "I'm really shook up over what happened, but last night I recalled how happy he had been Saturday, he was happier than I had ever seen him. I know it was you that made the difference. Thank you."

Connie began to cry again as the two clung desperately to one another.

Suzanna's futile attempt at composure crumbled the minute she had seen the casket. Now she wept uncontrollably against the rough shoulder of an old faded jean jacket. What a contrast it was, dark featured Suzanna in the very outfit she had chosen to please Denni, and fair haired Connie, thin and frail in her navy blue dress beneath Denni's old discarded jean jacket. She would never part with it now. The two had never been close friends but now they shared a common bond, Love. Love for one who had been so tragically taken from them.

Later that morning while Cindi and Suzanna worked with their mother in the Church kitchen, and Bob assisted by Luke set up the tables and chairs for the luncheon, Mike Shephard entered behind an artificial wreath of flowering plants from the funeral home.

"Well folks, Ginny wants these here for the funeral, where do you want them?"

Elizabeth looked desperately at Suzanna. "Suzanna dear, will you help Mike put the flowers out. Keep them around the front of the Sanctuary."

"Sure mom."

"I'll bring these in, but be prepared there's a whole truck full out there."

Suzanna hadn't seen so many flowers at one time ever before. Goregeous mums in deep reds, golds and oranges. Thick green plants in big sturdy planters. single roses, delicate carnations and a variety of other fresh cut flowers. Each time Suzanna thought she'd found a nice arrangement Mike would appear with another plant.

After what seemed an endless fifteen minutes, she had gained enough order to the arrangement to be satisfied. Standing back the two admired their work.

"That should do." Mike stated preparing to leave.

Suzanna just stared at the empty place where they would soon set Denni's casket.

"Will you be okay?" He asked.

"Sure Mike, Thanks for your help."

"Anytime, now you keep smiling."

"I may smile on the outside, but inside it's still storming."

"Talk to him about it." Mike pointed heavenward.

"I'll do that." She agreed as he left.

No one was quite prepared for the events that transpired during the 11:30 funeral service. The sun shone brightly through the windows of the small sanctuary, illuminating the bold colors of the plants and flowers the cascaded about the platform. Elizabeth Rhodes sat at the piano, softly playing as mourners gathered. Ben and Sarah with Nick accompanied by Richard McAllister were among the first to arrive. Judy Johnson and Steve Williams slowly entered and found a seat in the back. Jenny was with them. Doc Martin came too, with his wife; many others had silently slipped through the doors and slowly filled the small building. It was nearing the time to present the casket when the noise of a stifled crowd was heard as nearly the entire Junior class of John F. Kennedy High School entered led by Coach Johnson. Ushers quickly lined the walls with folding chairs to accomodate the overflowing attendance.

The preacher entered first, Solemn and burdened, he led the small procession down the familiar aisle to the platform. The casket followed in the capable hands of friends; Matt and Mark Rankin, Jeff Johnson, Mike Shephard, Tom VanDyke, and Pat Rhodes. His parents followed, so joined in their grief yet so apart in their lives. Together they walked jointly carrying the burden of their lost son. Connie followed having requested that Suzanna accompany her, the two walked slowly, clinging to each other for support. Behind, Den's grandparents, aunts, and uncles joined them. A small group yet grief stricken, had gathered to pay their last respects.

Old Bill Winters was the first to step forward. He spoke in a clear yet feeble voice as he read from Ecclesiastes.

> To everything there is a season,
> and a time for every purpose under heaven;
> A time to be born, and a time to die;
> A time to plant, and a time to pluck up that which is planted;
> A time to kill, and a time to heal;
> A time to break down, and a time to build up;
> A time to weep, and a time to dance;
> A time to cast away stones,
> and a time to gather stones together;
> A time to embrace and a time to refrain from embracing;
> A time to get, and a time to lose;

A time to keep, and a time to cast away;
A time to rend, and a time to sew;
A time to keep silent, and a time to speak;
A time of love, and a time of hate;
A time of war, and a time of peace;

As Bill returned to his seat beside Peggy and her friends, Brother Rhodes stepped to the pulpit. He stood there awhile and looked out at the multitude of faces that were unfamiliar to him. Young faces and Old faces. Faces of those who grieved the death of this young seventeen year old boy. Taking a deep breath he offered unto them what encouragement he could.

"To everything there is a season." He began hesitantly. "It's October, the season is autumn. It's a beautiful time of the year, the leaves create such a rainbow of colors for us to enjoy, the air seems so much fresher. But Autumn doesn't last forever. The beautiful leaves don't remain on the trees, one by one they fall to the earth. I've raked stacks of them in my yard, my children have gathered them through the years and pressed them in the pages of my pulpit commentaries. Some have burned them, others buried them, I myself cover my garden with them. These beautiful glorious leaves are soon forgotten. We forget the glory of their different colors in fall. We forget the shade they create during the long days of summer, the shelter they give to the birds, the homes they create for the squirrels."

"The leaves become forgotten. But the life of the one that lies before us will never be forgotten. We will long recall the days of his glory, of the comfort he gave us. Of his friendship, his love his patience. They will be with us although his presence is not."

"Spring will soon come, and new buds will appear on the trees, they will erupt in a lush green shelter once again. And so with Dennis, although no one will ever take the place of this young man, others will rise to become comforts to us, friends to us. Denni's life was short but it was full, he accomplished more in seventeen years than many do in a lifetime. We have a right to mourn over our loss, but we also have a right to rejoice, that we knew him, and loved him, and that he now stands before the God that he loved."

At that moment song broke forth, the musical strains of 'The Battle Hymn of the Republic' played by a group of young people, minus their trumpet player. Pat at the piano, Matt and Mark with sax and trombone. It wasn't perfect, but it was beautiful. Tears flowed freely as the congregation joined with the Junior class of Kennedy High in singing.

He has died to make men holy.
Let us live to make men free,
His truth is marching on.

As the last notes of the song echoed through the church, Sarah Daniels rose silently and made her way hesitantly toward the pulpit. Looking out upon the assembled crowd she began to read in a calm voice a piece she had written, just for that moment.

We gather on this solemn day,
in grief and sorrow.
For one who was so very young.
who will never see tomorrow.
His feet that no more walk upon,
the familiar paths he trod,
Are walking now on streets of Gold,
within the home of God.
We'll no more feel those hands clasp ours,
in their firm, unyielding shake,
but we can hope to see him someday
waiting by that pearly gate.
So young, and yet so full the life,
he offered to each friend,
As he was given from his God
He gave unto the end.
He's gone now, we grieve him
yet in ways we'll never part.

Denni, we'll always miss you,
But you're still in our hearts.

Headed south through Wisconsin farmland, putting as much behind him as possible drove young rebellious Brady Downing. The lad who had manipulated parents, teachers, and friends; the one who's smile had won him acceptance, connections won him favors, and money bought him anything within his grasp; drove resolutely away, unable to change the results of what his utter foolishness had caused.

For once Brady Downing wasn't in control. His desire became only to put as many miles as possible between him and his plights.

And thus, life continues on in Roberts Junction.

THE END

THE ADVENTURES IN
ROBERTS JUNCTION CONTINUE...

BOOK#2 - LOVE BEARETH ALL THINGS

June finds things changing around the little town of Roberts Junction. First we welcome Bob Morris into the Rhodes family after the wedding of Edward and Elizabeth's eldest daughter Cindi. We find their son Pat tossed in his decision to further his education, and also tossed in his feelings toward Michelle Morrison. We find Suzanna aboard a plane headed toward a two week vacation on a Mission in Brazil, and young Luke taking a week long seminar at Horseman's Unlimited.

Chrys Shephard, a chaperone for four teenage girls along the Amazon finds more than she bargains for when she meets David Rankin's oldest son Daniel, and her brother

Mike encounters his first experience with vandals. Our hearts are tore when Steve Williams finds Bill Winters' unconscious body on the floor of the tack room and we stand vigil for days with Ben Daniels. A stranger enters town in search of Rich McAllister, while in Alaska Joe Jamison fights more than mere forest fires.

BOOK #3 LET NOT MAN PUT ASUNDER

As September approaches and a new school year begins we find Suzanna Rhodes struggling with the changes that have taken place over the past year. First there was the death of Dennis Little in October, then her sister's marriage to Bob Morris in June, followed closely by the stroke that left Bill Winters confined to a nursing home and his granddaughter (Peggy) returning to live with her mother and stepfather in New York. Now Pat has left for college, and Luke is beginning to act like the Teen-ager he has become.

In the midst of this turmoil Drew Arnolds enters the scene. Drew is the second oldest of Angies brothers and has secured a job on the faculty of J.F.K. High. It is the prayerful efforts of Mike and Chrys Shephard and Suzanna's consistent stand amid the daily struggles that teens encounter that bring Drew to the place where he is able to consider the fact that somewhere there is a God.

BOOK#4 HEAPS UPON HEAPS

In fall of 1984 we follow Patrick Rhodes to Elliot University in pursuit of a College Education. Amid the struggles of college life, and his stands for truth we find him flourishing as a Christian. Enter C.U.E. or Christians United at Elliot, a club on campus that votes him in as their Vice President. It's not the power of the position but his love of music that causes him to become a modern day Samson.

BOOK #5 EXCEEDING GREAT JOY

Christmas is a wonderful time of the year,.. or is it? We find in the midst of the celebrating, gift giving, carol singing, and gingerbread baking, that this supposed Christian holiday is causing questions in the minds of some of the residents of Roberts Junction. Is there really a true meaning behind the holiday? Wynn Hawk seems to think so, and armed with Scriptures and Historical facts he confronts his pastor who deals with it prayerfully and with an open heart.

BOOK #6 FROM THE RISING OF THE SUN

January begins a new year for thirteen year old Luke Rhodes. In an attempt to correct his rebellious behavior he is sent to stay with his fathers good friend, Carl Seymour, who pastors a church in Maximum.

Determined to make his stay as miserable as possible, he launches into an all out campaign of practical jokes on both the others in the Seymour 'family' and the surrounding community, until something unexpected happens. Join him in his struggle to escape from the power of his families prayers only to find himself falling deeper into the pit he'd dug.

BOOK #7 HAVING DONE ALL TO STAND

Another school year begins, the third year in which we follow Suzanna Rhodes, (Now a Senior) to and from her classes. All her friends have graduated. Angie is no longer there to share secrets with and Mark and Jeff aren't standing by their lockers outside Mr. Arnolds classroom. The only thing that does appear to be the same is the fact that once again she is scheduled for Creative Writing during first hour every morning. Andrew Arnolds has changed for the better, but this fall finds him introducing a Student Teacher named Craig T. Barley. An extremely young an inexperienced teacher, Craig Barley struggles to find one student that shows any form of talent and focus's most of his comments and criticism on that one person. That person however, is Suzanna Rhodes. We struggle with her feelings of inferiority, and her attempt to stand for what she believes in the midst of the pressure she is receiving on all sides.

BOOK #8 - REDEEMING THE TIME

In late February 1993, Mark Rankin a reporter for the New York Current, finds himself questioning the deterioration of the press, and the morals of this country. In the midst of searching for answers he joins a campaign to find out what the Government is really doing at the small Mt. Carmel Complex in Waco Texas. Armed with a unique sense of right and wrong, and basic biblical teaching Mark, along with Attorney's Andrew and Margaret Clayton, seeks for truth amid the multitude of propaganda that the Government spews forth.

A continuation in the Adventures in Roberts Junction, Redeeming The Time reintroduces you to characters you've met in previous books, and follows Mark's writing career to the streets of New York, and the back roads of Texas.

THE APOSTOLIC KIDS SERIES

BOOK #1 - THE TRUTH SHALL MAKE YOU FREE

Rose Mary Hawk, a twelve year old Nez Perc Indian from Washington finds herself uprooted from her home and family and settling, reluctantly, in a small town in Wisconsin. Her mother (newly married) isn't much help; her step-father Mac a great guy seems to be keeping secrets; and then there's church. Rosie finds that she doesn't seem to fit anywhere, all she seems to come across in her search for acceptance are more and more questions. Where will she go to find answers? Will the time ever come when she can feel at home among these strangers? What is the secret behind the bearded man with the tattered army jacket and worn combat boots?

BOOK #2 - I GO TO PREPARE A PLACE FOR YOU

The second book in the Apostolic Kids series focuses on the life of young Nick Daniels. Nick is a dreamer, which to many is fine except when it begins to interfere with his work in school and his responsibilities at home. No one seems to understand, no one except maybe Tayler Spier. But does Nick understand Tayler as well as he thinks he does? Find out in the second book in the Apostolic Adventure Series.

BOOK #3 - GIVE AND SHALL BE GIVEN UNTO YOU

Mel O'Neal is twelve, and struggling with the age between being a kid and a teen. Her brothers no longer include her in their plans and her sisters are way to immature. In an attempt to be herself she begins a campaign to raise money to redecorate her bedroom. Along with her friends Aly Murphy and Rose Mary Hawk, Mel starts a catering business to earn money. Finally after weeks of cooking, cleaning, and all around kitchen duty, she has the money she wanted to save for a stereo. At this time a young couple, new to the evangelistic field, comes to preach their first revival. Mel's youngest sister Emily receives the Holy Ghost, and in the process Mel herself learns the blessing there is in giving when she sacrifices her hard earned money in a special offering.